COLLECTED EDITION

of

Heywood Broun

COLLECTED EDITION OF

Heywood Broun

Compiled by

HEYWOOD HALE BROUN

Essay Index Reprint Series

BOOKS FOR LIBRARIES PRESS
FREEPORT, NEW YORK

STANDARD BOOK NUMBER:

8369-1345-0

LIBRARY OF CONGRESS CATALOG CARD NUMBER:

70-90615

PRINTED IN THE UNITED STATES OF AMERICA

TO

MRS. HEYWOOD COX BROUN

PREFACE

BY HEYWOOD HALE BROUN

I don't know whether the pieces in this book are the best things Heywood Broun ever wrote. I used a much less resounding device than "best" for picking them. All I can say is that, as much as possible, these are things which Heywood Broun liked.

I didn't hear him express opinions on all of them, but I remember a few which he particularly asked me to read and others which he showed to Ruth Hale, whose judgment of his work he respected more than anyone else's. Then there are some which he mentioned to friends in the days when I was more often one of his subjects than one of his readers.

A number of the columns in the last third of this collection he selected himself for the book he had in preparation for Harcourt, Brace covering the years 1936 to 1939.

Old Broun readers will find a few articles which are very familiar. They are the ones which Heywood dug out of his clip files, fitted with a new lead, and used on days when he was catching trains, the races, or a speaking date. This seemed to me a fair guarantee of their permanency.

The reader is owed a partial apology in the matter of the excerpts from the novels. Excerpts are a very unsatisfactory business, by and large, and constitute the least attractive portions of anthologies. However, I felt that some part of *The Boy Grew Older* and *Gandle Follows His Nose* belong in any collection of Heywood Broun's writings. This is particularly true of *Gandle* which, though spectacularly unsuccessful, remained one of the things of which Heywood was proudest, and I am unwilling to let it pass into limbo without saving a part of it.

The Beau Broadway column, mentioned in The Old, Old

Telegraph as "the first item which I ever wrote for print," should rightly open this book, but unfortunately both the early *Telegraph* files of 1908 and the six copies of the paper which Heywood took home have disappeared.

The second selection, And the Greatest of These, is printed here as it was published by the editors of the 1909 *Harvard Advocate* over the misprinted signature "H. C. Brown," and not as later rewritten for the 1921 book, *Seeing Things at Night.*

There are one or two things which I did not include because they are still in current anthologies, but The Fifty-first Dragon deserves one more reprint to finish off the long career which is described in the preface to its *Nutmeg* edition.

The Christmas stories were a sort of common meeting-ground between the Broun-as-light-essayist fans and the Broun-as-political-commentator admirers. I have included all of them. They were executed with more loving care than almost anything else he wrote. Even to Judas appears with the *Nutmeg* preface which was added to it after the President had read it over the air as his Christmas message.

The material about H. 3rd was a little difficult for me to judge. Columns about child psychology as embodied in H. 3rd are too representative of the earlier Broun to be ignored in this collection as a gesture of false modesty on my part. On the other hand, I had an uneasy feeling that my enjoyment while re-reading them might be largely due to the part I played in them. I hope that the amount of H. 3rd data represents a fair balance.

I think the Sacco-Vanzetti series is the most important thing in this book. The case of the shoemaker and the fish-peddler represented for Heywood Broun a very definite turning-point. It would be overstating the case to say that he made overnight a conscious decision which changed him from a light essayist into a fiery crusader—he was something of each both before and after the Sacco-Vanzetti case—but for the first time he ran into public apathy on a large scale and realized more vividly than ever before that injustice is not knocked out in one round. Leaving the *World*, a paper on which he and many others had pinned hopes for the advance of liberal journalism, was a hard step to take but he felt that it was not enough merely to have "made his position clear," and he felt that way through a succession of causes, lost and won, until the day he died.

In an editorial in *Broun's Nutmeg* mildly chiding me for a long series of light stories in that paper he said that it's better to take a right hand swing and fall on your face than to try to win with nothing but a left jab. In the latter half of this book there are some jabs, but they are used, as he used them, to set up the solid smashes.

Some of those who regarded the "op. ed." page of the old *World*, with its collection of wits, as part of breakfast may feel that his light pieces have been slighted. Lest they accuse me of lack of appreciation of Heywood as a humorist, let me say that I would regard this volume as very incomplete without such columns as Apes and Elms and My First Nude and many others. Neither, I hope, have I been unmindful of Heywood Broun's stature as dramatic critic and sports writer.

It was Heywood Broun's greatest talent that he could join the ranks of the crusaders without losing his capacity for enjoyment and the ability to pass that enjoyment on in his writings but—"There is no vigor in expressing an opinion and then washing your hands."

A special word should be said about the *Connecticut Nutmeg*. As originally planned it was to be a sort of country weekly in which well-known authors could relax. The well-known authors dropped off at various stages, however, until it ended up as *Broun's Nutmeg*. The *Nutmeg* was never much of a financial success; in fact, it was never close to breaking even, but it was probably the freest press ever. As editor and publisher, Heywood used to accept all manuscripts by Broun no matter whose toes were stepped on. It was an experiment in the kind of personal journalism which he felt was increasingly lacking in the American press. It was a pretty good paper, and I think if he had been able to continue it, it might have become increasingly important. At any rate it is mentioned here so that nobody will look at the source section of this book and wonder what the *Nutmeg* was.

Except for the opening selection, the material of this book is arranged chronologically. I think that, taken as a whole, it gives a picture of Heywood Broun as a person, as well as of his development as a writer. I hope that this picture is not merely one of broad outlines and that there are no parts of this book of which it will be said, "Of course if you knew Heywood you'd get a bigger kick out of it." Rather let those who met him only in his columns or even in The Old, Old *Telegraph* feel that they know him as well as his oldest acquaintance when they have finished this book.

The Classification by Subject which follows the table of contents is, of course, purely arbitrary. There are a few uncomfortably placed pieces therein, but it seemed better to have such an index, even with its artificial divisions, than to leave the reader no guide save the names of the pieces.

Heywood Broun wrote only two pieces concerning his conversion to the Catholic faith, A Talk with a Friend and Not in This Issue. They were not written, or included here, as apologies. Despite numerous inquiries at the time, he did not rush into print with a statement. It was not an impulsive step and they are not impulsive pieces. They certainly belong here.

There has been no attempt to make Heywood Broun look like an infallible prophet. There are wrong guesses in this book. They're here because they were honest guesses and ones which we still might wish to be true. The column about Red Caps was written before the railroad companies discovered a method of making money out of employees, but it will be a good guide if ever the disgraceful system now in operation is abandoned. It represented at the time an honest effort at betterment of the porter's profession and as such is timeless.

Heywood Broun was a newspaperman for 31 years. Neither this book, nor one many times its size, can contain all the good work he did. In reading it over I have sometimes thought of others I wished I could have included; at the same time I have found none which I wished I had left out.

A preface about Heywood Broun should not look back but should rather look forward, as he did, to the world he hoped to see built. In the piece written on his fifty-first birthday he said: "The underdog can and will lick his weight in the wildcats of the world." Some of them he beat, others remain to be beaten. I hope this book will help.

ACKNOWLEDGMENTS

I wish to acknowledge the kindness of the following publishers, editors, and copyright holders in granting me permission to reprint some of Heywood Broun's writings in this volume:

D. APPLETON-CENTURY COMPANY: "Franco-American Honeymoon," part of chapter four of *The A.E.F.: With General Pershing and the American Forces*, copyright, 1918, by D. Appleton and Company.

DOUBLEDAY, DORAN AND COMPANY, INC.: Preface, chapters 4, 6, 8, 11, 12, 14, 20, 30, 37, 40, 42 of *Pieces of Hate and Other Enthusiasms*, copyright, 1922, by George H. Doran Company.

HARCOURT, BRACE AND COMPANY: Columns No. 6 to 15 from *Seeing Things at Night*, copyright, 1921, and columns No. 42 to 45, 47 to 49, 50a to 51, 53 to 91, and 93 to 96 from *It Seems to Me: 1925-1935*, copyright, 1935, by Harcourt, Brace and Company.

THE HARVARD ADVOCATE: "And the Greatest of These," copyright, 1909, by the editors of the *Harvard Advocate*.

HEYWOOD BROUN ESTATE: Chapters one and ten of *The Boy Grew Older*, copyright, 1922, by Heywood Broun, published by G. P. Putnam's Sons. Columns 30 to 41 from *Sitting on the World*, copyright, 1924, by Heywood Broun, published by G. P. Putnam's Sons.

LIVERIGHT PUBLISHING CORPORATION: Chapter two of *Gandle Follows His Nose*, copyright, 1926, by Boni & Liveright, Inc.

THE NATION: Columns 1, 54, 97, and 112.

THE NEW REPUBLIC: Columns 124, 128, 129, 130, 136, 140, 143, 170, 177.

THE NEW YORK POST: "The Last Column."

CHARLES SCRIBNER'S SONS: "Cease Firing," part of chapter twenty-five of *Our Army at the Front*, copyright, 1918, by Charles Scribner's Sons.

SCRIPPS-HOWARD NEWSPAPERS: Various columns from the *World*, *Telegram*, and *World-Telegram* as listed under Sources, p. 555.

H. H. B.

CONTENTS

PART FIVE: *1937 to 1939*

CLASSIFICATION BY SUBJECT

ART AND ARTISTS

AUTOBIOGRAPHICAL

BOOKS AND AUTHORS

BROUN FAMILY

CENSORSHIP

CHRISTMAS PIECES

LABOR

MISCELLANEOUS

WAR AND PEACE

PART ONE

1908-1919

1. THE OLD, OLD *TELEGRAPH*

Some of the striplings around the office occasionally ask me, "What was New York like back in the old days?" At such times I eye them coldly, but if a hat chances to drop I can be induced to talk. And while a single one remains to listen I like to reminisce about the old, old *Morning Telegraph*. The office was on Fiftieth Street and Eighth Avenue in what had been the stable of the adjacent street-car railway, which was electrified before my time. I refer to the summer of 1908. But the paper remained a publication devoted chiefly to horses and vaudeville actors.

The first item which I ever wrote for print was a contribution to the first-page column of the paper which was signed Beau Broadway. It was accepted and run at the top of the column. It was something about Francis Wilson as a golfer. As I remember, it was very comical. I took home six copies of the paper and felt that I was Beau Broadway. They started me on space and the first week I made $40, but of course that couldn't last. After that I was on a salary of $20, and it took me ten years to get back to the standard which I had originally set for myself.

Still, money wasn't everything because each night we played poker across the copy desk. We had two copy readers and they both sat in and read copy between pots. A story had to be very hot to get any attention after midnight. Even when I wanted to go home early I couldn't because Shep Friedman, the night editor, used to say, "I'm assigning you to the game, Broun." The reasons for this developed early in my ten months on the *Telegraph*. Shep was a good newspaperman but a terrible poker player. Most of the players in the game were printers, and when he tried to borrow money from them they would laugh

3

at him. But I was a cub reporter. We played with money, and Shep would reach over to my pile and say, "I'll raise you fifty cents." If I raised him he'd take another of my dollars and say, "I'll raise you again." Pretty soon I realized that even if I won I'd only get my money back.

But he was nice to me, and the second day I was on the paper he gave me an assignment to do an interview. I was to have a by-line on it, but the thing didn't pan out. My assignment was to go to Hammerstein's Victoria and interview Valeska Suratt. Irving Lewis, the managing editor, heard the instructions and he said, "I guess I'll walk down with you." On the way down Broadway he gave me a good deal of advice about newspaper work and suggested that I should imitate his style. As we got near the stage door of the theater he said, "I think I'll do this interview myself." Then he added, "You better wait outside. You know she always kisses me."

I doubt whether any newspaper in New York ever had quite the intimate atmosphere of the old *Telegraph*. It was like a tough *Emporia Gazette*. The city room was always cluttered up with all sorts of people who didn't seem to have any business there. Very often you couldn't get to your desk because there would be a couple of chorus girls sitting there waiting for a friend who was finishing an editorial. I used to write editorials myself and it made me feel very lonely. Everybody wrote editorials. Generally at the last minute somebody would remember that we didn't have any editorials. Then Bide Dudley and I would each write one. The editorials were not regarded as very important because the *Telegraph* had no policy about anything except that it was against reformers. Vaudeville reviews were very important because the actors advertised.

The *Morning Telegraph* was a very hard place to get any sleep because even when the poker game broke up it was not my custom to go home. Charlie and I used to go over to the Eldorado, which was a dance hall covering several acres. I was

young then and a basketball player. I'd hate to have to dance
once around that floor now. Charlie was the assistant foreman
of the composing room, and he and I were both somewhat smit-
ten with the exhibition dancer at the Eldorado. She had a part-
ner but she didn't care anything about him. She would sit with
us until it came time to do her turn and then she would hand
one or the other of us a silver dollar. This was not for keeps.
It was the coin which was supposed to start the silver shower at
the end of the act.

She would lock her arms around the neck of her partner, a
man named Oscar, and he would move faster and faster until
she was whirling around horizontally like one of those captive
airplanes at Coney Island. There was a good deal of art to it.
I mean on our part. Whichever one had the silver dollar had
to pick precisely the right psychological moment to toss the coin
out to the middle of the floor. If you picked the right time and
made it land with a clang, quarters and nickels and dimes would
follow.

I drifted apart from Elaine—I think her name was Elaine—
after I began to go to Sweeney's. Sweeney's was a good deal
tougher than the Eldorado. It was on the corner where Macy's
now stands. Sweeney is gone too. They say he stabbed a man
in the place one night. That's why I was so proud of having a
fight with him. We quarreled about a girl. I was her escort and
she was a stranger to him. He asked her to dance without first
requesting my permission. I declined for her. When he asked
a second time, I punched him in the nose. They say we made a
pretty picture rolling around on the floor together and that I
was wise to keep on rolling. A waiter stood close by intent upon
hitting me over the head with a bottle, but he couldn't tell
which head was which.

But I see that the last listener has fled. You must pardon the
garrulity of an old man. The melodies linger on. Here in my
forty-eighth year sometimes I grow a little homesick for the old,

old *Morning Telegraph* as I sit down to write a page about federal finances. And even now I can't say that I am sorry that I went to a car barn instead of a school of journalism.

2. "AND THE GREATEST OF THESE" *

Hans sat on the dyke beside the door of the low, gray stone cottage of Kahnale, the great magician. He looked out over the sea, which stretched away from the foot of the dyke as smooth as the meadows which encompassed Rothdam, the little town which lay half a mile behind him—its outline traced in ribbon-like canals shining with the modest gleam of unpolished silver.

Hans held in his hands the magic wand of Kahnale, which was known throughout the realms of Europe. But Hans was not afraid, for he was flushed with eighteen-year-old full-blooded health, which rose pink in his cheeks, shone bright in the clear blue of his eyes, and set golden in his touseled hair. Moreover, he believed more in the magic changes of sky and sea and meadow which he saw from day to day than in the prowess of his master, which was only hearsay to him. So he twirled the wand idly while he wrote names and drew pictures with it in the loose sand of the dyke top. Finally, he smoothed over his various sand creations and replaced them with a huge heart, in the center of which he wrote "Gretchen." Then he sighed and wondered when he might marry Gretchen, and he wished that he might be a great magician like Kahnale, to whom men paid gold in handfuls.

"But," he thought, "if I am to be like Kahnale, I must read

*Entitled "Red Magic" in a later version rewritten for *Seeing Things at Night*. This is the original as it appeared in the Spring of 1909 in the *Harvard Advocate*.—Ed.

the big leather books from the magic room instead of idling away time here on the dyke."

He pushed through the vines of crimson roses round the door as he went into the magic room, where the skeletons rattled as he passed by, and swung in white arcs through the violet haze which filled the room with pungent odor. Hans took down one of the books from the shelf. He picked it out because it was the largest of the wood-browned leather books fastened with great clasps of silver. He carried it out of the magic room to the dyke top, where he lay down at full length beside the sand pile as he read. The words were long and foreign looking, so Hans read them aloud to hear how they sounded. "Vunsamerles, Khublasamerlee, Sasamerlee."

In the meantime Kahnale, long, lean and yellow, was coming out of the city hall of Rothdam accompanied by Burgomeister Steinhert, who contrasted with his companion by his short squat figure and ruddy complexion; his doublet of crimson also was in contrast with the somber black of the magician. Kahnale looked at the western horizon and was surprised to see that the sky, which had been cloudless only a few minutes before, was marred with tier upon tier of oily clouds filled with purple wrath.

"We must hurry to your house, my learned friend," said the Burgomeister. But even as they hastened the purple clouds in front of them kept puffing and swelling greater and greater till they seemed to rain darkness in their path. Suddenly there was a tremor of the earth which rolled the level meadow into ripples. A crash of thunder shouted out, and a sudden breeze of salt air smote them in the face. A snake of orange fire zigzagged through the cloud bank in front of them. In the flash Kahnale saw the figure of Hans swaying to and fro on the dyke top, book in hand.

"The Devil call," cried Kahnale, "hasten, man, there may be time if he has not yet reached the final charm."

Spurred on by the tremendous applause of the heavens, they

raced against the growing breeze from the sea. As they reached the foot of the dyke Hans stopped swaying, and they could hear his voice even above the growing roar of the wind, though it sounded thin and soft—"Eb dewollah."

"Too late," shrieked the magician. "The Devil call, he has reached the final charm."

"What is it?" asked the Burgomeister, thoroughly frightened, despite his ignorance of the whole proceeding.

"Don't you hear? He is saying the Lord's Prayer backwards; he has reached 'hallowed be.' "

"But why should our Hans weave spells against us?"

"Hans! That is not Hans. Look!" The figure turned its head from side to side as if in the unrest of pain. Above the full throated cry of the wind came a moan in the thin soft voice. "See, it is the devil in Hans' body. The boy has repeated the Devil call and now the Fiend is workng out the final charm which will bring the destruction of the world."

"The destruction of the world! But then Rothdam will be destroyed," said the Burgomeister in almost incredulous alarm.

"Even so, look to the sea."

Kahnale led him to the dyke top at a distance from the moaning figure. Urged on by the whip of the wind, the sea was leaping, plunging, and rearing at the dyke. Every second its foothold would rise and a breaker would roll in and cover the newly gained position.

"Kill him, pitch him in the sea," shouted the Burgomeister, as he pointed to the figure which held the great book.

"Nonsense," said Kahnale, seizing him by the arm, "you might as well live your little while. The man that touches the devil dies quickly, surely."

"Let me go," yelled the Burgomeister, "let me call my guard and the priest," and he made as if to clamber down the dyke and rush to the village.

"Fool," said Kahnale, still restraining him, "I may be powerless before the Devil call, but I can summon your cattle for you."

He raised his arm to heaven, muttered thrice in a low tone, and pointed to the east. Up against the wind came a faint tinkle of the danger bell in the cathedral tower.

"Nevaeh ni," came the voice.

"In heaven," groaned the Burgomeister, "Oh that my priest were here." He looked seawards; the waves had only ten feet more to climb.

"Here come your people."

Down the road came the throng of the village, led by the priest flanked by two red-liveried guards bearing blunderbusses.

"Sorcery, holy father," called the Burgomeister, "Hans is possessed of the devil."

The priest clambered on to the dyke, accompanied by the guards. The rest of the people kept at a respectful distance.

"Die, Devil," called one of the guards, and he shot point blank at the charm weaver. The report was followed by an even greater roar of the heavens. A fire fang darted from the clouds and curled around the guard's head. He fell and lay still. From the gathering gloom came the thin voice; it was growing louder, "Tra ohw."

"Who art," said the Burgomeister, "the end is near," and he sank nerveless, face downward on the dyke top.

"Away, Fiend!" cried the priest as he walked close to the figure and sprinkled him with holy water from a bottle which he carried. But the water was no sooner in the air than each drop of it changed into a tiny tongue of flame leaping and dancing on the shoulders of the Devil servant. The priest recoiled in horror. Kahnale bared his yellow gums in a smile, "How now, sir priest, is your God as great as my Devil?"

A wave broke over the wall and drenched the Burgomeister. "My God," he cried, and rushed to the meadow below, followed by Kahnale, the remaining guard and the priest. The figure was alone; it could not be seen, but the moan was rising ever higher

above the wind. A wall of green water a hundred feet high rose
towering above the dyke top. The heavens split. The clouds of
purple were columns of floating fire. There was a frightful odor
borne on by the roaring wind—the dead of the sea.

"I come, master," shouted Kahnale.

A little girlish figure of white, all flaxen haired, sprang from
the crowd and clambered up the dyke.

"Hans," she cried, "it is I, Gretchen; save me, save me."

"Rehtaf," said the figure, in a voice which rang out amid a
sudden hush of the wind. But before he could utter the last
word, Gretchen was upon him. She threw her arms around his
neck and kissed his mouth. The wall of water advanced across
the dyke top and swallowed up both boy and girl.

The wave hung on the edge of the dyke like a banjo string
drawn tight. Then suddenly it faded away from view; the green
of the curled wave of water a hundred feet high dwindled into
a few tall grasses swaying gently in the breeze; the clouds of
fire faded into orange tinted mist around the sinking sun; the
odor of the rose bushes was heavy in the air. The crowd rushed
on to the dyke. The sea stretched away far below them, calm
as the meadows. The priest raised his hand, "God, I thank thee
for empowering me, thy servant, to quell the Fiend."

The Burgomeister drew himself up, "Tonight we will gather
in the cathedral and render thanks. Later there will be dancing
in the city hall. I will burn one hundred candles in honor of
the saving of Rothdam and its brave citizens."

That same evening Kahnale walked along the dyke top in
the moonlight. The light from the windows of the city hall
was borne dimly to him by the dying land breeze. The cathedral
bell tolled with a sententious ding dong.

"I wonder," he said to himself, "what stopped the working
of the final charm. I know all things that are in books, and no-
where is there any power mentioned to overcome the spell."

Just then the moon silvered some marks which lay in his path.

He stooped down. There on the wave-swept dyke top was a large heart drawn in the sand, and in the center of it was written "Gretchen."

3. THE FRANCO-AMERICAN HONEYMOON

The day after the Americans marched in Paris one of the French newspapers referred to the doughboys as "Roman Caesars clad in khaki." The city set itself to liking the soldiers and everything American and succeeded admirably. Even the taxicab drivers refrained from overcharging Americans very much. School children studied the history of America and *The Star-Spangled Banner*. There were pictures of President Wilson and General Pershing in many shops and some had framed translations of the President's message to Congress. In fact, so eager were the French to take America to their hearts that they even made desperate efforts to acquire a working knowledge of baseball. *Excelsior*, an illustrated French daily, carried an action picture taken during a game played between American ambulance drivers just outside of Paris. The picture was entitled: "A player goes to catch the ball, which has been missed by the catcher," and underneath ran the following explanation: "We have given in our number of yesterday the rules of baseball, the American national game, of which a game, which is perhaps the first ever played in France, took place yesterday at Colombes between the soldiers of the American ambulances. Here is an aspect of the game. The pitcher, or thrower of balls, whom one sees in the distance, has sent the ball. The catcher, or *attrapeur*, who should restrike the ball with his wooden club, has missed it, and a player placed behind him has seized it in its flight."

The next day *L'Intransigeant* undertook the even more hazardous task of explaining American baseball slang. During the parade on the Fourth of July some Americans had greeted the doughboys with shouts of "ataboy." A French journalist heard and was puzzled. He returned to his office and looked in English dictionaries and various works of reference without enlightenment. Several English friends were unable to help him and an American who had lived in Paris for thirty years was equally at sea. But the reporter worked it out all by himself and the next day he wrote: "Parisians have been puzzled by the phrase 'ataboy' which Americans are prone to employ in moments of stress or emotion. The phrase is undoubtedly a contraction of 'at her boy' and may be closely approximated by *au travail, garçon.*" The writer followed with a brief history of the friendly relations of France and America and paid a glowing tribute to the memory of Lafayette.

The name for the American soldiers gave the French press and public no end of trouble. They began enthusiastically enough by calling them the "Teddies," but General Pershing, when interviewed one day, said that he did not think this name quite fitting as it had "no national significance." The French then followed the suggestion of one of the American correspondents and began to call the soldiers "Sammies," or as the French pronounce it, "Sammees." Although this name received much attention in French and American newspapers it has never caught the fancy of the soldiers in the American Expeditionary Army. Officers and men cordially despise it and no soldier ever refers to himself or a comrade as a "Sammy." American officers have not been unmindful of the usefulness of a name for our soldiers. Major General Sibert, who commanded the first division when it arrived in France, posted a notice at headquarters which read: "The English soldier is called Tommy. The French soldier is called *poilu.* The Commanding General would like suggestions for a name for the American soldier." At the end of the week the following names had been written in answer to the

General's request: "Yank, Yankee, Johnnie, Johnny Yank, Broncho, Nephew, Gringo, Liberty Boy, Doughboy."

Now doughboy is a name which the soldiers use, but strictly speaking, it refers only to an infantryman. The origin of the name is shrouded in mystery. One officer, probably an infantry-man, has written that the infantrymen are called doughboys because they are the flower of the army. Another story has it that during some maneuvers in Texas an artilleryman, comfort-ably perched on a gun, saw a soldier hiking by in the thick sticky Texas mud. The mud was up to the shoetops of the in-fantryman and the upper part which had dried looked almost white. "Say," shouted the artilleryman, "what've you been do-ing? Walking in dough?" And so the men who march have been doughboys ever since.

Paris did not let the lack of a name come between her and the soldiers. The theaters gave the Americans almost as much recognition as the press. No musical show was complete without an American finale and each soubrette learned a little English, "I give you kees," or something like that, to please the dough-boys. The vaudeville shows, such as those provided at the Olympia or the Alhambra, gave an even greater proportion of English speech. The Alhambra was filled with Tommies and doughboys on the night I went. Now and again the comedians had lapses of language and the Americans were forced to let jokes go zipping by without response. It was a pity, too, for they were good jokes even if French. Presently, however, a fat comedian fell off a ladder and laughter became general and in-ternational. The show was more richly endowed with actresses than actors. The management was careful to state that all the male performers had fulfilled their military obligations. Thus, under the picture of Maurice Chevalier, a clever comedian and dancer, one read that Mons. Chevalier was wounded at the battle of Cutry, when a bullet passed between his lungs. The story added that he was captured by the Germans and held prisoner for twenty-six months before he escaped. It did not

seem surprising therefore that Chevalier should be the gayest of
funny men. Twenty-six months of imprisonment would work
wonders with ever so many comedians back home.

And yet we Americans missed the old patter until there came
a breath from across the sea. A low comedian came out and
said to his partner in perfectly good English: "Well, didja like
the show?" His partner said he didn't like the show. "Well,
didja notice the trained seals?" persisted the low comedian and
the lower comedian answered: "No, the wind was against 'em."
Laughter long delayed overcame us then, but it was mingled
with tears. We felt that we were home again. The French are
a wonderful people and all that, of course, but they're so darn
far away.

Later there was a man who imitated Eddie Foy imperfectly
and a bad bicycle act in which the performers called the orches-
tra leader "Professor" and shouted "Ready" to each other just
before missing each trick. This bucked the Americans up so
much that a lapse into French with Suzanne Valroger *dans son
répertoire* failed to annoy anybody very much. The doughboys
didn't care whether she came back with her repertoire or on it.
Some Japanese acrobats and a Swedish contortionist completed
the performance. There are two such international music halls
in Paris as well as a musical comedy of a sort called *The Good
Luck Girl*. The feature of this performance is an act in which
a young lady swings over the audience and invites the soldiers
to capture the shoe dangling from her right foot. The shoe is
supposed to be very lucky and soldiers try hard to get it, stand-
ing up in their seats and snatching as the girl swings by. An
American sergeant was the winner the night I went to the show,
for he climbed upon a comrade's shoulder and had the slipper
off before the girl had time to swing out very far. Later, when
he went to the trenches, the sergeant took the shoe with him
and he says that up to date he has no reason to doubt the value
of the charm.

The most elaborate spectacle inspired by the coming of the

Americans was at the Folies Bergère which sent its chorus out for the final number all spangled with stars. The leader of the chorus was an enormous woman, at least six feet tall, who carried an immense American flag. She almost took the head off a Canadian one night as he dozed in a stage box and failed to notice the violent manner in which the big flag was being swung. He awoke just in time to dodge and then he shook an accusing finger at the Amazon. "Why aren't you in khaki?" he said.

Restaurants as well as theaters were liberally sprinkled with men in the American uniform. The enlisted men ate for the most part in French barracks and seemed to fare well enough, although one doughboy, after being served with spinach as a separate course, complained: "I wish they'd get all the stuff on the table at once like we do in the army. I don't want to be surprised, I want to be fed." A young first lieutenant was scornful of French claims to master cookery. "Why, they don't know how to fry eggs," he said. "I've asked for fried eggs again and again and do you know what they do? They put 'em in a little dish and bake 'em."

Yet, barring this curious and barbarous custom in the cooking of eggs, the French chefs were able to charm the palates of Americans even in a year which bristled with food restrictions. There were two meatless days a week, sugar was issued in rations of a pound a month per person and bread was gray and gritty. The French were always able to get around these handicaps. The food director, for instance, called the ice cream makers together and ordered them to cease making their product in order to save sugar.

"We have been using a substitute for sugar for seven months," replied the merchants.

"Well, then," said the food director, "it will save eggs."

"We have hit upon a method which makes eggs unnecessary," replied the ice cream makers.

"At any rate," persisted the food director, "my order will save unnecessary consumption of milk."

"We use a substitute for that, too," the confectioners answered, and they were allowed to go on with their trade.

The cooks are even more ingenious than the confectioners. As long as they have the materials with which to compound sauces, meat makes little difference. War bread might be terrapin itself after a French chef has softened and sabled it with thick black dressing. Americans found that the French took food much more seriously than we do in America. Patrons always reviewed the *carte du jour* carefully before making a selection. It was not enough to get something which would do. The meal would fall something short of success if the diner did not succeed in getting what he wanted most. No waiter ever hurried a soldier who was engaged in the task of composing a dinner. He might be a man who was going back to the trenches the next day and in such a case this last good meal would not be a matter to be entered upon lightly. After all, if it is a last dinner a man wants to consider carefully whether he shall order *contrefilet à la Bourguignon* or *poulet rôti à l'espagnole*.

Whatever may be his demeanor while engaged in the business of making war or ordering a meal, the Frenchman makes his "permission" a real vacation. He talks a good deal of shop. The man at the next table is telling of a German air raid, only, naturally, he calls them Boches. A prison camp, he explains, was brilliantly illuminated so that the Boche prisoners might not escape under the cover of darkness. One night the enemy aviators came over that way and mistook the prison camp for a railroad station. They dropped a number of bombs and killed ten of their comrades. Everybody at the soldier's table regarded this as a good joke, more particularly as the narrator vivified the incident by rolling his war bread into pellets and bombarding the table by way of illustration, accompanied by loud cries of "Plop! Plop!"

Practically every man on "permission" in Paris is making love to someone and usually in an open carriage or at the center table of a large restaurant. Nobody even turns around to look if a soldier walks along a street with his arm about a girl's waist. American officers, however, frowned on such exhibitions of demonstrativeness by doughboys and in one provincial town a colonel issued an order: "American soldiers will not place their arms around the waists of young ladies while walking in any of the principal thoroughfares of this town."

Still it was not possible to regulate romance entirely out of existence. "There was a girl used to pass my car every morning," said a sergeant chauffeur, "and she was so good looking that I got a man to teach me *bon jour,* and I used to smile at her and say that when she went by and she'd say *bon jour* and smile back. One morning I got an apple and I handed it to her and said *pour vous* like I'd been taught. She took it and came right back with, 'Oh, I'm ever so much obliged,' and there like a chump I'd been holding myself down to *bon jour* for two weeks."

There could be no question of the devotion of Paris to the American army. Indeed, so rampant was affection that it was occasionally embarrassing. One officer slipped in alighting from the elevator of his hotel and sprained his ankle rather badly. He was hobbling down one of the boulevards that afternoon with the aid of a cane when a large automobile dashed up to the curb and an elderly French lady who was the sole occupant beckoned to him and cried: *"Premier blessé."* The officer hesitated and a man who was passing stepped up and said: "May I interpret for you?" The officer said he would be much obliged. The volunteer interpreter talked to the old lady for a moment and then he turned and explained: "Madame is desirous of taking you in her car wherever you want to go, because she says she is anxious to do something for the first American soldier wounded on the soil of France."

The devotion of Paris was so obvious that it palled on one or two who grew fickle. I saw a doughboy sitting in front of the Café de la Paix one bright afternoon. He was drinking champagne of a sort and smoking a large cigar. The sun shone

on one of the liveliest streets of a still gay Paris. It was a street
made brave with bright uniforms. Brighter eyes of obvious non-
combatants gazed at him with admiration. I was sitting at the
next table and I leaned over and asked: "How do you like
Paris?"

He let the smoke roll lazily out of his mouth and shook his
head. "I wish I was back in El Paso," he said.

I found another soldier who was longing for Terre Haute.
Him I came upon in the lounging room of a music hall called
the Olympia. Two palpably pink ladies sat at the bar drinking
cognac. From his table a few feet away the American soldier
looked at them with high disfavor. Surprise, horror and indig-
nation swept across his face in three waves as the one called
Julie began to puff a cigarette after giving a light to Margot.
He looked away at last when he could stand no more, and recog-
nizing me as a fellow countryman, he began his protest.

"I don't like this Paris," he said. "I'm in the medical corps,"
he continued. "My home's in Terre Haute. In Indiana, you
know. I worked in a drug store there before I joined the army.
I had charge of the biggest soda fountain in town. We used to
have as many as three men working there in summer sometimes.
Right at a good business corner, you know. I suppose we had
almost as many men customers as ladies."

"Why don't you like Paris?" I interrupted.

"Well, it's like this," he answered. "Nobody can say I'm
narrow. I believe in people having a good time, but—" and he
leaned nearer confidentially, "I don't like this Bohemia. I'd
heard about it, of course, but I didn't know it was so bad. You
see that girl there, the one in the blue dress smoking a cigarette,
sitting right up to the bar. Well, you may believe it or not, but
when I first sat down she came right over here and said, 'Hello,
American. You nice boy. I nice girl. You buy me a drink.' I
never saw her before in my life, you understand, and I didn't
even look at her till she spoke to me. I told her to go away
or I'd call a policeman and have her arrested. I've been in Paris

a week now, but I don't think I'll ever get used to this Bohemia business. It's too effusive, that's what I call it. I'd just like to see them try to get away with some of that business in Terre Haute."

The high tide in the American conquest of Paris came one afternoon in July. I got out of a taxicab in front of the American headquarters in the Rue Constantine and found that a big crowd had gathered in the Esplanade des Invalides. Now and again the crowd would give ground to make room for an American soldier running at top speed. One of them stood almost at the entrance of the courtyard of "Invalides." His back was turned toward the tomb of Napoleon and he was knocking out flies in the direction of the Seine. Unfortunately it was a bit far to the river and no baseball has yet been knocked into that stream. It was a new experience for Napoleon though. He has heard rifles and machine guns and other loud reports in the streets of Paris, but for the first time there came to his ears the loud sharp crack of a bat swung against a baseball. Since he could not see from out the tomb the noise may have worried the emperor. Perhaps he thought it was the British winning new battles on other cricket fields. But again he might not worry about that now. He might hop up on one toe as a French caricaturist pictured him and cry: "*Vive l'Angleterre!*"

One of the men in the crowd which watched the batting practice was a French soldier headed back for the front. At any rate he had his steel helmet on and his equipment was on his back. His stripes showed that he had been in the war three years and he had the Croix de Guerre with two palms and the Médaille Militaire. His interest in the game grew so high at last that he put down his pack and his helmet and joined the outfielders. The second or third ball hit came in his direction. He ran about in a short circle under the descending ball and at the last moment he thrust both hands in front of his face. The ball came between them and hit him in the nose, knocking him down.

His nose was a little bloody, but he was up in an instant

grinning. He left the field to pick up his trench hat and his equipment. The Americans shouted to him to come back. He understood the drift of their invitation, but he shook his head. *"C'est dangereux,"* he said, and started for the station to catch his train for the front.

4. CEASE FIRING

Although the German Army had begun to disintegrate by November 1, the Americans saw some hard fighting after that date. The task set for Pershing's men was in theory almost as difficult as clearing the Argonne Forest. The offensive was aimed at the Longuyon-Sedan-Mézières railway, which was one of the most important lines of communication of the German Army. Germany was aware of the gravity of this threat and used her very best troops in an effort to stop the Americans. For a time the Germans fought steadily, but their morale was waning at the end. The Americans found on several occasions that their second-day gains were greater than those of the first day, which was formerly an unheard of thing on the western front.

In the final days of the war the Americans had to go their fastest in an effort to reach Sedan before the armistice went into effect. During one phase of the battle doughboys mounted on auto-trucks went forward in a vain effort to establish contact with the enemy. The roads were so bad, however, that the Americans were unable to catch up with the fleeing Germans.

The third phase of the Meuse-Argonne campaign found the Americans absolutely confident of success. They knew their superiority over the Germans, and the American Army was constantly growing stronger while the Germans grew weaker. Pershing was able to send well-rested divisions into the battle.

The final advance began on November 1. American artillery was stronger than ever in numbers and much more experienced. Never before had our army seen such a barrage, and the German infantry broke before the advance of the doughboys. The German heart to fight had begun to develop murmurs, although there were some units among the enemy forces which fought with great gallantry until the very end. Aincreville, Doulcon, and Andevsnne fell in the first day of the attack. Landres et St. Georges was next to go, as the Fifth Corps, in an impetuous attack, swept up to Bayonville. On November 2, which was the second day of the attack, the First Corps was called in to give added pressure. By this time the German resistance was pretty well broken. It was now that the motor-truck offensive began. Behind the trucks the field-guns rattled along as the artillerymen spurred on their horses in a vain effort to catch up with something at which they could shoot. At the end of the third day of the attack the American Army had penetrated the German line to a depth of twelve miles. A slight pause was then necessary in order that the big guns might come up, but on November 5 the Third Corps crossed the Meuse. They met a sporadic resistance from German machine-gunners but swept them up with small losses. By the 7th of November the chief objective of the offensive thrust was attained. On that day American troops, among them the Rainbow Division, reached Sedan. Pershing's army had cut the enemy's line of communication. Nothing but surrender or complete defeat was left to him.

In estimating the extent of the American victory it is interesting to note that General Pershing reported that forty enemy divisions participated in the Meuse-Argonne battle. Our army took 26,059 prisoners and captured 468 guns. Colonel Frederick Palmer estimates that 650,000 American soldiers were engaged in the battle. This is a greater number than were engaged at St. Mihiel, and it was, of course, a new mark in the records of the American Army. Colonel Palmer has stated his opinion that

Meuse-Argonne was one of the four decisive battles of the war. The other three which he names are the first battle of the Marne, the first battle of Ypres, and Verdun.

Curiously enough, Château-Thierry looms larger in the mind of the average American than Meuse-Argonne, although the number of Americans engaged in the former battle was not half as great as those who battered their way through the forest. Of course the importance of a battle is not to be judged solely by the number of men engaged, but there seems to be no good reason for assigning a strategic importance to Château-Thierry which is denied to Meuse-Argonne. Most of the military critics are of the opinion that the widespread belief that the Americans saved Paris at the battle of Château-Thierry is not literally true. The American victory was a factor, to be sure. It was even an important factor. Perhaps, from the point of view of morale, it was vital, but judged by strict military standards there is no support for the frequent assertion that only a few marines stood between Paris and the triumphant entry of the German Army. Meuse-Argonne, on the other hand, was not only a campaign solely under American control but a large-scale battle which probably shortened the war by many months. This victory was America's chief contribution in the field to the cause of the Allies. It is on Meuse-Argonne that our military prestige will rest. The divisions engaged were the First, Second, Third, Fourth, Fifth, Twenty-sixth, Twenty-eighth, Twenty-ninth, Thirty-second, Thirty-third, Thirty-fifth, Thirty-seventh, Forty-second, Seventy-seventh, Seventy-eighth, Seventy-ninth, Eightieth, Eighty-second, Eighty-ninth, Ninetieth, and Ninety-first. The First, Fifth, Twenty-sixth, Forty-second, Seventy-seventh, Eightieth, Eighty-ninth, and Ninetieth were particularly honored by being put in the line twice during the campaign.

Though the armistice was now close at hand the war had not ended. The policy of Allied leadership was to fight until the last minute lest there should be some hitch. The American plans called for an advance toward Longwy by the First Army in co-operation with the Second Army, which was to threaten the Briey iron-fields. If the war had kept up, this would have been followed by an offensive in the direction of Château-Salins, with the ultimate object of cutting off Metz. The attack of the Second Army was actually in progress when the time came set in the armistice for the cessation of hostilities. At eleven o'clock the hostilities ceased suddenly, although just before that the Second Army was advancing against heavy and determined machine-gun fire, with both sides apparently unwilling to believe that the war was almost over. At other points in the line where no offensive was set for the last day, the artillerymen had the final word to say. Most of the American guns fired at the foe just before eleven o'clock, and in many batteries the gunners joined hands to pull the lanyards so that all might have a share in the final defiance to Germany.

When the war ended, the American position ran from Port-sur-Seille across the Moselle to Vandières, through the Wœvre to Bezonvaux, thence to the Meuse at Mouzay, and ending at Sedan. There were abroad or in transit 2,053,347 American soldiers, less the losses, and of these there were 1,338,169 combatant troops in France. The American Army captured about 44,000 prisoners and 1,400 guns. The figures on our losses are not yet entirely checked up at the time of this writing, but they were approximately 300,000 in killed, died of disease, wounded, and missing.

When he wrote his report to Secretary Baker, General Pershing reserved his final paragraph for a tribute to his men, and in it he said: "Finally, I pay the supreme tribute to our officers and soldiers of the line. When I think of their heroism, their patience under hardships, their unflinching spirit of offensive action, I am filled with emotion which I am unable to express. Their deeds are immortal, and they have earned the eternal gratitude of our country."

5. A NEW PREFACE TO AN OLD STORY

In this issue *Nutmeg* reprints The Fifty-first Dragon. This is done not on account of any popular clamor but solely at my own request.

The story itself is fairly familiar since it has been reprinted in several anthologies, including Christopher Morley's *Modern Essays*. Morley's book is being used in some high school English courses and two or three times a year I get a letter from some boy or girl saying: "Dear Mr. Brown:—I had to read your story The Fifty-first Dragon because Miss Baker, our teacher, assigned it to us. I could not make head or tail of it and when I asked Miss Baker what it meant she answered, 'Damned if I know.' I am enclosing three cents in stamps and a self-addressed envelope. Will you please explain what you were driving at."

Stamps you get that way never do you any good. They stick to the lining of my pockets and when the pants presser steams them out they are practically useless.

Now that it is too late I realize that I should have been more kindly and considerate in my correspondence on the subject of The Fifty-first Dragon. For several years it constituted my only royalty income. Originally the piece appeared in the magazine section of the old New York *Tribune* which was run at that time by F.P.A., the venerable columnist. Mr. Adams gave me the usual space rates which amounted, as I remember, to $13.20. This was the first piece of fiction I had ever sold with the exception of one or two news stories which I turned in while serving as a reporter on the *Tribune*. I went around to the old, old Press Club and bought a drink for Don Marquis who was already an established author and selling little masterpieces for $25 a throw as if they had been hot cakes.

I put my piece in a book along with other clippings and Chris Morley dug it out and added a little preface * in which he predicted that I would become famous in time as a writer of fanciful and imaginative stories. That was almost twenty-five years ago and, unless Chris is doing his predicting for the long pull, he and I are both out of luck. But for six or seven years the Dragon story was a little gold mine. Every six or seven months somebody would send in ten or twelve dollars for the reprint rights. By now the market has staled and although I never kept any exact books on the subject my thirteen-dollar caravel brought home a total of some two hundred dollars. It bobs up in strange places. Last winter, at the Miami-Biltmore, the bartender and I were talking about a possible daily double combination. He was an old and grizzled bartender who had followed racing successfully for at least twenty years. Suddenly he broke away from horses and said, "You once wrote a story called The Fifty-first Dragon, didn't you?"

I said that I had and added, "But why do you ask?"

"Well," said the bartender, "when I was a senior in high

* From Christopher Morley's anthology, *Modern Essays: First Series*, Harcourt, Brace and Company, 1921: "Heywood Broun, who has risen rapidly through the ranks of newspaper honor from sporting reporter and war correspondent to one of the most highly regarded dramatic and literary critics in the country, is another of these Harvard men, but, as far as this book is concerned, the last of them. Broun graduated from Harvard in 1910; was several years on the New York *Tribune*, and is now on the *World*. There is no more substantially gifted newspaperman in his field; his beautifully spontaneous humor and drollery are counterbalanced by a fine imaginative sensitiveness and a remarkable power in the fable or allegorical essay, such as the one here reprinted. His book, *Seeing Things at Night*, is only the first-fruit of truly splendid possibilities. If I may be allowed to prophesy, thus hazarding all, I will say that Heywood Broun is likely, in the next ten or fifteen years, to do as fine work, both imaginative and critical, as any living American of his era." Heywood Broun reprinted this preface in the *Nutmeg* of August 19, 1939, under the caption "The Joke's on You, Chris."—Ed.

school in Emporia, Kansas, a good many years ago we had to read that story in our English class and it just didn't make any sense to me. I'll tell you what—if you can give me an inkling of what you were driving at, this drink is on the house."

"Make mine a Martini," I answered wearily. "It goes like this, Charlie. I was pretty young at the time and I got hold of a quarter truth and expressed it in a flip and cynical manner which was my mood at the time. Of course the idea isn't new. It was done in popular form in a Harold Lloyd picture called *Grandma's Boy*. I might add that my dragon piece was written long before the picture. But of course the fundamental idea belongs to the ages.

"It is simply this—man is not sufficient unto himself. He must have a rallying cry, a slogan by which to die and by which to live. The story says that even an empty slogan is better than no slogan at all. There is some truth in that, but it is a doctrine on which some of the most dangerous causes in the world have been founded. The step forward is to write the story all over again and more ambitiously. Then the motto would read: faith is essential to life. Paradoxically enough, some of the most eloquent proofs of this lie in the curious passionate intensity of those who would destroy faith. There is no proselyter half so energetic as the hard-shelled atheist. He won't let you alone for a minute. He is, of course, looking for a faith. He tries to raise himself up to it by using negations as his bootstraps. Nobody talks so constantly about God as those who insist that there is no God. That doesn't make sense to me. And so in a fumbling kind of way The Fifty-first Dragon is psychologically correct. Without a belief man is helpless against the dragons. Do you get what I mean?"

"I make it a rule never to talk religion with customers," said Charlie, "but if I can switch it over to politics I think I get you. For instance if a man goes around doing nothing but bawl out the New Deal he's got no hope but only a holler. But I say, 'Re-elect Roosevelt.' I've got something. That's a slogan. That's something to fight for."

"Done and done," I answered. "This drink is on me."

6. THE FIFTY-FIRST DRAGON

Of all the pupils at the knight school Gawaine le Coeur-Hardy was among the least promising. He was tall and sturdy, but his instructors soon discovered that he lacked spirit. He would hide in the woods when the jousting class was called, although his companions and members of the faculty sought to appeal to his better nature by shouting to him to come out and break his neck like a man. Even when they told him that the lances were padded, the horses no more than ponies and the field unusually soft for late autumn, Gawaine refused to grow enthusiastic. The Headmaster and the Assistant Professor of Pleasaunce were discussing the case one spring afternoon and the Assistant Professor could see no remedy but expulsion.

"No," said the Headmaster, as he looked out at the purple hills which ringed the school, "I think I'll train him to slay dragons."

"He might be killed," objected the Assistant Professor.

"So he might," replied the Headmaster brightly, but he added, more soberly, "we must consider the greater good. We are responsible for the formation of this lad's character."

"Are the dragons particularly bad this year?" interrupted the Assistant Professor. This was characteristic. He always seemed restive when the head of the school began to talk ethics and the ideals of the institution.

"I've never known them worse," replied the Headmaster. "Up in the hills to the south last week they killed a number of peasants, two cows and a prize pig. And if this dry spell holds there's no telling when they may start a forest fire simply by breathing around indiscriminately."

"Would any refund on the tuition fee be necessary in case of an accident to young Coeur-Hardy?"

"No," the principal answered, judicially, "that's all covered in the contract. But as a matter of fact he won't be killed. Before I send him up in the hills I'm going to give him a magic word."

"That's a good idea," said the Professor. "Sometimes they work wonders."

From that day on Gawaine specialized in dragons. His course included both theory and practice. In the morning there were long lectures on the history, anatomy, manners and customs of dragons. Gawaine did not distinguish himself in these studies. He had a marvelously versatile gift for forgetting things. In the afternoon he showed to better advantage, for then he would go down to the South Meadow and practice with a battle-ax. In this exercise he was truly impressive, for he had enormous strength as well as speed and grace. He even developed a deceptive display of ferocity. Old alumni say that it was a thrilling sight to see Gawaine charging across the field toward the dummy paper dragon which had been set up for his practice. As he ran he would brandish his ax and shout, "A murrain on thee!" or some other vivid bit of campus slang. It never took him more than one stroke to behead the dummy dragon.

Gradually his task was made more difficult. Paper gave way to papier-mâché and finally to wood, but even the toughest of these dummy dragons had no terrors for Gawaine. One sweep of the ax always did the business. There were those who said that when the practice was protracted until dusk and the dragons threw long, fantastic shadows across the meadow, Gawaine did not charge so impetuously nor shout so loudly. It is possible there was malice in this charge. At any rate, the Headmaster decided by the end of June that it was time for the test. Only the night before a dragon had come close to the school grounds and had eaten some of the lettuce from the garden. The faculty decided that Gawaine was ready. They gave him a diploma and a new battle-ax and the Headmaster summoned him to a private conference.

"Sit down," said the Headmaster. "Have a cigarette."

Gawaine hesitated.

"Oh, I know it's against the rules," said the Headmaster. "But after all, you have received your preliminary degree. You are no longer a boy. You are a man. Tomorrow you will go out into the world, the great world of achievement."

Gawaine took a cigarette. The Headmaster offered him a match, but he produced one of his own and began to puff away with a dexterity which quite amazed the principal.

"Here you have learned the theories of life," continued the Headmaster, resuming the thread of his discourse, "but after all, life is not a matter of theories. Life is a matter of facts. It calls on the young and the old alike to face these facts, even though they are hard and sometimes unpleasant. Your problem, for example, is to slay dragons."

"They say that those dragons down in the south wood are five hundred feet long," ventured Gawaine, timorously.

"Stuff and nonsense!" said the Headmaster. "The curate saw one last week from the top of Arthur's Hill. The dragon was sunning himself down in the valley. The curate didn't have an opportunity to look at him very long because he felt it was his duty to hurry back to make a report to me. He said the monster —or shall I say, the big lizard?—wasn't an inch over two hundred feet. But the size has nothing at all to do with it. You'll find the big ones even easier than the little ones. They're far slower on their feet and less aggressive, I'm told. Besides, before you go I'm going to equip you in such fashion that you need have no fear of all the dragons in the world."

"I'd like an enchanted cap," said Gawaine.

"What's that?" asked the Headmaster, testily.

"A cap to make me disappear," explained Gawaine.

The Headmaster laughed indulgently. "You mustn't believe

all those old wives' stories," he said. "There isn't any such thing. A cap to make you disappear, indeed! What would you do with it? You haven't even appeared yet. Why, my boy, you could walk from here to London, and nobody would so much as look at you. You're nobody. You couldn't be more invisible than that."

Gawaine seemed dangerously close to a relapse into his old habit of whimpering. The Headmaster reassured him: "Don't worry; I'll give you something much better than an enchanted cap. I'm going to give you a magic word. All you have to do is to repeat this magic charm once and no dragon can possibly harm a hair of your head. You can cut off his head at your leisure."

He took a heavy book from the shelf behind his desk and began to run through it. "Sometimes," he said, "the charm is a whole phrase or even a sentence. I might, for instance, give you 'To make the'—no, that might not do. I think a single word would be best for dragons."

"A short word," suggested Gawaine.

"It can't be too short or it wouldn't be potent. There isn't so much hurry as all that. Here's a splendid magic word: 'Rumplesnitz.' Do you think you can learn that?"

Gawaine tried and in an hour or so he seemed to have the word well in hand. Again and again he interrupted the lesson to inquire, "And if I say 'Rumplesnitz' the dragon can't possibly hurt me?" And always the Headmaster replied, "If you only say 'Rumplesnitz,' you are perfectly safe."

Toward morning Gawaine seemed resigned to his career. At daybreak the Headmaster saw him to the edge of the forest and pointed him to the direction in which he should proceed. About a mile away to the southwest a cloud of steam hovered over an open meadow in the woods and the Headmaster assured Gawaine that under the steam he would find a dragon. Gawaine went forward slowly. He wondered whether it would be best to approach the dragon on the run as he did in his practice in the South Meadow or to walk slowly toward him, shouting "Rumplesnitz" all the way.

The problem was decided for him. No sooner had he come to the fringe of the meadow than the dragon spied him and began to charge. It was a large dragon and yet it seemed decidedly aggressive in spite of the Headmaster's statement to the contrary. As the dragon charged it released huge clouds of hissing steam through its nostrils. It was almost as if a gigantic teapot had gone mad. The dragon came forward so fast and Gawaine was so frightened that he had time to say "Rumplesnitz" only once. As he said it, he swung his battle-ax and off popped the head of the dragon. Gawaine had to admit that it was even easier to kill a real dragon than a wooden one if only you said "Rumplesnitz."

Gawaine brought the ears home and a small section of the tail. His school mates and the faculty made much of him, but the Headmaster wisely kept him from being spoiled by insisting that he go on with his work. Every clear day Gawaine rose at dawn and went out to kill dragons. The Headmaster kept him at home when it rained, because he said the woods were damp and unhealthy at such times and that he didn't want the boy to run needless risks. Few good days passed in which Gawaine failed to get a dragon. On one particularly fortunate day he killed three, a husband and wife and a visiting relative. Gradually he developed a technique. Pupils who sometimes watched him from the hill-tops a long way off said that he often allowed the dragon to come within a few feet before he said "Rumplesnitz." He came to say it with a mocking sneer. Occasionally he did stunts. Once when an excursion party from London was watching him he went into action with his right hand tied behind his back. The dragon's head came off just as easily.

As Gawaine's record of killings mounted higher the Headmaster found it impossible to keep him completely in hand. He fell into the habit of stealing out at night and engaging in long drinking bouts at the village tavern. It was after such a deba that he rose a little before dawn one fine August morning and started out after his fiftieth dragon. His head was heavy and his mind sluggish. He was heavy in other respects as well, for he had adopted the somewhat vulgar practice of wearing his medals, ribbons and all, when he went out dragon hunting. The decorations began on his chest and ran all the way down to his abdomen. They must have weighed at least eight pounds.

Gawaine found a dragon in the same meadow where he had killed the first one. It was a fair-sized dragon, but evidently an old one. Its face was wrinkled and Gawaine thought he had never seen so hideous a countenance. Much to the lad's disgust, the monster refused to charge and Gawaine was obliged to walk toward him. He whistled as he went. The dragon regarded him hopelessly, but craftily. Of course it had heard of Gawaine. Even when the lad raised his battle-ax the dragon made no move. It knew that there was no salvation in the quickest thrust of the head, for it had been informed that this hunter was protected by an enchantment. It merely waited, hoping something would turn up.

Gawaine raised the battle-ax and suddenly lowered it again. He had grown very pale and he trembled violently.

The dragon suspected a trick. "What's the matter?" it asked, with false solicitude.

"I've forgotten the magic word," stammered Gawaine.

"What a pity," said the dragon. "So that was the secret. It doesn't seem quite sporting to me, all this magic stuff, you know. Not cricket, as we used to say when I was a little dragon; but after all, that's a matter of opinion."

Gawaine was so helpless with terror that the dragon's confidence rose immeasurably and it could not resist the temptation to show off a bit.

"Could I possibly be of any assistance?" it asked. "What's the first letter of the magic word?"

"It begins with an 'r,'" said Gawaine weakly.

"'s see," mused the dragon, "that doesn't tell us much,

does it? What sort of a word is this? Is it an epithet, do you think?"

Gawaine could do no more than nod.

"Why, of course," exclaimed the dragon, "reactionary Republican."

Gawaine shook his head.

"Well, then," said the dragon, "we'd better get down to business. Will you surrender?"

With the suggestion of a compromise Gawaine mustered up enough courage to speak.

"What will you do if I surrender?" he asked.

"Why, I'll eat you," said the dragon.

"And if I don't surrender?"

"I'll eat you just the same."

"Then it doesn't mean any difference, does it?" moaned Gawaine.

"It does to me," said the dragon with a smile. "I'd rather you didn't surrender. You'd taste much better if you didn't."

The dragon waited for a long time for Gawaine to ask "Why?" but the boy was too frightened to speak. At last the dragon had to give the explanation without his cue line. "You see," he said, "if you don't surrender you'll taste better because you'll die game."

This was an old and ancient trick of the dragon's. By means of some such quip he was accustomed to paralyze his victims with laughter and then to destroy them. Gawaine was sufficiently paralyzed as it was, but laughter had no part in his helplessness. With the last word of the joke the dragon drew back his head and struck. In that second there flashed into the mind of Gawaine the magic word "Rumplesnitz," but there was no time to say it. There was time only to strike and, without a word, Gawaine met the onrush of the dragon with a full swing. He put all his back and shoulders into it. The impact was terrific and the head of the dragon flew almost a hundred yards and landed in a thicket.

"Le

Gawaine did not remain frightened very long after the death of the dragon. His mood was one of wonder. He was enormously puzzled. He cut off the ears of the monster almost in a trance. Again and again he thought to himself, "I didn't say 'Rumplesnitz'!" He was sure of that and yet there was no question that he had killed the dragon. In fact, he had never killed one so utterly. Never before had he driven a head for anything like the same distance. Twenty-five yards was perhaps his best previous record. All the way back to the knight school he kept rumbling about in his mind seeking an explanation for what had occurred. He went to the Headmaster immediately and after closing the door told him what had happened. "I didn't say 'Rumplesnitz,'" he explained with great earnestness.

The Headmaster laughed. "I'm glad you've found out," he said. "It makes you ever so much more of a hero. Don't you see that? Now you know that it was you who killed all these dragons and not that foolish little word 'Rumplesnitz.'"

Gawaine frowned. "Then it wasn't a magic word after all?" he asked.

"Of course not," said the Headmaster, "you ought to be too old for such foolishness. There isn't any such thing as a magic word."

"But you told me it was magic," protested Gawaine. "You said it was magic and now you say it isn't."

"It wasn't magic in a literal sense," answered the Headmaster, "but it was much more wonderful than that. The word gave you confidence. It took away your fears. If I hadn't told you that, you might have been killed the very first time. It was your battle-ax did the trick."

Gawaine surprised the Headmaster by his attitude. He was obviously distressed by the explanation. He interrupted a long philosophic and ethical discourse by the Headmaster with "If I hadn't of hit 'em all mighty hard and fast any one of 'em might have crushed me like a, like a—" He fumbled for a word.

"Egg shell," suggested the Headmaster.

"Like a egg shell," assented Gawaine, and he said it many times. All through the evening meal people who sat near him heard him muttering, "Like a egg shell, like a egg shell."

The next day was clear, but Gawaine did not get up at dawn. Indeed, it was almost noon when the Headmaster found him cowering in bed, with the clothes pulled over his head. The principal called the Assistant Professor of Pleasaunce, and together they dragged the boy toward the forest.

"He'll be all right as soon as he gets a couple more dragons under his belt," explained the Headmaster.

The Assistant Professor of Pleasaunce agreed. "It would be a shame to stop such a fine run," he said. "Why, counting that one yesterday, he's killed fifty dragons."

They pushed the boy into a thicket above which hung a meager cloud of steam. It was obviously quite a small dragon. But Gawaine did not come back that night or the next. In fact, he never came back. Some weeks afterward brave spirits from the school explored the thicket, but they could find nothing to remind them of Gawaine except the metal parts of his medals. Even the ribbons had been devoured.

The Headmaster and the Assistant Professor of Pleasaunce agreed that it would be just as well not to tell the school how Gawaine had achieved his record and still less how he came to die. They held that it might have a bad effect on school spirit. Accordingly, Gawaine has lived in the memory of the school as its greatest hero. No visitor succeeds in leaving the building to-day without seeing a great shield which hangs on the wall of the dining hall. Fifty pairs of dragons' ears are mounted upon the shield and underneath in gilt letters is "Gawaine le Coeur-Hardy," followed by the simple inscription, "He killed fifty dragons." The record has never been equaled.

7. SOME OF MY BEST FRIENDS
ARE YALE MEN

Oh, Harvard was old Harvard when Yale was but a pup,
And Harvard will be Harvard still when Yale has all gone up,
And if any Eli—

This is about as far as the old song should be carried. Perhaps it is too far. Our plea today is for something of abatement in the intensity of the rivalry between Harvard and Yale. To be sure we realize that the plea has been made before unsuccessfully by mightier men. Indeed it was Charles W. Eliot himself, president of Harvard, who rebuked the students when first they began to sing, "Three cheers for Harvard and down with Yale." This, he said, seemed to him hardly a proper spirit. He suggested an amendment so that the song might go, "Three cheers for Harvard and one for Yale." Such seventy-five per cent loyalty was rejected. Yale must continue to do its own cheering.

Naturally, it is not to be expected that Yale and Harvard men should meet on terms of perfect amity immediately and that the old bitterness should disappear within the time of our own generation. Such a miracle is beyond the scope of our intention. Too much has happened. Just what it was that Yale originally did to Harvard we don't profess to know. It was enough we suppose to justify the trial of the issue by combat four times a year in the major sports. Curiously enough, for a good many years Yale seemed to grow more and more right if judged in the light of these tests. But the truth is mighty and shall prevail and the righteousness of Harvard's cause began to be apparent with the coming of Percy Haughton. God, as some cynic has said, is always on the side which has the best football coach.

Our suggestion is that whatever deep wrong Yale once committed against Harvard, a process of diminution of feeling should be allowed to set in. After all, can't the men of Cambridge be broad-minded about these things and remember that nothing within the power of Yale could possibly hurt Harvard very much? Even in the days when the blue elevens were winning with great regularity there should have been consolation enough in the thought that Harvard's Greek department still held the edge. Seemingly nobody ever thought of that. In the 1906 game a Harvard half-back named Nichols was sent in late in the game while the score was still a tie. On practically the first play he dropped a punt which led directly to a Yale touchdown and victory.

Throughout the rest of his university career he was known in college as "the man who dropped the punt." When his brother entered Harvard two years later he was promptly christened and known for his next four years as "the brother of the man who dropped the punt."

Isn't this a little excessive? It seems so to us, but the emphasis has not yet shifted. Only a month or so ago we were talking in New Haven before an organization of Yale graduates upon a subject so unpartisan as the American drama—though to be sure Harvard has turned out ten playwrights of note to every one from Yale—and somehow or other the talk drifted around to football. In pleading for less intensity of football feeling we mentioned the man who dropped the punt and his brother and told how Yale had recovered the fatal fumble on Harvard's nineteen-yard line. Then, with the intention of being jocose, we remarked, "The Yale eleven with characteristic bulldog grit and courage carried the ball over the line." To our horror and amazement the audience immediately broke into applause and long cheers.

Some of my best friends are Yale men and there is no basis

for the common Harvard assumption that graduates of New Haven's leading university are of necessity inferior to the breed of Cambridge. Still, there is, perhaps, just a shade of difference in the keenness of perception for wit. Practically all the Harvard anecdotes about Yale which we know are pointed and sprightly, while Yale is content with such inferior and tasteless jibes as the falsetto imitation which begins, "Fiercely, fellows, sift through." Even the audience of graduates to which we referred was singularly cold to the anecdote about the difference in traditions which prevails at New Haven and at Cambridge. "When a Yale man is sick, the authorities immediately assume that he is drunk. When a Harvard man is drunk, the authorities assume that he is sick."

Nor were we successful in retelling the stirring appeal of a well-known organizer who was seeking to consolidate various alumni bodies into a vast unified employment agency for college men. "There should be," he cried, "one great clearing house. Then when somebody came for a man to tutor his children we could send him a Harvard man and if he needed somebody to help with the furnace, we'd have a Yale graduate for him."

Joking with undergraduates we found still more disastrous. After the last Harvard-Yale football game—score, Harvard 9, Yale 0, which doesn't begin to indicate the margin of superiority of the winning team—we wrote an article of humorous intent for a New York newspaper. Naturally our job as a reporter prevented us from being partisan in our account of the game. Accordingly, in a temperate and fair-minded spirit, we set down the fact that, through the connivance of the New York press, Yale has become a professional underdog and that any Harvard victory in which the score is less than 42 to 0 is promptly hailed as a moral victory for Yale.

Developing this news angle for a few paragraphs, we eventually came to the unfortunate fist fight between Kempton of Yale and Gaston of Harvard which led to both men being put out of the game. It was our bad luck to see nothing but the last half second of the encounter. As a truthful reporter we made this admission but naturally went on to add, "Of course, we assume that Kempton started it." For weeks we continued to receive letters from Yale undergraduates beginning, "My attention has been called to your article" and continuing to ask with great violence how a reporter could possibly tell who started a fight without seeing the beginning of it. Some letters of like import were from Princeton men.

Princeton is always quick to rally to the defense of Yale against Harvard. This suggests a possibly common meeting ground for Harvard and Yale. Of course, they can hardly meet on the basis of a common language, for the speech of Yale is quite alien. For instance, they call their yard a "campus." Also, there are obvious reasons why they cannot meet as equal members in the fellowship of educated men. Since this is a non-partisan article designed to promote good feeling it will probably be just as well not to go into this. Though football is the chief interest at New Haven, Yale men often display a surprising sensitiveness to attacks on the scholarship of their local archeologists. Nor will religion do as a unifier. Yale is evangelical and prays between the halves, while Harvard is mostly agnostic, if it isn't Unitarian. No, just one great cause can be discovered in which Harvard men and Yale men can stand shoulder to shoulder and lift their voices in a common cause. Each year some public-spirited citizen ought to hire Madison Square Garden and turn it over to all graduates and undergraduates of Harvard and of Yale for a great get-together meeting in which past differences should be forgotten in one deep and full-throated shout of "To Hell with Princeton!"

8. DEATH SAYS IT ISN'T SO

The scene is a sickroom. It is probably in a hospital, for the walls are plain and all the corners are eliminated in that peculiar circular construction which is supposed to annoy germs. The shades are down and the room is almost dark. A doctor who has been examining the sick man turns to go. The nurse at his side looks at him questioningly.

THE DOCTOR (*briskly*)—I don't believe he'll last out the day. If he wakes or seems unusually restless, let me know. There's nothing to do.

He goes out quietly, but quickly, for there is another man down at the end of the corridor who is almost as sick. The nurse potters about the room for a moment or two, arranging whatever things it is that nurses arrange. She exits l.c., or, in other words, goes out the door. There is just a short pause in the dark, quiet room shut out from all outside noises and most outside light. When the steam pipes are not clanking only the slow breathing of the man on the bed can be heard. Suddenly a strange thing happens.

The door does not open or the windows, but there is unquestionably another man in the room. It couldn't have been the chimney, because there isn't any. Possibly it is an optical illusion, but the newcomer seems just a bit indistinct for a moment or so in the darkened room. Quickly he raises both the window shades, and in the rush of bright sunlight he is definite enough in appearance. Upon better acquaintance it becomes evident that it couldn't have been the chimney, even if there had been one. The visitor is undeniably bulky, although extraordinarily brisk in his movements. He has a trick which will develop later in the scene of blushing on the slightest provocation. At that his color is habitually high. But this round, red, little man, peculiarly enough, has thin white hands and long tapering fingers, like an artist or a newspaper cartoonist. Very possibly his touch would be lighter than that of the nurse herself. At any rate, it is evident that he walks much more quietly. This is strange, for he does not rise on his toes, but puts his feet squarely on the ground. They are large feet, shod in heavy hobnail boots. No one but a golfer or a day laborer would wear such shoes.

The hands of the little, round, red man preclude the idea that he is a laborer. The impression that he is a golfer is heightened by the fact that he is dressed loudly in very bad taste. In fact, he wears a plaid vest of the sort which was brought over from Scotland in the days when clubs were called sticks. The man in the gaudy vest surveys the sunshine with great satisfaction. It reaches every corner of the room, or rather it would but for the fact that the corners have been turned into curves. A stray beam falls across the eyes of the sick man on the bed. He wakes, and, rubbing his eyes an instant, slowly sits up in bed and looks severely at the fat little man.

THE SICK MAN (*feebly, but vehemently*)—No, you don't. I won't stand for any male nurse. I want Miss Bluchblauer.

THE FAT MAN—I'm not a nurse, exactly.

THE SICK MAN—Who are you?

THE FAT MAN (*cheerfully and in a matter-of-fact tone*)—I'm Death.

THE SICK MAN (*sinking back on the bed*)—That rotten fever's up again. I'm seeing things.

THE FAT MAN (*almost plaintively*)—Don't you believe I'm Death? Honest, I am. I wouldn't fool you. (*He fumbles in his pockets and produces in rapid succession a golf ball, a baseball pass, a G string, a large lump of gold, a receipted bill, two theater tickets and a white mass of sticky confection which looks as though it might be a combination of honey and something— milk, perhaps.*) I've gone and left that card case again, but I'm Death, all right.

THE SICK MAN—What nonsense! If you really were I'd be frightened. I'd have cold shivers up and down my spine. My hair would stand on end like the fretful porcupine. I'm not afraid of you. Why, when Sadie Bluchblauer starts to argue about the war she scares me more than you do.

THE FAT MAN (*very much relieved and visibly brighter*)— That's fine. I'm glad you're not scared. Now we can sit down and talk things over like friends.

THE SICK MAN—I don't mind talking, but remember I know you're not Death. You're just some trick my hot head's playing on me. Don't get the idea you're putting anything over.

THE FAT MAN—But what makes you so sure I'm not Death?

THE SICK MAN—Go on! Where's your black cloak? Where's your sickle? Where's your skeleton? Why don't you rattle when you walk?

THE FAT MAN (*horrified and distressed*)—Why should I rattle? What do I want with a black overcoat or a skeleton? I'm not fooling you. I'm Death, all right.

THE SICK MAN—Don't tell me that. I've seen Death a thousand times in the war cartoons. And I've seen him on the stage —Maeterlinck, you know, with green lights and moaning, and that Russian fellow, Andreyeff, with no light at all, and hollering. And I've seen other plays with Death—lots of them. I'm one of the scene shifters with the Washington Square Players. This isn't regular, at all. There's more light in here right now than any day since I've been sick.

THE FAT MAN—I always come in the light. Be a good fellow and believe me. You'll see I'm right later on. I wouldn't fool anybody. It's mean.

THE SICK MAN (*laughing out loud*)—Mean! What's meaner than Death? You're not Death. You're as soft and smooth-talking as a press agent. Why, you could go on a picnic in that make-up.

THE FAT MAN (*almost soberly*)—I've been on picnics.

THE SICK MAN—You're open and above board. Death's a

sneak. You've got a nice face. Yes; you've got a mighty nice face. You'd stop to help a bum in the street or a kid that was crying.

THE FAT MAN—I have stopped for beggars and children.

THE SICK MAN—There, you see; I told you. You're kind and considerate. Death's the cruelest thing in the world.

THE FAT MAN (*very much agitated*)—Oh, please don't say that! It isn't true. I'm kind; that's my business. When things get too rotten I'm the only one that can help. They've got to have me. You should hear them sometimes before I come. I'm the one that takes them off battlefields and out of slums and all terribly tired people. I whisper a joke in their ears, and we go away, laughing. We always go away laughing. Everybody sees my joke, it's so good.

THE SICK MAN—What's the joke?

THE FAT MAN—I'll tell it to you later.

Enter the Nurse. She almost runs into the Fat Man, but goes right past without paying any attention. It almost seems as if she cannot see him. She goes to the bedside of the patient.

THE NURSE—So you're awake. You feel any more comfortable?

The Sick Man continues to stare at the Fat Man, but that worthy animated pantomime indicates that he shall say nothing of his being there. While this is on, the Nurse takes the patient's temperature. She looks at it, seems surprised, and then shakes the thermometer.

THE SICK MAN (*eagerly*)—I suppose my temperature's way up again, hey? I've been seeing things this afternoon and talking to myself.

THE NURSE—No; your temperature is almost normal.

THE SICK MAN (*incredulously*)—Almost normal?

THE NURSE—Yes; under a hundred.

She goes out quickly and quietly. The Sick Man turns to his fat friend.

THE SICK MAN—What do you make of that? Less than a hundred. That oughtn't to make me see things; do you think so?

THE FAT MAN—Well, I'd just as soon not be called a thing. Up there I'm called good old Death. Some of the fellows call me Bill. Maybe that's because I'm always due.

THE SICK MAN—Rats! Is that the joke you promised me?

THE FAT MAN (*pained beyond measure*)—Oh, that was just a little unofficial joke. The joke's not like that. I didn't make up the real one. It wasn't made up at all. It's been growing for years and years. A whole lot of people have had a hand in fixing it up—Aristophanes and Chaucer and Shakespeare, and Mark Twain and Rabelais—

THE SICK MAN—Did that fellow Rabelais get in—up there?

THE FAT MAN—Well, not exactly, but he lives in one of the most accessible parts of the suburb, and we have him up quite often. He's popular on account of his after-dinner stories. What I might call his physical humor is delightfully reminiscent and archaic.

THE SICK MAN—There won't be any bodies, then?

THE FAT MAN—Oh, yes, brand new ones. No tonsils or appendixes, of course. That is, not as a rule. We have to bring in a few tonsils every year to amuse our doctors.

THE SICK MAN—Any shows?

THE FAT MAN—I should say so. Lots of 'em, and all hits. In fact, we've never had a failure (*provocatively*). Now, what do you think is the best show you ever saw?

THE SICK MAN (*reminiscently*)—Well, just about the best show I ever saw was a piece called *Fair and Warmer*, but, of course, you wouldn't have that.

THE FAT MAN—Of course; we have. The fellow before last wanted that.

THE SICK MAN (*truculently*)—I'll bet you haven't got the original company.

THE FAT MAN (*apologetically*)—No, but we expect to get most of them by and by. Nell Gwynn does pretty well in the lead just now.

THE SICK MAN (*shocked*)—Did she get in?

THE FAT MAN—No, but Rabelais sees her home after the show. We don't think so much of *Fair and Warmer*. That might be a good show for New York, but it doesn't class with us. It isn't funny enough.

THE SICK MAN (*with rising interest*)—Do you mean to say you've got funnier shows than *Fair and Warmer*?

THE FAT MAN—We certainly have. Why, it can't begin to touch that thing of Shaw's called *Ah, There, Annie!*

THE SICK MAN—What Shaw's that?

THE FAT MAN—Regular Shaw.

THE SICK MAN—A lot of things must have been happening since I got sick. I hadn't heard he was dead. At that I always thought that vegetable truck was unhealthy.

THE FAT MAN—He isn't dead.

THE SICK MAN—Well, how about this *Ah, There, Annie!*? He never wrote that show down here.

THE FAT MAN—But he will.

THE SICK MAN (*enormously impressed*)—Do you get shows there before we have them in New York?

THE FAT MAN—I tell you we get them before they're written.

THE SICK MAN (*indignantly*)—How can you do that?

THE FAT MAN—I wish you wouldn't ask me. The answer's awfully complicated. You've got to know a lot of higher math. Wait and ask Euclid about it. We don't have any past and future, you know. None of that nuisance about keeping "shall" and "will" straight.

THE SICK MAN—Well, I must say that's quite a stunt. You get shows before they're written.

THE FAT MAN—More than that. We get some that never do get written. Take that one of Ibsen's now, *Merry Christmas*—

THE SICK MAN (*fretfully*)—Ibsen?

THE FAT MAN—Yes, it's a beautiful, sentimental little fairy story with a ghost for the hero. Ibsen just thought about it and never had the nerve to go through with it. He was scared people would kid him, but thinking things makes them so with us.

THE SICK MAN—Then I'd think a sixty-six round Van Cortlandt for myself.

THE FAT MAN—You could do that. But why Van Cortlandt? We've got much better greens on our course. It's a beauty. Seven thousand yards long and I've made it in fifty-four.

THE SICK MAN (*suspiciously*)—Did you hole out on every green or just estimate?

THE FAT MAN (*stiffly*)—The score is duly attested. I might add that it was possible because I drove more than four hundred yards on nine of the eighteen holes.

THE SICK MAN—More than four hundred yards? How did you do that?

THE FAT MAN—It must have been the climate, or (*thoughtfully*) it may be because I wanted so much to drive over four hundred yards on those holes.

THE SICK MAN (*with just a shade of scorn*)—So that's the trick. I guess nobody'd ever beat me on that course; I'd just want the ball in the hole in one every time.

THE FAT MAN (*in gentle reproof*)—No, you wouldn't. Where you and I are going pretty soon we're all true sportsmen and nobody there would take an unfair advantage of an opponent.

THE SICK MAN—Before I go I want to know something. There's a fellow in 125th Street's been awful decent to me. Is there any coming back to see people here? (*A pause.*)

THE FAT MAN—I can't explain to you yet, but it's difficult to arrange that. Still, I wouldn't say that there never were any slumming parties from beyond the grave.

THE SICK MAN (*shivering*)—The grave! I'd forgotten about that.

THE FAT MAN—Oh, you won't go there, and, what's more, you won't be at the funeral, either. I wish I could keep away from them. I hate funerals. They make me mad. You know, they say, "Oh, Death, where is thy sting?" just as if they had a pretty good hunch I had one around me someplace after all.

And you know that other—"My friends, this is not a sad occasion," but they don't mean it. They keep it sad. They simply won't learn any better. I suppose they'd be a little surprised to know that you were sitting watching Radbourne pitch to Ed Delehanty with the bases full and three balls and two strikes called. Two runs to win and one to tie.

THE SICK MAN—Will Radbourne pitch?

THE FAT MAN—Sure thing.

THE SICK MAN—And, say, will Delehanty bust that ball?

THE FAT MAN—Make it even money and bet me either way.

THE SICK MAN—I don't want to wait any longer. Tell me that joke of yours and let's go.

The light softens a little. The room is almost rose color now. It might be from the sunset. The Fat Man gently pushes the head of the Sick Man back on the pillow. Leaning over, he whispers in his ear briefly and the Sick Man roars with laughter. As his laughter slackens a little the Fat Man says, "I'll meet you in the press box," and then before you know it he's gone. The Sick Man is still laughing, but less loudly. People who did not know might think it was gasping. The Nurse opens the door and is frightened. She loudly calls "Doctor! Doctor!" and runs down the corridor. The Sick Man gives one more chuckle and is silent. The curtains at one of the windows sway slightly. Of course, it's the breeze.

(CURTAIN)

9. THE LIBRARY OF A LOVER

The responsibilities of a book reviewer, always heavy, sometimes assume a gravity which makes it quite impossible for them to be borne on any single pair of shoulders. We have received a letter today upon which so much depends that we hesitate to answer without requesting advice from readers. It is from a young man in Pittsburgh who identifies himself merely by the initials X.Q., which we presume to be fictitious. He writes as follows:

"As a reader of the book columns of the *Tribune* I am humbly requesting your assistance in the matter of a little experiment that I desire to perform. I find myself highly enamored of a superlatively attractive young lady who has, however, one apparent drawback to me. That lies in the fact that she has never cultivated a taste for really worth while reading. Such reading to me is one of the greatest of life's pleasures. Now, my idea is this: that this reading taste may be developed by the reading of a number of the best books in various lines. I have decided upon an experiment wherein a list of fifty books shall be furnished by you and a serious attempt made by the young lady to read them. When she has completed this reading I shall ask her to make a thoroughly frank statement as to whether a reading habit has been cultivated which will enable her to enjoy good literature. I would appreciate very much your furnishing me a list of fifty of the very best books which you consider suitable for the experiment which I have in mind. The lady in question has read but little, but has completed the regulation high school course and in addition has taken two years at one of the recognized girls' schools of the country."

Obviously, the making of such a list involves a responsibility which we do not care to assume. We do not like to risk the possibility that our own particular literary prejudices might rear a barrier between two fond hearts. After all, as somebody has said, fond hearts are more than Conrads. However, we do venture the suggestion that if the young man's intentions are honorable, fifty books is far too great a number for the experiment which he has in mind. We have known many a young couple to begin life with no possession to their name but a common fondness for the poems of W. E. Henley. We have known others to marry on Kipling and repent on Shaw.

Of course, it would be a great deal easier for us to advise the young man if we knew just what sort of a wife he wanted. If she likes *Dombey and Son* and *Little Dorrit* it seems to us fair to assume that she will be able to do a little plain mending and some of the cooking. On the other hand, if her favorite author is May Sinclair, we rather think it would be well to be prepared to provide hired help from the beginning. Should she prefer Eleanor H. Porter, we think there would be no danger in telling the paperhangers to do the bedroom in pink. After all, if she is a thorough-going follower of Pollyanna and the glad game, you don't really need any wallpaper at all. It would still be her duty to be glad about it.

But we are afraid that some of this is frivolous and beside the point, and we assume that the young man truly wants serious advice to help him in the solution of his problem. Since marriage is at best a gamble, we advise him earnestly not to compromise his ardor with any dreary round of fifty books. Let him chance all on a single volume. And what shall it be? Personally, we have always been strongly attracted by persons who liked *Joan and Peter*, but we know that there are excellent wives and mothers who find this particular novel of Wells's dreary stuff. There are certain dislikes which might well serve as green signals of caution.

A young man, we think, should certainly go slow if she does not like *An Inland Voyage*, or *Virginibus Puerisque*, or *The Ebb Tide* or *Sentimental Tommy*. He should take thought and ask himself repeatedly, "Is this really love?" if she confesses a distaste for *Tono Bungay*, or *Far from the Madding Crowd*, or *Caesar and Cleopatra*. And if she can find no interest in *Conrad in Quest of His Youth*, or *Mary Olivier* or *Huckleberry Finn*, let him by all means stipulate a long engagement. But if she dislikes *Alice in Wonderland* let the young man temporize no more. It is then his plain duty to tell her that he has made a mistake and that what he took for love was no more than the passing infatuation of physical passion.

10. INASMUCH

Once there lived near Bethlehem a man named Simon and his wife Deborah. And Deborah dreamed a curious dream, a dream so vivid that it might better be called a vision. It was not yet daybreak, but she roused her husband and told him that an angel had come to her in the vision and had said, as she remembered it, "Tomorrow night in Bethlehem the King of the World will be born." The rest was not so vivid in Deborah's mind, but she told Simon that wise men and kings were already on their way to Bethlehem, bringing gifts for the wonder child.

"When he is born," she said, "the wise men and the kings who bring these gifts will see the stars dance in the heavens and hear the voices of angels. You and I must send presents, too, for this child will be the greatest man in all the world."

Simon objected that there was nothing of enough value in the house to take to such a child, but Deborah replied, "The King of the World will understand." Then, although it was not yet light, she got up and began to bake a cake, and Simon went beyond the town to the hills and got holly and made a wreath. Later in the day husband and wife looked over all their belongings, but the only suitable gift they could find was one old toy, a somewhat battered wooden duck that had belonged to their eldest son, who had grown up and married and gone away to live in Galilee. Simon painted the toy duck as well as he could, and Deborah told him to take it and the cake and the wreath of holly and go to Bethlehem. "It's not much," she said, "but the King will understand."

It was almost sunset when Simon started down the winding road that led to Bethlehem. Deborah watched him round the first turn and would have watched longer except that he was walking straight toward the sun and the light hurt her eyes. She went back into the house and an hour had hardly passed when she heard Simon whistling in the garden. He was walking very slowly. At the door he hesitated for almost a minute. She looked up when he came in. He was empty handed.

"You haven't been to Bethlehem," said Deborah.

"No," said Simon.

"Then, where is the cake, and the holly wreath, and the toy duck?"

"I'm sorry," said Simon, "I couldn't help it somehow. It just happened."

"What happened?" asked Deborah sharply.

"Well," said Simon, "just after I went around the first turn in the road I found a child sitting on that big white rock, crying. He was about two or three years old, and I stopped and asked him why he was crying. He didn't answer. Then I told him not to cry like that, and I patted his head, but that didn't do any good. I hung around, trying to think up something, and I decided to put the cake down and take him up in my arms for a minute. But the cake slipped out of my hands and hit the rock, and a piece of the icing chipped off. Well, I thought, that baby in Bethlehem won't miss a little piece of icing, and I gave it to the child and he stopped crying. But when he finished he began to cry again. I just sort of squeezed another little piece of icing off, and that was all right, for a little while; but then I had to give him another piece, and things went on that way, and all of a sudden I found that there wasn't any cake left. After that he looked as if he might cry again, and I didn't have any more cake and so I showed him the duck and he said 'Ta-ta.' I just meant to lend him the duck for a minute, but he wouldn't give it up. I coaxed him a good while, but he wouldn't let go. And then a woman came out of that little house and she began to scold him for staying out so late, and so I told her it was my fault and I gave her the holly wreath just so she wouldn't be mad at the child. And after that, you see, I didn't have anything to take to Bethlehem, and so I came back here."

Deborah had begun to cry long before Simon finished his story, but when he had done she lifted up her head and said, "How could you do it, Simon? Those presents were meant for the King of the World, and you gave them to the first crying child you met on the road."

Then she began to cry again, and Simon didn't know what to say or do, and it grew darker and darker in the room and the fire on the hearth faded to a few embers. And that little red glow was all there was in the room. Now, Simon could not not even see Deborah across the room, but he could still hear her sobbing. But suddenly the room was flooded with light and Deborah's sobbing broke into a great gulp and she rushed to the window and looked out. The stars danced in the sky and from high above the house came the voice of angels saying, "Glory to God in the highest, and on earth peace, good will toward men."

Deborah dropped to her knees in a panic of joy and fear. Simon knelt beside her, but first he said, "I thought maybe that the baby in Bethlehem wouldn't mind so very much."

11. H. 3RD: THE REVIEW OF
A CONTINUOUS PERFORMANCE

March 1, 1919: "Do you know how to keep the child from crying?" began the prospectus. "Do you know how always to obtain cheerful obedience?" it continued. "To suppress the fighting instinct? To teach punctuality? Perseverance? Carefulness? Honesty? Truthfulness? Correct pronunciation?"

We wondered. Obviously, our rejoinder must be: "In reply to questions Nos. 1, 2, 3, 4, 5, 6, 7, 8 and 9 the answer is in the negative."

The prospectus said that all this would be easy if you bought the book.

"Instead of a hardship," the advertisement said, "child training becomes a genuine pleasure, as the parent shares every confidence, every joy and every sorrow of the child, and at the same time has its unqualified respect. This is a situation rarely possible under the old training methods. And what a source of pride now as well as in after years! To have children whose every action shows culture and refinement—perfect little gentlemen and gentlewomen."

This gave us pause. After all, we were not certain that we wanted a little gentleman who washed behind the ears, wore blue velvet and took his baths with a broad "a." We felt that he might expect too much from us. It might cramp our style to live with a person entirely truthful, punctual, persevering, honest and careful. Also, we were a little abashed about sharing confidences. The privilege of becoming a confidant would involve a return in kind, and it would not be a fair swap. It seemed to us that the confessions of the truthful, honest, careful and persevering child could never be half so interesting as our own.

We were also a little bit discouraged over the promise to suppress the fighting instinct. We did not feel qualified for the job of making it up to him by chastising the parents of the various boys along the block who drubbed him. And yet we were not entirely dissuaded until we read something of the manner in which the new method should be applied. It was hard to thrust aside the knowledge of how to keep the child from crying. But, then, the book said: "No matter whether your child is still in

the cradle or is eighteen years old, this course will show how
to apply the right methods at once. You merely take up the
particular trait, turn to the proper page and apply the lessons
to the child. You are told exactly what to do."

It wasn't that we were afraid that somebody else around the
house might get hold of the book and turn it on us. That risk
we might have faced. But a quotation from Abraham Lincoln
in the prospectus itself brought complete disillusion. "All that
I am and all that I ever hope to be I owe to my mother." That's
what Abraham Lincoln said, according to the prospectus. It
seemed, perhaps, like halving the proper acknowledgments, and
yet it lay in the right direction. But what of the punctual, per-
severing and truthful child brought up under the new method?
We could see only one acknowledgment open to him. We pic-
tured his first inaugural address, and seemed to hear him say:
"All that I am today I owe to Professor Tunkhouser's book
on *The Training of Children*. If I am honest you have only to
look on page 29 to know the reason. It is true that I have per-
severed to gain this high office, and why should I not, seeing
.that I was cradled in page 136?"

Of course, if he had not overlooked the chapter on proper
gratitude he might upon maturity return the purchase price of
Professor Tunkhouser's volume. That seemed almost the most
to be expected.

And so we let him cry, and are going on in the old, careless
way, hoping to be able, unscientifically enough, to lick a work-
ing amount of truth and general virtue into him at such time
as that becomes necessary. However, we did write to the pub-
lisher to ask him if by any chance he had a book along the same
lines about Airedale puppies.

September 3, 1919: H. 3rd lay back in his carriage with his
arms folded across his stomach and said nothing. I tried to make
conversation. I pointed out objects of interest, but met no re-
sponse. He smiled complacently and was silent. Even carefully

rehearsed bits of dialogue such as "Who's a good boy?" to which the answer is "Me," and "Is your face dirty?" to which the answer is "No," failed to move him to speech. I tried him in new lands with strange sights and pointed out the camels, and buffaloes and rhinoceri of the zoo, hoping that he would identify some one of them in his all-embracing "dog," which serves for every member of the four-footed family. But still he smiled complacently and was silent. I began to feel as if I were an Atlantic City Negro wheeling a tired business man down the Boardwalk.

Suddenly the possible value of suggestion came to me, and I turned to the right and finally brought up at the foot of Shakespeare's statue in the mall. And here again I sought to interest him in the English language. "Man," said I, rather optimistically, pointing to the bronze. H. 3rd looked intently, and taking his hands from his stomach answered, "Boy." "Man," I repeated. "Boy," said H. 3rd. And so the argument continued for some time without progress being made by either side. At last I stopped. Is it possible, I thought, that in this curious statue the sculptor has succeeded in giving some suggestion of "sweetest Shakespeare, fancy's child," which is communicated to H. 3rd and fails to reach me? I looked again and gave up this theory for one more simple and rational. Without question it was the doublet and hose which confused him. Never, I suppose, had the child seen me, or the janitor, or the iceman or any of his adult male friends clad in close-fitting tights such as Shakespeare wore. And then I looked at the doublet. No, there was no denying that in this particular statue it appeared uncommonly like a diaper.

December 17, 1919: We read Floyd Dell's *Were You Ever a Child?* today and found him remarking: "People talk about children being hard to teach and in the next breath deplore the facility with which they acquire the 'vices.' That seems strange. It takes as much patience, energy and faithful application to become proficient in a vice as it does to learn mathematics. Yet consider how much more popular poker is than equations! But did a schoolboy ever drop in on a group of teachers who had sat up all night parsing, say, a sentence in Henry James, or seeing who could draw the best map of the North Atlantic states? And when you come to think of it, it seems extremely improbable that any little boy ever learned to drink beer by seeing somebody take a tablespoonful once a day."

Most of this is true. The only trouble with all the new theories about bringing up children is that it leaves the job just as hard as ever.

We believe in the new theories for all that. They work, we think, but, like most worth while things, they are not always easy. For instance, H. 3rd came into the parlor the other day carrying the carving knife. Twenty years ago I could have taken it away and spanked him, but then along came the psychologists with their talk of breaking the child's will, and sensible people stopped spanking. Ten years ago I could have said, "Put down that carving knife or you'll make God feel very badly. In fact, you'll make dada feel very badly. You'll make dada cry if you don't obey him." But then the psychoanalysts appeared and pointed out that there was danger in that. In trying to punish the child by making him feel that his evil acts directly caused suffering to the parent there was an unavoidable tendency to make the child identify himself with the parent subconsciously. That might lead to all sorts of ructions later on. The child might identify himself so completely with his father that in later life he would use his shirts and neckties as if they were his own.

Of course, I might have gone over to H. 3rd and, after a short struggle, taken the carving knife away from him by main force, but that would have made him mad. He would at length have suppressed his anger and right away a complex would begin in his little square head.

Picture him now at thirty—he has neuralgia. Somebody mentions the theory of blind abscesses and he has all his teeth pulled out. No good comes of it. He goes to a psychoanalyst and the doctor begins to ask questions. He asks a great many over a long period of time. Eventually he gets a clue. He finds that when H. 3rd was eight years old he dreamed three nights in succession of stepping on a June bug.

"Was it a large, rather fat June bug?" asks the doctor carelessly, as if the answer was not important.

"Yes," says H. 3rd, "it was."

"That June bug," says the doctor, "was a symbol of your father. When you were twenty months old he took a carving knife away from you and you have had a suppressed anger at him ever since. Now that you know about it your neuralgia will disappear."

And the neuralgia would go at that. But by that time I'd be gone and nothing could be done about this suppressed feud of so many years' standing. My mind went through all these possibilities and I decided it would be simpler and safer to let H. 3rd keep the carving knife as long as he attempted nothing aggressive. A wound is not so dangerous as a complex.

"And, anyhow," I thought, "if he can make that carving knife cut anything he's the best swordsman in the flat."

January 21, 1920: When the rest went out and left me alone in the house, they said that H. 3rd would surely sleep through the evening. Nobody remembered that he had ever waked up to cry. But he did this night. I didn't quite know what to do about it. I sang *Rockabye Baby* to him, but that didn't do any good, and then I said, "I wouldn't cry if I were you." This, too, had no effect, and, in fact, no sooner had I uttered it than I recognized it as a piece of gratuitous impertinence. How could I possibly tell whether or not I would cry if the safety pins were in wrong or anything else of that sort was not quite right?

Nor was it even fair to assume that H. 3rd was crying for any such personal reasons. After all, he lives in a state which has recently suspended five duly elected assemblymen, and in which as fine a book as *Jurgen* has aroused the meddlesome attention of the Society for the Suppression of Vice, and his country has gone quite hysterical on the subjects of "Reds" and "Red" propaganda and I haven't paid him back yet for that $50 Liberty Bond of his which I sold.

And after I had thought of these things it seemed to me that he was entirely justified in crying, and that I ought to be ashamed of myself because I didn't cry, too, since there were so many wrong things in the world to be righted. Humbly I left him to continue his dignified protest without any further unwarranted meddling on my part.

April 6, 1920: Some time ago I wrote a bitter attack on H. 3rd, the reactionary, in which I stated that his political emotions made it necessary for his parents to avoid the use of "proletariat" and such words except when disguised by the expedient of spelling out "p-r-o-l-e-t-a-r-i-a-t." And it is only fair to say that the device takes a good deal of the zest out of sedition. I also stated at the time that we had been able to keep the picture of Trotsky over the mantelpiece in the red room by mendaciously telling H. 3rd that it was a portrait of Nicholas Murray Butler.

It now becomes necessary for me to make a public apology to H. 3rd. It is perhaps a tasteless proceeding for me to drag his private political views into print, but the retraction ought to have as much publicity as the original slander. H. 3rd is not a reactionary. He is a liberal. It would have been perfectly safe for us to have said "proletariat" right out and to have confessed the identity of Trotsky. H. 3rd might not have been altogether in support, but he would have been interested.

I discovered that he was a liberal early on Sunday morning while we were walking in Central Park. We happened to go near the merry-go-round and H. 3rd, drawn by the strains of

Dardanella, dragged me eagerly toward the pavilion. I supposed, of course, that he wanted to ride and had just time to strap him on top of a camel before the platform began to move. No sooner were we in motion round and round, slow at first and then faster and faster as the revolutions increased in violence, than H. 3rd began to cry. As soon as possible I lifted him back to the firm and stable ground and briskly started to walk away from the scene of his harrowing experience. I thought he wanted to get as far away from it as possible, but after a few steps I noticed that he was not following me. Instead he was hurrying back to the merry-go-round as fast as his legs would carry him. "Perhaps," I thought, "he intends to discipline his will and is going to ride that merry-go-round again just because he is so much afraid of it." I knew that people sometimes did things like that because I had read it in *The Research Magnificent.* H. 3rd is not among them. He howled louder than before when I tried to put him on the camel again. I even tested the fantastic possibility that it was the camel and not the carrousel to which he objected, but he yelled just as vigorously when offered a horse and later a unicorn.

Then, I ceased to interfere and resolved to watch. When the merry-go-round began to whirl H. 3rd edged up closer and closer with a look of the most intense interest which I have ever seen on his face. He was fascinated by the sight of men, women and children engaged in a wild and, perhaps, a debauching experiment. Hitherto he had observed that people went forward and back in reasonably straight lines, but this progress was flagrantly rotary. I could not get him away. He stood his ground firmly. He would not retreat a step, nor would he go any nearer. In fact, he was already so close to the carrousel that he could have leaped on board with no more than a hop. By leaning just a little he could have touched it. But he did neither. He preferred a combination of the closest possible proximity and stability. And after a while I realized just what it was of which he reminded me. He was an editor of the *New Republic* watching the Russian Revolution. The mad whirling thing lay right at his feet, but his interest in it and even its imminence never disturbed his tranquillity. The lines of communication with the safe and sane rear remained unbroken. He could retreat the minute the carrousel attempted to become overly familiar.

And so we knew that H. 3rd was and is a liberal.

June 15, 1920: "Heywood Broun 3rd," writes a correspondent who signs no name, "is, fortunately for him, a very young son; Heywood Broun is a very young father—both will grow up. May the boy grow in grace free from *Jurgen's* influence and may the father find his materialism Dead Sea fruit in time to set such an example that H. B. 3rd will act upon the Fifth Commandment. It can't be done on smutty fiction or carnal knowledge."

It may be, as the writer suggests, that we shall grow in grace. However, that is beside the point, for, in the words of the beautiful christening service, a child takes his father "for better or worse." Even now we are of the opinion that all the Commandments should be observed in decent moderation. We think we are correct in assuming that the Fifth is, "Honor thy father and thy mother, that thy days may be long upon the land which the Lord thy God giveth thee." We intend to serve notice on H. 3rd not to make this his favorite Commandment. If he must break one of them, by all means let it be the Fifth. Even though we become much better than we are now, it is going to make us distinctly uncomfortable if he goes about the house honoring us. It will seem too ridiculous, and we doubt very much if he can do it with a straight face. Whenever he feels that he simply must honor his parents we hope that he will do it in an underhand way behind our backs. Although we hope never to spank him, he will be running a great risk if he makes his honoring frank and flagrant.

And, anyway, why should he want to? Hasn't he got *Jack the Giant Killer*, and *Dick Whittington*, and *Aladdin* and *Captain Kidd*? Let him honor them. They are all too dead and too deserving to be annoyed by it.

PART TWO

1920-1924

12. SOUTHPAWS

Our text today is from the fifteenth verse of the third chapter of the Book of Judges, in which it is written: "And afterwards they cried out to the Lord, who raised them up a saviour called Aod, the son of Gera, the son of Jemini, who used the left hand as well as the right."

As a matter of fact, it seems probable that the old chronicler was simply trying to spare the feelings of Aod by describing him merely as an ambidexterous person, for there is later evidence, in the Book of Judges, that Aod actually favored his left hand and was—to be blunt and frank—just a southpaw.

Aod, as you may remember, was sent to Eglon, the king of Moab, ostensibly to bear gifts from the Children of Israel, but, in reality, to kill the oppressor. "Aod," continues the vivid scriptural narrative, "went in to him: now he was sitting in a summer parlor alone, and he said: I have a word from God to thee. And he forthwith rose up from his throne. And Aod put forth his left hand, and took the dagger from his right thigh, and thrust it into his belly with such force that the haft went in after the blade into the wound, and was closed up with the abundance of fat."

When some great scholar comes to write the long-neglected book entitled *A History of Left-handers from the Earliest Times*, it may well be that Aod will be discovered to be the first of the great line to be definitely identified in ancient history. He is the only left-hander mentioned by name in the Bible, although this physical condition—or is it a state of mind?—is referred to in another chapter (Judges 20) in which we hear of a town which seems to have been inhabited entirely by left-handers. At any rate the Bible says: "The inhabitants of Gabaa, who were seven hundred most valiant men, fighting with the left hand as well as with the right and slinging stones so sure that they could hit even a hair, and not miss by the stone's going on either side."

It is interesting to note that these left-handers are again described as ambidexterous, but it is safe to assume that they too were in reality southpaws. It may even be that Gabaa was a town specially set aside for left-handed people, a place of refuge for a rather undesirable sort of citizen.

This surmise is made in all seriousness, for there was a time in the history of the world when left-handedness was considered almost a crime. Primitive man was unquestionably ambidexterous, but, with the growth of civilization, came religious and military customs and these necessitated at certain points in drill or ceremonial a general agreement as to which hand should be used. Man, for some reason unknown, chose the right. That is why ninety per cent of the people in the world today are right-handed. Then with the development of business there soon came to be a conventionally correct hand for commerce. Early dealings of a business nature were carried on by men who held the shield in the left hand and bargained with the right. The shield proved convenient in case the deal fell through. Men who reversed the traditional use of the hands were regarded as queer folk or even a little worse than that. After all, left-handedness was impious in religion, subversive to discipline in military affairs and unlisted in business. It is not to be wondered at then that there is testimony that centuries ago left-handed children were severely beaten and the offending arm often tied down for years.

And yet the southpaw has persisted in spite of persecution. The two men most widely known in America today are both left-handed. I assume that nobody will dispute the pre-eminence in fame of Charlie Chaplin and Babe Ruth, both of whom are completely and fervently left-handed. And to top that off it may be added that the war was won by a left-hander, Marshal Ferdinand Foch, a southpaw, or, as the French have it, *gaucher*.

It is interesting to note that the prejudice against left-handedness has manifested itself and endures in our language. We speak of forbidding things as "sinister," and of awkward things as "gauche," but we left-handers can afford to smile contemptuously at these insults knowing, as we do, that Leonardo da Vinci was one of us. Gauche indeed!

On account of the extent and the duration of the ill will to left-handers there has come to be definitely such a thing as a left-handed temperament. This is no more than natural. The left-hander is a rebel. He is the descendant of staunch ancestors who refused to conform to the pressing demands of the church, the army and the business world. Even today left-handers are traditionally poor business men and Babe Ruth has been obliged to bring suit against the company with which he made a moving picture contract. They are apt to be political radicals, and it has been freely rumored that Charlie Chaplin is social-minded. They are illogical or rather they rise above logic, as did Foch in his famous message: "My left is broken, my right has been driven back, I shall attack at dawn." That is a typically left-handed utterance. It has in it all of the fine rebellion of folk who have refused to conform even to such hard things as facts. If the sculptor had been a little more astute the lady who stands at the entrance of our harbor would have borne the torch aloft in her left hand. Liberty is a southpaw.

So strong is the effect of the left hand upon the temperament that it may even be observed in the case of converts. Such an instance is afforded by the case of Daniel Vierge, the great Spanish artist, and by the recent conduct of James M. Barrie, a right-hander of years' standing, who finally developed writer's cramp and switched to the use of the left hand. What happened? He wrote *Mary Rose*, a play which deals symbolically with death and, instead of giving his audiences the conventional Barrie message of hope and charm and sweetness, he straightway set forth the doctrine that the dead didn't come back and that if they did they and the folk they left behind couldn't get on at all. Time, said the new Barrie, destroys all things, even the most ardent of affections. This was a strange and startling doctrine from Barrie. It was a left-handed message.

Today, of course, left-handers are pretty generally received socially; occasionally they are elected to office, and there is no longer any definite provision against intermarriage. But anybody who thinks that prejudice has died out completely has only to listen to a baseball player when he remarks: "Why, him—he's a left-hander!" There is also the well authenticated story of a young left-handed golfer in our Middle West who played a match with Harry Vardon, in which he made a brilliant showing. Indeed, the youngster was so much elated that at the end of the round he asked the great pro: "Who's the best left-handed golfer you ever saw?" "There never was one that was worth a damn," answered Vardon sourly.

The estimate is not quite fair, for Brice Evans is left-handed and, though it seems hardly patriotic to dwell upon it, our own Chick Evans was put out of the English amateur championship several years ago by Bruce Pierce, a southpaw from Tasmania. Still, left-handed golfers of any consequence are rare. Football has a few southpaw or rather southfoot heroes. Victor Kennard won a game against Yale for Harvard with a left-footed field goal. He and Felton were two of Harvard's greatest punters, and both cf them were left-footed kickers. There must have been some others, but the only one I can think of at the moment was Lefty Flynn of Yale, who was hardly a great player.

Almost all boxers adopt the conventional right-handed form of standing with the left arm advanced, but Knockout Brown, for a few brief seasons, puzzled opponents by boxing left-handed. He jabbed with his right and kept his left hand for heavy work. Of all the men nominated as possibilities for the international polo match only one is left-handed, Watson Webb, the American, and one of the greatest and prettiest horsemen that America has turned out in many a year. In tennis we have done better, with Norman Brookes, Lindley Murray, Dwight Davis and Beals Wright.

But the complete triumph of the left-hander comes in baseball. Tris Speaker, greatest of outfielders and manager of the world's champion Cleveland Indians, is left-handed. So is Babe Ruth, the home-run king, and George Sisler, who led the American League in batting. Ty Cobb, like the Roman emperor before whom Paul appeared, is almost persuaded. He bats left-handed. Almost half the players in both leagues adopt this practice since it gives them an advantage of about six feet in running to first base. And yet, in spite of this fact, thousands of meddling mothers all over the country are breaking prospective left-handers into dull, plodding, conventional right-handedness. Babe Ruth was fortunate. He received his education in a protectory where the good brothers were much too busy to observe which hand he used. His spirit was not broken nor his natural proclivities bent. Accordingly he made fifty-four home runs last season and earned over one hundred thousand dollars. The world has sneered at us all too long. Even a left-hander will turn in time.

13. A ROBE FOR THE KING

Hans Christian Andersen once wrote a story about the tailors who made a suit for a King out of a magic cloth. The quality of the cloth was such, so the tailors said, that it could be seen by nobody who was not worthy of the position he held. And so all the people at court declared that they could see the cloth and admired it greatly, but when the King went out to walk a little boy cried: "Why, he hasn't got anything on." Then everybody took up the cry, and the King rushed back to his palace, and the two tailors were banished in disgrace. Information has recently been discovered which casts new light on the story. According to this information there was only one tailor, and his adventure with the King was about as follows:

AN IMPERIAL FOOTMAN—There's a man at the gate who says he's a tailor and that he wants to see your majesty.

THE KING—Explain our constitution to him. Tell him that all bills for revenue originate in the lower House, and point out that on account of a vicious bipartisan alliance of all the traitors in the kingdom I'm kept so short of money that I can't possibly afford any new clothes.

THE IMPERIAL FOOTMAN—He didn't say anything about money, your majesty.

THE KING—Well, I won't give him a bealo down and a bealo a week either. Tell him to wait until I've got a clear title to the pianola.

THE IMPERIAL FOOTMAN—What he said was that he had a valuable gift for the most enlightened ruler in the world.

THE KING—Well, why didn't you say so in the first place? What was the use of keeping me waiting? Send him up right away. (*Exit the Footman.*)

THE KING (*speaking in the general direction of the Leading Republican*)—Fortunately, my fame rises above petty slanders. The common people, they know me and they love me.

THE LEADING REPUBLICAN—They love your simplicity, your majesty, your lack of ostentation, your tractability. (*Enter the Tailor.*)

THE TAILOR—I have come a far journey to see your majesty.

THE KING—I am honored.

THE TAILOR—For a long time I have been journeying to find an enlightened sovereign, a sovereign who was fitted in all respects for his high office. I stopped in Ruritania; he was not there. He was not in Pannonia or in Gamar. You are my hope, majesty.

THE KING—I trust this may indeed be the end of your journey. I think I may say that Marma is a model kingdom. As you doubtless know, the capital city is Grenoble, with a population of 145,000, according to the last census. We have modern waterworks, a library with more than 10,000 volumes, an art museum, a tannery, three cathedrals, two opera houses and numerous moving picture theaters. The principal industries, as you may recall, are salt fish, woolen blankets, pottery, dried raisins and shrapnel.

THE TAILOR—Your majesty will pardon me if I say that I don't give a fig for your raisins or your dried fish or the cathedrals, or even the library with the 10,000 volumes. What I am seeking is a man with eyes to see.

THE KING—No one has better eyes than myself, I'm sure. I have shot as many as a hundred pheasants in an afternoon, and, if you will pardon the allegorical allusion, I can see loyalty and virtue though they reside in the breast of the most distant and humble subject in my kingdom.

THE TAILOR—Perhaps, then, you can see my cloth. It is a marvelous cloth. It was one of the gifts the wise men brought to the Child. It lay across his feet in the manger. But in order that its richness should not attract the attention of Herod, the wise men decreed that the cloth should be invisible to everyone who was not worthy of his station in the world. See, your majesty, and judge for yourself. (*He puts his hand into the bag and brings it forth, apparently empty, although he seems to be holding up something for the King and the courtiers to admire.*) Is it not a brave and gallant robe, gentlemen?

(*All look intently at the hand of the tailor. There is a long silence, in which many sly glances are cast from one to another to ascertain if it is possible that somebody else sees this thing which is invisible to him. The King looks slowly to the right and slowly to the left to scan the faces of his subjects, and then he gazes straight at the Tailor in high perplexity. Of a sudden the Leading Republican pulls himself together and speaks in an assured and certain tone.*)

THE LEADING REPUBLICAN—It is a magnificent robe. It is a robe for a King. It is so fine a robe that no king should wear it but our beloved monarch, Timothy the Third.

THE LEADING DEMOCRAT (*very hastily*)—Oh, I say, that is nice. So shiny and bright, and good serviceable stuff, too. That would make a mighty good raincoat. (*Briskly*) Say, now, Mr. Tailor, how would you like to form the Wonder Cloth Limited Company? You'd be president, of course, and hold thirty-three and one-third per cent of the stock, the same amount for the King, and the rest to be divided equally among my friends of the opposition here and myself.

THE TAILOR—There will never be any more of the cloth. Only a little is left. Much has been lost. It lies in lonely places, in forests, at the bottom of the sea, in city streets. I have searched the world for this cloth, and I have found no more than I could carry in this bag, a robe for the King (*he holds his hand up*), this square piece you see, and this long twisted piece that might be a rope. Yes, it might be a rope, for it is stronger than hemp.

THE LEADING DEMOCRAT—That robe there, as near as I can judge, should be pretty much of a fit for his majesty. He might wear it for his regular afternoon walk through the city today.

THE KING—Oh, I don't think I'll take my exercise today. There's rather a nasty bite to the air.

THE LEADING DEMOCRAT—Don't forget, you're a constitutional monarch.

THE TAILOR—If the King will wear my robe today I can go on with my journey to find the cloth the world has lost. Already I have found a King who can see, and it only remains to discover whether there is vision in his people, too.

THE KING (*musing*)—Hum! If the people can see it, hey? That's a bit of a risk now, isn't it? When I wear that robe of your magic cloth it might be a good idea to have something warm and substantial underneath. It wouldn't do to have any mistakes, you know. After all, I don't want a lot of stupid louts thinking I'm parading around in my B.V.D.'s.

THE LEADING DEMOCRAT—Does your majesty mean to suggest that the common people of Marma, from whom he derives all his just powers, are not to be trusted?

THE KING—You know I didn't mean that. Of course I trust the people. I realize perfectly well that they'd die for me and all that, but, after all, you can't be sure of everybody in a big crowd. There'll be fishwives, you know, and Socialists and high-waymen and plumbers and reporters and everything.

THE LEADING DEMOCRAT—It all gets down to this, your majesty: do you trust the people, or don't you?

THE KING—I trust them as much as you do, but I don't go to excess. I don't see any good reason why I shouldn't wear an ordinary business suit under this magic royal robe. A King can't take chances, you know. He must play it safe.

THE TAILOR—Don't say that, your majesty. You're a King, your majesty. Think of that. You mustn't tap in front of you, like a blind man with a stick. You mustn't fear to bump your head. If you hold it high, you know, there'd be nothing to fear but the stars.

THE KING—You are eloquent, O stranger from a far country, and what do you mean?

THE TAILOR—Only this: if you wear my robe you must cast off compromise and expediency.

THE KING—Oh, that's all right. I was only thinking about trousers.

THE TAILOR—They were a compromise of Adam's, your majesty.

THE KING—Quite true, but I hope you wouldn't go so far as to object to essentials. It's mesh stuff, you know, and very thin. Practically nothing at all. Just one piece. Somehow or other I don't believe I'd feel easy without it. Sort of a habit with me.

THE TAILOR—If you wear my robe you must put aside every other garment.

THE KING—But this is December.

THE TAILOR—Your majesty, the man who wears this cloth will never fear cold.

THE LEADING DEMOCRAT—It seems to me that the only question is, Does his majesty trust the people fully and completely?

THE KING—Of course I trust the people.

THE LEADING DEMOCRAT—Then why are you afraid to show yourself before them in this magnificent new robe? Is there any reason to believe that they who are the real rulers of Marma cannot see this cloth which the Tailor sees, which I see and admire so much and (*pointedly*) which your majesty, Timothy the Third, cannot conceivably fail to see? It would be unfortunate if it became a matter of news that your majesty did not believe in the capabilities and worthiness of the people.

THE KING—Oh, I believe all right.

THE LEADING DEMOCRAT—Then why are you afraid?

THE KING—Give me the robe. I am not afraid. (*The Tailor stoops and seems to take something out of a bag. He extends the invisible object to the King, who clumsily pretends to hang it over his arm.*)

THE TAILOR—Oh, not that way, your majesty. It will wrinkle. (*Painstakingly he smooths out a little air and returns it to the astonished monarch.*)

THE KING (*to the Leading Republican, the Leading Democrat and the two Courtiers*)—You will meet me at the great gate of the palace in three minutes and accompany me on my promenade through the city. (*Exit the King. The Leading Republican draws close to the first Courtier.*)

LEADING REPUBLICAN—Wonderful fabric that, was it not?

FIRST COURTIER—Much the finest I have ever seen.

LEADING REPUBLICAN—Now, what shade should you say it was? It's hard to tell shades in this light, isn't it?

FIRST COURTIER—I had no trouble, sir. The robe is a bright scarlet.

LEADING REPUBLICAN—Scarlet, eh? (*He moves over close to the second Courtier.*)

LEADING REPUBLICAN—Wonderful fabric that we saw just now, wasn't it?

SECOND COURTIER—It was like a lake under the moonlight.

LEADING REPUBLICAN—Moonlight?

SECOND COURTIER—Yes, it was easy to see that it was a miraculous fabric. Man could never have achieved that silver green.

LEADING REPUBLICAN—Yes, it was a mighty fine color. (*Raising his voice.*) I think we had better join his majesty now, gentlemen, and I believe we shall have an interesting promenade. Good-by until later, Mr. Tailor.

ALL—Good-by, Mr. Tailor!

(*The Tailor moves to a great window at the back of the stage and opens it. He leans out. He bows low to someone who is passing by underneath. The rattle of wagons may be heard distinctly, and the rumble of cars, with occasionally the honk of an automobile horn. Suddenly there is a noise much louder and shriller than any of these. It is the voice of a child, and it cries: "He hasn't got anything on!" Voice after voice takes up the shout. Seemingly thousands of people are shouting, "He hasn't got anything on!" Finally the shouting loses all coherence; it is just a great, ugly, angry noise. A shot breaks the glass of the window just above the Tailor's head. Quickly he protects himself from further attack in that direction by swinging two iron shutters together and fastening them. Then he locks the great door through which the King and the Courtiers have just passed.*)

THE TAILOR (*in sorrow and anger*)—More blind men. (*He moves to his bag and, dipping his hands in, raises them again to fondle an invisible something. As he is so engaged a little door at the right opens and a meanly dressed girl of about eighteen enters.*)

THE TAILOR—Keep your distance. I won't be taken alive. Not until I can find someone to care for my cloth.

THE GIRL FROM THE KITCHEN—Oh, please, don't hurt me,

mister. I just ran up here because there were soldiers down in the garden, and shooting and things.

THE TAILOR—Who are you?

THE GIRL FROM THE KITCHEN—I'm the sixth assistant helper of the cook.

THE TAILOR—The sixth?

THE GIRL FROM THE KITCHEN—Yes, I clean the butter plates.

THE TAILOR—And that's all you do? Just clean butter plates? How terrible!

THE GIRL FROM THE KITCHEN—But it isn't. The cook says I'm the best butter dish cleaner in the world. I like butter. I like to touch it. There's no color in the world so beautiful. It's like that bit of cloth you have in your hands.

THE TAILOR—You see the cloth?

THE GIRL FROM THE KITCHEN—Of course I see it. Why, it's right there in your hands. And it's yellow like the butter.

THE TAILOR—Or gold. (*He reaches into the bag again.*) And what's this? (*He holds his right hand high above his head.*)

THE GIRL FROM THE KITCHEN—Why, it's a yellow rope.

THE TAILOR—Yes, that's it, a rope. I'm going to give you the other piece of cloth now, and later the rope, too. You must guard it as carefully, as carefully as you would watch one of your butter dishes. Do you understand?

THE GIRL FROM THE KITCHEN—I wouldn't lose it. It's pretty.

THE TAILOR—Yes, it's pretty and the world mustn't lose it. You will find that most people can't see. I know only two, you and I, but there must be others. That's your task now, finding people who can see the cloth and cleaning butter plates, of course. (*There is a loud pounding on the great door and a shout of "Open, in the King's name!" The knocking increases in violence and the command is repeated. Then men begin to swing against the door with heavy bars and hatchets.*)

THE TAILOR—Here (*he makes a gesture toward the girl*), take the cloth. Go quickly to the kitchen. Then come back in a moment and save the rope, too.

THE GIRL FROM THE KITCHEN—But what do they want?

THE TAILOR—They want to kill me.

THE GIRL FROM THE KITCHEN—They mustn't.

THE TAILOR—They won't if you get out and leave me alone. Here, hurry. (*He half pushes her out the little door. Then he returns to the bag and seems to pull out something. He looks to the ceiling and finds a hook fairly in the middle of it. He moves his hand upward as if tossing something, and goes through the motions of tying a knot around his neck. Then the Tailor takes a chair and moves it to the center of the room. He stands upon it. The violent assault upon the door begins with renewed vigor. Some of the axes bite through the wood. The Tailor steps off the chair and dangles in the air. He floats in space, like a man in a magic trick, but one or two in the audience, dramatic critics, perhaps, or scullery maids, may see that round his neck and fastened to the hook in the ceiling is a yellow rope.*)

(CURTAIN)

14. HOLDING A BABY

When Adam delved and Eve span, the fiction that man is incapable of housework was first established. It would be interesting to figure out just how many foot-pounds of energy men have saved themselves, since the creation of the world, by keeping up the pretense that a special knack is required for washing dishes and for dusting, and that the knack is wholly feminine. The pretense of incapacity is impudent in its audacity, and yet it works.

Men build bridges and throw railroads across deserts, and yet they contend successfully that the job of sewing on a button is beyond them. Accordingly, they don't have to sew buttons.

It might be said, of course, that the safety of suspension bridges is so much more important than that of suspenders that the division of labor is only fair, but there are many of us who have never thrown a railroad in our lives, and yet swagger in all the glory of masculine achievement without undertaking any of the drudgery of odd jobs.

Probably men alone could never have maintained the fallacy of masculine incapacity without the aid of women. As soon as that rather limited sphere, once known as woman's place, was established, women began to glorify and exaggerate its importance, by the pretense that it was all so special and difficult that no other sex could possibly begin to accomplish the tasks entailed. To this declaration men gave immediate and eager assent and they have kept it up. The most casual examination will reveal the fact that all the jokes about the horrible results of masculine cooking and sewing are written by men. It is all part of a great scheme of sex propaganda.

Naturally there are other factors. Biology has been unscrupulous enough to discriminate markedly against women, and men have seized upon this advantage to press the belief that, since the bearing of children is exclusively the province of women, it must be that all the caring for them belongs properly to the same sex. Yet how ridiculous this is.

Most things which have to be done for children are of the simplest sort. They should tax the intelligence of no one. Men profess a total lack of ability to wash baby's face simply because they believe there's no great fun in the business, at either end of the sponge. Protectively, man must go the whole distance and pretend that there is not one single thing which he can do for baby. He must even maintain that he doesn't know how to hold one. From this pretense has grown the shockingly transparent fallacy that holding a baby correctly is one of the fine arts; or, perhaps even more fearsome than that, a wonderful intuition, which has come down after centuries of effort to women only.

"The thing that surprised Richard most," says a recent woman novelist, "was the ease and the efficiency with which Eleanor handled Annabel. . . . She seemed to know, by instinct, things that Richard could not understand and that he could not understand how she came by. If she reached out her hands to take Annabel, her fingers seemed, of themselves, to curve into the places where they would fit the spineless bundle and give it support."

At this point interruption is inevitable. Places indeed! There are one hundred and fifty-two distinctly different ways of holding a baby—and all are right! At least all will do. There is no need of seeking out special places for the hands. A baby is so soft that anybody with a firm grip can make places for an effective hold wherever he chooses. But to return to our quotation: "If Richard tried to take up the bundle, his fingers fell away like the legs of the brittle crab and the bundle collapsed, incalculable and helpless. 'How do you do it?' he would say. And he would right Annabel and try to still her protests. And Eleanor would only smile gently and send him on some masculine errand, while she soothed Annabel's feelings in the proper way."

You may depend upon it that Richard also smiled as soon as he was safely out of the house and embarked upon some masculine errand, such as playing eighteen holes of golf. Probably, by the time he reached the tenth green, he was too intent upon his game to remember how guile had won him freedom. Otherwise, he would have laughed again, when he holed a twenty-foot putt over a rolling green and recollected that he had escaped an afternoon of carrying Annabel because he was too awkward. I once knew the wife of the greatest billiard player in the world, and she informed me with much pride that her husband was incapable of carrying the baby. "He doesn't seem to have the proper touch," she explained.

As a matter of fact, even if men in general were as awkward as they pretend to be at home, there would still be small reason for their shirking the task of carrying a baby. Except that right side up is best, there is not much to learn. As I ventured to suggest before, almost any firm grip will do. Of course the child may cry, but that is simply because he has become over-particular through too much coddling. Nature herself is cavalier. Young rabbits don't even whimper when picked up by the ears, and kittens are quite contented to be lifted by the scruff of the neck.

This same Nature has been used as the principal argument for woman's exclusive ability to take care of the young. It is pretty generally held that all a woman needs to do to know all about children is to have some. This wisdom is attributed to instinct. Again and again we have been told by rapturous grandmothers that: "It isn't something which can be read in a book or taught in a school. Nature is the great teacher." This simply isn't true. There are many mothers in America who have learned far more from the manuals of Dr. Holt than instinct ever taught them—and Dr. Holt is a man. I have seen mothers give beer and spaghetti and Neapolitan ice-cream to children in arms, and, if they got that from instinct, the only conclusion possible is that instinct did not know what it was talking about. Instinct is not what it used to be.

I have no feeling of being a traitor to my sex, when I say that I believe in at least a rough equality of parenthood. In shirking all the business of caring for children we have escaped much hard labor. It has been convenient. Perhaps it has been too convenient. If we have avoided arduous tasks, we have also missed much fun of a very special kind. Like children in a toy shop, we have chosen to live with the most amusing of talking-and-walking dolls, without ever attempting to tear down the sign which says, "Do not touch." In fact we have helped to set it in place. That is a pity.

Children mean nothing at long range. For our own sake we ought to throw off the pretense of incapacity and ask that we be given a half share in them. I hope that this can be done without its being necessary for us to share the responsibility of dishes also. I don't think there are any concealed joys in washing dishes. Washing children is quite a different matter. After you have washed somebody else's face you feel that you know him better. This may be the reason why so many trained nurses marry their patients—but that is another story. A dish is an unresponsive thing. It gives back nothing. A child's face offers competitive possibilities. It is interesting to see just how high a polish can be achieved without making it cry.

There is also a distinct sense of elation in doing trifling practical things for children. They are so small and so helpless that they contribute vastly to a comforting glow in the ego of the grown-up. When you have completed the rather difficult task of preparing a child for bed and actually getting him there, you have a sense of importance almost divine in its extent. This is to feel at one with Fate, to be the master of another's destiny, of his waking and his sleeping and his going out into the world. It is a brand-new world for the child. He is a veritable Adam and you loom up in his life as more than mortal. Golf is well enough for a Sunday sport, but it is a trifling thing beside the privilege of taking a small son to the zoo and letting him see his first lion, his first tiger and, best of all, his first elephant. Probably he will think that they are part of your own handiwork turned out for his pleasure.

To a child, at least, even the meanest of us may seem glamorous with magic and wisdom. It seems a pity not to take the fullest advantage of this chance before the opportunity is lost. There must come a day when even the most nimble-witted father has to reply, "I don't know." On that day the child comes out of Eden and you are only a man again. Cortes on his lonely peak in Darien was a pigmy discoverer beside the child eating his first spoonful of ice-cream. There is the immediate frightened and angry rebellion against the coldness of it, and then the amazing sensation as the strange substance melts into magic of pleasant sweetness. The child will go on to high adventure, but

I doubt whether the world holds for anyone more soul-stirring surprise than the first adventure with ice-cream. No, there is nothing dull in feeding a child.

There is less to be said for dressing a child, from the point of view of recreation. This seems to us laborious and rather tiresome, both for father and child. Still I knew one man who managed to make an adventure of it. He boasted that he had broken all the records of the world for changing all or any part of a child's clothing. He was a skilled automobile mechanic, much in demand in races, where tires are whisked on and off. He brought his technic into the home. I saw several of his demonstrations. He was a silent man who habitually carried a mouthful of safety pins. Once the required youngster had been pointed out, he wasted no time in preliminary wheedlings but tossed her on the floor without more ado. Even before her head had bumped, he would be hard at work. With him the thrill lay in the inspiration of the competitive spirit. He endeavored always to have his task completed before the child could begin to cry. He never lost. Often the child cried afterward, but by that time my friend felt that his part of the job was completed—and would turn the youngster over to her mother.

15. JUST AROUND THE CORNER

We sometimes wonder just how and what Joseph Conrad would have written if he had never gone to sea. It may be that he would never have written at all if he had not been urged on by the emotion which he felt about ships and seas and great winds. And yet we regret sometimes that he is so definitely seastruck. After all, Conrad is a man so keen in his understanding of the human heart that he can reach deep places. It is sometimes a pity, therefore, that he is so much concerned with researches which take him down into nothing more than water, which, even at its mightiest, is no such infinite element as the mind of man.

Typhoons and hurricanes make a brave show of noise and fury, but there is nothing in them but wind. No storm which Conrad ever pictured could be half so extraordinary as the tumult which went on in the soul of Lord Jim. We notice at this point that we have used heart and mind and soul without defining what we meant by any of them. We mean the same thing in each case, but for the life of us we don't know just what it is. *Lord Jim,* of course, is a great book, but to our mind the real battle is a bit obscured by the strangeness and the vividness of the external adventures through which the hero passes. There is danger that the attention of the reader may be distracted by silent seas and savage tribes and jungles from the fact that Jim's fight was really fought just behind his forehead; that it was a fight which might have taken place in Trafalgar Square or Harlem or Emporia.

Naturally, we have no right to imply that nothing of consequence can happen in wild and strange places. There is just as much romance on Chinese junks as on Jersey Central ferryboats. But no more. Here is the crux of our complaint. Conrad and Kipling and the rest have written so magnificently about the far places that we have come to think of them as the true home of romance. Indeed, we have almost been induced to believe that there is nothing adventurous west of Suez. Hereabouts, it seems as if one qualified as a true romancer simply from the fact of living in Shanghai or Singapore, or just off the island of Carimata. And yet we suppose there are people in Shanghai who cobble shoes all day long and sleep at nights, and that there are dishes to be washed in Singapore.

For our own part, we remember that we once spent ten days in Peking, and our liveliest recollection is that one night we held a ten high straight flush in hearts against two full houses. One of them was aces and kings. That was adventure, to be sure, and yet we have held a jack high straight flush in clubs against four sixes in no more distant realm than West Forty-fourth Street.

Adventure is like that. It always seizes upon a person when he least expects it. There is no good chasing to the ends of the earth after romance. Not if you want the true romance. It moves faster than tramp steamers or pirate schooners. We hold that there is no validity in the belief that a little salt will assist the capture; no, not even when it is mixed with spume, or green waves, or purple seas. Only this year we saw a play about a youngster who pined away to death because he neglected to accept an opportunity to sail around the world. He wanted adventure. He starved for romance. He felt sure that it was in Penang and not in the fields of his father's farm. It was not reasonable for him thus to break his heart. If Romance had marked him for her own the hills of Vermont would have been no more a barrier to her coming than the tops of the Andes.

16. PREFACE TO *PIECES OF HATE*

The trouble with prefaces is that they are partial and so we have decided to offer instead an unbiased review of *Pieces of Hate*. The publishers have kindly furnished us advance proofs for this purpose.

We wish we could speak with unreserved enthusiasm about this book. It would be pleasant to make out a list of three essential volumes for humanity and suggest the complete works of William Shakespeare, the Bible and *Pieces of Hate*, but Mr. Broun's book does not deserve any such ranking. Speaking as a critic of books, we are not at all sure that we care to recommend it. It seems to us that the author is honest, but the value of that quality has been vastly overstressed in present-day reviewing.

We are inclined to say, "What of it?" There would be nothing particularly persuasive if a man should approach a poker game and say, "Won't you let Broun in; I can assure you he's honest." Why should a recommendation which is taken for granted among common gamblers be considered flattering when applied to a writer?

Anyhow, it does not seem to us that Broun carries honesty to excess. There is every indication that most of the work in *Pieces of Hate* has been done so hurriedly that there has been no opportunity for a recount. If it balances at any given point luck must be with him as well as virtue. All the vices of haste are in this book of stories, critical essays and what not. The author is not content to stalk down an idea and salt it. Whenever he sees what he believes to be a notion he leaves his feet and tries to bring it down with a flying tackle. Occasionally there actually is an exciting and interesting crash of flying bodies coming into contact. But just as often Mr. Broun misses his mark and falls on his face. At other times he gets the object of his dive only to find that it was not a genuine idea after all, but only a straw man, a sort of tackling dummy set up to fool and educate novices.

And Broun does not learn fast. Like most newspaper persons he is an extraordinary mixture of sophistication and naïveté. At one moment he will be found belaboring a novelist or a dramatist for sentimentality and on the next page there will be distinct traces of treacle in his own creative work. Seemingly, what he means when he says that he does not like sentimentality is that he doesn't like the sentimentality of anybody else. He would restrict the quality to the same narrow field as charity.

The various forms introduced into the book are a little confusing. Seemingly there has been no plan as to the sequence of stories, essays, dramatic criticism and the rest. Possibly the author regards this as versatility, but here is another vastly overrated quality. We once had a close friend who was a magician and after we had watched him take an omelet out of his high hat, and two white rabbits, and a bowl of goldfish, it always made us a little uneasy when he said, "Wait a minute until I put on my hat and I'll walk home with you."

The fear constantly lurked in our mind that he might suddenly remember, in the middle of Times Square, that he had forgotten a trick and be compelled to pause and take a boa-constrictor from under the sweat-band. We suggest to Mr. Broun that he make up his mind as to just what he intends to do and then stick to it to the exclusion of all sidelines.

Perhaps he has promised, but we are prepared to wager nothing on him until we are convinced that he has begun to drive for something. He may be a young man but he is not so young that he can afford to traffic any further with flipness under the impression that it is something just as good as humor. And we wish he wouldn't pun. The publisher informs us that he had to plead with Broun to make him leave out a chapter on the ugliness of heirlooms and particularly old sofas. Apparently the piece was written for no other purpose than to carry the title The Chintz of the Fathers.

We also find Mr. Broun's pose as the professional Harvard man a little bit trying, particularly as expressed in his essay The Bigger the Year. We suppose he may be expected to outgrow this in time but he has been long enough about it.

17. G. K. C.

The ship news man said that Gilbert K. Chesterton was staying at the Commodore and the telephone girl said he wasn't, but we'd trust even a ship news man before a hotel central and so we persisted.

In fact, we almost persuaded her.

"Maybe he's connected with one of the automobile companies

that are exhibiting here," she suggested, helpfully. For a moment we wondered if by any chance the hotel authorities had made an error and placed him in the lobby with the ten-ton trucks. It seemed too fantastic.

"He's not with any automobile company," we said severely. "Didn't you ever hear of *The Man Who Was Thursday?*"

"He may have been here Thursday, but he's not registered now," she answered with some assurance. We didn't seem to be getting on. "It's a book," we shouted. "He wrote it."

"Not in this hotel," said central with an air of finality and rang off before we could try her out on *Man Alive* or *The Ball and the Cross*. Still, it turned out eventually that she was right, for it was the Biltmore which at last acknowledged Mr. Chesterton somewhat reluctantly after we had spelled out the name.

"Not in his room, but somewhere about the hotel," was the message.

"You can find him," said the city editor with confidence. "Just take this picture with you. He's sort of fat and he speaks with an English accent."

We had a more helpful description than that in our mind, because we remembered Chesterton's answer when a sweet girl admirer once remarked, "It must be wonderful to walk along the streets when everybody knows who you are."

"Yes," said Chesterton; "and if they don't know they ask."

He wasn't in the bar, but we found him in the smoking room. He was giving somebody an interview without much enthusiasm. It seemed to be the last round. Chesterton was beginning to droop. Every paradox, we feared, had been hammered out of him. He rose a little wearily and started for the elevator. We chased him. At last we had the satisfaction of finding someone we could outrun. He paused, and now we know the look which the Wedding Guest must have given to the Ancient Mariner.

"It's for the New York *Tribune*," we said.

"How about next week?" suggested Mr. Chesterton.

"It's a daily newspaper," we remonstrated. "You know—Grantland Rice and The Conning Tower and When a Feller Needs a Friend."

Something in the title of the Briggs series must have touched him. "Tomorrow, perhaps," he answered. Feeling that the mountain was about to come through, we stood our ground like another Mahomet. Better than that, we rose to one of the few superb moments in our life. Looking at Mr. Chesterton coldly we said slowly, "It must be now or never." And we used a gesture. The nature of it escapes us, but it was something appropriate. Later we wondered just what reply would have been possible if he had answered, "Never." After the danger had passed we realized that we had been holding up the visitor with an empty gun. It must have been our manner which awed him, and he stopped walking and almost turned around.

"The press men have been here since two o'clock," he complained more in sorrow than in anger. "What is it you want to know?"

At that stage of the interview the advantage passed to him. The whole world lay before us. Dimly we could hear the problems of a great and unhappy universe flapping in our ears and urging us with unintelligible, hoarse caws to present their cases for solution. And still we stood there unable to think of a single thing which we wanted to know.

Mostly we had read Chesterton on rum and religion, but there were too many people passing to give the proper atmosphere for any such confidential questions. Moreover, if he should question us in turn we realized that we would be unable to give him any information as to when to boil and when to skim, nor did we feel sufficiently well disposed to let him in on the name of the drug store where you stay, "I'm a patient of Dr. Brown's" and are forthwith allowed to buy gin.

All the questions we had ever asked anybody in our life passed rapidly before us. "What do you think of our tall buildings?" "Have you ever thought of playing Hamlet?" "Why

are you called the woman with the most beautiful legs in Paris?"
We remembered that the last had seemed silly even when we
first used it on Mistinguette. On second thought we had told the
interpreter to let it drop because the photographers were anxious
to begin. There seemed to be even less sense to it now. Indeed
none of our familiar inquiries struck us as appropriate.

"What American authors do you read?" we ventured timidly,
and added "living ones," hoping to get something about *Main
Street* for Wednesday's book column.

"I don't read any," he answered.

That seemed to us a possible handicap in pursuing that line
of inquiry.

"I don't read any living English authors, either," Mr. Ches-
terton added hastily, as if he feared that he had trod upon our
patriotism. "Nothing but dead authors and detective stories."

That we had expected. In the march up to the heights of
fame there comes a spot close to the summit in which man reads
"nothing but detective stories." It is the Antaean touch which
distinguishes all Olympians. As you remember, Antaeus was the
demigod who had to touch the earth every once and so often to
preserve his immortality. Probably he did it by reading a good
murder story.

"Can you tell me what *Mary Rose* is all about?" we sug-
gested, still fumbling for a literary theme.

"I haven't seen *Mary Rose*," said Mr. Chesterton, although
he did go on to tell us that Barrie had done several excellent
plays. Probably there was a long pause then while we tried to
think up something provocative about the Irish question.

"If you really will excuse me, I must go to my room," he
burst out. "The press men have been here ever since two
o'clock."

This, of course, is no land in which to stand between a man
and his room, where heaven knows what solace may await the
distinguished visitor who has been spending two and a half

hours with the press men. We stepped aside willingly enough. Still, we must confess a slight disappointment in Gilbert K. Chesterton. He's not as fat as we had heard.

18. CHIVALRY IS BORN

Every now and then we hear parents commenting on the fearful things which motion pictures may do to the minds of children. They seem to think that a little child is full of sweetness and of light. We had the same notion until we had a chance to listen intently to the prattle of a three-year-old. Now we know that no picture can possibly outdo him in his own fictionized frightfulness.

Of course, we had heard testimony to this effect from Freudians, but we had supposed that all these horrible blood lusts and such-like were suppressed. Unfortunately, our own son is without reticence. We have a notion that each individual goes through approximately the same stages of progress as the race. Heywood Broun, 3d, seemed not yet quite as high as the cavemen in his concepts. For the last few months he has been harping continuously, and chiefly during meal times, about cutting off people's noses and gouging out eyes. In his range of speculative depredations he has invariably seemed liberal.

There seemed to us, then, no reason to fear that new notions of horror would come to Heywood Broun, 3d, from any of the pictures being licensed at present in this State. As a matter of fact, he has received from the films his first notions of chivalry. Of course, we are not at all sure that this is beneficial. We like his sentimentalism a little worse than his sadism.

After seeing *Tol'able David*, for instance, we had a long argument. Since our experience with motion pictures is longer than his we often feel reasonably certain that our interpretation of the happenings is correct and we do not hesitate to contradict H. 3d, although he is so positive that sometimes our confidence is shaken. We knew that he was all wrong about *Tol'able David* because it was quite evident that he had become mixed in his mind concerning the hero and the villain. He kept insisting that David was a bad man because he fought. Pacifism has always seemed to us an appealing philosophy, but it came with bad grace from such a swashbuckling disciple of frightfulness as H. 3d.

However, we did not develop that line of reasoning but contended that David had to fight in order to protect himself. Woodie considered this for a while and then answered triumphantly, "David hit a woman."

Our disgust was unbounded. Film life had seared the child after all. Actually, it was not David who hit the woman but the villainous Luke Hatburn, the terrible mountaineer. That error in observation was not the cause of our worry. The thing that bothered us was that here was a young individual, not yet four years of age, who was already beginning to talk in terms of "the weaker vessel" and all the other phrases of a romantic school we believed to be dying. It could not have shocked us more if he had said, "Woman's place is in the home."

"David hit a woman," he piped again, seeming to sense our consternation. "What of it?" we cried, but there was no bullying him out of his point of view. The fault belongs entirely to the motion pictures. H. 3d cannot truthfully say that he has had the slightest hint from us as to any sex inferiority of women. By word and deed we have tried to set him quite the opposite example. We have never allowed him to detect us for an instant in any chivalrous act or piece of partial sex politeness. Toasts such as "The ladies, God bless 'em" are not drunk in our house, nor has Woodie ever heard "Shall we join the ladies?" "the fair sex," "the weaker sex," or any other piece of patronizing masculine poppycock. Susan B. Anthony's picture hangs in his bedroom side by side with Abraham Lincoln and the big elephant. He has led a sheltered life and has never been allowed to play with nice children.

But, somehow or other, chivalry and romanticism creep into each life even through barred windows. We have no intention of being too hard upon the motion pictures. Something else would have introduced it. These phases belong in the development of the race. H. 3d must serve his time as gentle knight just as he did his stint in the role of sadistic caveman. Presently, we fear, he will get to the crusades and we shall suffer during a period in which he will try to improve our manners. History will then be our only consolation. We shall try to bear up, secure in the knowledge that the dark ages are still ahead of him.

We hoped that the motion pictures might be used as an antidote against the damage which they had done. We took H. 3d to see Nazimova in *A Doll's House*. There was a chance, we thought, that he might be moved by the eloquent presentation of the fact that before all else a woman is a human being and just as eligible to be hit as anybody else. We read him the caption embodying Nora's defiance, but at the moment it flashed upon the screen he had crawled under his seat to pick up an old program and the words seemed to have no effect. Indeed when Nora went out into the night, slamming the door behind her, he merely hazarded that she was "going to Mr. Butler's." Mr. Butler happens to be our grocer.

The misapprehension was not the fault of Nazimova. She flung herself out of the house magnificently, but Heywood Broun, 3d, insisted on believing that she had gone around the corner for a dozen eggs.

In discussing the picture later, we found that he had quite missed the point of Mr. Ibsen's play. Of Nora, the human being, he remembered nothing. It was only Nora, the mother, who had impressed him. All he could tell us about the great and stimulating play was that the lady had crawled on the floor with her little boy and her little girl. And yet it seems to us that Ibsen has told his story with singular clarity.

D'Artagnan Woodie likes very much. He is fond of recalling to our mind the fact that D'Artagnan "walked on the roof in his nightshirt." H. 3d is not allowed on the roof nor is he permitted to wander about in his nightshirt.

Perhaps the child's introduction to the films has been somewhat too haphazard. As we remember, the first picture which we saw together was called *Is Life Worth Living?* The worst of it is that circumstances made it necessary for us to leave before the end and so neither of us found out the answer.

19. THE BIGGER THE YEAR

As soon as we heard that *The Big Year—A College Story* by Meade Minnigerode was about Yale we knew that we just had to read it. Tales of travel and curious native customs have always fascinated us. According to Mr. Minnigerode the men of Yale walk about their campus in big blue sweaters with "Y's" on them, smoking pipes and singing college songs under the windows of one another. The seniors, he informs us, come out on summer afternoons on roller skates.

Of course, we are disposed to believe that Mr. Minnigerode, like all travelers in strange lands, is prone to color things a little more highly than exact accuracy would sanction. We felt this particularly when he began to write about Yale football. There was, for instance, Curly Corliss, the captain of the eleven, who is described as "starting off after a punt to tear back through a broken field, thirty and forty yards at a clip, tackling an opposing back with a deadliness which was final—never hurt, always smiling—a blond head of curly hair (he never wore a headguard) flashing in and out across the field, the hands clapping together, the plaintive voice calling, 'All right, all right, give

me the ball!' when a game was going badly, and then carrying
it alone to touchdown after touchdown."

Although we have seen all of Yale's recent big games we
recognized none of that except "the plaintive voice" and even
that would have been more familiar if it had been used to say,
"Moral victory!" We waited to find Mr. Minnigerode explain-
ing that of course he was referring to the annual contest with
the Springfield Training School, but he did no such thing and
went straight ahead with the pretense that football at Yale is
romantic. To be sure, he attempts to justify this attitude by let-
ting us see a good deal of the gridiron doings through the eyes
of a bull terrier who could not well be expected to be captious.
Champ, named after the Yale chess team, came by accident to
the field just as Curly Corliss was off on one of his long runs.
Yes, it was a game against the scrubs. "Someone came tearing
along and lunged at Curly as he went by, apparently trying to
grab him about the legs. Champ cast all caution to the winds.
Interfere with Curly, would he? Well, Champ guessed not!
Like an arrow from a bow Champ hurled himself through the
air and fastened his jaws firmly in the seat of the offender's
pants, in a desperate effort to prevent him from further molest-
ing Curly."

Champ was immediately adopted by the team as mascot. It
seems to us he deserved more, for this was the first decent piece
of interference seen on Yale field in years. The associate mascot
was Jimmy, a little newsboy, who also took football at New
Haven seriously. His romanticism, like that of Champ, was un-
derstandable. Hadn't Curly Corliss once saved his life? We
need not tell you that he had. "Jimmy," as Mr. Minnigerode
tells the story, "started to run across the street, without noticing
the street-car lumbering around the corner . . . and then be-
fore he knew it Jimmy tripped and fell, and the car was almost
on top of him grinding its brakes. Jimmy never knew exactly
what happened in the next few seconds, but he heard people
shouting, and then something struck him and he was dragged

violently away by the seat of the pants. When he could think connectedly again he was sitting on the curb considerably battered—and Curly was sitting beside him, with his trousers torn, nursing a badly cut hand."

We remember there was an incident like that in Cambridge once, only the man who rescued the newsboy was not the football captain but a substitute on the second team. We have forgotten his name. Unlike Corliss of Yale, the Harvard man did not bother to pick up the newsboy. Instead he seized the street car and threw it for a loss.

The first half was over and Princeton led by a score of 10 to 0. Things looked blue for Yale. Neither mascot was on hand. Yale was trying to win with nothing but students. Where was little Jimmy the newsboy? If you must know he was in the hospital, for he had been run over again. The boy could not seem to break himself of the habit. Unfortunately he had picked out the afternoon of the Princeton game when all the Yale players were much too busy trying to stop Tigers to have any time to interfere with traffic. It was only an automobile this time and Jimmy escaped with a mere gash over one eye. Champ, the bull terrier who caused the mixup, was uninjured. "I'm all right now," Jimmy told the doctor, "honest I am—can I go—I gotta take Champ out to the game—he's the mascot and they can't win without him—please, Mister, let me go—I guess they need us bad out there."

Apparently the crying need of Yale football is not so much a coaching system as a good leash to keep the mascots from getting run over. Champ and Jimmy rushed into the locker room just as the big Blue team was about to trot out for the second half. After that there was nothing to it. Yale won by a score of 12 to 10. "Curly clapped his hands together," writes Mr. Minnigerode in describing the rally, "and kept calling out, 'Never mind the signal! Give me the ball' in his plaintive voice"—

This sounds more like Yale football than anything else in the book. However, it sufficed. Curly made two touchdowns and all the Yale men went to Mory's and sang, "Curly Corliss, Curly Corliss, he will leave old Harvard scoreless." It is said that a legend is now gaining ground in New Haven that Yale will not defeat Harvard again until it is led by some other captain whose name rhymes with "scoreless." The current captain of the Elis is named Jordan. The only thing that rhymes with that is "scored on."

Still, as Professor Billy Phelps has taught his students to say, football isn't everything. Perhaps something of Sparta has gone from Yale, for a few years or forever, but just look at the Yale poets and novelists all over the place. There is a new kindliness at New Haven. Take for instance the testimony of the same *Big Year* when it describes a touching little scene between Curly Corliss, the captain of the Yale football team, and his roommate as they are revealed in the act of retiring for the night:

" 'Angel!'

" 'Yeah,' very sleepily.

" 'They all seem to get over it!'

" 'Over what?'

" 'The fellows who have graduated,' Curly explained. 'I guess they all feel pretty poor when they leave, but they get over it right away. It's just like changing into a new suit, I expect.'

" 'Yeah, I guess so' . . .

" 'Well, goo' night, little feller' . . .

" 'Goo' night, Teddy.' "

But we do wish Mr. Minnigerode had been a little more explicit and had told us who tucked them in.

20. SPORT FOR ART'S SAKE

For years we had been hearing about moral victories and at last we saw one. This is not intended as an excuse for the fact that we said before the fight that Carpentier would beat Dempsey. We erred with Bernard Shaw. The surprising revelation which came to us on this July afternoon was that a thing may be done well enough to make victory entirely secondary. We have all heard, of course, of sport for sport's sake but Georges Carpentier established a still more glamorous ideal. Sport for art's sake was what he showed us in the big wooden saucer over on Boyle's dirty acres.

It was the finest tragic performance in the lives of ninety thousand persons. We hope that Professor George Pierce Baker sent his class in dramatic composition. We will be disappointed if Eugene O'Neill, the white hope of the American drama, was not there. Here for once was a laboratory demonstration of life. None of the crowds in Greece who went to somewhat more beautiful stadia in search of Euripides ever saw the spirit of tragedy more truly presented. And we will wager that Euripides was not able to lift his crowd up upon its hind legs into a concerted shout of "Medea! Medea! Medea!" as Carpentier moved the fight fans over in Jersey City in the second round. In fact it is our contention that the fight between Dempsey and Carpentier was the most inspiring spectacle which America has seen in a generation.

Personally we would go further back than that. We would not accept a ticket for David and Goliath as a substitute. We remember that in that instance the little man won, but it was a spectacle less fine in artistry from the fact that it was less true to life. The tradition that Jack goes up the beanstalk and kills his giant, and that Little Red Ridinghood has the better of the wolf, and many other stories are limited in their inspirational quality by the fact that they are not true. They are stories that man has invented to console himself on winter's evenings for the fact that he is small and the universe is large. Carpentier showed us something far more thrilling. All of us who watched him know now that man cannot beat down Fate, no matter how much his will may flame, but he can rock it back upon its heels when he puts all his heart and his shoulders into a blow.

That is what happened in the second round. Carpentier landed his straight right upon Dempsey's jaw and the champion, who was edging in toward him, shot back and then swayed forward. Dempsey's hands dropped to his side. He was an open target. Carpentier swung a terrific right-hand uppercut and missed. Dempsey fell into a clinch and held on until his head cleared. He kept close to Carpentier during the rest of the fight and wore him down with body blows during the infighting. We know of course that when the first prehistoric creature crawled out of the ooze up to the beaches (see *The Outline of History* by H. G. Wells, some place in the first volume, just a couple of pages after that picture of the big lizard) it was already settled that Carpentier was going to miss that uppercut. And naturally it was inevitable that he should have the worst of it at infighting. Fate gets us all in the clinches, but Eugene O'Neill and all our young writers of tragedy make a great mistake if they think that the poignancy of the fate of man lies in the fact that he is weak, pitiful and helpless. The tragedy of life is not that man loses but that he almost wins. Or, if you are intent on pointing out that his downfall is inevitable, that at least he completes the gesture of being on the eve of victory.

For just eleven seconds on the afternoon of July 2 we felt that we were at the threshold of a miracle. There was such flash and power in that right-hand thrust of Carpentier's that we believed Dempsey would go down, and that fate would go with him and all the plans laid out in the days of the oozy friends of Mr. Wells. No sooner were the men in the ring together than it seemed just as certain that Dempsey would win as that the sun would come up on the morning of July 3. By and by we were not so sure about the sun. It might be down, we thought, and also out. It was included in the scope of Carpentier's punch, we feared. No, we did not exactly fear it. We respect the regularity of the universe by which we live, but we do not love it. If the blow had been as devastating as we first believed, we should have counted the world well lost.

Great circumstances produce great actors. History is largely concerned with arranging good entrances for people; and later exits not always quite so good. Carpentier played his part perfectly down to the last side. People who saw him just as he came before the crowd reported that he was pitifully nervous, drawn, haggard. It was the traditional and becoming nervousness of the actor just before a great performance. It was gone the instant Carpentier came in sight of his ninety thousand. His head was back and his eyes and his smile flamed as he crawled through the ropes. And he gave some curious flick to his bathrobe as he turned to meet the applause. Until that very moment we had been for Dempsey, but suddenly we found ourself up on our feet making silly noises. We shouted, "Carpentier! Carpentier! Carpentier!" and forgot even to be ashamed of our pronunciation. He held his hands up over his head and turned until the whole arena, including the five-dollar seats, had come within the scope of his smile.

Dempsey came in a minute later and we could not cheer, although we liked him. It would have been like cheering for Niagara Falls at the moment somebody was about to go over in a barrel. Actually there is a difference of sixteen pounds between the two men, which is large enough, but it seemed that afternoon as if it might have been a hundred. And we knew for the first time that a man may smile and smile and be an underdog.

We resented at once the law of gravity, the Malthusian

theory and the fact that a straight line is the shortest distance between two points. Everything scientific, exact, and inevitable was distasteful. We wanted the man with the curves to win. It seemed impossible throughout the first round. Carpentier was first out of his corner and landed the first blow, a light but stinging left to the face. Then Dempsey closed in and even the people who paid only thirty dollars for their seats could hear the thump, thump of his short hooks as they beat upon the narrow stomach of Carpentier. The challenger was only too evidently tired when the round ended.

Then came the second and, after a moment of fiddling about, he shot his right hand to the jaw. Carpentier did it again, a second time, and this was the blow perfected by a lifetime of training. The time was perfect, the aim was perfect, every ounce of strength was in it. It was the blow which had downed Bombardier Wells, and Joe Beckett. It rocked Dempsey to his heels, but it broke Carpentier's hand. His best was not enough. There was an earthquake in Philistia but then out came the signs "Business as usual!" and Dempsey began to pound Carpentier in the stomach.

The challenger faded quickly in the third round, and in the fourth the end came. We all suffered when he went down the first time, but he was up again, and the second time was much worse. It was in this knockdown that his head sagged suddenly, after he struck the floor, and fell back upon the canvas. He was conscious and his legs moved a little, but they would not obey him. A gorgeous human will had been beaten down to a point where it would no longer function.

If you choose, that can stand as the last moment in a completed piece of art. We are sentimental enough to wish to add the tag that after a few minutes Carpentier came out to the center of the ring and shook hands with Dempsey and at that moment he smiled again the same smile which we had seen at the beginning of the fight when he stood with his hands above his head. Nor is it altogether sentimental. We feel that one of the elements of tragedy lies in the fact that Fate gets nothing but the victories and the championships. Gesture and glamor remain with Man. No infighting can take that away from him.

Jack Dempsey won fairly and squarely. He is a great fighter, perhaps the most efficient the world has ever known, but everybody came away from the arena talking about Carpentier. He wasn't very efficient. The experts say he fought an ill-considered fight and should not have forced it. In using such a plan, they say, he might have lasted the whole twelve rounds. That was not the idea. As somebody has said, "Better four rounds of—" but we can't remember the rest of the quotation.

Dempsey won and Carpentier got all the glory. Perhaps we will have to enlarge our conception of tragedy, for that too is tragic.

21. JACK THE GIANT KILLER

All the giants and most of the dragons were happy and contented folk. Neither fear nor shame was in them. They faced life squarely and liked it. And so they left no literature.

The business of writing was left to the dwarfs, who felt impelled to distort real values in order to make their own pitiful existence endurable. In their stories the little people earned ease of mind for themselves by making up yarns in which they killed giants, dragons and all the best people of the community who were too big and strong for them. Naturally, the giants and dragons merely laughed at such times as these highly drawn accounts of imaginary happenings were called to their attention.

But they laughed not only too soon but too long. Giants and dragons have died and the stories remain. The world believes today that St. George slew the dragon, and that Jack killed all those giants. The little man has imposed himself upon the world. Strength and size have come to be reproaches. The world has been won by the weak.

Undoubtedly, it is too late to do anything about this now. But there is a little dim and distant dragon blood in our veins. It boils when we hear the fairy stories and we remember the true version of Jack the Giant Killer, as it has been handed down by word of mouth in our family for a great many centuries. We can produce no tangible proofs, and we are willing to admit that the tale may have grown a little distorted here and there in the telling through the ages. Even so it sounds much more plausible to us than the one which has crept into the story books.

Jack was a Celt, a liar and a meager man. He had great green eyes and much practice in being pathetic. He could sing tenor and often did. But it was not in this manner that he lived. By trade he was a newspaperman, though he called himself a journalist. In his shop there was a printing press and every afternoon he issued a newspaper which he called *Jack's Journal*. Under this name there ran the caption, "If you see it in *Jack's Journal* you may be sure that it actually occurred." Jack had no talent for brevity and little taste for truth. All in all he was a pretty poor newspaperman. We forgot to say that in addition to this he was exceedingly lazy. But he was a good liar.

This was the only thing which saved him. Day after day he would come to the office without a single item of local interest, and upon such occasions he made a practice of sitting down and making up something. Generally, it was far more thrilling than any of the real news of the community which clustered around one great highroad known as Main Street.

The town lay in a valley cupped between towering hills. On the hills, and beyond, lived the giants and the dragons, but there was little interchange between these fine people and the dwarfs of the village. Occasionally, a sliced drive from the giants' golf course would fall into the fields of the little people, who would ignorantly set down the great round object as a meteor from heaven. The giants were considerate as well as kindly and they made the territory of the little people out of bounds. Otherwise, an erratic golfer might easily have uprooted the first national bank, the Second Baptist Church, which stood next door, and *Jack's Journal* with one sweep of his niblick. If by any chance he failed to get out in one, the total destruction of mankind would have been imminent.

Once upon a time, a charitable dowager dragon sought to bring about a closer relationship between the peoples of the hills and the valley in spite of their difference in size. Hearing of a poor neglected family in the village, which was freezing to death because of want of coal, she leaned down from her mountain and breathed gently against the roof of the thatched cottage. Her intentions were excellent but the damage was $152,694, little of which was covered by insurance. After that the dragons and the giants decided to stop trying to do favors for the little people.

Being short of news one afternoon, Jack thought of the great gulf which existed between his reading public and the big fellows on the hill and decided that it would be safe to romance a little. Accordingly, he wrote a highly circumstantial story of the manner in which he had gone to the hills and killed a large giant with nothing more than his good broadsword. The story was not accepted as gospel by all the subscribers, but it was well told, and it argued an undreamed of power in the arm of man. People wanted to believe and accordingly they did. Encouraged, Jack began to kill dragons and giants with greater frequency in his newspaper. In fact, he called his last evening edition *The Five Star Giant Final* and never failed to feature a killing in it under great red block type.

The news of Jack's doings came finally to the hill people and they were much amused, that is all but one giant called Fee Fi Fo Fum. The Fo Fums (pronounced Fohum) were one of the oldest families in the hills. Jack supposed that all the names he was using were fictitious, but by some mischance or other he happened one afternoon to use Fee Fi Fo Fum as the name of his current victim. The name was common enough and undoubtedly the thing was an accident, but Mr. Fo Fum did not see it in that light. To make it worse, Jack had gone on in his story with some stuff about captive princesses just for the sake of sex appeal. Not only was Mr. Fo Fum an ardent Methodist, but his wife was jealous. There was a row in the Fo Fum home (see encyclopedia for Great Earthquake of 1007) and Fee swore revenge upon Jack.

"Make him print a retraction," said Mrs. Fo Fum.

"Retraction, nothing," roared Fee, "I'm going to eat up the presses."

Over the hills he went with giant strides and arrived at the office of *Jack's Journal* just at press time. Mr. Fo Fum was a little calmer by now, but still revengeful. He spoke to Jack in a whisper which shook the building, and told him that he purposed to step on him and bite his press in two.

"Wait until I have this last page made up," said Jack.

"Killing more giants, I presume?" said Fee with heavy satire.

"Bagged three this afternoon," said Jack. "Hero Slaughters Trio of Titans."

"My name is Fo Fum," said the giant. Jack did not recognize it because of the trick pronunciation and the visitor had to explain.

"I'm sorry," said Jack, "but if you've come for extra copies of the paper in which your name figures I can't give you any. The edition is exhausted."

Fo Fum spluttered and blew a bale of paper out of the window.

"Cut that out," said Jack severely. "All complaints must be made in writing. And while I'm about it you forgot to put your name down on one of those slips at the desk in the reception room. Don't forget to fill in that space about what business you want to discuss with the editor."

Fo Fum started to roar, but Jack's high and pathetic tenor cut through the great bass like a ship's siren in a storm.

"If you don't quit shaking this building I'll call Julius the office boy and have him throw you out."

"Take the air," added Jack severely, disregarding the fact that Fo Fum before entering the office had found it necessary to remove the roof. But now the giant was beginning to stoop a little. His face grew purple and he was swaying unsteadily on his feet.

"Hold on a minute," said Jack briskly, "don't go just yet. Stick around a second."

He turned to his secretary and dictated two letters of congratulation to distant emperors and another to a cardinal. "Tell the Pope," he said in conclusion, "that his conduct is admirable. Tell him I said so."

"Now, Mr. Fo Fum," said Jack turning back to the giant, "what I want from you is a picture. There is still plenty of light. I'll call up the staff photographer. The north meadow will give us room. Of course, you will have to be taken lying down because as far as the *Journal* goes you're dead. And just one thing more. Could you by any chance let me have one of your ears for our reception room?"

Fo Fum had been growing more and more purple, but now he toppled over with a crash, carrying part of the building with him. Almost two years before he had been warned by a doctor of apoplexy and sudden anger. Jack did not wait for the verdict of any medical examiner. He seized the speaking tube and shouted down to the composing room, "Jim, take out that old head. Make it read, 'Hero Finishes Four Ferocious Foemen.' And say, Jim, I want you to be ready to replate for a special extra with an eight-column cut. I'll have the photographer here in a second. I killed that last giant right here in the office. Yes, and say, Jim, you'd better use that stock cut of me at the bottom of the page. A caption, let me see, put it in twenty-four point Cheltenham bold and make it read 'Jack—the Giant Killer.'"

22. FRANKINCENSE AND MYRRH

Once there were three kings in the East and they were wise men. They read the heavens and they saw a certain strange star by which they knew that in a distant land the King of the world was to be born. The star beckoned to them and they made preparations for a long journey.

From their palaces they gathered rich gifts, gold and frankincense and myrrh. Great sacks of precious stuffs were loaded upon the backs of the camels which were to bear them on their journey. Everything was in readiness, but one of the wise men seemed perplexed and would not come at once to join his two companions, who were eager and impatient to be on their way in the direction indicated by the star.

They were old, these two kings, and the other wise man was young. When they asked him he could not tell why he waited. He knew that his treasuries had been ransacked for rich gifts for the King of Kings. It seemed that there was nothing more which he could give, and yet he was not content.

He made no answer to the old men who shouted to him that the time had come. The camels were impatient and swayed and snarled. The shadows across the desert grew longer. And still the young king sat and thought deeply.

At length he smiled, and he ordered his servants to open the great treasure sack upon the back of the first of his camels. Then he went into a high chamber to which he had not been since he was a child. He rummaged about and presently came out and approached the caravan. In his hand he carried something which glinted in the sun.

The kings thought that he bore some new gift more rare and precious than any which they had been able to find in all their treasure rooms. They bent down to see, and even the camel drivers peered from the backs of the great beasts to find out what it was which gleamed in the sun. They were curious about this last gift for which all the caravan had waited.

And the young king took a toy from his hand and placed it upon the sand. It was a dog of tin, painted white and speckled with black spots. Great patches of paint had worn away and left the metal clear, and that was why the toy shone in the sun as if it had been silver.

The youngest of the wise men turned a key in the side of the little black and white dog and then he stepped aside so that the kings and the camel drivers could see. The dog leaped high in the air and turned a somersault. He turned another and another and then fell over upon his side and lay there with a set and painted grin upon his face.

A child, the son of a camel driver, laughed and clapped his hands, but the kings were stern. They rebuked the youngest of the wise men and he paid no attention but called to his chief servant to make the first of all the camels kneel. Then he picked up the toy of tin and, opening the treasure sack, placed his last gift with his own hands in the mouth of the sack so that it rested safely upon the soft bags of incense.

"What folly has seized you?" cried the eldest of the wise men. "Is this a gift to bear to the King of Kings in the far country?"

And the young man answered and said: "For the King of Kings there are gifts of great richness, gold and frankincense and myrrh.

"But this," he said, "is for the child in Bethlehem!"

23. THE UNKNOWN SOLDIER

They call him "the unknown hero." It is enough, it is better that we should know him as "the unknown soldier." "Hero" suggests a superman and implies somebody exalted above his fellows. This man was one of many. We do not know what was in his heart when he died. It is entirely possible that he was a fearful man. He may even have gone unwillingly into the fight. That does not matter now. The important thing is that he was alive and is dead.

He was drawn from a far edge of the world by the war and in it he lost even his identity. War may have been well enough in the days when it was a game for heroes, but now it sweeps into the combat everything and every man within a nation. The unknown soldier stands for us as symbol of this blind and far-reaching fury of modern conflict. His death was in vain unless it helps us to see that the whole world is our business. No one is too great to be concerned with the affairs of mankind, and no one too humble.

The unknown soldier was a typical American and it is probable that once upon a time he used to speak of faraway folk as "those foreigners." He thought they were no kin of his, but he died in one of the distant lands. His blood and the blood of all the world mingled in a common stream.

The body of the unknown soldier has come home, but his spirit will wander with his brothers. There will be no rest for his soul until the great democracy of death has been translated into the unity of life.

24. THE YOUNG PESSIMISTS

Bert Williams used to tell a story about a man on a lonely road at night who suddenly saw a ghost come out of the forest and begin to follow him. The man walked faster and the ghost increased his pace. Then the man broke into a run with the ghost right on his heels. Mile after mile, faster and faster, they went until at last the man dropped at the side of the road exhausted. The ghost perched beside him on a large rock and boomed, "That was quite a run we had." "Yes," gasped the man, "and as soon as I get my breath we're going to have another one."

Our young American pessimists see man at the moment he drops beside the road, and without further investigation decide that it is all up with him. To be sure, they may not be very far wrong in the ultimate fate of man, but at least they anticipate his end. They do not stick with him until the finish; and this second-wind flight, however useless, is something so characteristic of life that it belongs in the record. I have at least a sneaking suspicion that now and again there happens along a runner so staunch and courageous that he keeps up the fight until cock-crow and thus escapes all the apparitions which would overthrow him. Of course, it is a long shot and the young pessimists are much too logical to wait for such miraculous chances. As a matter of fact, they don't call themselves pessimists but prefer to be known as rationalists, realists, or some such name which carries with it the hint of wisdom.

And they are wise up to the very point of believing only the things they have seen. However, I am not sure they are quite so wise when they go a notch beyond this and assert roundly that everything which they have seen is true. For my own part I don't believe that white rabbits are actually born in high hats.

The truth is quicker than the eye, but it is hardly possible to make any person with fresh young sight believe that. Question the validity of some character in a play or book by a young rationalist and he will invariably reply, "Why she lived right in our town," and he will upon request supply name, address, and telephone number to confound the doubters.

"Let the captious be sure they know their Emmas as well as I do before they tell me how she would act," wrote Eugene O'Neill when somebody objected that the heroine of *Diff'rent* was not true. This, of course, shifts the scope of the inquiry to the question, "How well does O'Neill know his Emmas?" Indeed, how well does any bitter-end rationalist know anybody? Once upon a time we lived in a simple age in which when a man said, "I'm going to kick you downstairs because I don't like you," and then did it, there was not a shadow of doubt in the mind of the person at the foot of the stairs that he had come upon an enemy. All that is changed now. During the war, for instance, George Sylvester Viereck wrote a book to prove that every time Roosevelt said, "Viereck is an undesirable citizen," or words to that effect, he was simply dissembling an admiration so great that it was shot through and through with ambivalent outbursts of hatred. Mr. Viereck may not have proved his case but he did, at least, put his relations into debatable ground by shifting from Philip conscious to Philip subconscious.

In the new world of the psychoanalysts there is confusion for the rationalist even though he is dealing with something so inferentially logical as a science. For here, with all its tangible symbols, is a science which deals with things which cannot be seen or heard or touched. And much of all the truth in the world lies in just such dim dominions. The pessimist is very apt to be stopped at the border. For years he has reproached the optimist with the charge that he lived by dreams rather than realities. Now, wise men have come forward to say that the key to all the most important things in life lies in dreams. Of course, the poets have known that for years, but nobody paid any attention to them because they only felt it and offered no papers to the medical journals.

It would be unfair to suggest that no dreamer is a pessimist. The most prolific period of pessimism comes at twenty-one, or thereabouts, when the first attempt is made to translate dreams into reality, an attempt by a person not over-skillful in either language. Often it is made in college where a new freedom inspires a somewhat sudden and wholesale attempt to put every vision to the test. Along about this time the young man finds that the romanticists have lied to him about love and he bounces all the way back to Strindberg. Maybe he gets drunk for the first time and learns that every English author from Shakespeare to Dickens has vastly overrated it for literary effect. He follows the formulae of Falstaff and instead of achieving a roaring joviality he goes to sleep.

Personally tobacco sent me into a deep pessimism when I first took it up in a serious way. Huck's corncob pipe had always seemed to me one of the most persuasive symbols of true enjoyment. It seemed to me that life could hold nothing more ideal than to float down the Mississippi blowing rings. After six months of experimenting I was ready to believe that maybe the Mississippi wasn't so much either. Romance seemed pretty doubtful stuff. Around this time, also, the young man generally discovers, in compulsory chapel, that the average minister is a dull preacher; and of course that knocks all the theories of the immortality of the soul right on the head. He may even have come to college with a thirst for knowledge and a faith in its exciting quality, only to have these emotions ooze away during the second month of introductory lectures on anthropology.

Accordingly, it is not surprising to find F. Scott Fitzgerald's Amory Blaine looking at the towers of Princeton and musing:

Here was a new generation, shouting the old cries, learning the old creeds through a revery of long days and nights; destined finally to go out into that dirty gray turmoil to follow love and pride; a new generation dedicated more than the last to the fear of poverty and the worship of success; grown up to find all Gods dead, all wars fought; all faiths in man shaken. . . .

Nobody wrote as well as that in Copeland's course at Harvard but there was a pretty general agreement that life—or rather Life—was a sham and a delusion. This was expressed in poems lamenting the fact that the oceans and the mountains were going to go on and that the writer wouldn't. Generally he didn't give the oceans or the mountains very long either. All the short stories were about murder and madness. We cut our patterns into very definite conclusions because we were pessimists and sure of ourselves. It was the most logical of philosophies and disposed of all loose ends.

One of my pieces (to polish off a theme on the futility of human wishes) was about a man who went stark raving mad, and Copeland sat in his chair and groaned and moaned, which was his substitute for making little marks in red ink. He had been reading Sheridan's *The Critic* to the class with the scene in which the two faithless Spanish lovers and the two nieces and the two uncles all try to kill each other at the same time, and are thus thrown into the most terrific stalemate until the author's ingenious contrivance of a beefeater who cries, "Drop your weapons in the Queen's name." At any rate, when I had finished, the little man ceased groaning and shook his head about my story of the man who went mad. "Broun," he said, "try to solve your problems without recourse to death, madness—or any other beefeater in the Queen's name."

And it seems to me that the young pessimists, generally speaking, have allowed themselves to be bound in a formula as tight as that which ever afflicted any Pollyanna. It isn't the somberness with which they imbue life which arouses our protest, so much as the regularity. They paint life not only as a fake fight in which only one result is possible but they make it again and again the selfsame fight.

25. THE ORTHODOX CHAMPION

The entire orthodox world owes a debt to Benny Leonard. In all the other arts, philosophies, religions and what nots conservatism seems to be crumbling before the attacks of the radicals. A stylist may generally be identified today by his bloody nose. Even in Leonard's profession of pugilism the correct method has often been discredited of late.

It may be remembered that George Bernard Shaw announced before "the battle of the century" that Carpentier ought to be a fifty to one favorite in the betting. It was the technique of the Frenchman which blinded Shaw to the truth. Every man in the world must be in some respect a standpatter. The scope of heresy in Shaw stops short of the prize ring. His radicalism is not sufficiently far reaching to crawl through the ropes. When Carpentier knocked out Beckett with one perfectly delivered punch he also jarred Shaw. He knocked him loose from some of his cynical contempt for the conventions. Mr. Shaw might continue to be in revolt against the well-made play, but he surrendered his heart wholly to the properly executed punch.

But Carpentier, the stylist, fell before Dempsey, the mauler, in spite of the support of the intellectuals. It seemed once again that all the rules were wrong. Benny Leonard remains the white hope of the orthodox. In lightweight circles, at any rate, old-fashioned proprieties are still effective. No performer in any art has ever been more correct than Leonard. He follows closely all the best traditions of the past. His left-hand jab could stand without revision in any textbook. The manner in which he feints, ducks, sidesteps and hooks is unimpeachable. The crouch contributed by some of the modernists is not in the repertoire of Leonard. He stands up straight like a gentleman and a champion and is always ready to hit with either hand.

His fight with Rocky Kansas at Madison Square Garden was advertised as being for the lightweight championship of the world. As a matter of fact much more than that was at stake. Spiritually, Saint-Saens, Brander Matthews, Henry Arthur Jones, Kenyon Cox, and Henry Cabot Lodge were in Benny Leonard's corner. His defeat would, by implication, have given support to dissonance, dadaism, creative evolution and bolshevism. Rocky Kansas does nothing according to rule. His fighting style is as formless as the prose of Gertrude Stein. One finds a delightfully impromptu quality in Rocky's boxing. Most of the blows which he tries are experimental. There is no particular target. Like the young poet who shot an arrow into the air, Rocky Kansas tosses off a right-hand swing every once and so often and hopes that it will land on somebody's jaw.

But with the opening gong Rocky Kansas tore into Leonard. He was gauche and inaccurate but terribly persistent. The champion jabbed him repeatedly with a straight left which has always been considered the proper thing to do under the circumstances. Somehow or other it did not work. Leonard might as well have been trying to stand off a rhinoceros with a feather duster. Kansas kept crowding him. In the first clinch Benny's hair was rumpled and a moment later his nose began to bleed. The incident was a shock to us. It gave us pause and inspired a sneaking suspicion that perhaps there was something the matter with Tennyson after all. Here were two young men in the ring and one was quite correct in everything which he did and the other was all wrong. And the wrong one was winning. All the enthusiastic Rocky Kansas partisans in the gallery began to split infinitives to show their contempt for Benny Leonard and all other stylists. Macaulay turned over twice in his grave when Kansas began to lead with his right hand.

But traditions are not to be despised. Form may be just as tough in fiber as rebellion. Not all the steadfastness of the world belongs to heretics. Even though his hair was mussed and his nose bleeding, Benny continued faithful to the established order. At last his chance came. The young child of nature who was challenging for the championship dropped his guard and Leonard hooked a powerful and entirely orthodox blow to the conventional point of the jaw. Down went Rocky Kansas. His past life flashed before him during the nine seconds in which he remained on the floor and he wished that he had been more faithful as a child in heeding the advice of his boxing teacher. After all, the old masters did know something. There is still a kick in style, and tradition carries a nasty wallop.

26. PROFESSOR GEORGE PIERCE BAKER

A great many persons speak and write about Professor George Pierce Baker, of Harvard, as if he were a sort of agitator who made a practice of luring young men away from productive labor to write bad plays. There is no denying the fact that a certain number of dramatists have come out of Harvard's English 47, but the course also has a splendid record of cures. Few things in the world are so easy as to decide to write a play. It carries a sense of satisfaction entirely disproportionate to the amount of effort entailed. Even the failure to put a single line on paper brings no remorse, for it is easy to convince yourself that the thing would have had no chance in the commercial theater.

All this would be well enough except that the author of a phantom play is apt to remain a martyr throughout his life. He makes a very bad husband and father and a worse bridge partner. Freudians know the complaint as the Euripidean complex. The sufferer is ailing because his play lies suppressed in his subconscious mind.

Professor Baker digs these plays out. People who come to English 47 may talk about their plays as much as they choose, but they must write them, too. Often a cure follows within forty-eight hours after the completion of a play. Sometimes it is enough for the author to read the thing through for himself, but if that does not avail there is an excellent chance for him after his play has been read aloud by Professor Baker and criticized by the class. If a pupil still wishes to write plays after this there is no question that he belongs in the business. He may, of course, never earn a penny at it but, starve or flourish, he is a playwright.

Professor Baker deserves the thanks of the community, then, not only for Edward Sheldon, and Cleves Kincaid, and Miss Lincoln and Eugene O'Neill and some of the other playwrights who came from English 47, but also for the number of excellent young men who have gone straight from his classroom to Wall Street, and the ministry, and automobile accessories with all the nascent enthusiasm of men just liberated from a great delusion.

In another respect Professor Baker has often been subjected to much undeserved criticism. Somebody has figured out that there are 2.983 more rapes in the average English 47 play than in the usual non-collegiate specimen of commercial drama. We feel comparatively certain that there is nothing in the personality of Professor Baker to account for this or in the traditions of Harvard, either. We must admit that nowhere in the world is a woman quite so unsafe as in an English 47 play, but the faculty gives no official encouragement to this undergraduate enthusiasm for sex problems. One must look beyond the Dean and the faculty for an explanation. It has something to do with Spring, and the birds, and the saplings and "What Every Young Man Ought to Know" and all that sort of thing.

When I was in English 47 I remember that all our plays

dealt with Life. At that none of us regarded it very highly. Few respected it and certainly no one was in favor of it. The course was limited to juniors, seniors and graduate students and we were all a little jaded. There were times, naturally, when we regretted our lost illusions and longed to be freshmen again and to believe everything the Sunday newspapers said about Lillian Russell. But usually there was no time for regrets; we were too busy telling Life what we thought about it. Here there was a divergence of opinion. Some of the playwrights in English 47 said that Life was a terrific tragedy. In their plays the hero shot himself, or the heroine, or both, as the circumstances might warrant, in the last act. The opposing school held that Life was a joke, a grim jest to be sure, cosmic rather than comic, but still mirthful. The plays by these authors ended with somebody ordering "Another small bottle of Pommery" and laughing mockingly, like a world-wise cynic.

Bolshevism had not been invented at that time, but Capital was severely handled just the same. All our villains were recruited from the upper classes. Yet capitalism had an easy time of it compared with marriage. I do not remember that a single play which I heard all year in 47, whether from Harvard or Radcliffe, had a single word of toleration, let alone praise, for marriage. And yet it was dramatically essential, for without marriage none of us would have been able to hammer out our dramatic tunes upon the triangle. Most of the epigrams also were about marriage. "Virtue is a polite word for fear"—that is the sort of thing we were writing when we were not empowering some character to say, "Honesty is a bedtime fairy story invented for the proletariat," or "The prodigal gets drunk; the Puritan gets religion."

But up to date Professor Baker has stood up splendidly under this yearly barrage of epigrams. With his pupils toppling institutions all around him he has held his ground firmly and insisted on the enduring quality of the fundamental technic of the drama. When a pupil brings in a play in favor of polygamy,

Baker declines to argue but talks instead about peripety. In other words, Professor Baker is wise enough to realize that it is impossible that he should furnish, or even attempt to mold in any way, the philosophy which his students bring into English 47 each year. If it is often a crude philosophy that is no fault of his. He can't attempt to tell the fledgling playwrights what things to say and, of course, he doesn't. English 47 is designed almost entirely to give a certain conception of dramatic form. Professor Baker "tries in the light of historical practice to distinguish the permanent from the impermanent in technic." He endeavors, "by showing the inexperienced dramatist how experienced dramatists have solved problems similar to his own, to shorten a little the time of apprenticeship."

When a man has done with Baker he has begun to grasp some of the things he must not do in writing a play. With that much ground cleared all that he has to do is to acquire a knowledge of life, devise a plot and find a manager.

27. CENSORING THE CENSOR

Mice and canaries were sometimes employed in France to detect the presence of gas. When these little things began to die in their cages the soldiers knew that the air had become dangerous. Some such system should be devised for censorship to make it practical. Even with the weight of authority behind him no bland person, with virtue obviously unruffled, is altogether convincing when he announces that the book he has just read or the moving picture he has seen is so hideously immoral that it constitutes a danger to the community. For my part I always feel that if he can stand it so can I. To the best of my knowledge and belief, Mr. Sumner was not swayed from his usual course of life by so much as a single peccadillo for all of

Jurgen. His indignation was altogether altruistic. He feared for the fate of weaker men and women.

Every theatrical manager, every motion picture producer, and every publisher knows, to his sorrow, that the business of estimating the effect of any piece of imaginative work upon others is precarious and uncertain. Genius would be required to predict accurately the reaction of the general public to any set piece which seems immoral to the censor. For instance, why was Mr. Sumner so certain that *Jurgen,* which inspired him with horror and loathing, would prove a persuasive temptation to all the rest of the world? Censorship is serious and drastic business; it should never rest merely upon guesswork and more particularly not upon the guesses of men so staunch in morals that they are obviously of distant kin to the rest of humanity.

The censor should be a person of a type capable of being blasted for the sins of the people. His job can be elevated to dignity only when the world realizes that he runs horrid risks. If we should choose our censors from fallible folk we might have proof instead of opinions. Suppose the censor of *Jurgen* had been someone other than Mr. Sumner, someone so unlike the head of the vice society that after reading Mr. Cabell's book he had come out of his room, not quivering with rage, but leering and wearing vine leaves. In such case the rest would be easy. It would merely be necessary to shadow the censor until he met his first dryad. His wink would be sufficient evidence and might serve as a cue for the rescuers to rush forward and save him. Of course there would then be no necessity for legal proceedings in regard to the book. Expert testimony as to its possible effects would be irrelevant. We would know and we could all join cheerfully in the bonfire.

To my mind there are three possible positions which may logically be taken concerning censorship. It might be entrusted to the wisest man in the world, to a series of average men,—or be abolished. Unfortunately it has been our experience that there is a distinct affinity between fools and censorship. It seems to be one of those treading grounds where they rush in. To be sure, we ought to admit a prejudice at the outset and acknowledge that we were a reporter in France during the war at a time when censors seemed a little more ridiculous than usual. We still remember the young American lieutenant who held up a story of a boxing match in Saint-Nazaire because the reporter wrote, "In the fourth round MacBeth landed a nice right on the Irishman's nose and the claret began to flow." "I'm sorry," said the censor, "but we have strict orders from Major Palmer that no mention of wine or liquor is to be allowed in any story about the American army."

Nor have we forgotten the story of General Pétain's mustache. "Why," asked Junius Wood of the *Globe*, "have you held up my story? All the rest have gone."

"Unfortunately," answered the courteous Frenchman, "you have twice used the expression General Pétain's 'white mustache.' I might stretch a point and let you say 'gray mustache,' but I should much prefer to have you say 'blond mustache.'"

"Oh, make it green with purple spots," said Junius.

The use of average men in censorship would necessitate sacrifices to the persuasive seduction of immorality, as I have suggested, and moreover there are very few average men. Accordingly, I am prepared to abandon that plan of censorship. The wisest man in the world is too old and too busy with his plays and has announced that he will never come to America. Accordingly we venture to suggest that in time of peace we try to get along without any censorship of plays or books or moving pictures. I have no desire, of course, to leave Mr. Sumner unemployed—it would perhaps be only fair to allow him to slosh around among the picture postcards.

Once official censorship had been officially abolished, a strong and able censorship would immediately arise consisting of the playgoing and reading public. It is a rather offensive error to assume that the vast majority of folk in America are rarin' to get to dirty books and dirty plays. It is the experience of New

York managers that the run of the merely salacious play is generally short. The success which a few nasty books have had has been largely because of the fact that they came close to the line of things which are forbidden. Without the prohibition there would be little popularity.

To save myself from the charge of hypocrisy I should add that personally I believe there ought to be a certain amount of what we now know as immoral writing. It would do no harm in a community brought up to take it or let it alone. It is well enough for the reading public and the critic to use terms such as moral or immoral, but they hardly belong in the vocabulary of an artist. I have heard it said that before Lucifer left Heaven there were no such things as virtues and vices. The world was equipped with a certain number of traits which were qualities without distinction or shame. But when Lucifer and the heavenly hosts drifted into their eternal warfare it was agreed that each side should recruit an equal number of these human, and at that time unclassified, qualities. A coin was tossed and, whether by fair chance or sharp miracle, Heaven won.

"I choose Blessedness," said the Captain of the Angels. It should be explained that the selection was made without previous medical examination, and Blessedness seemed at that time a much more robust recruit than he has since turned out to be. A tendency to flat foot is always hard to detect.

"Give me Beauty," said Lucifer, and from that day to this the artists of the world have been divided into two camps—those who wished to achieve beauty and those who wished to achieve blessedness, those who wanted to make the world better and those who were indifferent to its salvation if they could only succeed in making it a little more personable.

However, the conflict is not quite so simple as that. Late in the afternoon when the Captain of the Angels had picked Unselfishness and Moderation and Faith and Hope and Abstinence, and Lucifer had called to his side Pride and Gluttony and Anger and Lust and Tactlessness, there remained only two more qualities to be apportioned to the contending sides. One of them was Sloth, who was obviously overweight, and the other was a furtive little fellow with his cap down over his eyes.

"What's your name?" said the Captain of the Angels.

"Truth," stammered the little fellow.

"Speak up," said the Captain of the Angels so sharply that Lucifer remonstrated, saying, "Hold on there; Anger's on my side."

"Truth," said the little fellow again but with the same somewhat indistinct utterance which has always been so puzzling to the world.

"I don't understand you," said the Captain of the Angels, "but if it's between you and Sloth I'll take a chance with you. Stop at the locker room and get your harp and halo."

Now today even Lucifer will admit, if you get him in a corner, that Truth is the mightiest warrior of them all. The only trouble is his truancy. Sometimes he can't be found for centuries. Then he will bob up unexpectedly, break a few heads, and skip away. Nothing can stand against him. Lucifer's best ally, Beauty, is no match for him. Truth holds every decision. But the trouble is that he still keeps his cap down over his eyes, and he still mumbles his words, and nobody knows him until he is at least fifty years away and moving fast. At that distance he seems to grow bigger, and he invariably reaches into his back pocket and puts on his halo so that people can recognize him. Still, when he comes along the next time and is face to face with any man of this world, the mortal is pretty sure to say, "Your face is familiar but I can't seem to place you."

There is no denying that he isn't a good mixer. But for that he would be an excellent censor.

28. *THE BOY GREW OLDER*, CHAPTER I

"Your son was born ten minutes ago," said the voice at the other end of the wire.

"I'll be up," replied Peter Neale, "right away."

But it wasn't right away. First he had to go upstairs to the card room and settle his losses. Indeed he played one more pot, for when he returned to the table his deal had come around again. He felt that it was not the thing to quit just then. The other men might think he had timed his departure in order to save the dollar ante. He dealt the cards and picked up four spades and a heart. Eventually, he paid five dollars to draw and again he had four spades and a heart. Nevertheless, he bet ten dollars, but it was no go. His hands shook as he dropped the two blue chips in the center of the table. The man with a pair of jacks noticed that and called. Peter threw his cards away.

"I've got nothing—a busted flush. I want to cash in now. I owe for two stacks. That's right, isn't it? I haven't any chips left. If somebody'll lend me a fountain pen I'll make out a check. I guess I need a check too. Any kind'll do. I can cross the name off."

"Why are you quitting so soon?" asked the banker as Peter waved the check back and forth to let it dry. "We're all going to quit at seven o'clock."

"Two rounds and a consolation pot," corrected somebody across the table.

Peter was curiously torn between reticence and an impulse to tell. He felt a little as if he might begin to cry. When he spoke his voice was thick. "I've got to go up to see my son," he said. "He's just been born."

He shoved the check over to the banker and was out of the room before anybody could say anything.

He thought that the banker said, "Congratulations," as he slammed the door behind him, but he could not be certain of it.

All the way up in the taxi he worried. The hospital was half a mile away. He wished that the nurse had said, "A fine boy," but he remembered it was just "Your son was born ten minutes ago."

"If anything had been wrong," he thought, "she wouldn't have said it over the telephone."

"Is everything all right?" was his first question when a nurse came to the door of the small private hospital and let him in. "My name's Peter Neale," he explained. "My son's just been born half an hour ago."

"Everything's fine, Mr. Neale," she said and she smiled. "The baby weighs nine pounds. Mrs. Neale is fine too. You can see them both, but she's asleep now. You can't really see her today, but I think they'll let you have a good look at your son. He's a little darling."

Peter was reassured but irritated. Formula was all over the remark, "He's a little darling." He thought she ought not to use it until she had learned to do it better. Some place or other he had read that babies were fearfully homely. Still it didn't look so bad when he came into the room. Black was smudged all around the eyes, which gave the child a rakish look.

"Miss Haine," said the nurse who brought him in, "this is Mr. Neale."

"Mr. Neale," she added, "meet your son." Then she went out.

"Is he all right, Miss Haine?" was Peter's first question as soon as the door closed. After all, the other woman was just supposed to answer the bell. Miss Haine might know more about it.

"He's a cherub," said Miss Haine.

"How did his eyes get blacked?" Peter wanted to know.

"Oh, that's just the silver nitrate. We always put that on a baby's eyes to make sure— Look what a fine head he has."

Peter bent closer. The baby was not nearly so red as he had expected. As for the head he didn't see why it was fine. He had no notion of just what made a head fine anyway. The child kept wrinkling up its face, but it was not crying. There was nothing about his son to which Peter could take specific exception, but somehow he was disappointed. When he had said down at the New York Newspaper Club, "I've got to go up and see my son," the phrase "my son" had thrilled him. But this wasn't "my son." It was just a small baby. It seemed to him as distant as a second cousin.

"He is sweet," remarked Miss Haine.

"Yes," said Peter, but he felt that any extension of the discussion would merely promote hypocrisy on both sides. "Can I see my wife?" he asked.

"Come this way," said Miss Haine. "You can only stay a second. I'm pretty sure she's asleep."

Maria was asleep and snoring hard. Miss Haine took up one arm which was flung outside the cover and found the pulse of the sleeping girl, and as she felt it she smiled reassuringly. "Yes," she said, "she's doing fine."

"And now," she added, "I'm going to bundle you off. There really isn't anything around here for a father to do. This isn't your job, you know. I'm going to let you come back in the morning, but not before ten."

Peter learned later that one of the strongest factors in Maria's resentment against having a baby was that he was implicated in the affair so slightly. He tried to tell her that she ought to blame biology and not him, but she said there was nothing in the scheme of creation which arranged that fathers should be playing cards when their sons were born. It had an air of reckless indifference about it which maddened her. Peter knew that he could not explain to her that he had not been free in spirit during the afternoon. He simply could not bear to stay out of a single pot. Hour after hour he kept coming in on middle straights and three flushes. Never before had he done anything like that. But she knew so little about poker that there was no use in telling her any of this. Indeed he realized that he had made a mistake in venturing his one answer. Maria was in nowise pacified when he said, "But I lost fifty dollars."

29. *THE BOY GREW OLDER*, CHAPTER X

The baby carriage was kept in the kitchen and Peter did not see "it" again until Sunday, his first Sunday at home. Kate left the flat very early. Peter could not very well object to that because she said she was going to Mass. He wished that she might be converted to one of the eleven o'clock denominations, but he supposed at her age there was small hope of that. She would be gone, she told him, until nine or ten o'clock in the evening. Her niece, the one who lived in Jamaica, had a new baby five weeks old. Kate was going there right after church. Peter thought that if he had Kate's job he would prefer to spend his day off at an old folks' home or some other spot exclusively mature.

Still he could understand the psychology of it. Out in Jamaica, Kate could sit around and when the baby cried she need not move hand or foot. She could watch other people bustle around and fulfill its needs. And then every now and then she might give advice and see it carried out. He himself had spent many a day off in the office of the *Bulletin* sitting on the desk of somebody who was working and interrupting him.

Before Kate left she gave Peter a complete list of directions for the baby's day and also a problem for him to ponder over. "What will I be calling the boy?" she wanted to know. "I find it hard to be talking to him and him with no name."

"I'll think it over," Peter told her. After she left he did think it over. He went into the baby's room and looked at him as he lay there to see if the child suggested any name in particular. Being asleep he seemed a little more impersonal than usual. Of course, Peter Neale was a pretty good name, but there didn't seem to be any point in calling him that unless in some way or other he seemed to be Peter. He did sleep with his head buried face down in the pillow but that was an insufficient bond. Perhaps there were millions of people in the world who slept that way. Probably there were no statistics on the subject.

Maybe one Peter Neale was enough. It did mean something. After all it was Peter Neale who had written in the *Bulletin:* "If Horace Fogel goes through with his plan of making a first baseman out of Christy Mathewson he will be committing the baseball crime of the century. Mathewson, or Matty as his team mates call him, is still green, but he has in him the makings of one of the greatest pitchers the world has ever known. He has the speed and control and more than that he has a head on his shoulders. Horace Fogel hasn't."

And they didn't switch Matty to first base after all and now everybody was beginning to realize that he was a great pitcher. But Peter Neale knew it first of all. More than that, it was Peter Neale who had begun his round by round story of the Gans-Nelson fight, only two weeks ago, with the memorable line, "The Dane comes up like thunder." He had invented the name of "Hooks" for George Wiltse and had written that "Frank Bowerman runs the bases like somebody pulling Grover Cleveland in a rickshaw." And Peter was still progressing. He would go on, years hence, to make the most of McGraw's practice of starting games with Rube Schauer and finishing them with Ferdie Schupp by contriving the lead, "It never Schauers but it Schupps." Perhaps he had prevision enough to realize that it was he, Peter Neale, who would eventually ascribe to Jack Dempsey the motto, "Say it with cauliflowers," and write after a Crimson disaster on the Thames, "Harvard's most perplexing race problems appear to be crewish and Jewish."

He looked at the sleeping child and wondered if there were any leads like that in the little head. By and by, of course, the baby would grow up and in some newspaper there would be articles under his name. Peter would like to see the articles before he was willing to have them signed "By Peter Neale." Every now and then somebody wandered into his office at the *Bulletin* and asked him to use his good influences with the managing editor. Peter always said, "Will you let me see something you've written?" Here in front of him was a candidate not only for a job but for his job. And the applicant had nothing to show.

It was a hot bright Sunday and Kate had recommended that the baby go out. The carriage was deplorable. Peter had not bothered to look at it before, but now he examined it and found it wholly lacking in distinction. It could not be that all the things which were wrong with it had resulted from his falling over it a few mornings back. That had hurt him much more than the carriage. The paint was splotchy and all the wheels squeaked. Kate must have seized the first available vehicle in the neighborhood. What with that carriage and his heavily bandaged head he felt that the caravan which he was about to conduct would be disreputable. The numerous chin straps which held the bandages in place made it difficult for Peter to shave. In order to avoid that difficulty Peter hadn't shaved. He only hoped that nobody in the Park would stop the procession and ask him to accept a quarter. Peter practiced an expression of scorn in front of a mirror in order to be ready for some such contingency. Nature had endowed him with a loose scalp. He could wiggle both ears, together or separately. So far this had never been of much use although he found that it helped him enormously to qualify as a nursery entertainer. But there was another maneuver which he used habitually and successfully to indicate utter disagreement and contempt. He could elevate his right eyebrow without disturbing the other. This never failed to strike terror to all observers. Peter had that so well in hand that he needed no mirror practice to perfect it. He worked on curling his lip, a device which was new to him. Combined with an elevated eyebrow an effect was produced ample to carry off the handicaps of both carriage and bandages.

Nevertheless, he felt a little conspicuous when he started for the Park. And pushing a carriage was dull work. There was no future to it, no competitive value, no opportunity for advancement. One could not very well come to the point of being able to say, "I can wheel a carriage a little bit better than anybody else in New York." The thing was without standards. Of all outdoor sports this was the most dreary and democratic. But in spite of the ease of manipulation he was under the impression that a carriage required constant attention. Quite by accident he discovered that it would space nicely between shoves if he happened to let go of the handlebar. This led to the creation of a rather amusing game. Peter called it putting the sixteen pound carriage.

Not far from the Sixty-fifth Street entrance of the Park he found a large hill and for a moment it was clear of pedestrians. Standing at the foot of this hill Peter gave the carriage a violent shove and let go. Up the hill it sped until its momentum was exhausted and then it rolled back again. The game was to try and make it reach the top. Peter never succeeded in that although he came within four feet eight inches of accomplishing the feat which he had set for himself. He was handicapped by the fact that he did not quite dare to put all his back and shoulders into the preliminary shove. Indeed on his best heave, the one which took the missile within four feet eight inches of the top, the carriage careened precariously. More than that it almost hit a stout woman who was coming down the hill. She stopped and spoke to Peter. "Haven't you got any better sense than to do a thing like that?" she said. "That carriage almost upset. I've a good mind to follow you home and tell the father of that baby some of the things you're doing with his child. Aren't you ashamed of yourself, a grown man carrying on like that. And on Sunday too."

Peter didn't want her to follow him home and so he merely said, "Yes, ma'am, I won't do it any more."

And for that day he kept his word. However, the baby did not seem to mind much. It continued to sleep. Peter pushed the carriage aimlessly about for a little while, never letting go of the handlebar. He felt like an Atlantic City Negro with a wheel chair hired for the day by a tired business man. There was nobody to whom he could talk. The baby had slept so long by now that Peter began to worry that something might be wrong with him. Bending over the carriage, he ascertained that the child was still breathing. He wished it would wake up. Of course he might not actually be company if aroused but he seemed even less animated when asleep.

Perhaps Christy would be a good name for him. Christopher Mathewson Neale had a fine resounding swing to it. Still maybe Matty wouldn't turn out to be a great pitcher after all. Peter was tremendously confident about him, but it might be best to wait until time had tested him. After a World's Series or something like that, one could be absolutely certain. No good taking chances until then. It was still within the bounds of possibility that Matty might be a bloomer and it would hardly be fair to name the child after somebody in the Three I League.

Finding a tree and a bench, Peter sat down to continue his speculations. How about a newspaper name? Greeley Neale wouldn't be so bad. Yes, it would. Everybody would be sure to make it Greasy Neale. A prizefight name offered possibilities. Nelson Neale, for instance, had alliteration. Peter had given the lightweight a name—the Durable Dane was his invention—and it seemed no more than a fair exchange to take his in return. Still he had never been convinced that Nelson was a really first class man. He had neither speed nor a punch. It was just stamina which carried him along. The youngster ought not to go through life head down. Besides a name like that would serve to remind Peter of his return from Goldfield and the flight of Maria.

Just then a sound came from the carriage. It was a gurgle. Peter pushed back the hood. The baby looked at him fixedly and Peter fancied that there was a certain trace of emotion in the small face. Surprise seemed to be indicated. And it was not altogether agreeable surprise for as Peter returned the stare the baby's right eyebrow went up and the left one didn't.

"God!" said Peter, "he is Peter Neale."

But there must be more ceremony than that. Peter looked around to see that he and the baby were alone. Then he spoke to him distinctly although emotionally. He realized now that his intuition had been sound when he had said way back weeks ago at the Newspaper Club, "My son has just been born." He had never had any doubt about his physical paternity but that did not seem important. It was spiritual kinship which counted and an eyebrow like that was a thing of the spirit.

"You're my son all right," said Peter, "and you're going to have my name. Peter Neale, that's your name."

He thought it would complicate things to go into the question of whether he should be Peter Neale, Jr., or Peter Neale, 2nd. The Peter Neale was the important part of it. "I guess maybe you can do a lot more with that name than I have, but I've made it a good newspaper name. You can make it a better one maybe. We'll wait and see." He reached out and took the small hand of Peter Neale and shook it. The prayer which went with it was silent. "O God, give him some of the breaks and I will." That completed the christening. It was all that young Peter ever got.

The red-headed boy up the block who had contributed disturbing ideas in other fields also threw a bombshell into Peter's boyhood theology. "Can God do anything?" was his catch question. "Of course He can," replied Peter. "Well, I'll just bet you a million billion dollars He can't make a trolley car go in two directions at the same time." Peter didn't see how He could.

He puzzled over the problem for months and at last he decided that maybe God could work it by making the trolley car like an elastic so that it could be stretched uptown and downtown at the same time. It was not an entirely satisfactory solution of the problem. If a passenger stood in the middle of the car he wouldn't get any place at all.

But for the moment Peter was not much concerned with the potential relationship between the Deity and young Peter. He could bide his time and think up an answer for the day when the child should ask him, "Who's God?" The immediate problem was what place he should fill on the *Bulletin*. Eventually, of course, he would conduct the column called Looking Them Over With Peter Neale. Already there were thirty-one papers in the syndicate and some day Peter could step down and the column would still be Looking Them Over With Peter Neale.

It would be pleasant not to die in the office but to have ten years or so with no worries as to whether Jim Jeffries could have beaten John L. Sullivan in his prime. And he didn't want to go on forever writing on the question of whether more nerve was required to hole a ten-foot putt in a championship match or bring down a halfback on the five-yard line. In those last ten years he would have all the fun of reading a Peter Neale column without having to write it. The job had come to him by the merest chance. But young Peter could be trained from the beginning for the work. "I'll start his education right now," Peter resolved and then he looked at the baby and decided that there didn't seem to be anything specific which could be done immediately. Still an early start was possible. Long division ought to be easy and interesting for a child who knew that it was something used in computing batting averages. Of course young Peter would receive an excellent general education. There wasn't any reason why a sporting writer shouldn't be a person of well-rounded culture. Sometimes Peter regretted that his Harvard career had lasted only a year. Probably his sporting poems might have been better if he had been able to go on and take that course in versification. Fine arts and history would not be a waste of time.

There was never any telling when some stray scrap of information could be pressed into service for a sporting story. For instance Peter had been struck by that quotation from Walter Pater about the Mona Lisa which he had happened upon in a Sunday newspaper story. Two years later he had been able to use it about Ed Dunkhurst, the human freight car, by paraphrasing the line to read, "Here is the head upon which all the jabs of the world have come and the eyelids are a little weary."

The quotation had given distinction to the story. Sporting writing ought to be just as distinguished as a man could make it. The days of the lowbrow commentator were disappearing. Young Peter might very well carry on and expand the tradition which he had begun. To be sure, there wasn't any hurry about giving him the job. Twenty-five years more for himself would be about right. By that time young Peter would be just twenty-five years and three weeks old. A year or so of general work on the city staff of the *Bulletin* might be good for him. Indeed anything on the newspaper would do for a start. That was, anything real. Book critics and people like that weren't really newspaper men. On his fiftieth birthday, perhaps, Peter would go to the managing editor and say, "I'm through and there's just one thing I want from the *Bulletin*. I think it's only fair that you should let me name my successor."

And the managing editor would say, "Why, of course, Neale, who is it to be?"

"His name is Peter Neale."

Naturally, the managing editor would express some regrets. He would pay a warm tribute to the worth and career of Peter Neale, at the end of which Peter would remark, "I'm glad you feel that way about it, sir." After that formality the substitution would be accepted. The line of Neale would remain unbroken.

Kate's ten o'clock turned out to be past midnight. Shortly before her return the baby went to sleep.

"How did you find your niece's child?" asked Peter.

"Oh, she's fine," said Kate. "She's a girl. A fine little girl, but she's not a patch on himself."

"He's got a name now," said Peter. "We won't have to be saying 'him,' and 'it' and 'the baby' any more. His name's Peter Neale."

30. THE DECLINE AND FALL OF HUMPTY-DUMPTY

Frankly, we have never been entirely clear as to what it was which made Rome fall. We have heard feminism blamed and liquor and the Continental Sabbath. Others have mentioned easy divorce and machine politics. We even have a vague memory that one of the historians took particular pains to point out that the decay began a little after the Romans abandoned whole-wheat bread. However, there seems to be a pretty general agreement that Rome did fall, and numberless public orators have behaved as if it were a personal calamity.

We have not wept for Rome, nor has the example served to frighten us much. So far as we can remember, no mad impulse of ours has ever been thwarted by the sudden recollection, "That's just the sort of business that was responsible for the fall of Rome." We are reconciled to the fact that nations do fall. All of them. Nothing can be done about it.

"Strangers will enter the land if we do not have better ideals, if we do not seek to live on a higher plane," said Archbishop Hayes last Sunday in the *Tribune*. "They will take it from us. We shall be wiped out."

Yes, and if we do adopt every one of the principles which Archbishop Hayes regards as "higher ideals" it seems to us entirely probable that in time the same annihilation will occur. There is always the possibility of the discovery of still higher ideals.

But why, we wonder, do orators never dwell on the fact that Sparta also fell? And after that fall there was not even enough left to justify an issue of picture postcards. The battle in the pass, the boy who waited patiently for the fox to see the evil of his ways, and "Come back with your shield or on it," comprise practically all that is left in memory of Sparta.

The austere do decline and die. Now that it is all over, it seems that Rome chose the better way. At least, that empire was a good fellow while it had it. Time has elevated its importance far beyond all the strangers who overthrew it. Rome was ready to fall. It had made its peace with posterity. "After me," the falling Roman might well say, "the scholars and the tourists."

To be sure, all the King's horses and all the King's men couldn't put Rome together again. It was like that with Humpty-Dumpty, but he has remained one of the most inspiring tragic figures of all time. No doubt he could have gone on quite a little longer if he had been content merely to pace up and down the narrow pathway on the top of his high wall. There were those in authority who told him it was an ideal, but he knew it for a wall. He wanted more of life, and he reached out toward the horizon and slipped and fell.

In the first second he traveled sixteen feet, and that wild swoop with green grass rushing up to meet him and wind pounding in his ears may very well have been worth an eternity of life on the wall. As he fell he brushed against a tree-top and the leaves which pounded upon his back seemed to say, " 'Ataboy, Humpty-Dumpty!" There was such a singing in his ears that he hardly felt the blow which came before the silence and the darkness.

"Nature of death—accidental; cause—multiple contusions," wrote the court physician, who came with all convenient haste.

"Can't anything be done about it?" asked the King, who arrived a little later. "Glands, or something like that?"

"We might," said the court physician. "But say, listen, Your Majesty," and he beckoned the King to come closer so that not even the Generals could hear.

"What is it?" whispered the King, after assuring the Prime Minister that it actually was a private matter.

"I could fix him up," murmured the court physician.

"Fine and dandy," said the King.

"Shush! Your Majesty," hissed the doctor, placing a restraining hand upon the arm of his sovereign. "Bodily, the problem is simple. The Garfunkle Intraligamentary Glue operation would fix him right as a—right as a trivet."

"Paste him together, you mean?"

"Well, that's near enough for a layman. From just looking at him you could never tell the difference. That's the physical side of it. But the mind. There's something else. He's had a great shock. I could put him together again, but I give it as my professional opinion that he'd never be quite normal. I mean, I doubt very much whether you could ever get him to go up on the wall again."

The King gave a low whistle.

"Exactly," said the court physician. "It wouldn't look well, would it? After all, we have the state to consider. How would you like your subjects to know that living on top of a high ideal is mighty uncomfortable business? We'd have to draft him and he'd fall off again at the first opportunity. Still, it isn't for me to decide. That's up to you."

"Miss Jimpson," roared the King, and his secretary ran forward.

"Take a statement for the Associated Press. Ready? 'Humpty-Dumpty sat on a wall. Humpty-Dumpty had a great fall. All the King's horses and all the King's men couldn't put Humpty together again.' "

31. JOE GRIM

Joe Grim, a small catfish or bullhead, was hooked in the lake north of Stamford at 3:30 o'clock Saturday afternoon. He would have been thrown back at once because of his meagerness, but H. 3d, who had assisted in the capture a little, protested. This was his first fish and he wanted to take it home.

The hook remained in the mouth of Joe Grim, and for a time he swung suspended by a loop of line over a nail in the wall of a local cabin. He was then wrapped in tissue paper and placed in a heavy burlap bag on the back seat of a small sedan. The journey to town consumed two hours and a half, and the springs of the car are not so good.

H. 3d also insists that I sat on Joe Grim during the greater part of the journey, but I don't think so. I am pretty sure it was the chocolate cake.

At half-past six Joe was taken out of the burlap bag in the kitchen of the town house, and to the surprise and consternation of all beholders it was observed that he still breathed. Immediately the hook was removed from his mouth and he was placed in a laundry tub. Once in water, Joe Grim not only revived but swam about furiously, and within half an hour ate a hearty meal of shredded wheat, which was supplied to him at my suggestion, as there were no worms available in the house at the moment.

Joe Grim is still alive and, as far as I can tell, happy. His career has been an inspiration to me. When water was denied to him during the long ordeal in the automobile, he breathed and lived on will power. His gills clamped tight as iron doors each time that the spirit within him pounded to be let out of torrid torture into the empty glare of nothingness. Perhaps he had been told of cool, green, muddy pools which are eternal. But Joe gasped and choked to hang on to the now which he knew. And after watching this little catfish I feel that anybody is a damn fool to die.

I plan to put Grim into a pail of water and take him back to the lake north of Stamford. Of course, he doesn't actually have to have water. He could sit up on the driver's seat or even wriggle along behind this car, which has a good deal of carbon in the engine. Still, I think a pail of water would be a courtesy.

When Joe Grim gets back to his lake, what tales he will have to tell! After the first month or so I rather fear that he may grow a little tiresome. Because he suffered so much he will inevitably have to garnish his adventure with significance. There will be a moral, a purpose, a philosophy. Perhaps Joe will tell the other bullheads that he fought in a war to end war.

And naturally he will organize. By and by belatedly, he will run for something and be opposed by bullheads who have never ridden in sedans or lived in laundry tubs. This will bring in the religious issues, and Joe will be badly defeated.

However, in his community there need be no protracted period of waiting for the coming of a younger generation, and every new fish born into the lake alive will be compelled to hear at least once the tale of the covered wagon and the trek across the continent. And these little catfish will be allowed to swim close and gaze at the scar across the mouth of old Joe Grim, who fought and bled back in the days when bullheads were bullheads.

Joe has rather dampened my enthusiasm for fishing. Certainly I shall never venture to eat any catfish caught in the lake north of Stamford. If the filet so much as bobbled under the knife I would draw back from the table with the horrible conviction that here again was Joe Grim and that he had somehow survived the frying pan and the bread crumbs.

But even beyond that I am disturbed by the evidence that fish so much want to live on. There is no such passion in my angling. It is not fair that I should thwart and crush great eagerness for existence for the sake of the extremely mild diversion which I get from fishing. They told me that the fish cared very little and that they were cold blooded and felt no pain. But they were not fish who told me.

Fishing is something less than the duel pictured by the complete angler. The matchmaking decidedly is open to criticism.

"But sometimes the fish gets away," explains the angler.

That is not enough. A good draw or, at the very best, a moral victory is the most a fish can expect. The rules should be altered. If there is to be adequate chivalry in the pastime no man should be allowed a rod and line until he has first signed an agreement that every time he fails to pull a hooked fish out of water he himself will accept and signalize defeat by jumping into the lake. The man gets the fish or the fish gets the man. I can see no other fair way.

And even after my amendment has been adopted there must be a congress to consider justice to the worm. He is exploited by both fish and fishermen. For him there is not so much as the cold comfort of a moral victory. He stakes his life upon a roulette wheel which carries just two numbers. One is zero and the other is double zero. The worm may be taken with the hook or without the hook. You can't expect a worm to get excited about a sport with such limited potentialities as far as he is concerned.

And my experience is that he doesn't get excited. I have seen many a worm carry his complete boredom right into the jaws of an onrushing fish. He will neither fight nor fly. He tries to dignify his death by being sullen about it.

"But," I can imagine a fish saying in rebuttal, "your remarks are most unfair. Worming is a truly sporting proposition. Sometimes you don't get the whole worm."

32. IN WHICH HE REHEARSES

I've lost my amateur standing. It was one of the proud moments of my life. Our show, *Round the Town*, had its dress rehearsal in Newark Sunday night. In the beginning the omens seemed to be set against me. A heavy rain drenched the alley. The theater appeared to be locked front and back, but I rattled the knob of the stage door and at last a man flung it open and growled, "Quit making all that noise. Don't you know we're having a rehearsal here?"

That was the cue for my proud moment. I drew myself up to my full width and answered, "I'm one of the actors." And he let me in.

Nobody can possibly have any adequate conception of what occurred during the creation week described in Genesis unless he has seen a musical revue in the making. Of course, I have no intention of comparing the two productions. Ours took more time, four weeks against one, but I doubt very much whether it will have anything like so long a run.

Still, from watching the rehearsal of a revue one gets some idea of what the word chaos means. The nature of man is stripped bare. Intellect is banished as emotion clashes with emotion and passion bumps against passion. In my unsophistication I foresaw a hundred bloody brawls. During a rehearsal, it seems, it is customary for the actor every little while to toss away his part and then catch it again on the first bound. Even a Republican Cabinet could hardly offer the spectacle of so many resignations flung out in fury.

After a bit I got the hang of it. I found that when one of my fellow actors said, "All right, I'll quit," he merely meant to say no more than a simple "Is that so!" And when one of the many producers replied, also according to the formula, "If you don't like it we'll get somebody else," nothing more was intended than a soothing "Don't get excited."

But I didn't feel quite confident enough of this to get into the game and offer any resignations on my own account. Instead, I remained most respectful to all the producers. Here I think Genesis was more shrewdly administered. Cross purposes were reduced to a minimum through single control. The government of a musical show during rehearsal seems to be modeled on the old moot court or, in our own day, the New England town meeting. Nor is it numbers so much which prevail as vocal vigor. The one who shouts the loudest carries the point. Some day an essay should be written on The Effect of Chest Tones upon the Esthetic Development of American Dramatic Art.

I think I understand now from what quarters musical comedies draw their audiences during the first three or four weeks after an opening. These people who fill the orchestra are the producers, the directors, the composers, the scene designers, the dance manipulators. They like to return to revisit the battlefields.

Although I did not understand much that was going on, I did not behave exactly like a dumb fool. The order had been that I was to be ready at eleven o'clock. Getting ready in this case didn't require anything more than taking off my hat and clearing my throat. And I was ready; but nothing happened. There seemed to be some difficulty about the lights. That I believe is also part of the tradition. "Let there be light," was enough in Genesis, but it isn't as simple as that in creating a revue. Apparently there are all kinds of lights in a theater except the particular sort which the director wants at any given moment. The mind of the director is always a little quicker than the hand of the electrician at the switchboard. When it is necessary for the sun to go down like thunder all the preliminary efforts result in nothing more than a long Nordic twilight.

Then there is the question of artistic effect. I listened to a long and really fundamental argument between two directors who stood as symbols of opposing schools of art. One said of the combination of foots and spots (or whatever they were), "It's very pretty." To which the other replied, "But you can't see anything."

I was afraid they might never come through this divergence, as it is a vexed problem which has agitated warring esthetes ever since the first cave man chalked pictures on a wall. While the debate raged I went out into the rain and brought back ham sandwiches and distributed them around to chorus girls who were not at that precise moment engaged in rehearsal. That was where I was smart. When they called for my act I received a vigorous round of applause at the start. I only wish I could supply ham sandwiches for the entire audience on the opening night.

The chief director said that the turn was a little short. "It ran nine minutes and forty-five seconds," he told me.

That objection I was able to meet with a highly professional reply. "When there's an audience," I replied, "I think, with the laughs, it will run to almost ten minutes."

Unless somebody laughs it's going to be mighty lonely business out on that great bare stage. They've got lights for me too. There's one that they flash in my eyes to blind me. I believe it's a baby spot. And so I stagger around sightless as Samson. I hope somebody in the audience coughs so that I will know I am not wholly cut off from all human communication.

As a matter of fact, I'm not very far on the stage yet. Three feet is the extent of my invasion. That gives me an opportunity to lean against the proscenium arch, and I can practically fall off when the moment comes.

If I ever live through this I'm going to be a mighty lenient critic from now on.

Along about four in the morning we all gathered on the stage for coffee, and I found that in spite of the tumult there was plenty of school spirit in our company. One of the chorus girls told me that she had been in the show business for ten years and this was the most trying rehearsal she'd ever been through, and I said it was just the same with me. And I remembered that David Garrick had been an actor, and Shakespeare and Molière, and this seemed just the place a person ought to be at four o'clock in the morning, even if it was only Newark. And I realized that I too belonged among the troupers and I knew that the life had got me.

33. DARE DEVIL OLIVER

A man stopped at the city desk yesterday and left a flaring poster announcing that "Dare Devil" Oliver is coming to Paradise Park and will "thrill the crowds by his marvelous dive of 104 feet into 54 inches of water." Mr. Oliver will thrill twice a day. We are grateful for the news about Oliver. Although our paths have not crossed for more than a year, he has remained a vivid memory. When we saw him he was performing in the shadow of an event which loomed high above his 104-foot ladder. Indeed, his route brought him to Atlantic City only a few days before Jack Dempsey broke camp to take part in the battle of the century.

As a consequence, the first-night crowd which permitted Oliver to thrill it consisted of nine people. It was bleak, gloomy weather with a stiff gale blowing in from the ocean. The leap itself was magnificent, but there was a facet of the performance still more striking. We found to our intense surprise that Oliver was among the authentic artists of our day.

He seemed utterly indifferent to the fact that there were but nine of us. He abated not a single foot from his ladder nor an inch from the tank of water. Every rite in the ritual was duly observed. The band played gay tunes as Oliver strolled about the foot of the ladder and looked up anxiously to the top where the wind whipped and jerked a little flag. Suddenly a large man stepped forward and hushed the clarinets. And the drums rested.

He was the announcer, and the early portion of his talk was expository. He dealt with facts—the height of the ladder and the depth of the tank. He spoke of it as "four foot of water." Perhaps that was for oratorical effect. We are a little hurt to discover at this late date that it was actually fifty-four inches. Possibly Mr. Oliver grows older and has decided to increase his margin of safety.

In any case, there was not much passion or human appeal in the opening part of the address. The ascent from the impersonal scientific attitude to the human note came suddenly. The big man paused for a count of one, two, three and no one broke into the silence. Then he raised his right hand high above his head.

"And now, Mr. Oliver," he said, sinking his voice to a rumbling whisper, "you may go whenever you are ready."

Again he paused and added, as if in a spontaneous burst of after-thinking, "And we all wish you the best of luck!"

On the printed page the phrase may sound like an agreeable expression of good will, but the announcer was able to allow larger implications to rush in between his words. We who stood there knew that the announcer felt that it was most unlikely that Oliver would have good luck. You could tell that he was thinking of the 104 feet of ladder and the four feet of water. It almost seemed as if he was striving to assure himself the memory of having said the right thing in case anything happened to Oliver.

The will may have been good, but it was also distinctly gloomy. The speaker had emotionalized himself so completely that for several seconds he forgot to lower his right arm. Then he took it down, and Oliver began to climb the ladder. The band, now feverishly gay, played Oliver up to his diving platform.

The opportunity for irony gaped so prodigiously at the event in hand that we feared the worst. During the theatrical season just closed we had seen a number of the plays of Eugene O'Neill, and aspects of life had also been disclosed to us in other quarters. The pattern of existence almost demanded that "Dare Devil" Oliver should die because only nine spectators had paid for admission that evening. The uselessness of it all menaced the moment. None of the nine could have protested if Oliver had said, "No show this evening."

He continued to climb and the wind managed to shake the ladder, even though his weight was on it. "What a silly thing it will be if he gets killed," we said, and we thought of the morning of the armistice and other things which reminded us that death remains the most poorly motivated of all happenings which we know.

Oliver, the climb finished, went about his business slowly. He kept looking at the flag and for several moments he held his hand up against the wind. But the matter of the leap itself was wholly settled in his mind. He was merely calculating and amending the details.

At last he came to the front of the diving platform and turned his back toward the tank. He leaned slowly. There was still time to stop. Now there wasn't. He had begun to fall. The movement was still slow, but it had become inevitable. The familiar and useful rule which we learned in school that a body falls sixteen feet the first second and then much faster didn't seem to work. Oliver's body turned an important but highly casual somersault in the air and with a sudden sprint his feet hit the water squarely in the middle of the tank and the spray flew over our heads.

The next thing we knew Oliver was blowing water out of his mouth. The band took up approximately where it had left off. Oliver bowed politely to rapturous eighteen-handed applause, slipped on a bathrobe and skipped away. He was absolutely free until 3:30 o'clock on the following afternoon.

After Oliver didn't get killed we began to wonder why and decided that it was because he was an artist. The high dive was his own affair and he went through with it in exactly the same manner for nine people as for 900. Even 1,000, more or less, could contribute nothing nor subtract nothing from the curved line of his back just before the fall clutched him. It was beauty strictly of his own making.

We had exaggerated in our mind the temptation which he offered to all ironic high gods. They couldn't play jokes on Oliver. He was much too engrossed in the job in hand to care whether his final fall came before a Monday night crowd or a Saturday one. It is more likely, we suppose, that some day he will trip on a curbing.

But if a man is a complete artist, and maybe Oliver is, even that sort of thing is not so funny. A person actually inspired to high diving or anything else which brings beauty into the world ought to be so set in his purposes that his life is all one piece. Once that has been accomplished he can have much the best of any joshing back and forth with the old ladies of the scissors and thread. He need only say to the one who snips, "You may cut whenever you are ready."

34. THE LAST REVIEW

Whenever an artist thinks that the community does not sufficiently appreciate him, he takes an appeal to posterity. I wonder where this notion comes from, that posterity is equipped with superior judgment and wisdom? Just how does it get that way? Posterity is as likely to be wrong as anybody else. The artist of today who seeks this deferred judgment is merely appealing to the grandchildren and the great grandchildren of folk who thought that *Abie's Irish Rose* was one of the finest plays ever produced in America.

For all I know, *Abie's Irish Rose* may endure through the centuries, and then the professors will assert that it must be great because it has survived so sturdily. I think it is entirely possible that a number of things which have been established as classics through sheer persistency are no great shakes. I cannot read Greek tragedy in the original, but much of it seems dull stuff in English translation. And perhaps it is. Life does not inevitably purify itself like a running stream. There is terrific stamina in stuff and nonsense. A thing is neither true nor beautiful merely because the world has clung to it for a thousand years. Centuries of belief in the flatness of the world were not enough to make it flat, and it may well be that certain works of art upon which permanence has been conferred really are flat, even though they have been hailed as complete and rounded by generations of critics.

Some geniuses have lived and died without recognition, only to be discovered and honored by later and less preoccupied generations. And others never have been recognized at all in any age and never will be. I am willing to grant that the sum total of wisdom in ten generations tends to rise higher than the wisdom of any single generation. But wisdom has very little to do with artistic appreciation. That must be to some extent a matter of emotional sensitivity, and the emotional content of the world remains about the same no matter how many dark ages and light ones are thrown in for good measure.

But if posterity is not completely competent to set things straight, who is? I believe the correct answer is nobody. No critic can fashion measuring rods and other devices for accurate survey. The whole matter will have to be taken up, along with much other business, on Judgment Day. I have faith that there will be critics in heaven. There only can injustices be ironed out. An adjective will be taken away from one poet and added to the store of some other whom the world held more lightly. Angels will be set to whittling down superlatives. And as they whittle they will chuckle and sometimes laugh out loud at things which mankind insisted on calling eternal, transcendental and supreme.

I trust that some large section of reserved seats will be set aside for newspaper critics. I think that the revelation of Divine wisdom in regard to books and plays will be even more interesting than the manifestation of heavenly standards in regard to souls. I am more eager to know whether Thackeray was actually greater than Dickens than I am to find out whether Henry Ford was on the whole a better citizen of the cosmos than Napoleon Bonaparte.

Possibly some standing of the critics after the manner of the scheme instituted by *Variety* will be displayed on a huge heavenly blackboard. There are almost sure to be upsets. It is even possible that these final, five-star-edition reviewers will decide that Macaulay didn't have a good style at all. They may hand down the decision that the worth of the King James Bible as English literature was slightly exaggerated. Consider the sensation if this Supreme Court should establish by a vote of five to four that Marlowe was a more eloquent dramatic poet than William Shakespeare!

You see this court will be quite unabashed by all previous traditions. It will be tradition. Angels have no inhibitions. They will, if they choose, flick away with one finger everything which Stuart P. Sherman has said. Even the name of Mencken will be less than dust. When George Jean Nathan attempts to strike awe and terror into the hearts of all present by telling what he saw in Das Grossespiel Haus in Prague in the summer of 1905, he will be pushed back into his seat. If this court of supercritics thinks that *The Show-Off* is more fun than *As You Like It*, that is precisely what it will say. It will be a great day.

But probably I am far too optimistic in suggesting that these critical decisions will be accepted as final beyond the hope of argument. The true artist will remain a rebel when awards go against him. The one who is slighted is almost sure to appeal to some group of opinion which lies behind and beyond immortality. The novelist who is insufficiently appreciated in that court of last resort will unquestionably contend that he has not been understood. He will assert that this is not his true public, and with shoulders thrown back and head erect he will stalk away from the gold bar of heaven and seek a road to hell, where he may find enough subtlety of intelligence and sensitivity of feeling to make it possible for him to gain a friendly hearing.

Under certain circumstances I will be much inclined to follow the rebel novelists. There will be small comfort for me in heaven unless that grandest jury decides that Dickens sniveled inordinately, and that Shaw was worth ten of Barrie.

It might be, although I have no great faith in the matter, that the inspired reviewers, along toward the dusk of whittling day, will get around to saying something pleasant about *The Sun Field* and *The Boy Grew Older*. That would be agreeable, but it would come much too late to help royalties.

35. BETHLEHEM, DEC. 25

When we first came into the office it looked like a dreary Christmas afternoon. To us there is something mournful in the sight of a scantily staffed city room. Just two men were at work typing away at stories of small moment. The telegraph instruments appeared to be meditating. One continued to chatter along, but there was nobody to set down what it said.

Its shrill, staccato insistence seemed momentous. But telegraph instruments are always like that. Their tone is just as excited whether the message tells of mighty tremors in the earth or baby parades at Asbury Park. Probably a job in a newspaper office is rather unhealthy for a telegraph instrument. The contrivance is too emotional and excitable to live calmly under the strain. Even an old instrument seldom learns enough about news values to pick and choose suitable moments in which to grow panicky. As soon as a story begins to move along a wire the little key screams and dances. It is devoid of reticence. Every distant whisper which comes to it must be rattled out at top voice and at once. Words are its very blood stream and for all the telegraph instrument knows one word is just as good and just as important as another.

And so the one restless key in the telegraph room shrieked, and whined, and implored listeners. We tried to help by coming close and paying strict attention, but we could not get even the gist of the message. It seemed to us as if the key were trying to say, with clicking tumult, that some great one, a King perhaps, was dead or dying. Or, maybe, it was a war and each dash and dot stood for some contending soldier moving forward under heavy fire. And again, it might be that a volcano had stirred and spit. Or great waves had swept a coast. And we thought of sinking steamers and trains up-ended.

Certainly it was an affair of great moment. Even though we discounted the passion and vehemence of the machine there was something almost awe-inspiring in its sincerity and insistence. After a time it seemed to us as if this was in fact no long running narrative, but one announcement repeated over and over again. And suddenly we wondered why we had assumed from the beginning that only catastrophes were important and epoch-making. By now we realized that though the tongue was alien we did recognize the color of its clamor. These dots and dashes were seeking to convey something of triumph. That was not to be doubted.

And in a flash we knew what the machine said. It was nothing more than, "A child is born." And of course nobody paid any attention to that. It is an old story.

36. BE-KIND-TO-ADJECTIVES WEEK

But at least we profited artistically at the races. The sport exercises a tremendous influence for good in the community and it might do an even nobler service if every critic were compelled to attend at least once a year. From the horsemen we might all learn something of high respect for adjectives. The true follower of the turf enforces a precision of speech which is not known elsewhere in this country.

One afternoon we happened to win a bet, and in the careless, impulsive way which so often fastens itself upon dramatic critics, we remarked: "That's a great horse."

At the moment the horse seemed all of that. Unfortunately, we addressed the remark to a man confirmed in racegoing and he regarded us with cold hostility and then walked away without explanation. Another member of the group was more charitable in recognizing our inexperience and undertook to point out the grave blunder we had committed.

"King Solomon's Seal," he said, "happens to be a fair plater, but if you had been speaking of Zev or My Own your remark would have been offensive to a true turfman. Down here we are most punctilious about using the phrase 'a great horse.' It isn't done more than about once in a decade. I think you might call Man O' War a great horse, although there are a few who wouldn't even concede that. The rest that have been running in your time are good horses or bad horses."

This attitude seemed to us merely swanky. Possibly we have an unfortunate tendency always to suspect the sincerity of persons who insist upon precision in expression, but in this case the standard claimed by our turf friend was confirmed the next day. At the Music Box Revue we found Max Hirsch in the seat just in front of us. Hirsch trains Sarazen, the gre—we mean the promising two-year-old owned by Mrs. W. K. Vanderbilt. Sarazen has won all his races in most impressive style, upon every sort of track, and has conceded pounds to his competitors. The man next to Hirsch leaned over and asked him confidently: "What do you really think of Sarazen?"

The trainer thought hard and considered his words carefully and then he replied with bubbling enthusiasm, "I think he's a nice horse."

And that suggests to us a method by which we may in time cure ourself of adjectival recklessness. First of all, we will establish in our mind a picture of the great dormitory in which the adjectives live. At midnight, when the time comes for writing dramatic criticisms, these adjectives are all asleep. Libidinous lies cot to cot with Fragile. Whimsical sleeps with his feet on the pillow and his head under the blanket. Freudian, that foreign fellow, has a smile on his lips. Perhaps he dreams.

But there is no smile upon the face of the sleeper in the next bed or any sign of life save the slightly wheezy breathing of one worn to exhaustion by protracted and constant toil. And he has earned his rest, for this is Intriguing. The bed of Charming has been placed apart in an alcove at the request of the other adjectives, for she snores a little. And to the right we find a poor fellow whose cot is within easy distance of the brass pole which descends through an aperture to the street level. His trousers are tucked inside his boots and he has retired without removing his socks. This is Thrilling.

After witnessing the peaceful domesticity of the adjectives at midnight we shall begin to picture that other scene which must occur every evening as the dramatic critics get to work. Such a tumult and a roaring. The dormitory of the adjectives is agog and more. Preposterous has made off with the shirt of Quaint. Good and Clean collide upon the pole only to discover that their haste was unnecessary, since they must wait for Wholesome, who can't find his trousers. Theatrical has been and gone these many hours and Artificial is on his toes awaiting the signal. Sophisticated stirs, but turns over and sleeps again, for he knows that it is a John M. Golden opening. Advanced and Shocking sit up and josh back and forth, confident that they too are in for the night. Surefire is the butt of their merriment and he sadly declines a wager of 50 to 1 that his name will be drawn before the evening is out.

With all this in mind we shall pause the next time the impulse comes to use an adjective. We will not forget the fatigue upon the face of Intriguing or the drooping shoulders of Wholesome. No, when we come again to review a show we will bear in mind the woes of all the adjectives and exclaim, "Let them sleep."

37. HE DIDN'T KNOW IT WAS LOADED

"You cannot argue great poetry or great characterization," says the *Evening Post*, in taking us to task for lack of enthusiasm about *Antony and Cleopatra;* "you cannot even teach it unless there is some response. Cleopatra did not live in the Bronx, but if she had, the Bronx would undoubtedly have supposed her ill-contrived. She could not talk prose as the modern newspaper conceives prose; she was incapable of sentimentality, even of Mr. Shaw's mild latter-day variety; she was the kind of romantic that Broadway could neither create nor comprehend.

"Broadway and the Bronx have been too much for the usually excellent judgment of Mr. Broun. They do not understand tragedy."

It is our notion that the most poignantly tragic figures must always be drawn from the ranks of the uncomprehending. Very often the edge of our pity is dulled because most of Shakespeare's children of misfortune are too articulately aware of their own dramatic stature. We could weep more for Hamlet if he were not so exceedingly well prepared to weep for himself. No harm is done if we fail to feel the whole weight of Cleopatra's sorrow. She is fully competent to appreciate her own suffering and has small need of sobbing from the sidelines.

In many of the Shakespearian tragedies the major part of our sympathy goes to one of the lesser figures. We are moved by the plight of those people at whom Fate lunges suddenly and without preliminary fanfare.

When we read *Romeo and Juliet* for the first time, we realized from the beginning that no enduring good could come to the young man or the young woman. The black spot had been tipped to them even before they stood in the moonlight and talked of love. The road to the rendezvous stretched straight away to the edge of the shadow. And, as they walked, the lovers saw quite plainly the end of their journey. Accordingly, they said nothing which was not wholly and self-consciously suitable for travelers on such a road.

Mercutio met his fate around the bend of a horseshoe curve. For him there was no breathing spell in which he might posture and thus make the mighty accident of destruction seem no more than an appropriate figure in a pattern of his own design. His was an aimless death. No lofty pertinence softened its absurdity. Even his last words were a stammered half-phrase from a sentence.

The dying Romeo said (in part):

> Come, bitter conduct, come, unsavory guide!
> Thou desperate pilot, now at once run on
> The dashing rocks thy sea-sick weary bark!
> Here's to my love!—O true apothecary!
> Thy drugs are quick. Thus with a kiss I die.

Now, that is admirable, of course, but decidedly it is not impromptu. One cannot help realizing that Romeo must have rehearsed his death a little in advance. When the moment came he was magnificently prepared. Indeed, he accepted it so superbly that it is only reasonable to believe that he must have enjoyed his own proficiency in the art of dying.

The *Evening Post* is entirely correct. Broadway and the Bronx cannot quite understand. They may even resent it a little. When death comes to Broadway and the Bronx it invariably presents the rough edges, the incoherence, the awkwardness of a first performance.

Shakespeare could not conceive of tragedy except as a full stop. He needed shears as well as pen. To him, tragedy meant being killed, committing suicide or going mad. The deeper and more deadly tragedy of the man or woman who lives on was not in his repertoire. Younger dramatists have found that often there is more poignancy in a tale of an individual into whose life there enters nothing of violence. He may be truly tragic even though he seems to suffer not at all. Perhaps the most pitiful of all protagonists is the person who is fully resigned to his fate.

A squirrel tearing around in his little circular tread-mill is evidently having no end of fun. He is quite convinced that he is off on a journey. To him the illusion of progress is so perfect that he may quite possibly crinkle his nose, wag his tail or indicate delight by any other mannerism customary to squirrels. But still he is a tragic figure. And a man may smile and smile.

Just once Shakespeare did write a tragic play about a character who lived on after the final curtain. He told one tale in which the plight of the central figure depended on the fact that the man had to continue and play out a role to which he was neither suited nor accustomed. Length of days merely served to heighten the pitifulness of his harsh fate. Shylock left the courtroom condemned to be a Christian.

38. MY SORT OF GOD

I wish I could write it down. Of course I can't. To define God is to limit Him. Still it seems inevitable that man should do that in order to get some edge to which his mind may cling. All religion is concerned with this process of scaling down God into the realm of finite comprehension.

And so, although the various churches insist that the God confined in their own particular dogma is a Deity of absolute perfection, it seems to me that in every case there has been a minification. Perfection itself is a conception quite a bit beyond the range of mortal mind.

Orthodoxy has burdened Jehovah with human attributes. Anger and vengeance are attributed to Him because these are failings which we ourselves experience and can therefore understand.

And in the churches they also talk of God as all-powerful, but it does not seem to me that they quite mean that either. The conception of an all-powerful Deity has been decidedly qualified by the belief that His creature man got out of hand and could be saved from perdition only by the sacrifice of Christ, the son of God. An all-powerful God could have created Adam and Eve without sin and without the desire of sin. The existence of such a place as hell would be an indication of the fallibility of God. If souls were really lost it would be hard to acquit God of mislaying them.

But most of all I quarrel with the fundamentalist who insists that he "loves God." I don't believe him for a minute. Into love there must enter some slight solace of equality. Adoration and love I hold to be imperfect synonyms. No human being could possibly be at ease with the God of the dogmas. He could pray to such a God, but he could not explain, or argue, or have a joke. Fear tarnishes love. I could not love a God who held one hand behind his back and in that hand had hell. But, naturally, if I believed in such a God I would try very hard to feign love.

No, I do not think that man may ever expect to know God and to define Him. But there is an extraordinary something which happens now and again in the human spirit. There comes to the soul a second wind. A man gets the chance to say to himself, and to say truthfully, "This thing I have done is magnificent. I didn't know I had it in me."

The achievement need not be anything so tangible as the creation of music or poetry. It might be something which made people laugh. It could be a tingle, a taste, a hope, the sight of leaves in a wind, a caress. But in this moment there would be gusto. And the man upon whom the spell came would be for his little time valuable and important.

Something marching catches him up. Ahead are the banners and the bugles and we are all marching, marching away. Away —that's enough for anyone who feels the swing of it.

Oh, I can't define God, but I'm not an atheist.

Somebody may come along and say, "But you're not talking about God at all. You're talking about the will to live, or a good dinner, or a sunny day, or the subconscious."

I don't care what name is used because it really is God.

39. A TEETH-GRITTER FAILS

The defeat of Molla Bjurstedt Mallory by Suzanne Lenglen was a heartening event to us. It set a limit upon the potentialities of determination. It was generally conceded by all observers, even before the match, that Lenglen was infinitely superior in skill, but the issue remained in doubt because Molla is so richly endowed with the will to win. Suzanne's brilliance, we feared, might get splashed and spattered by the shock of meeting character in full collision. Such a result would have tightened upon existence the tyranny of the teeth-gritters.

In the modern world a man without will or character travels naked through a jungle. In our own case, for instance, we live in constant danger of being carried off by insurance agents, stock promoters and men with genuine stray bits of authentically smuggled English woolens. At the present moment we own several bales of cloth, much of it with green stripes. The only factor which protects us is that probably we haven't character enough to take any of this stuff to the tailor to have it made up into suits.

We knew perfectly well that we didn't want any of the cloth the day we bought it. The green stripes were plainly visible, but behind them lay a dominant personality. Whenever we said "No" the man just banged it right back at us. There was no passing him with the most skillfully placed negative. He kept storming in until we surrendered and agreed to take the four bolts offered. After that he said that it would be a great saving for us if we bought two more bits he had in his bag and made it an even half dozen.

It has been our misfortune to find ourself constantly associated with determined people. Maybe they are not really so determined. Possibly the contrast only makes it seem so. All day long in this office we hear that menacing, crunching sound which indicates to us that somebody near by is gritting his teeth about something. The worst of it is that we are entirely surrounded by persons in executive capacities. When they set their jaws it is pretty safe to assume that they have clamped upon affairs other than their own individual concerns. We are never free for a moment from the notion that some one of them has just decided that it would be a good thing to develop us.

Before Suzanne beat Molla it was our impression that beyond

flight or hiding there was no possible defense against the onrush of the determined. The Frenchwoman seems to have hit upon a solution. Apparently she was able to sidestep every now and then enough to let the force of Molla's will sweep the ball right out of the court.

Some such system as that may prove useful to us. We ought to realize by this time that we are incapable of saying "No." We toss it back so feebly that it presents an easy opportunity for a kill. Hereafter we purpose to say nothing at all. Then when somebody grits his teeth he will have no word of ours to masticate.

If any reader happens to know the name and address of some conspicuously weak-willed person and sends it to us he may be a factor in enabling his friend to obtain six bolts of genuine imported English cloth at a ridiculously low figure.

None of the champions whose success rested upon determination ever made any appeal to us. Battling Nelson, for instance, was almost without boxing skill. He had nothing but perseverance. In him character was developed to such a remarkable extent that he was able to wear down opponents by hitting their fists with his face.

But for the gleam of hope which is aroused by the occasional downfall of a teeth-gritter, as in the case of the Mallory-Lenglen match, think of the fearful things which might happen in our own community. If a man can become lightweight champion of America for no particular reason except that he is determined to be, what is to prevent all the high and desirable posts from falling into the hands of go-getters?

It is easy to conceive of a time when not only the Government but all the arts will have been taken over by virtue of virility. We can imagine a visitor from a strange land inquiring, "Why on earth has that man been chosen as the leading tenor of the Metropolitan Opera House?" and receiving the answer, "What's the matter with your ear? Aren't you thrilled by his persistency?"

40. THE INCOME OF H. THIRD

"Yes, I think every child should have an allowance," says Angelo Patri in an interview in the *Evening World*. "An allowance teaches a child how to spend and how to save. . . . It is surprising how much confidence a child will acquire, how proud he will be, if he is allowed to save money. He will figure out for himself how he can save a penny here and a penny there, to add to his savings. And if he starts to save very early, he will have a snug little bank account by the time he is fifteen years old.

"But it is up to his parents to teach him how to save. He must not be allowed to grow selfish and egotistical in his savings. The time may come when the money a child has saved may be extended toward the use of the family. He must not be allowed to grow so selfish in his savings that in the event of such circumstances he will refuse to part with the money."

We find much consolation in the last remark of Mr. Patri's. The time to which he refers is rapidly approaching in our house. Although we don't exactly make H. 3d an allowance, we did buy him a dime bank. It has been very amusing to watch the assurance with which he has approached all visitors and asked them for money. Of course he prefers dimes, but at our suggestion he refuses nothing. We help him out in his childish schemes and whenever he gets a quarter we supply two dimes in exchange. Even the penny which the plumber gave him was not disdained.

Apparently, H. 3rd derives no end of pleasure from putting dimes in the bank and watching the figures change on the dial. The fund has mounted with amazing rapidity. Often while we are away for a day at the office we find that as much as a dollar or so has been added to the total during our absence.

There is no possible way of getting money out until $10 has been deposited. When that sum is reached the tin door opens automatically—at least such is the promise of the directions on the back of the contraption. There has been some little dispute as to what is to be the disposal of the money when it gushes out. We can't see what on earth H. 3rd could possibly do with $10. And after all, he has had all the fun of putting the money in. We haven't handled a single dime of it.

Moreover, we did buy the bank. As Angelo Patri says, a child ought not to be allowed to become selfish and egotistical. We hope to be able to effect a compromise. It is our notion that H. 3rd will undoubtedly be willing to let us have the $10 if we promise to return the bank immediately after it has disgorged and agree to let him start out on a new campaign to fill it up again.

As for "the snug little bank account" which the saving child might acquire by the time he is fifteen we have reserved judgment. We want the respect of our child when he grows up. There would be no particular point in raising up somebody to comment on our shiftlessness. If we let the money accumulate until his fifteenth year it might be a great deal harder to get it away from him. Business transactions are much simpler when only one party in the deal is able to count.

And worse than that, we have the fear that the possession of a fortune might put notions into the head of H. 3rd. We seem to see a morning eleven years hence. H. 3rd is now fifteen years old and is reading the *World*. He appears to be looking over the columns of the page opposite the editorials. For a time he chuckles to himself and we know that he is still on the Conning Tower. Then he begins to shake his head doubtfully. Protesting wrinkles appear in his forehead. He looks across the table and smiles indulgently at us.

"Still muddling around with that old-fashioned radicalism," he says not unkindly.

Now his tone is friendly but firmer. "Heywood," he says, picking his words carefully, "you can't seem to get it into your head that private property also has its rights. Liberty, yes, we can agree on that, but not license.

"Here," he adds, tossing over a segment of the paper, "you can have it all but the financial section. I want to see what Pressed Steel Car preferred did yesterday."

"He should be given an allowance when he begins to need money for simple, everyday needs," continues Mr. Patri in his discussion of juvenile finance. "Sometimes this allowance can start when he is four years old. And from the time he first starts to save he should be taught to keep an account book of his spendings and savings. If he spends two cents for a stamp, he should have a small blank book and jot down 'two cents for a stamp.' Then at the end of a week he should figure out how much he has spent and how much he has saved. The child's parents should guide him in the keeping of this book—show him where he may save and where he might have spent a little more judiciously."

When it comes to stamps, we have always believed in people's accepting the first price quoted by the drug-store man. Haggling doesn't get you enough to make it worth while. Of course the child might be shown how he could have obtained two green ones instead of a single red for his two pennies, but it seems to us unsound to make a child too shrewd about such things. The first thing you know he might grow up to be a Rockefeller. According to our plan, H. 3rd is going to be a column conductor when he gets old enough. It would be fatal to instill in him any such slavish respect for stamps as Mr. Patri suggests. It would just break his heart in a job like this. He couldn't possibly get any work done because of his belief in his obligation to soak the stamps off the self-addressed envelopes sent in by readers.

More than that, it would shock us a great deal to find any four-year-old child jotting things down in a little notebook. His father's system of bookkeeping is plenty good enough for H. 3rd. A couple of times a week he can go to the window and ask the teller, "Have I got any more money left in this bank?" All the banks we have ever dealt with have been very obliging in letting us know when it was all gone.

Anyhow, why should H. 3rd want a stamp except to stick it on the wall, or something like that? Even in a columnist's household, where stamps are free, they ought not to be plastered around so carelessly. H. 3rd hasn't got anybody to write to as far as we know. It's possible, of course, that he might want to send a letter to Santa Claus and in that case we might be able to point out to him "where he might save." No matter what rate the Government quotes on the delivery, we will guarantee to do it not only cheaper but more expeditiously.

41. CONVENTION STUDIES

CLEVELAND, June 10 [1924]—When Theodore E. Burton made his keynote speech for the Republicans this morning he waved every now and again, as emotion lagged, the name of Lincoln. And then he was done, and after a little while there came on to the platform a man who had seen Lincoln and known him.

Addison G. Proctor of St. Joseph, Mich., is the last living delegate who voted for Lincoln when he was nominated by the Republicans in 1860. He came to tell what he remembered of these things of sixty-four years ago.

His shoulders stooped, but he walked with high head and did not need the arm offered by one of the convention clerks. Mr. Proctor stepped beyond the amplifiers, for these had not been known at that other convention. Mr. Burton steered him into place and the voice of the old man rose loud, strong and impassioned, for he spoke of slavery and of how he and his fellows had decided that it must go no further.

"We wanted to save the West," he cried, and he flung out his hand to indicate some distant horizon beyond the last row of the deep convention hall. It seemed as if this was again the year 1860 in the mind of the last delegate.

He spoke of Lincoln as a man who lived, and not as a framed portrait perched upon the bunting back of the platform. He explained why Seward would not do, and again he cried out, "We had to save the West," and thrust out his hands.

A curious thing happened. The delegates who had sat through Burton's long speech began to wriggle and to rustle. It was time for lunch and many got up to go. The feet of the old man were firmly set back beyond the half-century mark. Nineteen twenty-four was not interested in 1860. It was only too evident that nothing pertinent was in the mind of the man of memories.

From the name of Lincoln he would draw no moral of the evils of reckless investigation in the matter of oil lands. And when he spoke of saving the West he had no thought of the protection of sound business threatened by the raids of radical agitators.

He wanted to make the picture step out of the gold frame. It seemed to be within his hope to resurrect the dead leader and set to marching down the aisle in the full light of day a tall gaunt figure. That would have been interesting.

For if the figure from the frame had left the wall and walked into the convention he would have passed, quite closely, John T. Adams. And then if he proceeded straight ahead he might have brushed by Burton, who had spoken well of him.

Down from the platform and up the aisle and at his elbow sits Henry Cabot Lodge. It might have been necessary for the gaunt man to stoop a little in order to see the Senator from Massachusetts. One step more and Nicholas Murray Butler is beside him; Wadsworth, Smoot, Longworth, Sutherland, Weeks and all the giants among his fellow Republicans.

The clerk upon the platform plucked at the sleeve of Addison G. Proctor and whispered to him. Evidently the clerk mumbled that it was not necessary to go on and tell precisely what sort of a person was this Lincoln. It was enough to have mentioned the name. The speaker nodded. He stood with both hands outspread.

"It had to be Lincoln," he said, "because we knew that we needed somebody bigger than all the others." Again the clerk plucked at the sleeve of Proctor, and the delegates laughed at the old man, who wanted to talk about a living Lincoln. They applauded, but they edged toward the doors at the same time.

Proctor stopped and Burton patted him on the back and said he had done nicely. He reassured the man who knew Lincoln that he had talked just the right length. He pointed out that it was almost lunch time. But he forgot to add that anyhow this was a convention that was going to nominate Calvin Coolidge.

MADISON SQUARE GARDEN, June 25 [1924]—"The organization known as the Ku Klux Klan."

It was named in a voice which rang out through the convention hall. At last a man had walked straight forward and stood face to face with the ghost in the haunted garden.

A slight man, tight-lipped, with sharp bridged nose of fighting stock, slashed clean through the conspiracy of silence. His name is Forney Johnson and he comes from Alabama. He took the platform to place in nomination Oscar Underwood.

Many another speaker at the convention has mentioned "religious liberties" and "constitutional guarantees" and "equality," but this was not enough to lay the specter which stalked the aisles.

Until Forney Johnson spoke, the delegates of the Democratic Party lived and moved in the thick vapor of a wizard's spell. It was held, and apparently believed, that the nature of the charm was such that the name of the sorcerer must not be spoken aloud. One might, if he liked, speak ill of necromancy and whisper behind his hand that he, personally, had no use for black magic. But to cry aloud the name of the wizard's crew was to bring down damnation, sudden, curious and terrible.

The magic wand had drawn a circle, and in this hall of the trolls all must walk roundabout and talk roundabout. Forney Johnson stepped across this circle and bisected it.

No wall crumbled. No doom descended. A great shout rose from throats loosed out of the spell. In the aisle beside the Colorado standard one man punched another in the nose. And that other was a Klansman. When his nose was punched it bled and he grew angry and hit back.

And now it was known that these sometimes sheeted figures were neither gods nor devils, but merely instructed delegates. And perhaps many remembered that the great Wizard of the order is not truly a man of magic but a "painless dentist."

Nor were the usual mundane processes of the law ineffective in dealing with the disturbance aroused by the laying of the ghost. The Klansman battling to hold the Colorado standard was for the moment in a bad way, though he may have been even a Kleagle. In the scuffle the head of the Ku Kluxer became wedged in the metal frame of the standard of his State. It seemed either that he must completely follow the pole, which was being dragged out into the aisle, or at least allow his head and neck to make the journey.

But help was at hand. Not goblins or ghostly riders galloped to his aid, but Lieut. Martin Noonan of the New York police. Noonan tugged the head from the metal noose and garroting ceased. He pushed the combatants apart.

"Mr. Rickard won't let you fight here," said Noonan, "unless you've got a contract."

And so ended the first battle of the Colorado.

It was not the last, for the delegation of that State is split in half—six for Smith and six for McAdoo—and whenever the impulse comes to demonstrate, the toughness of the standard pole is tested. They should have chosen a staff of elastic instead of pine.

Dramatically, the present convention is made. It has now achieved one of the finest thrills known to any modern convention. Before the fog lifted, doings were dull. Senator Walsh's speech was wholly ineffective. There was a faint cheer at the announcement that Charles the First had lost his head, but the rest was silence.

Richard Enright, Police Commissioner, took the platform to make announcements, and informed the delegates that Sparta had no walls, but they refused to get excited about it.

Forney Johnson captured little attention in the beginning of his speech when he took the platform after Gov. Brandon had announced, according to traditional form, "Alabama responds." But in handling his Klan attack Johnson was a master playwright. He built up to it slowly and surely, working from the general to the particular.

"Above all," he said, "does the candidate we represent condemn the massed action of secret political orders in furtherance of any objective which is plainly contrary to the spirit of the Constitution."

That was applauded, but still he had not yet named the name. He did it by reading the text of Underwood's own proposal for the platform. It is not new. It had already been printed. But for the first time it was spoken in public and out loud.

The demonstration which followed was not the longest of the convention. Many a carefully prepared uproar will outlast it in the mere matter of time. But this was a sudden cheer, a real cheer and it ran deep, deep as the grave of the ghost which once had walked in the garden.

MADISON SQUARE GARDEN, June 30 [1924]—It is related in St. Mark that Jesus came to a place called Gethsemane and it was a garden. And to this garden went Judas, "And as soon as he was come, he goeth straightway to him, and saith, Master, Master; and kissed him."

In Madison Square Saturday night William Jennings Bryan testified his love of Christ and voted for the Ku Klux Klan.

Mr. Bryan explained his vote by saying that he did not think the Ku Klux Klan should be advertised in the platform of the Democratic Party. And as he pleaded against giving publicity to the Klan he stood in the glare of ten great Klieg spotlights while 15,000 in the hall, and millions outside, listened to the debate on the most fiery issue presented to any National Convention in fifty years. It was a little as if Noah, on the twenty-ninth day, had said, "Let's hush up the matter that there's been quite a spell of rain around here lately."

"You may call me a coward if you will," Mr. Bryan continued in developing his argument, "but there is nothing in my life to justify the charge that I am a coward."

That's as it may be, but it is true that Saturday night Mr. Bryan's betrayal of his country was not actuated by fear. No such kindly explanation is possible. The poor frightened woman from Georgia who changed her vote over to the forces of the Klan was afraid. She could hardly whisper the "no" which helped largely to decide the result. But Bryan spoke fearlessly in a loud, clear voice with oratorical interludes. He did that which he wanted to do.

For William Jennings Bryan is the very type and symbol of the spirit of the Ku Klux Klan. He has never lived in a land of men and women. To him this country has been from the beginning peopled by believers and heretics. According to his faith mankind is base and cursed. Human reason is a snare, and so Bryan has made oratory the weapon of his aggressions.

When professors in precarious jobs have disagreed with him about evolution, Mr. Bryan has never argued the issue, but instead has turned bully and burned fiery crosses at their doors. Once he wrote to a friend: "We will drive Darwinism from the schools. The agnostics who are undermining the faith of our students will be glad enough to teach anything the people want taught when the people speak with emphasis. My explanation is that a man who believes he has brute blood in him will never be a martyr. Only those who believe they are made in the image of God will die for a truth. We have all the Elijahs on our side."

Of course, that is not quite true. William Jennings Bryan was a pacifist for the glory of God. Eugene V. Debs was a pacifist for the glory of man. It was Mr. Debs who went to jail.

But, true or untrue, Mr. Bryan's letter is revelatory. Jesus Christ was the first and greatest teacher of democracy because his mission in the world was to win belief. He made faith the test of the human soul. Mr. Bryan is content to compel conformity.

In the present convention the Ku Klux Klansmen were not in the least concerned with what the delegates thought about them. They were only interested in what was said. The demand was simply that the platform should be silent. Mr. Bryan can understand that philosophy.

I said that Mr. Bryan spoke fearlessly, but I will not say that he spoke truthfully. He said many things which were obviously false. His capacity for folly and misconception is great, but even so, I think he knew that he spoke falsely.

"There is not a State in the Union," he said, "where anybody whose rights are denied cannot go and find redress."

If a Negro in Mr. Bryan's Florida went to the polls and tried to vote, where could he go when his right was denied? Not to William Jennings Bryan, for Mr. Bryan is on record as giving complete approval to the policy of his adopted State in handling the race question. And so in this instance Mr. Bryan knew that he did not speak the truth.

And again he said, "Anybody can fight the Ku Klux Klan, but only the Democratic Party can stand between the common people and their oppressors in this land."

Mr. Bryan did not specify just where one might look for a

political champion against the Klan. No voice was raised in Cleveland and the defiance which might have been sounded here was stilled by Mr. Bryan himself. And as yet no one knows whether La Follette will speak out on the Fourth of July.

"The Catholic Church," said Mr. Bryan, "does not need a great party to protect it from 1,000,000 men. The Jews do not need this resolution. They have Moses. They have Elijah. They have Elisha."

Well, personally, I wouldn't have Elisha if I could. He was another spiritual Ku Kluxer, who, when little children mocked him, sent she-bears to devour them instead of turning them over to the duly constituted authorities of the Juvenile Court. And I have not Moses or the Catholic Church. Do I, therefore, sacrifice my right to stand against the Klan?

"The Democratic Party has never taken the side of one church against another," said Mr. Bryan in perhaps the most monstrous falsification of the issue which occurred in his whole speech. He knows it is not an issue between church and church. In the convention he heard speaker after speaker declare that though the Klan might not be against himself he was against the Klan.

Underwood is not colored, Catholic, Jewish nor foreign born, but he was the first man in the convention to come out against the Klan. It is impertinent to say, as some have said: "Why, some of the best people in the Catholic Church don't want the Klan named in the platform." That is nothing to me. Is Mr. Bryan's conception of civic duty and patriotism so feeble that he thinks one should fight only those who fight him? After all, the dragon had done nothing to St. George personally. It was St. George's own idea to go out and slay the monster.

Anatole France once wrote a story of a juggler who lived in the days of St. George, and this juggler was possessed of a magic formula by which he could change himself at will into a fiery dragon. But then he heard of what had happened to one dragon, and after that he changed himself into a rabbit. Mention "Republican" to Bryan and he too can puff himself up into a great avenging monster who roars and breathes fire. And after that, just for the sake of the experiment, whisper to him "Ku Klux Klan."

"Three words were more to them than the welfare of a party in a great campaign," said Bryan. As it happens the phrase *Liberty, Equality, Fraternity* also consists of three words.

Every now and then I get letters which begin, "Although I am not a member of the Klan" and go on to say, "Why do you condemn this order without a fair hearing? Do you know anything about it except what you have read in the lying newspapers?"

I do. With my own eyes I have seen the Klan at work. I saw the knights riding on Saturday night, full tilt, to serve a cause. And did they ride against some monstrous oppressor, this devoted little band, only fifty-five strong? Well, not exactly. They were charging down upon one woman in the Georgia delegation who happened to have voted against them. She was faint, frightened and of feeble will. They called on her to change her vote and when she slumped back into her seat without speaking they dragged at her arm and pulled her up again. And when with a last despairing flutter she tried still to keep silent the men of Georgia, the knights of the Klan bawled out for her the word which they had commanded that she should speak.

And Mr. Bryan asked us in Madison Square Garden to recognize the honesty of the Ku Klux Klan.

There was a man who aided Bryan in the betrayal. It does not matter much that his name is McAdoo. For a time during the coming week he will be heard of as a small minority party bickers to see which of its sons shall be named to take a licking in November. And in four years the question will be asked, "Who was McAdoo?"

But Bryan I know will persist. His addiction to delivering lectures has undermined the semblance of sincerity which was once an effective factor in his performances. His power for evil dwindles, but I have no hope but that he will wriggle until sundown.

PART THREE

1925-1930

42. "WIFE OF LOT"

In Sunday School I often found myself on the side of the Old Testament villains and against some of the Old Testament heroes. Esau is inevitably a more attractive man than Jacob, and among the women Vashti is finer grained than Esther. But in examining over Genesis in preparation for the great trial, I find still another Biblical character who seems to me deserving honor not yet accorded to her in any generous measure.

She is a woman without a name and nothing which she said in life has been recorded. Yet her fame should endure. That she was kinswoman to Eve is evident enough, for in her, too, there blazed the spirit of research. Indeed, if it had not been for Eve and this other, science might not have come into this world ever. But for them, these mothers of science (it never seems to have had a father of any great significance), Dayton's ball park might have gone on to the end of time without echoing to the eloquence of any ideal more lofty than the familiar "Kill the umpire!"

Like Mr. Scopes, she was a person of an inquiring mind. She had to know in spite of penalties. The one vital incident in her life is related in a single sentence: "But his wife looked back from behind him, and she became a pillar of salt."

Generally it is assumed that this was a doom, a punishment visited upon the wife of Lot because she turned to watch the fire and brimstone as it rained from the skies upon Sodom and upon Gomorrah. It is true that the commandment, "Look not behind thee," had been imposed upon Lot, but it is not altogether clear that this prohibition was also issued to the wife of Lot. However, the point is not important. I believe she would have looked in any case and I am not at all prepared to admit that her end was of a sort to make mankind shudder and draw back in the future from other courageous investigation.

It is at least debatable as to whether this was not canonization rather than punishment which fell upon her. The estate of being a white and shining column in this flat country of the plains may have been by a great margin more desirable than the station—"Wife of Lot." It is not easy for any woman to lose her identity in the shadow of a great man and it is worse when she has to play a supporting role to a husband of distinctly minor quality. Lot does not seem to have been a very prepossessing person. When the mob besieged his house in Sodom he was overready to suggest a cowardly compromise. You may remember that he offered to turn his daughters over to the ruffians. Later, when informed of the impending destruction of his home city, he quailed before the advice that he should flee to the mountains and suggested that he be allowed to escape to Zoar, because that was a city and, as he meachingly added, "Is it not a little one?" From town to suburb was about the most to which Lot could nerve himself. He had not the hardihood to dare the mountains.

Subsequently, to be sure, he did make the trip and again it was great fear that moved him. Under the rigors of primitive life in a cave he seemed to have gone pretty much to pieces, and the Bible records that he became drunken and degenerate.

It was not, then, altogether tragic to leave off being the wife of Lot and become instead a towering white shaft of cleanly salt. Even in life she may well have been a little contemptuous of this man of hers. We know that "she looked back from behind him." Evidently, in his terror at the destruction which rained from the heavens, Lot was going as fast as his legs would carry him towards safety. If he had ever known of "Women and children first" he forgot it in his fright.

But she asked no favors of him. Nor for that matter of anyone. Her desire to know the nature of this fiery phenomenon was more passionate than any terror. I hope we may assume that when she looked back she had opportunity to see clearly and to record in her mind the facts concerning the mighty convulsion. This I think is so, for symbolically her fate conforms to this conception. The achievement of knowledge is a crystallization.

The seed of Lot was preserved in the world by incestuous sin, following the flight from Sodom, but I will not grant that the wife of Lot ceased ever as a continuing influence upon the life and thought of mankind. She brought to life a savor. It endures.

After the fire and the brimstone peace came again to the plains where once the city stood. Under stars and moon the pillar of salt gleamed bright. And over it blew the mountain breeze. From behind a star Prometheus looked down and bowed low. He called her name. I don't know what that is, but I am quite certain it was something other than "Wife of Lot."

43. THEY BURIED THE BEARDED LADY

There was a funeral on Thursday in Drummond, Okla., for Mme. Sidonia Barsey, "the bearded lady." The author of the brief dispatch wrote under the seeming impression that she was the last and only representative of her profession. There must be, here and there, other bearded ladies, but Mme. Barsey may well have been the best known of all. "She had excited the wonder of countless thousands in the side shows of circuses."

No explanation was given of the manner in which she came to die in this tiny place, for "Drummond is a town of 200 inhabitants, south of Enid." To me Enid conveys no more than Drummond, but, since the local correspondent uses it as a point of orientation, this may be a settlement large enough to afford hospitality to a passing circus.

Still, there was no mention in the story of other show folk. Mme. Barsey seems to have died a lonely freak, surrounded by the drab normality of a little town. Possibly Drummond served her as a retreat. The wonder of countless thousands may come in time to throb unpleasantly.

But from this point of view a small town seems a poor place for privacy. Any sensitive person, stricken with beard or other blemish, would more readily find solace in a city. The healing compassion of indifference is known only in the haunts of the many. The beard of Mme. Barsey was "iron gray and heavy." In Drummond, Okla., that could hardly have failed to excite comment and attention. A stroll along Broadway might have been accomplished with far less tribulation than a walk down Main Street.

"It is," the cynical New Yorker would say to himself, "only a false beard, and if I turn about I shall find an advertising display. Why should I buy another safety razor?"

But in saying this the cynical New Yorker would be less than truthful. Of course, as a matter of fact, he isn't really cynical. Here we are crowded so close that we must in sheer self-protection overlook the beams and motes in the eyes of brothers.

Once I saw a two-headed calf led down Broadway and nobody followed after it. Maybe Broadway was under the delusion that all calves are so. Even so, if ever I grow an eye in the middle of my forehead, I shall live close to crowds, for there I may hope to find a curiosity more kindly than that which grows wild in the open spaces.

To be sure, I may be all wrong in assuming that Mme. Barsey disliked excited wonder. After all, she had lived with it at her elbow for many seasons. In the beginning she traded off embarrassment for bread and butter. But bearded ladies do not live by bread alone. For nineteen years Mme. Barsey went up and down the countryside bowing to those who passed her chair upon a high platform and selling her own photographs. She came, I suppose, to think of herself as an artist, and in conver-

sation with others of the tent colony she spoke of these appear-
ances as "my work."

In her heart she believed that the secret of her success was
personality. It is worth noting that she allowed the beard to go
gray and made no attempt to retouch it. Still she can hardly
have escaped the afflicting thought, some time or other before
the nineteen years were done, that there was no future in this
job of hers. She had gone as far as possible.

Perhaps in her spare time she was writing a book. Certainly
she was equipped to reveal a highly specialized point of view.
How does life seem to a bearded lady? Would it be a bitter
book, I wonder, or did she feel that all was right with the
world?

And what did she think of the modern girl with her addiction
to cigarettes and knickerbockers? Mme. Barsey, I feel sure, was
impatient at all the newer rowdiness of women. That attitude
would inevitably be forced upon her by circumstances. After all,
her post with the circus depended, among other things, upon the
fact that she was a lady.

They buried her in Drummond and a pastor of the Congre-
gational Church offered a prayer and gave a short sermon. Un-
fortunately, nothing of his discourse was reported in the news
dispatches. I am eager to know what he said. It was a difficult
but a stimulating opportunity. The church was crowded. Many
more than Drummond's 200 edged their way in. Any funeral
is an event in rural Oklahoma, and this was a service to com-
memorate the death of a bearded lady.

I hope that with his first words the young preacher stilled the
ribald hum in the church. Mme. Barsey was, in this world, a
freak and she was not yet free from her stigma of strangeness.
Farmer boys grinned across the aisles at their fellows. "A major-
ity of the spectators," says the news dispatch, "attended only to
get a last look at the bearded lady."

It was the very necessary task of the preacher to bring home
to the shuffling crowd the fact that a share in the dignity of

mortality must no longer be denied to the person of whom he spoke. She who had lived a bearded lady became in death a woman and no longer an exile.

44. THE MIRACLE OF DEBS

Eugene V. Debs is dead and everybody says that he was a good man. He was no better and no worse when he served a sentence at Atlanta.

I imagine that now it would be difficult to find many to defend the jailing of Debs. But at the time of the trial he received little support outside the radical ranks.

The problem involved was not simple. I hated the thing they did to Debs even at the time, and I was not then a pacifist. Yet I realize that almost nobody means precisely what he says when he makes the declaration, "I'm in favor of free speech." I think I mean it, but it is not difficult for me to imagine situations in which I would be gravely tempted to enforce silence on anyone who seemed to be dangerous to the cause I favored.

Free speech is about as good a cause as the world has ever known. But, like the poor, it is always with us and gets shoved aside in favor of things which seem at some given moment more vital. They never are more vital. Not when you look back at them from a distance. When the necessity of free speech is most important we shut it off. Everybody favors free speech in the slack moments when no axes are being ground.

It would have been better for America to have lost the war than to lose free speech. I think so, but I imagine it is a minority opinion. However, a majority right now can be drummed up to support the contention that it was wrong to put Debs in prison. That won't keep the country from sending some other Debs to jail in some other day when panic psychology prevails.

You see, there was another aspect to the Debs case, a point of view which really begs the question. It was foolish to send him to jail. His opposition to the war was not effective. A wise dictator, someone like Shaw's Julius Caesar, for instance, would have given Debs better treatment than he got from our democracy.

Eugene Debs was a beloved figure and a tragic one. All his life he led lost causes. He captured the intense loyalty of a small section of our people, but I think that he affected the general thought of his time to a slight degree. Very few recognized him for what he was. It became the habit to speak of him as a man molded after the manner of Lenin or Trotzky. And that was a grotesque misconception. People were constantly overlooking the fact that Debs was a Hoosier, a native product in every strand of him. He was a sort of Whitcomb Riley turned politically minded.

It does not seem to me that he was a great man. At least he was not a great intellect. But Woodward has argued persuasively that neither was George Washington. In summing up the Father of His Country, this most recent biographer says in effect that all Washington had was character. By any test such as that Debs was great. Certainly he had character. There was more of goodness in him than bubbled up in any other American of his day. He had some humor, or otherwise a religion might have been built up about him, for he was thoroughly Messianic. And it was a strange quirk which set this gentle, sentimental Middle-Westerner in the leadership of a party often fierce and militant.

Though not a Christian by any precise standard, Debs was the Christian-Socialist type. That, I'm afraid, is outmoded. He did feel that wrongs could be righted by touching the compassion of the world. Perhaps they can. It has not happened yet. Of cold, logical Marxianism, Debs possessed very little. He was never the brains of his party. I never met him, but I read many of his speeches, and most of them seemed to be second-rate utterances. But when his great moment came a miracle occurred. Debs made a speech to the judge and jury at Columbus after his conviction, and to me it seems one of the most beautiful and moving passages in the English language. He was for that one afternoon touched with inspiration. If anybody told me that tongues of fire danced upon his shoulders as he spoke, I would believe it.

Whenever I write anything about churches, ministers write in and say: "But of course you have no faith in miracles and the supernatural." And that is a long way off the target. For better or worse I can't stand out for a minute against mysticism. I think there are very few ministers ready to believe in as many miracles as I accept, because I cannot help myself. The speech which Debs made is to me a thing miraculous, because in it he displayed a gift for singing prose which was never with him on any other day of his life. And if you ask me, I'll also have to admit that I don't see how Lincoln came to the Gettysburg Address by any pathway which can be charted. There was in that nothing to suggest the utterance of a man who had been a small-time politician and who might reasonably be expected to have formed his habits of speech in the rough and tumble school of give and take political debate in which his formative years were spent.

Something was in Debs, seemingly, that did not come out unless you saw him. I'm told that even those speeches of his which seemed to any reader indifferent stuff, took on vitality from his presence. A hard-bitten Socialist told me once, "Gene Debs is the only one who can get away with the sentimental flummery that's been tied onto Socialism in this country. Pretty nearly always it gives me a swift pain to go around to meetings and have people call me 'comrade.' That's a lot of bunk. But the funny part of it is that when Debs says 'comrade' it's all right. He means it. That old man with the burning eyes actually believes that there can be such a thing as the brotherhood of man. And that's not the funniest part of it. As long as he's around I believe it myself."

With the death of Debs, American Socialism is almost sure to grow more scientific, more bitter, possibly more effective. The party is not likely to forget that in Russia it was force which won the day, and not persuasion.

I've said that it did not seem to me that Debs was a great man in life, but he will come to greatness by and by. There are in him the seeds of symbolism. He was a sentimental Socialist, and that line has dwindled all over the world. Radicals talk now in terms of men and guns and power, and unless you get in at the beginning of the meeting and orient yourself, this could just as well be Security Leaguers or any other junkers in session.

The Debs idea will not die. To be sure, it was not his first at all. He carried on an older tradition. It will come to pass. There can be a brotherhood of man.

45. MY FIRST NUDE

My first nude sold the other day for a price which was not made public, but which is reported to have been 25 cents. Personally, I felt that it was a $3 picture; but a creative artist may be too indulgent with himself and since 25 cents was the best offer I let it go.

In this case the profit was not great, although I do believe in quick and frequent sales. My biggest money-maker is "Tempest on a Wooded Coast." This has never fetched more than $2.35 but I have sold it four times already. There is a point in almost every party at my house in which somebody gets the notion that he wants to buy "Tempest on a Wooded Coast" and pay cash. But it seems to be the sort of picture men forget. When the purchaser goes he always leaves the painting behind

him although it is quite dry. Whether this is second thought or
inadvertence, I don't profess to know. I merely stick it back
upon the shelf and wait for another buyer to come along.

The purchase of paintings for speculation is not the noblest of
all motives, though there is nothing snide in it, and I have al-
ways wondered why the dealers did not seek to encourage this
sort of patronage through publicity. Many a true story could
be told.

There is the familiar anecdote about Van Gogh, who took a
still life of some sabots to his butcher in Paris and let him have
it for five francs. And as the artist was coming from the shop
a beggar in dire need accosted him and got the money. This
same picture sold at auction later for $20,000, and by now is
worth even more.

Then there was Rousseau, the postal clerk in Paris who drew
as kindergarten children do and showed his brilliant pictures
around to friends, who promptly had a good laugh at these
crudities. Indeed, it is said that once, when Rousseau was taken
into court because of indorsing someone's note, his lawyer pro-
duced some of the pictures and showed them to the judge in an
effort to prove that his client was not wholly adult-minded. And
he won the case. It may have been one of this very lot which
sold at an auction of John Quinn's collection for $50,000.

The chances of any casual visitor's picking up a potential
Van Gogh or Rousseau in some little gallery are somewhat
slight, but people will buy lots in Florida and stock in oil wells.
And though the certificates are often pretty, few of them may
be classed as works of art.

A dealer told me just the other day that he'd had a happy
afternoon because he sold a picture to a customer who bought
it for the very simple reason that he liked it. This, so the dealer
said, is very rare. According to his theory, people buy pictures
from a snobbish desire to be regarded as patrons of the arts or
from the hope that the thing they buy will appreciate in value.

"Snobbish" was his word, but I wouldn't call it quite that. To me it is more reasonable for a wealthy man to make a display by collecting pictures than by assembling leather books, horses or assorted shirt studs.

The graphic arts languish in America because not one per cent of the present population ever buys a painting for any reason whatsoever. And yet for prints in tacky gilt frames there is always a ready market.

I have my doubts as to whether picture dealers rank among the smartest men in this community. Possibly they are adept enough in making a bargain once a customer has come prepared to buy, but certainly they do not pull them in. The average man of middling means has not the slightest notion of how to buy a painting, even if he happens to think he'd like one. Most of the galleries I know are forbidding and aloof and the stranger within the gates is made to feel as if he ought to have a letter from his pastor, and excellent social references as well, before he even ventures to ask anybody in the shop how much some certain picture costs.

A large department store, which will not be nameless, called Macy's, undertook some time ago to maintain a department devoted to the paintings of young and little-known Americans. My impression is that the store has not kept up this innovation, though to my mind the idea was excellent. The hope of the American painter should be in getting his pictures into department stores, butchers', druggists' or delicatessen shops. Here people would come and buy who never by any chance venture inside a gallery.

46. *GANDLE FOLLOWS HIS NOSE,*
   CHAPTER 2

At first he blinked and could not see, for the room was filled with purple vapor and a pungence not known in the forest. Presently he detected something white moving in the mist. It went and returned and went again. There was a rhythm, but no wind or any sound. Gandle came closer to find out about this and saw that it was a skeleton. And even so he could not account for its uneasiness. As he peered up and down to learn, if he might, why the thing would not rest there came a voice from across the room. "Your name is Bunny Gandle," said the voice and that, too, was remarkable. First there was only a voice and a second later a fat man in a purple gown appeared from nowhere.

Baoz was a little chagrined because Gandle showed no surprise at this feat of magic, but how could Gandle recognize it as magic? For all he knew this might be the custom of the town. And in the forest things were not so very different. Gandle had seen a deer vanish and reappear out of a swamp almost as quickly. Those who spend a childhood close to dragons seldom swoon in later life.

Next Baoz took three slivers, cut from carrots, and dropped them into a bowl of water where instantly they became goldfish. From this trick Gandle derived an erroneous conception of biology. He had long wondered by just what process the small perch in the lake behind his uncle's house came into being. Now he remembered having seen the old man peel an orange along that shore.

But after that Baoz did lay hold upon the mind of Gandle

and made him shudder in surprise. He motioned to the boy to come close to a great crystal ball on a table in the center of the room. They huddled and bent over it and in the glass Gandle saw himself trudging a long road. Undeniably it was Gandle and in the crystal the trees and the hills swept past as he walked. Presently, he stood still at a fork in the road. To the right and to the left ran highways of equal promise.

"Now," said Baoz, "pay strict attention and you shall see what my magic can mean to you."

The tiny toy doll of a Gandle turned down the road at the left and before he had gone a little way there came a man to meet him, a man in steel with a sword blinking in the sun. There was talk between the two and up flashed the sword and fell upon the shoulder of the dream Gandle. Red spurted out till the whole circle of the crystal was crimson. And Gandle grew faint and swayed, for this was his own blood. Baoz waved his hand and the picture faded. There was nothing now but the reflection of the white skeleton which kept up its rounds behind them.

"So," said Baoz. "There is such a crossroads. You will come to it. I have let you see the evil of the wrong road. Maybe you felt the pain in your shoulder as the sword fell."

And, as he spoke, he put his hand on Gandle's shoulder. It was a soft, fat hand which grew heavier. And there was a chill from it and again Gandle swayed as if he felt the bite of metal. Before, it had been a single, sharp stroke, but the hard and crushing hand of the sorcerer continued to cut so that he would have jerked himself free if these fingers had not now become iron.

"The right road is the good road," continued Baoz. "There your fortune lies and no ill adventure."

Gandle was born again into the life of the crystal. He saw himself walking a long, straight road with none to oppose him, but he fancied that the figure moving through the dust swung shoulders not so free as the other Gandle who had chosen to turn left. It was almost as if the fingers under which he himself sagged rested upon the back of the little Gandle imprisoned within the glass. He felt that this time the traveler was not alone, though he seemed solitary. Baoz took from under the robe a cap of white cloth and with a quick movement set it upon his own head. There was no wizard. But his chuckle could be heard and the grip of his fingers did not relax. Gandle knew, then, that just such a one walked with him and leaned upon him in the journey along the road called good. Out of nothing popped Baoz back again into the room, but Gandle was just as quick. The price of the safe road was too high. He wanted to free his small blood brother and he swung his right hand against the crystal so that it leaped from off the table. Like a puffball it spattered. Smoke, which seemed the very dust of the conjured road, writhed high as the heel of the skeleton. But then the glass lay dead and in fragments.

One of the two Gandles was free. Danger menaced the other. Close and closer came the big, gray face of Baoz. The cold hand burned into the flesh of Gandle. With all his soul and shoulders he wrenched to get away and there was a might in his young back which brought him clear from the magic fingers. At this same moment he snatched for the white cap and won, for it was only in the right hand that Baoz was potent. Upon all his left side he was ancient. Gandle put on the cap as the magician had done a minute before. He did not know whether or not he was invisible and anyway even such a state was insufficient meagerness to keep him safe from sorcery. The purple haze concealed from him the direction of the door and so he sought escape by going up. As the skeleton swung over head Gandle leaped and seized the shoulder-blades. His legs he drew after him and wrapped them round the skull. Weight made no difference in the pattern of this pendulum. Even though the heft of life was now upon it, the skeleton continued to swing unceasingly.

From the wall Baoz took down a curved sword and cut and

thrust in every corner of the room. It swished too loud and swirled too fast to please the wizard, for he knew that even so sharp a sword could not slash, thus, through flesh and bone. If he could but reach Gandle with the blade he could mar him sight unseen. And truly Gandle was close at hand. Now and again he might have reached down from the arc and touched the head of Baoz, but instead he clung all the closer to the skeleton. With a word and a gesture of the hand, the wizard caused a flame to sweep along the whole length of the floor, but it did not rise high enough to scorch Gandle. Still, he realized that even on the back of a skeleton he was not safe and now he saw the door. Part of the leap was his own and a little was from the momentum of his uneasy and bony benefactor. Upon his toes he made a landing and thrust both hands ahead of him against the door. It swung open. Gandle was loose in the world. With no more than a stumble he clicked into his stride. He ran. He ran as if all the dragons he had ever seen were chirping behind him. His heart battered his ribs and no air came except a little which he bolted in agony. And farther he would have gone if he had not tripped and fallen into soft grass. There Gandle lay and fed upon the wind which came to his mouth.

His course had carried him to a hilltop and when he had strength enough to turn upon his side he saw, at a great distance, the house of Baoz. As he watched, there was a burst of flame and the house was gone. The wizard had blown it up by magic, hoping thus to kill Gandle. His old eyes had not seen the swing of the door as Gandle fled. Nor did Baoz have apparatus with which to find the fugitive. The crystal ball was not of his own making, but came from a city sorcerer who made such things in quantity. Gandle knew none of this and yet he felt quit of Baoz. Even dragons could kill only such as were within range of their claws. When his wind returned he whistled and climbed down the hill to a fine, fair highroad. Evidently he was not invisible in the eye of a searching sun and his forehead chafed against the rough texture of the cap. Soon he took it off, for it seemed more friendly to move openly and to join in with so kindly a landscape.

And he came to a crossroads. This Gandle had seen before and he hesitated. The left was the road of danger and misfortune. Baoz had said that he should by all means take the right. Baoz was an unpleasant man and Gandle swung resolutely to the left. Evil it might be, but it was also the road upon which Baoz would not expect to find him if he took up the pursuit. But most of all Bunny Gandle turned left because this road was his own idea. He himself chose it. That made it his.

47. A SERMON FROM SAMUEL

There is, we are told by many, a fundamentalist conflict between science and religion, and yet the creed of every scientist and seeker after truth is stated eloquently in the Bible out of the mouth of one of the greatest heroes of the Old Testament. Look into the seventeenth chapter of the First Book of Samuel and read the two paragraphs which describe the preparations of David for his battle against Goliath. Here you will read:

"And Saul armed David with his armor, and he put an helmet of brass upon his head; also he armed him with a coat of mail. And David girded his sword upon his armor, and he assayed to go; for he had not proved it. And David said unto Saul, I cannot go with these; for I have not proved them. And David put them off him."

As you know, David killed Goliath with a pebble of his own choosing. He knew the heft of that rock, for he thumbed it over and tested it before he took it into battle. In a fight for life David was not disposed to depend on hearsay and hand-me-downs.

Now the armor of the King undoubtedly looked good. It is

fair to assume that it was highly polished and blinked at the sun. And the helmet was all gold and glittering. But the man who was to meet Goliath had to be sure. The big Philistine was a pretty fine old skeptic on his own account and not one to bow down and surrender to the first brass hat who challenged him. David, in borrowed metal, would very probably have been no more than a hickory nut in the hands of the giant.

Pictorially, the gear was an excellent suggestion. Upon the fine young body of the boy this armor of the King set well. And, for many, the gift of Saul would have had great psychic significance. It would be a charm and a talisman. Very likely there was magic in it. More than that, the armor held the weight of authority. Saul recommended it. But, even with all this, something vital was missing in the accouterments. Nothing out of David's own experience sanctioned it.

As guardian of his father's sheep he had killed a lion and a bear. Against those savage beasts he went unhampered by any such trappings. And the methods which worked in animal experimentation should, in the light of reason, be efficacious against Philistines.

Throughout the story David is pictured as moving with the utmost confidence.

"The Lord has delivered me out of the paw of the lion, and out of the paw of the bear," he said. "He will deliver me out of the hand of this Philistine."

David was then a mystic, but not to excess. There was no disposition on his part to say, "Let God do it," and take no pains on his own account. Had he felt that he was no more than a pawn in the proceedings he would hardly have bothered his head to put off the armor once Saul had strapped it on. God could help a man in mail as easily as one who went naked into battle.

And when David went from Saul on his way to the front he "chose him five smooth stones out of the brook." Nothing was left to chance in this. It was an enlightened faith which ani-

mated David. You may be sure he took the stones best fitted
for his purpose, and did not say, like our own Fundamentalists,
"It is enough for me to lean upon the Rock of Ages."

God was not vexed at these precautions. He does not frown
on those who tincture faith with ruddy drops of hearty reason.
This has been so from the beginning. The first inhalation Adam
knew was the breath of God, but into this ancestor lungs were
created, and from that time on it became the business of the man
to do his breathing for himself.

It may be that there were smiles in heaven at the extent and
precision of David, scientist, who was about to risk his life for
the glory of his God. After all, there is no getting away from
the fact that David did take "five smooth stones." Had he been
addicted to a lean-back, lazy faith, one would have sufficed. And
some who do negate all power and virtue of the human will
would face Goliath with no rock at all, feeling that man is a
poor thing and wholly powerless to help himself. David was not
like that. He felt it entirely possible that he might miss with his
first shot, and after that he was prepared to go on firing and
firing with all the strength of soul and shoulders until the time
came for him to meet his God. I doubt if he thought of himself
as a miserable sinner, or cared to acknowledge that there was no
health in him.

"And David put his hand in his bag, and took thence a stone,
and slang it, and smote the Philistine in his forehead, that the
stone sunk into his forehead; and he fell upon his face to the
earth."

For this victory David did give thanks to God, but first he
ran and cut off Goliath's head to round out the accomplishment
and make it certain. The comment of the chronicler misses, to
my mind, some of the significance of the event.

"So David prevailed over the Philistine with a sling and with
a stone, and smote the Philistine, and slew him; but there was
no sword in the hand of David."

If I read the intention of this comment aright, the chronicler means to imply that it was the greater miracle that David succeeded in his mission without the use of a sword. That interpretation of the incident does not appeal to me. Had David come to grips with Goliath, I think the result might well have been quite different. In swordplay he could not match the giant. Goliath killed hundreds of godly folk who attempted to stand up to him toe to toe and exchange blows. That was not the way to conquer him. Granted that the scheme of God was made manifest in the final result, I still maintain that David was chosen champion of Israel not only because he possessed faith but also in reward for the undoubted fact that he used his intelligence in the solution of the problem. I hold with none of the theologians who seem to maintain that God is contemptuous of the wisdom of man and that he honors those who proceed quite aimlessly about the business of kingdom coming.

But to abandon the theological aspects of the incident, it seems to me there is an excellent moral in David's decision to wear nothing which he could not prove. Most of us prance into battle quite readily in any shining raiment which is tossed to us. Helmets which look enough like gold are pulled down over our ears, so that even the possibility of proof is shut out from the mind of man. And so we move heavily and clumsily weighted down with beliefs and suppositions and theories which simply are not so. Never mind what King or Kleagle has handed out this stuff. Let's put it off until we know.

48. WOOING BY WIRE

They say a corporation has no soul, but I say look at the Western Union. Last Christmas the company sent me a folder showing how I could wire Christmas greetings simply by mentioning a number at any branch office. The wording of the good cheer was already prepared by a company official called, I suppose, Assistant Supervisor of Sentiment.

And now Valentine's Day approaches. I make this statement not on my own authority, but through the assurance of the Western Union. In this bitter world, sweating and striving in the struggle for existence, I might easily forget February 14. I'm a business man, and my days and nights are often given over to concern and wonder as to whether I have any money in the bank. I make big deals by day and dream of them by night. My spirits are apt to rise and fall with American Sumatra Tobacco. Often I wake in a cold sweat after some nightmare in which I have watched our entire currant crop destroyed by the boll weevil.

And in this harsh world it is well that there should be some organization not limited and bound by thought of profit and loss. It was with a distinct thrill, then, that I opened the envelope yesterday morning and perceived in the very center of the little folder a great red heart inscribed, "For my valentine," and underneath it, "Western Union." I never knew they cared.

My assumption had been that our relations were purely professional and perfunctory. The last time I entered one of the branch offices the young woman in charge did not so much as wink at me. She seemed entirely cool and distant as she asked: "And so you want it to go collect?" It's true I heard from the back of the room a distinctly rhythmic pulsation, but I never took it for heart throbs. I thought it was merely the clatter of telegraph keys.

And so once again Valentine's Day approaches. In all truth I will confess I probably should not have remembered save for the fact that the Western Union nudged me.

"In the old days," says the folder, "Valentine sentiments were framed in lacy frills and furbelows, and then dropped to rest in the depths of a mail box; there was no better way.

"Today the distinctive valentine is a telegraph billet-doux

that speeds swiftly and true as Cupid's dart. It is then delivered on a special blank—in a special envelope."

Some might object that the Western Union in taking over the functions of Eros is too meddlesome, but this is decidedly captious, for a large range of choice is left to anyone who wishes to lay his heart by wire at any feet. Nor do I understand that the company places any limit upon the number or destination of protestations of complete affection which any individual may send. If you choose to be poetic the Western Union will serve as your bard. And if you bridle at this form of expression the list of numbered messages also contains sentiments expressed in good, bluff, manly fashion. Consider, for instance, Number 6:

> *I lost my heart around somewhere;*
> *Just give me yours, and I'll call it square.*

You don't like that, eh? You say that you are no great mush like the Western Union Telegraph Company? All right, be patient and look at Number 11:

> *No fuss or feathers, no Cupids or hearts. Just a warm friendly greeting on Valentine's Day.*

The latter message I would call a good business man's valentine but for the fact that it goes six words over the traditional ten. Still, in the end this might be much cheaper than some of the other messages on the company's list. I don't see how it would be possible to take anybody into court on the basis of "Just a warm friendly greeting." Not always is the Western Union so careful to keep passion and definite commitment out of the telegrams it recommends to its clients. There's dynamite in Number 2:

> *I like you, I love you, I want you all the time, so please wire me back that you'll be my valentine.*

Here the company has been guilty of a slight oversight. No-where in the folder is there any list of suggestions for the use of those who contemplate answers to the form vaientines. Such a list would have taken very little space. It might simply read:

    1. Yes.
    2. No.

Still, to me the "I like you, I love you" valentine is the most appealing of the whole Western Union dozen. I rather suspect that there's a tender little story behind it. The Assistant Supervisor of Sentiment for the Eastern Division is still a young man. He was, as I have already intimated, chosen for his sensitivity and his sympathy for the love problems of others. Very probably he ran an Advice to the Lovelorn column before his services were snapped up by the great corporation. Obviously, the Western Union possesses a soul, but just as obviously life in its service cannot be continually a round of romance. It has its stocks and bonds and wire troubles. As Valentine's Day, 1927, approached the Assistant Supervisor of Sentiment was worried. "Am I growing hard?" he said to himself. "Cannot it be that the life has got me?"

Sitting at his great flat-topped desk he summoned Miss Higgins, and undertook to dictate to her a line of valentine verse for the spring rush. "When I have been here twenty-five years will I, too, be as efficient as Miss Higgins?" The Assistant Supervisor thought to himself, "I wonder where she gets shoes as common sense as that." There seemed to be no snap or fire in the telegrams which he devised. Wearily he said: "That'll be all, Miss Higgins," and, then, as a new thought struck him, "Will you please ask Miss Sylvia Darcy to step in."

He heard the rustle and the crinkle of her as she approached. Looking up was too dangerous. "Miss Darcy, will you take a letter," he said, in the same firm tone that had been suggested in the course he once took in "How to get ahead in business." Sharply he rapped his right forefinger on the glass-top desk. That was also in the course.

"I like you," he began, and then hesitated. "Business is business" was the phrase which pounded in his head, but up behind it came another rider with a different and a louder clatter, drowning out the slogan to which he clung. Everything seemed to go black before his eyes. He was only whispering when he said, "I love you, I want you all the time." They are to be married in May, and that's how Number 2 on the Western Union's list of valentine suggestions came to be written.

Has the legal department of the company ever considered the possibility of having to defend a suit brought by someone who was induced to marry on account of one of its recommended valentines? There is at least the possibility that one might woo by Western Union and repent by Postal.

49. SACCO AND VANZETTI: 1

When at last Judge Thayer in a tiny voice passed sentence upon Sacco and Vanzetti, a woman in the courtroom said with terror: "It is death condemning life!"

The men in Charlestown Prison are shining spirits, and Vanzetti has spoken with an eloquence not known elsewhere within our time. They are too bright, we shield our eyes and kill them. We are the dead, and in us there is not feeling nor imagination nor the terrible torment of lust for justice. And in the city where we sleep smug gardeners walk to keep the grass above our little houses sleek and cut whatever blade thrusts up a head above its fellows.

"The decision is unbelievably brutal," said the Chairman of the Defense Committee, and he was wrong. The thing is worthy to be believed. It has happened. It will happen again, and the shame is wider than that which must rest upon Massachusetts. I have never believed that the trial of Sacco and Vanzetti was one set apart from many by reason of the passion and prejudice which encrusted all the benches. Scratch through the varnish of any judgment seat and what will you strike but hate thick-clotted from centuries of angry verdicts? Did any man ever find power within his hand except to use it as a whip?

Gov. Alvan T. Fuller never had any intention in all his investigation but to put a new and higher polish upon the proceedings. The justice of the business was not his concern. He hoped to make it respectable. He called old men from high places to stand behind his chair so that he might seem to speak with all the authority of a high priest or a Pilate.

What more can these immigrants from Italy expect? It is not every prisoner who has a President of Harvard University throw on the switch for him. And Robert Grant is not only a former Judge but one of the most popular dinner guests in Boston. If this is a lynching, at least the fish peddler and his friend the factory hand may take unction to their souls that they will die at the hands of men in dinner coats or academic gowns, according to the conventionalities required by the hour of execution.

Already too much has been made of the personality of Webster Thayer. To sympathizers of Sacco and Vanzetti he has seemed a man with a cloven hoof. But in no usual sense of the term is this man a villain. Although probably not a great jurist, he is without doubt as capable and conscientious as the average Massachusetts Judge, and if that's enough to warm him in wet weather by all means let him stick the compliment against his ribs.

Webster Thayer has a thousand friends. He has courage, sincerity and convictions. Judge Thayer is a good man, and when he says that he made every effort to give a fair trial to the Anarchists brought before him, undoubtedly he thinks it and he means it. Quite often I've heard the remark: "I wonder how that man sleeps at night?" On this point I have no first hand information, but I venture to guess that he is no more beset with uneasy dreams than most of us. He saw his duty and he thinks he did it.

And Gov. Fuller, also, is not in any accepted sense of the word a miscreant. Before becoming Governor he manufactured bicycles. Nobody was cheated by his company. He loves his family and pays his debts. Very much he desires to be Governor again, and there is an excellent chance that this ambition will be gratified. Other Governors of Massachusetss have gone far, and it is not fantastic to assume that some day he might be President. His is not a master mind, but he is a solid and sub-stantial American, chiming in heartily with all our national ideals and aspirations.

To me the tragedy of the conviction of Sacco and Vanzetti lies in the fact that this was not a deed done by crooks and knaves. In that case we could have a campaign with the slogan "Turn the rascals out," and set up for a year or two a reform Administration. Nor have I had much patience with any who would like to punish Thayer by impeachment or any other process. Unfrock him and his judicial robes would fall upon a pair of shoulders not different by the thickness of a fingernail. Men like Holmes and Brandeis do not grow on bushes. Popular government, as far as the eye can see, is always going to be ad-ministered by the Thayers and Fullers.

It has been said that the question at issue was not the guilt or innocence of Sacco and Vanzetti, but whether or not they received a fair trial. I will admit that this commands my in-terest to some extent, but still I think it is a minor phase in the whole matter. From a Utopian point of view the trial was far from fair, but it was not more biased than a thousand which take place in this country every year. It has been pointed out that the Public Prosecutor neglected to call certain witnesses because their testimony would not have been favorable to his case. Are there five District Attorneys, is there one, in the whole country who would do otherwise?

Again Prof. Frankfurter has most clearly shown that the

prosecution asked a trick question in regard to the pistol, and made the expert seem to testify far more concretely than he was willing to commit himself. That was very wrong, but not unique. Our judicial processes are so arranged that it is to the interest of District Attorneys to secure convictions rather than to ascertain justice, and if it would profit his case, there is not one who would not stoop to confuse the issue in the minds of the jurymen.

Eleven of the twelve who convicted Sacco and Vanzetti are still alive, and Gov. Fuller talked to them. He reports somewhat naively that they all told him that they considered the trial fair. Did he expect them to report, "Why, no, Governor, we brought in a verdict of guilty just out of general depravity"?

By now there has been a long and careful sifting of the evidence in the case. It is ridiculous to say that Sacco and Vanzetti are being railroaded to the chair. The situation is much worse than that. This is a thing done cold-bloodedly and with deliberation. But care and deliberation do not guarantee justice. Even if every venerable college president in the country tottered forward to say "guilty" they could not alter facts. The tragedy of it all lies in the fact that though a Southern mountain man may move more quickly to a dirty deed of violence, his feet are set no more firmly in the path of prejudice than a Lowell ambling sedately to a hanging.

I said of Calvin Coolidge that I admired his use of "I do not choose," but he was dealing with a problem wholly personal and had every right to withhold his reasons. For Gov. Fuller I can't say the same. These are the lives of others with which he is dealing. In his fairly long statement he answers not a single point which has been made against the justice of the conviction. The deliberations of himself and his associates were secret, and seemingly it is his intention that they shall remain secret. A gentleman does not investigate and tell.

I've said these men have slept, but from now on it is our business to make them toss and turn a little, for a cry should go

up from many million voices before the day set for Sacco and
Vanzetti to die. We have a right to beat against tight minds
with our fists and shout a word into the ears of the old men.
We want to know, we will know—"Why?"

50. SACCO AND VANZETTI: 2

Several points in the official decision of Gov. Fuller betray
a state of mind unfortunate under the circumstances. It seems
to me that the whole tone of Gov. Fuller's statement was apol-
ogetic, but this perhaps is debatable. There can be no question,
however, that he fell into irrelevancies.

"The South Braintree crime was particularly brutal," he
wrote, and went on to describe the manner in which the robbers
pumped bullets into a guard who was already wounded and
helpless. Surely this is beside the point. Had this been one of
the most considerate murders ever committed in the State of
Massachusetts, Sacco and Vanzetti would still have been deserv-
ing of punishment if guilty. The contention of the defense has
always been that the accused men had no part in the affair. The
savagery of the killing certainly is wholly extraneous to the
issue.

But these references of the Governor are worse than mere
wasted motion. Unconsciously he has made an appeal to that
type of thinker who says: "Why all this sympathy for those two
anarchists and none for the unfortunate widow of the pay-
master's guard?" But those of us who are convinced that Sacco
and Vanzetti are innocent certainly pay no disrespect to the woes
of the widow.

Again Gov. Fuller writes: "It is popularly supposed that he
(Madeiros) confessed to committing the crime." Surely this
gives the impression that no such statement ever came from the

condemned criminal. The Governor may be within his rights in
deciding that Madeiros lied, and for some self-seeking reason,
but it is not only popularly supposed but also true that he did
make a confession.

"In his testimony to me," the Governor explains, "he could
not recall the details or describe the neighborhood."

This, I must say, seems to me a rather frowsy sort of psy-
chology. Assuming that Madeiros took part in the crime, fired
some shots and sped quickly away in an automobile, how could
he be expected to remember the happenings in any precise de-
tail? I have known men who ran seventy yards across the goal
line in some football game and after this was over they knew
little or nothing of what happened while excitement gripped
them. I would be much more inclined to believe Madeiros a liar
if he had been able to give a detailed and graphic account of
everything which happened during the flurry.

And again, the Massachusetts Executive is far too cavalier
in dealing with Sacco's alibi.

"He then claimed," says the Governor, "to have been at the
Italian Consulate in Boston on that date, but the only confirma-
tion of this claim is the memory of a former employee of the
Consulate who made a deposition in Italy that Sacco among
forty others was in the office that day. This employee had no
memorandum to assist his memory."

In this brief paragraph I think I detect much bias. By speak-
ing of the witness as "a former employee," Gov. Fuller seems
to endeavor to discredit him. And yet the man who testified
may be wholly worthy to be believed, even though he eventu-
ally took another job. Nor does the fact that his deposition was
made in Italy militate against it. Truth may travel even across
an ocean.

Assuming that Sacco did go to the Consulate as he has said,
why should it be expected that his arrival would create such a
stir that everyone there from the Consul down would have

marked his coming indelibly? And this witness for the defense, according to Fuller, "had no memorandum to assist his memory." Why in Heaven's name should it be assumed that he would? There were other witnesses to whom the Governor gave credence who did not come with blueprints or flashlight photographs of happenings. Memory was all that served them and yet Fuller believed because he chose to.

One important point the Governor neglected to mention in dealing with the testimony of the Consulate clerk. The employee happened to fix Sacco in his mind by reason of a striking circumstance. The laborer, ignorant of passport requirements, brought with him to the Consulate not the conventional miniature but a large-sized crayon enlargment. And to my mind this should have been a clinching factor in the validity of the alibi.

Gov. Fuller has vindicated Judge Thayer of prejudice wholly upon the testimony of the record. Apparently he has overlooked entirely the large amount of testimony from reliable witnesses that the Judge spoke bitterly of the prisoners while the trial was on. The record is not enough. Anybody who has ever been to the theater knows it is impossible to evaluate the effect of a line until you hear it read. It is just as important to consider Thayer's mood during the proceedings as to look over the words which he uttered.

Since the denial of the last appeal, Thayer has been most reticent, and has declared that it is his practice never to make public statements concerning any judicial matters which come before him. Possibly he never did make public statements, but certainly there is a mass of testimony from unimpeachable persons that he was not so careful in locker rooms and trains and club lounges.

Nor am I much moved at the outcries of admiration from editorial writers who have expressed delight at the courage of the Governor of Massachusetts. Readily I will admit that by his decision he has exposed himself to the danger of physical violence. This is courage, but it is one of the more usual varieties. To decide in favor of Sacco and Vanzetti would have required a very different sort of courage. Such action upon Fuller's part might very possibly have blasted his political future.

I am afraid there is no question that a vast majority of the voters in the Bay State want to see the condemned men die. I don't know why. Clearly it depends upon no careful examination of the evidence. Mostly the feeling rests upon the fact that Sacco and Vanzetti are radicals and that they are foreigners. Also the backbone of Massachusetts, such as it is, happens to be up because of criticism beyond the borders of the State. "This is only our business," say the citizens of the Commonwealth, and they are very wrong.

Five times as many telegrams of praise as those of censure have come to the Governor, according to the official statement of his secretary. In such circumstances it seems to me that his courage in the business is of no great importance.

From now on, I want to know, will the institution of learning in Cambridge which once we called Harvard be known as Hangman's House?

50a. REGARDING MR. BROUN

The WORLD *has always believed in allowing the fullest possible expression of individual opinion to those of its special writers who write under their own names. Straining its interpretation of this privilege, the* WORLD *allowed Mr. Heywood Broun to write two articles on the Sacco-Vanzetti case, in which he expressed his personal opinion with the utmost extravagance.*

The WORLD *then instructed him, now that he had made his own position clear, to select other subjects for his next articles.*

Mr. Broun, however, continued to write on the Sacco-Vanzetti case. The WORLD, *thereupon, exercising its right of final decision as to what it will publish in its columns, has omitted all articles submitted by Mr. Broun.*

RALPH PULITZER
Editor, the WORLD

50b. A LETTER FROM MR. BROUN

Aug. 15, 1927

MR. RALPH PULITZER
THE *World*
PULITZER BUILDING
NEW YORK, N. Y.

DEAR SIR:

I am inclosing herewith the statement as to my position concerning our differences over the material submitted by me for the column heretofore conducted under my name.

I would greatly appreciate your printing my inclosed statement in this column under its former caption, and, in the event that you feel that you might be waiving any legal rights which you may have by accepting this as material from me, hereby waive any rights which may so accrue to me, it merely being my intention should you use this material in your column, that I, of course, shall not be entitled to compensation therefor, but that you would be extending me the courtesy of giving me the same publicity which you received concerning the cause of my failure to appear as special writer in the *World*.

Should you be disinclined to print my statement in the column, I have no objections to it appearing as a communication addressed to your paper, together with the other communications which appear on the editorial page.

I assume, of course, that if any comments or corrections are made you will submit the same to me prior to printing them. I am giving no publicity to this statement at the present time but have no objection to your giving this to the other papers if you see fit.

Yours very truly,
HEYWOOD BROUN

51. SACCO AND VANZETTI: 3

Naturally I was interested in the column which Ralph Pulitzer wrote and which appeared in my old shop window. I was grateful to him for writing it. This seemed to me a fair and frank statement of the issue. But upon one or two points I would like the privilege of stating my own attitude. "The *World*," wrote Mr. Pulitzer, "then instructed him, now that he had made his own position clear, to select other subjects for his next articles."

My recollection is that no official notice was issued. An executive of the paper remarked rather casually that it might be better for me not to write any more about Sacco and Vanzetti. The point is not important. Even though my instructions had been definite I would still have been unable at that time to write about anything but this case. Mr. Pulitzer unintentionally does me an injustice when he suggests that I should have been satisfied to make my own position clear and then keep silent. I felt and I feel passionately about the issue. The men were not yet dead. I was not simply trying to keep my own record straight. That's not good enough.

"When Pilate saw that he could prevail nothing, but that rather a tumult was made, he took water, and washed his hands

before the multitude, saying, I am innocent of the blood of this
just person; see ye to it."

The judgment of the world has been that Pilate did not do
enough. There is no vigor in expressing an opinion and then
washing your hands.

And after all Pilate was only a sort of Governor and I'm a
newspaperman. The *World* would not be satisfied to declare
itself upon some monstrous injustice and then depart saying,
"See ye to it." If Mr. Pulitzer believes that I have any respect
for the traditions of his paper how could he expect me to behave
like that?

I do respect the traditions of the *World*. It has carried on fine
fights and will continue to do so. That it is in every respect
superbly a liberal newspaper I cannot say. Still, it more nearly
approaches this ideal than any other New York daily in its field.

The curious part about the commotion lies in the fact that
fundamentally the *World* and I were on the same side. The
responsible heads of the paper were disturbed, I think, not so
much at my opinion as at my manners and my methods of con-
troversy. Mr. Pulitzer has said that I expressed my personal
opinion "with the utmost extravagance." I spoke only to the
limit of my belief and passion. This may be extravagance, but
I see no wisdom in saving up indignation for a rainy day. It was
already raining. Besides, fighters who pull their punches lose
their fights.

Once there was a pitcher on the Giants who was sued for
breach of promise, and fortunately this suit resulted in his love-
letters being made public. The memory of one of these I have
always treasured. He wrote, "Sweetheart, they knocked me out
of the box in the third inning, but it wasn't my fault. The day
was cold and I couldn't sweat. Unless I can sweat I can't pitch."

I realize that I have been a special writer who sometimes
embarrassed his newspaper. However, I wish to correct the
impression that in the Sacco-Vanzetti case I went completely
roaring mad after twice being generously afforded the privilege

of vehement expression. I am sorry to say that the two subsequent columns which the *World* refused contained no fiery phrases. Although I would like it very much, I have been around long enough to realize that no columnist can possibly be accorded the right to say whatever comes into his mind. There is libel, there is obscenity, there is blasphemy; and there are policies and philosophies which his paper happens to hold especially dear. I do not anticipate that the *World* or any other newspaper would give me license to scoff at every campaign to which it committed itself. And I have not. Of course, I have always contended that in It Seems to Me I expressed my own opinions and did not commit the paper. This, to be sure, would not be true in case of libel, but that has already been referred to and I did not ever involve the *World* in any suit. Ralph Pulitzer said that the *World* has always believed in "allowing the fullest possible expression of individual opinion to those of its special writers who write under their own names." And yet he also says that I was ordered not to write about the Sacco-Vanzetti case at all after I had twice gone on record. In other words, in this case the paper was prepared to censor what I might have to say even before it had been written. How full is the fullest?

There is no use in my pretending that I do not believe myself right and the *World* wrong in the present controversy. As far as Sacco and Vanzetti went, both the paper and the individual wanted an amelioration of the sentence. Nothing less than a pardon or a new trial was satisfactory to me. Apparently, the *World* believed that if life imprisonment was all that could possibly be won from Gov. Fuller, that would be better than nothing. Here an interesting point in tactics arises. The editorial strategy of the *World* seemingly rested upon the theory that in a desperate cause it is well to ask a little less than you hope to get. I think you should ask more.

Rigorously the *World* excluded from its editorial columns all invectives. To call names, the *World* felt, would merely stiffen the resistance of Fuller and his advisers. I did call names, and this might possibly have embarrassed the *World* in the precise sort of campaign which it deemed it wise to make. Again, the *World* undoubtedly felt anxious about the bomb outrages. With passions so high, sparks were undoubtedly to be avoided. But in spite of silly crimes of violence I felt and feel that the most tragic factor of the Sacco-Vanzetti case is the general apathy. In ten minutes' time I will guarantee to fetch from the streets of New York one hundred persons who have never heard of the case and thousands who have not the slightest idea what it is all about. This could have been a duet with the editorial page carrying the air in sweet and tenor tones while in my compartment bass rumblings were added.

By now I am willing to admit that I am too violent, too ill-disciplined, too indiscreet to fit pleasantly into the *World's* philosophy of daily journalism. And since I cannot hit it off with the *World* I would be wise to look for work more alluring. I am still a member of Actors' Equity, the top floor is well stocked with early Brouns and I know a card-trick. In farewell to the paper I can only say that in its relations to me it was fair, generous and gallant. But that doesn't go for the Sacco-Vanzetti case.

51a. A STATEMENT BY MR. PULITZER

Mr. Broun's temperately reasoned argument does not alter the basic fact that it is the function of a writer to write and the function of an editor to edit. Ninety-nine times out of a hundred I publish Mr. Broun's articles with pleasure and read them with delight; but the hundredth time is altogether different.

Then something arises like the Sacco-Vanzetti case. Here Mr. Broun's unmeasured invective against Gov. Fuller and his committee seemed to the WORLD *to be inflammatory, and to encour-*

age those revolutionists who care nothing for the fate of Sacco and Vanzetti, nor for the vindication of justice, but are using this case as a vehicle of their propaganda. The WORLD, *for these reasons, judged Mr. Broun's writings on the case to be disastrous to the attempt, in which the* WORLD *was engaged, of trying to save the two condemned men from the electric chair.*

The WORLD *could not conscientiously accept the responsibility for continuing to publish such articles.*

For the theory that the opinions of a columnist are wholly disassociated from the principles of a paper is ingenious but not practical. Mr. Broun himself concedes this to the considerable extent of libel, obscenity, blasphemy and Presidential elections. He concedes it to the full extent in signing a contract in which, as the party of the second part, he agrees that he "shall and will carry out the directions of the party of the first part or its executive editors in the discharge of his duties."

I am sure Mr. Broun will be the first to declare that he has never been directed to write a single word against his conscience. The issue is simply whether or not he may direct the WORLD *to publish his column against its conscience.*

The WORLD *still considers Mr. Broun a brilliant member of its staff, albeit taking a witch's Sabbatical. It will regard it as a pleasure to print future contributions from him. But it will never abdicate its right to edit them.*

RALPH PULITZER
Editor, the WORLD

52. THE RABBIT THAT BIT THE BULLDOG

Heywood Broun used to be fond of saying in his column that there was one theme upon which he was competent to speak with complete authority. By some happy chance it was his favorite subject. He maintained that he was an expert on Heywood Broun.

This boast was groundless. Although the most thorough-going practitioner of personal journalism in New York, he managed in ten years' time to fashion a wholly erroneous picture of himself. Particularly false was the impression created during the recent controversy between the columnist and his employer, Ralph Pulitzer, the owner of the *World*. Broun compared himself to a pitcher who had to achieve a fine frenzy of perspiration before he could lay the ball anywhere near the plate, and Pulitzer aided in the deception by gravely observing that his hired hand had an unfortunate tendency to express his personal opinion "with the utmost extravagance."

Accordingly, the legend grew that here was an untamed spirit bubbling over with the spirit of revolt and obstreperousness. All of which is distinctly news to those residents under the golden dome who have heard the meek and anxious tone of Heywood Broun as he replied, "Yes, Mr. Swope," in answer to some booming remark from the executive editor.

The truth of the matter is that Broun belongs among the exceptionally timorous. Almost any mouse can frighten this elephant. A confirmed hypochondriac, he fears open places, closed places, high places, angina pectoris, cows, darkness and all loud voices. His collection of doctors is one of the finest ever acquired by a private connoisseur. When the mood is on him he has been known to visit as many as three specialists a day and he is completely craveneted against reassurance.

In all fairness, it should be said that Broun seems to regard a typewriter as a sort of barricade. When crouched before a keyboard he does manage to assume an audacity which he could not possibly maintain against anyone who said "Boo" in his presence. But he has been known to be less than stalwart in carrying out precepts which he set for himself in print. A few years ago the columnist worked up a mighty rage against the Ku Klux Klan and attacked it with Biblical fury. By some coincidence a Connecticut Klavern chose this particular time to burn a fiery cross within a few hundred yards of Broun's small farmhouse north of Stamford. He was in New York, but when informed of the incident he assumed that the rite was intended as a personal warning. Immediately he wrote a piece for his paper in which he said, in effect, "If the Klan thinks it can terrorize me I want them to know that I will be in the farmhouse alone this Saturday night and let them come and get me if they dare."

Some of his Algonquin friends remonstrated saying, "I think that's a bad idea, Heywood. You know they really might come and maul you."

"Don't be silly," said Broun, "I just wrote that. I'm not going anywhere near the place. Next Saturday I'm going to be right here playing poker."

However, the thing is a little more subtle than this. Like all timorous people the very large young man has occasional fits of recklessness. People who refuse for years on end to expend any courage are apt, upon occasion, to blow their savings on a single spree. Broun's pattern seems to be one rash act every seven years. In his early undergraduate days he engaged quite eagerly in a rough-and-tumble battle with a dance-hall proprietor famous for his skill in smashing heads with empty bottles. Broun explained his own escape from injury on the ground that he and Sweeney kept rolling over so fast that he managed always to present a moving target.

At the duly appointed peak of the cycle seven years later the columnist accepted an invitation from two subway rowdies to get off at the next station and show them what business it was of his. This argument arose over a problem in etiquette. Broun contended that the men had no right to address two cabaret singers from Joel's without an introduction. His opponents were both small men, but with the aid of a ticket-chopper's chair and a subway lantern they managed to give him quite a beating which sent him back into the ways of timidity for another seven years.

The war found him a very frightened correspondent with the American army, and one of his bitterest memories concerns an enthusiastic conducting officer who exulted over the fact that he had prevailed upon the authorities at Verdun to allow this reportorial group to get nearer to the actual combat than newspaper representatives had ever before been permitted at this point. Broun went grudgingly, and fortunately for his peace of mind the afternoon turned out quiet and there was very little shelling. A few landed close to the tourists when they were on their way back and just about to embark in some automobiles concealed behind a convenient cliff. "None of us ran," Broun says, "but we all walked briskly. And I didn't take the lead either. I was merely a good strong third, but I never let them pocket me and I was always in a swell position to win that race if I had to."

A few years later the conventional period of lying low ended and the columnist hissed loudly at an Irish-Republican street-corner meeting because the orator of the evening said that Michael Collins, one of Broun's heroes, had "sold out for British gold." And, to make his attitude of disapprobation a little clearer, the embattled rabbit pressed close to the speaker and threw three pennies in his face. It was his intention to cap this gesture by walking away contemptuously, but four partisans collared him within fifty yards and he received one of the most extensive black eyes which have been known on Broadway.

The recent row with the *World* was inevitable. Broun's planetary course of quietude had passed. The stars sang to him to take a sock at someone and to the surprise of many, including himself, he bit the hand that fed him. There was, however, more than a tidal condition to account for his madness. The *World* undertook to shush him at a moment when his emotions were deeply involved in the cause of Sacco and Vanzetti. For years he had complained with some reason of an inability to work up a satisfactory amount of hate. And now he had it. The first piece which he wrote against Lowell and Fuller was by all odds, to his mind, the best he had ever done for his paper. Nor had his momentum quite subsided when editorial censorship set in. It was a little as if somebody shouted to a pole vaulter in mid-career, "Please go no further."

In saying that Broun has small capacity for setting down indignation I do not mean to suggest that he feels none. Possibly the falsest item in the portrait of himself which he created was the expression of amiability. Heywood Broun is not in any fundamental sense a kindly person. He merely palms off timidity as something just as good as affability. Most of the people who read him had the feeling that he was Falstaffian. Hamletish would be closer, for his blood runs thinner than that of the fat knight and much more acid. Only by the grossest misapprehension could he ever be classified as belonging to even the lower orders of the fraternity of wits and humorists. To some extent he was engulfed in the generalization which the public made concerning what used to be known as "the little Algonquin group." There was an impression that everybody who happened to lunch at a certain round table was of necessity cynical, jaded and intent upon the making of smart lines.

In this category Broun distinctly does not belong. His capacity for humorous invention is of the slightest. Although for seven years a regular attendant at a weekly poker game rather devoted to the making of wisecracks, he is remembered by his associates for only one joke, and that they could hardly forget because he trotted it out so often. It had something to do with some home-made wine proffered by a player upon a certain rainy evening. The integrity of the beverage was open to question and Broun remarked, "Well, any port in a storm." The jest was rendered all the more feeble by the fact that the wine was really sherry.

The exigencies of a newspaper job sometimes made it necessary for the columnist to try his hand at frivolity, but he did it badly, for he has no true lightness of touch. Probably he was not unaware of this fact. Heywood Broun has always taken himself very seriously. Even his attempts at painting in oil, about which he has joked defensively, seem to him a weighty activity. "Cynical" fits him not at all, for he is too romantic and too immature for any such point of view. Although seldom identified by the public as one of the uplifters, this is the class in which Broun belongs by nature. If he ever grows more articulate in expression he will be readily identified as belonging to the reform group. To some he has seemed a somewhat pallid Mencken, but he is in fact a lesser Don Marquis. Like his more gifted model, his real interests lie in serious and even somber fantasy. Of his several ventures into story-telling Broun took no pride in any book to which he set his name except a short novel called *Gandle Follows His Nose*. Such critics as read it stamped the little book as thin and humorously intended, but Broun was savagely in earnest in his defeatist fairy tale. Man, so his theme went, lives in a circle and when he has been all the way around he might as well call it a day.

However, he undoubtedly believes that he himself has not yet completed the range of his lap. No reference to the girth of the columnist is intended. As a matter of fact he is hardly as fat as the caricaturists would have him. But for an habitual stoop he would easily be recognized as the tallest New York newspaperman since Spike Hunt went Cosmopolitan. What I mean to say was that Heywood Broun is an intensely ambitious man whose hopes of making a name for himself are seriously compromised by a monstrous inertia. Some years ago it was rather the thing to do to refer to him as a promising young writer. He is no longer young, and he has not yet been graduated out of the promising stage, so nothing may come of his aspirations.

And laziness has not been his only handicap. He was never the type to conduct a daily newspaper column without suffering injury. If he has a gift it falls within rather narrow limits and it became his columnar practice to boil over and over again the same material.

To some his present alliance with the *Nation* may seem a little incongruous. Indeed it is to the extent that Broun is in no sense an intellectual. Mr. Villard's readers from now on are likely to be somewhat startled by references to Babe Ruth, Bob Meusel and other characters with whom they can hardly be familiar. But in another sense Broun does belong under the banner of Garrison's grandson. In the secret places of his heart he is a crusader riding out to do battle even though he dreads it. Still, when his time and tide come round he may yet swing a mace and crack a skull.

53. WHIMS

Bruce Barton in a recent syndicated editorial speaks ill of whims. "Convictions," he writes, "are splendid when they relate to important matters; they are a public nuisance when they provoke a row over a petty detail."

I think Mr. Barton is ever so wrong, nor is his case strengthened by the examples he offers. He speaks of a friend of his with a taste for eggs boiled two and one-half minutes. Against three-minute eggs and two-minute eggs he made constant protest. And Mr. Barton says that thirty seconds make very little difference. Here is rank heresy. No one but a man insensitive to eggs could utter such a sentiment. Let Mr. Barton stand silent in his room some morning and toll off thirty seconds. He will find it a period of existence at which no connoisseur of time or cookery can afford to sneeze. Save in Chicago three heavyweight boxing championships could pass in thirty seconds. Thousands of touchdowns have been made with no longer than that to go. Salvation itself has been gained in shorter compass.

And remember all the time the water was boiling. Thirty seconds make a lot of difference to an egg, no matter how it affects Mr. Barton. Let him, indeed, put his finger in a kettle and decide after that whether half a minute is an inconsiderable interval.

A chef of genius should never attempt even the simplest dish without a stop-watch. And eggs are not a simple dish. To a man who really cares the precise extent of coagulation is a matter of the greatest moment. A three-minute egg is nothing like a two-minute egg. The difference is deeper than a grave and wider than any church door. As a matter of fact, both varieties are inferior. An egg should be boiled four and one-half minutes if it is to be encountered in its finest estate. Then only does it appear half-yielding and half-resisting, like a poet being interviewed about his private life.

Broad is the theme of the egg and its nature, but the question of whims is even more extensive. Bruce Barton speaks of convictions as if they came into life full grown. Nothing like it. Every conviction was a whim at birth. If I remember what was taught to me in school, Christopher Columbus proved the world was round by making an egg stand on one end. I don't quite understand the pertinence of this, and maybe I've grown muddled about the whole business and the egg incident referred to something else. Anyhow, the scheme of Columbus must have been modest in the beginning. The eyes of Isabella were bright, or maybe it was her jewels. Out of little things like that could come caravels and a new continent.

Orville Wright as a little boy had a kite and fussed over it so much that everybody said, "Oh, don't be silly. What difference does it make if the thing stays up a minute or ten seconds?" And today Ruth Elder is a star in vaudeville.

The tax on tea was tiny. No more was required of William Tell than that he should take off his hat to somebody. India had a mutiny because of grease in cartridges, and the fact that it is possible to rhyme Maine and Spain induced America to intervene in Cuba. This last is perhaps a little beside the point, but let it go. What I am trying to say is that a conviction about a seeming trifle may be momentous. Of course, it may be a nuisance. But that is just as true about a conviction relating to a matter called important.

I happen to know a woman who chooses to retain her own name though married. Very many have said, "What does it matter?" The woman in question has several answers to that, but the best one is, "It matters to me." And in the technique of maintaining her point I believe she takes a position which is unassailable. Never does she allow any person, however casual the contact, to call her "Mrs. Howard Browne" without correcting him. It is a nuisance. She knows that. Some near and dear to her have suggested, "Oh, can't you let it pass just once?" And she can't, nor can anybody with a cause afford to make exceptions. Let just a little water trickle through a dyke and presently you've got the ocean.

I'm surprised at Bruce Barton, for he knows his Bible well. The heresy which he promotes was rebuked most strikingly in the New Testament. When they asked Peter if he knew the Nazarene he pretended not to be a follower. Quite properly Peter might have said that his testimony at the moment was of no particular consequence. To stand there and declare his faith could constitute a nuisance. In days before one was allowed to bow down in the house of Rimmon. It won't do. When a man has a conviction, great or small, about eggs or eternity, he must wear it always in plain sight, pulled down tight upon his forehead. I don't think a man should check even a tiny conviction in any corridor. When it comes time to go out into the world again there is too much danger that it will be missing. And often they will hand you the wrong one.

Worst of all is Mr. Barton's complaint that people afflicted by loyalty to little purposes come to be nuisances. Whenever in history did a conviction roost on top of the world without its toll of turmoil? William Lloyd Garrison, who freed the slaves, was probably the most unmitigated nuisance America has ever seen. He talked of nothing else, and always in a loud voice. It was his purpose to be heard. Nobody expects to find comfort and companionability in reformers. Of course, Mr. Barton may say that I have distorted his contention. He spoke of cranks and I've referred to prophets. But there is no lantern by which the crank may be distinguished from the reformer when the night is dark. Just as every conviction begins as a whim so does every emancipator serve his apprenticeship as a crank. A fanatic is a great leader who is just entering the room.

I can remember back to the day when woman suffrage seemed to most people in America just about as important as two-minute eggs. Most of the credit for success goes now to the placid and patient people in the movement who frowned upon disorder. But it was the rowdy women who put it over. Centuries of persuasion would never have accomplished as much as was gained by those who kicked and screamed and picketed. Of course they were nuisances. No body politic is in a healthy state till it begins to itch.

Maybe they will never raise a monument to Bruce Barton's friend who fought to get his eggs boiled two minutes and thirty seconds, but he is a cousin, possibly distant, of all the men and women who have nagged the world a little closer to the heart's desire. Consider the egg agitator: suppose he said, "This is three minutes. That's only thirty seconds wrong—what of it?" Well, the next day they might slip him a four-minute egg, and later one done six or even seven. Before he knew it he would be accepting any hard-boiled thing and saying meekly, "Better not make a fuss."

54. THE PIECE THAT GOT ME FIRED

There ought to be a place in New York City for a liberal newspaper. No daily has ventured into the vast territory which lies between the radical press and the New York *World*. The radicals themselves are meagerly served in English-language papers. There will be no argument, I think, that the *World* comes closest to being an American *Manchester Guardian*, but it is at best on the outer rim of the target. Possibly the contention may be raised that there are not enough liberals in New York to support a daily paper. It seems to me the try is worth making. Liberals need not be born. They can be trained by care and kindness.

The word "liberal" itself has fallen into disrepute. To a radical it is a label for a man who professes friendship and then rushes away for his thirty pieces of silver as soon as the crisis comes. In the eyes of the conservatives a liberal is a dirty Red who probably bought his dinner coat with Russian gold. Neither interpretation is accurate and it should not be impossible to expose the fallacy of such reasoning. First of all, there must be a tradition and that takes time. There was the possibility of an enduring association of political liberals when Theodore Roosevelt started the Progressive Party. The leadership was not ideal and many of the followers who clustered around the Colonel were about as liberal as Frank A. Munsey. Still it was effective leadership and we have none now.

Lacking a political haven, the liberal of America might still be rallied into the support of some powerful daily paper content to run the risk of expressing minority thought. This discussion is confined to the New York field. Perhaps in some other city such a paper does exist. I do not know its name, though possibly the Baltimore *Sun* lives up to the requirements. The *World* does not because it switches front so frequently. Nobody has a right to demand that an editor shall never change his mind. New facts on any given situation may require a complete right-about-face. But the *World* on numerous occasions has been able to take two, three, or even four different stands with precisely the same material in hand. So constant were the shifts during the Sacco-Vanzetti case that the paper seemed like an old car going up a hill. In regard to Nicaragua the *World* has thundered on Thursdays and whispered on Monday mornings. Again and again the paper has managed to get a perfect full-Nelson on some public problem only to let its opponent slip away because its fingers were too feeble.

It does not seem to me that the paper possesses either courage or tenacity. Of the honest intentions of all its executives I have not the slightest doubt. I think the fault lies in a certain squeamishness. That there should be some reaction from the flagrant pornography of the tabloids is no more than reasonable, but this development in journalism cannot be met with prudishness. To be specific I cite a *World* editorial on the recent squabble about the proposed birth-control exhibit at the Parents' Exposition in Grand Central Palace. In the beginning Mrs. Sanger's organization was promised a place and this promise was later rescinded at the demand of the Board of Education. The advice of the *World* to the birth controllers was that they should go quietly and make no commotion. "Now it is quite obvious," said the *World*, "that a building swarming with children is no place for a birth-control exhibit."

It may be obvious to the *World*, but I must insist that the reasons for exclusion are not so evident to me. I should think that a building swarming with children ought to be a very logical place for a birth-control exhibit. The fact of the matter is that in the mind of the *World* there is something dirty about birth control. In a quiet way the paper may even approve of the movement, but it is not the sort of thing one likes to talk about in print. Some of the readers would be shocked, and the *World* lives in deadly terror of shocking any reader. As a matter of fact, Mrs. Sanger and her associates intended nothing more dreadful than an exhibit of charts showing population curves and such statistical material. It is the term "birth control" which frightened the newspaper. Not so long ago a Sunday editor insisted on editing a contribution to one of the newspaper columns. Somebody had written in to say that before the triumphs of Lindbergh most Americans had regarded all Scandinavians as dull-witted. "Heywood," said the responsible editor, "don't you realize that our Swedish readers would be offended?"

During the war the *World* was active in attacking hyphenated loyalty, but to the paper's credit it should be remarked that it indulged in far less red-baiting than any of its rivals. Now that hostilities have ended, the *World* cannot get over a certain group consciousness. It has, in addition to "Swedish readers," "Methodist readers," "Baptist readers," "Italian readers," and, perhaps above all, "Catholic readers." When somebody gets angry and sends me a scurrilous postal card he almost always attacks the *World* on the ground that it is under Jewish influence and therefore Bolshevist. This, of course, is ridiculously wide of the mark. The *World* of today has few roots in the Jewish community. Very probably it does command a considerable circulation among the young intellectual group of the East Side, but the *Times* is very obviously the Bible of the arrived and successful Jewish citizen of New York. As a matter of fact, it is my experience that there is very little clannishness among the Jews of New York. There is less standardization than in any other group. Save for downright abuse there is no resentment.

The Irish are quite a different proposition. Admitting the danger of generalities I would contend that the Irish are the cry-babies of the Western world. Even the mildest quip will set them off into resolutions and protests. And still more precarious is the position of the New York newspaperman who ventures any criticism of the Catholic Church. There is not a single New York editor who does not live in mortal terror of the power of this group. It is not a case of numbers but of organization. Of course, if anybody dared, nothing in the world would happen. If the church can bluff its way into a preferred position the fault lies not with the Catholics but with the editors. But New York will never know a truly liberal paper until one is founded which has no allegiance with and no timidity about any group, racial, religious or national. Perhaps the first thing needed for a liberal paper is capital, but even more important is courage.

55. GANDLE THE OBSCURE

Fame has jogged on by and left me jilted. A chance has gone to ride, even as far as posterity perhaps, by clinging to another's coat-tails.

Deems Taylor's announcement that he has dropped the tragic fantasy which was to have been his second opera for the Metropolitan finds me the pitiful protagonist. It was my novel *Gandle Follows His Nose* upon which Mr. Taylor planned to found his musical drama. In the beginning this was supposed to be a secret, but I never did keep it well, and at this late date I see no reason why I should not rend my clothing in the market place.

If Bunny could have gone on in this new form he would have been a sort of Cinderella man. The book in which he lived and died fell like a pin in some great foundry. Indeed, the publisher had predicted as much, for he wrote me when he received the manuscript that it was a puny and feeble work and that it might be better for me to destroy it. "Our reputation can stand it," he added, "but I don't know whether yours can."

Tersely I telegraphed, "Go to press!"

And throughout the years I had saved up Mr. Liveright's bleak letter, purposing to wave it in his face on the great night when the violins began to sob and Bunny, clad in purple tights, bowed to the diamond horseshoe.

And I would be sitting somewhere in back because Mack's tailcoat does not fit me so very well. After Taylor and the conductor and all the singers had taken the requisite number of bows I felt that there might be a shout for "Broun!" In fact, I knew it, for I planned to start it. Now I shall never know just what one does when roses are thrust upon him suddenly.

Nor will I get the cigarette case. In the beginning it was to have been gold. When Deems told me that he planned to make an opera out of *Gandle* I was delighted, and when he added, "Now, as to the financial part of it"—I stopped him with a lordly gesture.

"This is sheer luck for me," I said, "so don't let's mention money. I will be perfectly satisfied if I get a gold cigarette case out of this."

"A gold cigarette case!" answered Deems, incredulous. "I guess you have some misconception as to the rewards of music."

But, anyhow, I won't get the silver-plated case.

This opera was in no sense planned as a collaboration. Deems Taylor simply took the book to use as much or as little as he liked and in his own words. In hope of unearned prestige I sold Bunny down the river, and perhaps my present frustration is a punishment quite justified.

Some little time after the first conference Deems read me his scenario of the operatic version. Still in conciliatory mood, I said, "I think that's very good," though at every change, however minor, the wounds of Bunny bled afresh, while I had slight twinges in the shoulder. Gandle did not rise up from his grave with that same body which he had worn in life. Already I could see that my beautiful hero was in a fair way of becoming merely the shell for an operatic tenor.

"Nobody can remember who first called him Bunny. That

name he seems almost to have brought with him into the world. It was coined out of his skin, white as a rabbit, and there was a twitch to his nose, and his eyes swept right and left. But his shock of hair was black as a dragon's belly."

Now nobody in the Metropolitan would ever look like that, and Agatha was "the fairest and most virtuous lady in all the world," which is asking too much of any soprano.

Moreover, there was Yom to think of. Genie-like, it was his custom to sit on a mountain and rest his feet upon some lower hill across the valley. At Mr. Kahn's place they would have been compelled to make him a bass-baritone perched precariously on stilts. And the elephants and the mighty armies of King Helgas, winding up the mountain road toward Kadia, would all of them have been minified.

Still I did hope to hear the music for the moment when the bugles blew and the elephants all trumpeted because the way was steep.

It was then that Gandle's voice rose high as he cried out, "It is no use. We have no chance. Let's go and fight them in the pass." And that time, even though the others ran away, he did turn back the host of Helgas.

Yes, I still think my Gandle was quite a fellow, and probably he is better off up in the mountains with an arrow through his heart than strutting around before the box-holders and bickering out an aria with the first flute making pace.

"Danger had come a second time as if it were a season." Bunny could not turn back Helgas again, and when they tossed his body to one side so that no passing elephant might slip and stumble he opened his eyes and said, "I am still here."

In a measure Gandle spoke the truth. Lacking orchestral accompaniment, his survival is meager. Few read the book when it first appeared, and there now remains just one devoted follower. Every year along about this time I take the little novel down and read it through. And then, with an egotism pardonable when one remembers that he and I are quite alone, I say to myself, "I must have been damned good when I wrote that."

So here's to you, Bunny, and here's to me. To hell with the fiddles!

56. CANON SHOCKS COLUMNIST

For the first time in some ten or twenty years I have been definitely shocked by a piece of writing about sex. Undoubtedly the three paragraphs are not obscene in the eyes of the law, for I draw the quotation from a widely circulated bulletin published by the International Reform Federation. Moreover, the author is Canon William Sheafe Chase, clergyman and a lifelong crusader for censorship of plays and books.

Indeed, I beg you to be indulgent with the Canon and not judge him too harshly. It is well kown that denunciation of things held to be pornographic will often inflame a reformer to a point where he quite unconsciously violates good taste.

Speaking of Mary Ware Dennett's *The Sex Side of Life,* Canon Chase writes:

"The pamphlet does not correctly speak of sex desires as a longing for motherhood and fatherhood but as an opportunity for 'an unsurpassed joy' and 'the very greatest pleasure in all human experience.' Why did Mrs. Dennett misstate this to her children?

"Ask a mother how it compares with the pleasure of nursing her own baby, and she will tell you the pamphlet is criminally deceiving the young she is trying to teach.

"Ask a fine athlete how the act compares with the joy of winning an athletic contest, and he will say that the writer of such advice to the young is not only incorrect but must be abnormal."

Now, I ask you to compare this statement of the good Canon

with what Mary Ware Dennett has to say on the same subject. And remember that the Canon's bulletin is freely circulated, while Mrs. Dennett has been sentenced to spend three hundred days in jail.

"The sex attraction is the deepest feeling that human beings know," writes Mrs. Dennett on page 9 of her pamphlet. "It is far more than a mere sensation of the body. It takes in the emotions and the mind and the soul, and that is why so much of our happiness is dependent upon it."

And may I ask you on this evidence which seems to you the clean, the healthy and the normal mind?

The Dennett case went deep into the roots of communal psychology. The defendant was convicted because she dared to say that love was beautiful. Some reformers hold that this is true but that the fact should be kept quiet in the presence of adolescents. Canon Chase, somewhat more logically, holds that it shouldn't be said because it isn't true. At least, he holds that love is not to be compared to the ecstasy of winning your "Y" in the hammer throw.

This, of course, is a pretty broad subject, and I do not see how it can be decided in a debate between Canon Chase and me. In the first place, I do not know whether he qualifies as an expert witness, for in the record books there is no mention of the races he has run. However, I contend that if Mrs. Dennett errs she has erred in company with Shakespeare, Milton, Wagner, Shelley, and the author of *The Song of Solomon*. Respectfully I urge Canon Chase to turn to that part of his Bible and decide for himself whether the Scriptural poet is talking of lacrosse.

Even if it so happens that the Brooklyn pastor cannot qualify as one fitted to give expert testimony I must admit the same about myself. I hold no medals. But years ago I got a pewter mug for winning the tennis championship of the North Entry of Thayer Hall. And, in spite of that vivid and joyful recollection, I still will cast my vote to string along with Shakespeare and with Shelley.

If Canon Chase is right, then Romeo was a fool and Juliet no better than abnormal. And Ruth, who gleaned, should have tended her sheaves and left Boaz alone. And Father Adam, who could not possibly have been corrupted by Mrs. Dennett (known to the press as "the old gentlewoman"), seems to have given up Eden because of the love of woman. But in those days there was no intercollegiate football and the A.A.U. was not yet founded.

If Canon Chase is right all lyric poetry had better be burned by the public hangman and there will hardly be an opera left fit for performance before any who can't abide misstatements.

Gone, too, will be the old verities celebrated in the legends. The prince in the story did not wake the sleeping princess, but rather, left her to sweet slumber's anesthesia and went upon his way to pitch horseshoes at a neighboring palace. And wasn't Ulysses naïve to fill the sailors' ears with wax lest they hear the song of sirens? Had Canon Chase been on that bridge he would have summoned all hands aft to play deck shuffleboard.

And yet the question raised by Canon Chase is not one to be lightly dismissed. If love is but a minor thing, then the world has been wrong-headed from the very beginning. Of course, Canon Chase may say that he has no desire to minimize that love which is of the spirit. It seems to me that soul and body are subtly interwoven. What God hath joined together let no dogmatic parson put asunder.

Canon William Sheafe Chase is not the first pessimist to insist that nature has tricked us all into a sorry mess and that sex is a fundamental blunder of creation. In that case Hamlet was quite right in urging a nunnery upon Ophelia, but the Canon is almost the first critic to insist that the melancholy Dane was altogether normal.

But is it really true that Nurmi knows more of the joy of life than Bobby Burns or any of the Bonnie Prince Charlies? History would be the poorer if Canon Chase is sound in his contention. I'd hate to hear that Antony actually asked for waivers on Cleopatra and finally traded her for a left-hand pitcher and a utility infielder from the Three I League.

57. A SHEPHERD

The host of heaven and the angel of the Lord had filled the sky with radiance. Now, the glory of God was gone, and the shepherds and the sheep stood under dim starlight. The men were shaken by the wonders they had seen and heard, and, like the animals, they huddled close.

"Let us now," said the eldest one of the shepherds, "go even unto Bethlehem and see this thing which has come to pass, which the Lord hath made known unto us."

The City of David lay behind a far, high hill, upon the crest of which there danced a star. The men made haste to be away, but as they broke out of the circle there was one called Amos who remained. He dug his crook into the turf and clung to it.

"Come," cried the eldest of the shepherds, but Amos shook his head. They marveled, and called out: "It is true. It was an angel. You heard the tidings. A Saviour is born."

"I heard," said Amos. "I will abide."

The eldest walked back from the road to the little knoll on which Amos stood.

"You do not understand," the old man told him. "We have a sign from God. An angel has commanded us. We go to worship the Saviour, who is even now born in Bethlehem. God has made His will manifest."

"It is not in my heart," replied Amos.

And now the eldest of the shepherds was angry.

"With your eyes," he cried out, "you have seen the host of heaven in these dark hills. And you heard, for it was like the thunder when 'Glory to God in the Highest' came ringing to us out of the night."

And again Amos said, "It is not in my heart."

Another then broke in: "Because the hills still stand and the sky has not fallen it is not enough for Amos. He must have something louder than the voice of God."

Amos held more tightly to his crook and answered, "I have need of a whisper."

They laughed at him and said, "What should this voice say in your ears?"

He was silent, and they pressed about him and shouted mockingly: "Tell us now. What says the God of Amos, the little shepherd of a hundred sheep?"

Meekness fell away from him. He took his hands from off the crook and raised them high.

"I, too, am a God," said Amos in a loud, strange voice, "and to my hundred I am a savior."

And when the din of the angry shepherds about him slackened Amos pointed to his hundred.

"See my flock," he said. "See the fright of them. The fear of the bright angel and of the voices is still upon them. God is busy in Bethlehem. He has no time for a hundred sheep. They are my sheep. I will abide."

This the others did not take so much amiss, for they saw that there was a terror in all the flocks, and they, too, knew the ways of sheep. And before the shepherds went away on the road to Bethlehem toward the bright star each one talked to Amos and told him what he should do for the care of the several flocks. And yet one or two turned back a moment to taunt Amos before they reached the dip in the road which led to the City of David. It was said, "We shall see new glories at the throne of God, and you, Amos—you will see sheep."

Amos paid no heed, for he thought to himself, "One shepherd the less will not matter at the throne of God." Nor did he have time to be troubled that he was not to see the Child who was come to save the world. There was much to be done among the flocks, and Amos walked between the sheep and made under his tongue a clucking noise, which was a way he had, and to his hundred and to the others it was a sound finer and more friendly than the voice of the bright angel. Presently the animals ceased to tremble and began to graze as the sun came up over the hill where the star had been.

"For sheep," said Amos to himself, "the angels shine too much. A shepherd is better."

With the morning the others came up the road from Bethlehem, and they told Amos of the manger and of the wise men who had mingled there with shepherds. And they described to him the gifts—gold, frankincense and myrrh. And when they were done they said, "And did you see wonders here in the fields with the sheep?"

Amos told them, "Now my hundred are one hundred and one," and he showed them a lamb which had been born just before the dawn.

"Was there for this a great voice out of heaven?" asked the eldest of the shepherds.

Amos shook his head and smiled, and there was in his face that which seemed to the shepherds a wonder even in a night of wonders.

"To my heart," he said, "there came a whisper."

58. LIFE AND LOWELL

Harvard University has discharged twenty scrubwomen rather than raise their wages from thirty-five to thirty-seven cents an hour. The scrubwomen themselves asked for no increase in salary, but it so happens that the State of Massachusetts has a minimum wage law which provides boards to set certain standards of pay for women and minors in certain industries.

When the board called the university's attention to the fact that it was underpaying its scrubwomen Harvard's answer was to discharge them. The university has announced that it will replace them with men who may perhaps be able to do a greater amount of work, and there is no minimum wage for men. Possibly ten men will be able to do the work of twenty middle-aged and elderly women.

This will result in a considerable saving to the university. Had it paid the women a legal living wage the sum would have amounted to almost $600 a year. Equipment for the scrub football team hardly costs that much in a season.

But the most interesting element in the problem is not the bare economic details but the human phase. A. Lawrence Lowell, president of Harvard, has passed upon the issue, and his attitude is interesting. William M. Duvall, a young Methodist clergyman in East Cambridge, was disturbed by the plight of one of his parishioners. Mrs. Emma Trafton had been employed by Harvard for thirteen years. She was discharged without notice on November 1. The college was kinder to Mrs. Katherine Donahue, who had worked for Harvard for thirty-three years. She was not discharged until the Saturday before Christmas. Mr. Duvall wrote to Mr. Lowell and received the following reply:

"I have inquired into the discharge of Mrs. Emma Trafton from the Widener Library, and I find that the Minimum Wage Board has been complaining of our employing women for these purposes at less than thirty-seven cents an hour, and hence the university has felt constrained to replace them with men. Some of them—I hope many of them—will be able to be employed at some other work in the university."

In other words, the reward of thirty-three years of work for Harvard University is the pious hope of the president that possibly something will turn up.

We used to have a song about how the football team was sweeping down the field and that we would do or die with the Crimson until the last chalk line was passed. The precise phrasing escapes me, but the words were to that effect. Well, Mrs. Katherine Donahue has had thirty-three years of sweeping. One might suppose at the end of that time she would have passed the last chalk line and landed in some haven of honor or security.

But it seems not. She carries with her into a bleak and cheerless world merely the tepid hope of a Lowell. Just try to warm your toes with that!

Thirty-three years is a long time to work for a college, whether the job be scrubbing or teaching. In my opinion, Mrs. Donahue has done rather more to tidy up the place than even A. Lawrence Lowell himself. She left no dark and clotted stains behind her.

It is said unofficially that some of the women had grown too old and too feeble to do their work with competence. One never does grow younger in scrubbing 'round under the book shelves for thirty-three years. In old Gore Hall and later in the new Widener Library Mrs. Donahue may have paused now and then for a second to look up at the battalions of books. They reached from floor to ceiling. In them was the stuff to make one free. But they were not for the likes of her. This was fodder for the Lodges and the Lowells and the Cabots.

And yet I would not say that the education of A. Lawrence Lowell had been altogether successful. He has failed to learn that there are things which men and colleges may not do with honor.

Myself, I did not frequent much the premises kept neat by Mrs. Donahue. My four years brought me no degree. No, not even a note from President Lowell. Accordingly, I cannot say that as an alumnus I demand humanity from Lowell and from Harvard.

But I will demand it just the same. This is no private fight.

"I hope," says A. Lawrence Lowell. And I say "hope" be damned! Unless Harvard takes immediate steps to fix a pension system for its veteran employees it will forfeit any right to stand as a leader in enlightenment. A university is a living organism, and, when the heart has ceased to beat, death and corruption of the flesh set in.

"The veterans of industry are entitled to a pension as well as the veterans of war." I quote from a leaflet issued on this case by the Harvard University Socialist Club. And the story was first called to public attention by Gardner Jackson, who has written about it in the current *Nation*.

Already, I am told, certain prominent alumni of the university have taken steps to right the wrong. That's good. It's up to Harvard to choose between life and Lowell.

59. IN THE IMAGE OF GOD

The text for my sermon is to be found in the twenty-sixth verse of the first chapter of Genesis: "And God said, Let us make man in Our image, after Our likeness: and let them have dominion—"

And if I were a clergyman I would preach a great many sermons on this text and similar ones, because the churches are too much inclined to cast man down rather than raise him up. It was the serpent which crawled upon his belly. Adam came in this world standing on his own two feet, and that's where he belongs.

He need not sit in shamefaced silence and let anybody tell him that he is puny and a miserable sinner. Man is a first-class job. Indeed, the first chapter of Genesis ends with the statement, "And God saw every thing that He had made, and, behold, it was very good."

It is not my notion that man represents the ultimate and crowning achievement of creation. Give him a few more million years and he can add cubits to his stature and raise the roof of his head to make room for bigger and better cranial convolutions. But he will do until the superman arrives.

Often parsons exhort us to look at the sun and other bodies and realize our own insignificance. The sun is pretty bright and pretty big, but man can put his hand out and catch all its essential properties in a lamp of violet rays. It does not seem to me that man need take back-talk from any of the planets. Mere size should not make him craven. He has outstayed the mammoth and is well on his way to conquer those even vaster forces of sea and sky.

Now and then the earth does rise up to smite him. The greatest disaster of our time was the Japanese earthquake, and it moved thousands of editorial writers and other preachers to musing on the mightiness of nature and the puniness of man.

But it seems to me that this was by no means the only possible interpretation of the event. Far from scoring against man and his mightiness, the episode furnished still one more proof of human tenacity. Thousands died in Tokio, but millions lived. Across that plain where the city lies the earthquakes roll like sluggish waves. Each year hundreds or more tug at the roots of Tokio. When bamboo quivers there it is not the wind.

So it has gone on for centuries. This is, perhaps, the mightiest yet of all recorded assaults, and man remains. In a thousand years nature has not been able to shake him off. Though the ground has rocked and swayed beneath him like a broncho, the little Japanese sits tight. And across the world of water from his fellow men there should come a mighty and defiant shout, "Ride him, cowboy!"

The boxing writers have named Johnny Risko the rubber man because he springs up again when borne down by blows. But this is not a unique distinction. There's a lot of gutta-percha even in the worst of us. It seems to me that resiliency is an almost universal trait in human kind. Within a year the tea houses stood in the streets where the dead did lie. Geishas sang once more of Johnkeen. "Yokohama, Nagasaki, Kobe, maru hoi!" And when any Babylon falls don't be surprised to see it bounce.

Who says that man is puny? He falls asleep and dies awhile and then he is up again. The stream of life force has not been dammed in our time and will not till the earth crumbles. Even then I rather expect that it will change to the car ahead and still continue. After the wave and the hurricane and the earthquake life crawls out from under the debris and starts on another lap.

One of the most fascinating things in *The Green Pastures* is the scene in which the ark comes finally to rest upon its mountain top. Up comes the sun, and up rise men and elephants. Noah opens the back door, and you hear the beasts rush out in search of life and lampposts. I am not one who can accept the fact that this particular flood was factually true, but it is authentic in a more important sense. It is spiritually true. Man does come through catastrophes and fill the ranks again.

What permanent victory has nature ever won from us? Neither ice nor fires nor floods have checked the succession of human kind. Other species have given up the fight, but man is the finest animal of the lot. The sun cannot drive him from the tropics, and beyond the Arctic in barren lands, where even the microbe cannot live, he sets his foot down and sends back pictures for Sunday rotogravure sections.

To be sure, our perch upon the earth is precarious. Only the crust has been completely won. Flame and water menace from beneath, and above are mighty bodies capable of flipping the whole globe into the dustbin. But they haven't done it yet. Nature has the weight and nature has the punch, but whom did she ever lick? Man has staggered and bled and reeled from hammer blows, but he hasn't been counted out as yet.

Until the final ten has been tolled who dares to say that he is puny?

60. BILL BOLITHO

Bolitho's dead at Avignon. There has passed, I think, the most brilliant journalist of our time. This is not the overstatement of one who mourns a friend. While he flourished I expressed the opinion that Bolitho's best was far and away beyond the topmost reach of any newspaper competitor.

It was pleasant to praise him because he lent some of his glory and achievement to all the rest. I think that there is no reporter or critic or columnist who does not smart under the popular and snobbish assumption that anybody who sets his stuff down day by day is of necessity a hack. All men live under the hope that one day they may touch greatness, and it is essential for them to feel that when they drive home the thrust the medium in which they live and labor shall be sufficient for their purpose.

It is not inevitable that today's strip of newsprint should be no more than tattered scraps in tomorrow's dustbin. The man who writes well enough and thinks through the thing before him can win his immortality, even though his piece appears obscurely in a Wall Street edition. Most of us on papers, for all our swagger, are at least five and a half times too humble. We are apt to say, "Oh, I'm just a newspaperman." When called upon to justify ourselves we smirk and behave as if the thing we did were really of but small importance.

We know better than that. There is no reason why a first-rate man on any newspaper should yield precedence to every novelist and minor poet and little essayist. In city rooms I've known the whole crowd to gape at some member of the staff in considerable awe and whisper behind his back, "He's written a book."

There's no special magic in getting between boards. Last year's novel is just as dead as last year's paper. Indeed, I know few sights more horrible than second-hand book stalls on which dead volumes are exposed to wind and weather, completely dead and lacking only decent burial.

Bolitho, to be sure, had his fling in bound sheets, but much of his finest appeared in the New York *World*. And these essays will still remain, though he is dead at Avignon.

From the standpoint of the old-fashioned school Bolitho could hardly be called a newspaperman at all, let alone a leader in the first rank. There still endure graybeards who detest frills and shake their heads to say that news is all and that anything else which creeps into a paper is so much folly.

But these graybeards employ a tight and tenuous definition of news. They mean no more than the report of the thing which has happened. They feel that it is the part of newspapermen to behave like members of the Light Brigade and refuse to reason why.

Such a definition would have excluded William Bolitho almost completely. He was far more interested in the explanation than in the event. Many had better eyes to see and ears to hear but less of analytical power. Sometimes, like an overeager shortstop who throws before the ball is in his hands, Bolitho began to interpret episodes which were still in motion. It is hard for any interpreter to remain patient until the play has been completed.

Yet news must be a deeper and a more significant thing than a mere recital of names, addresses and the doctor's diagnosis. Causes, however far beneath the surface they may lie, are distinctly within the province of journalism. That is, if journalism is to be a kingdom and not a little parish.

For instance, I mean just this: Some little time ago a group of Jewish internes were cruelly hazed in a public hospital. Naturally, all the papers reported the facts of this incident. There they stopped, and I say they stopped because they did not have a sufficiently keen vision to see the whole way to the uttermost boundaries of journalistic territory. It is not enough to discuss the symptom. The disease itself must be investigated. It was the function of papers then, and it is the function of papers now, to get at the root of conditions which underlie strife and prejudice and turmoil. The story of Gastonia should not have ended just because the strike ceased.

It was as the leader of journalistic exploration, deep into the human heart and mind, that Bolitho made his mark. If the standard which he set can even be approximated it may well be that seekers after education will not turn to some five-foot shelf or scrapbook, but find their road to knowledge in the living, daily record of things which lie about them. Indeed, I would call a man well read if he could hold the dinner table spellbound with an accurate discussion of the dispatches from Russia. That would mean much more than if he lived up to the advertisements by giving the date of Walt Whitman's birth and a few lines from his best-known poems.

Indeed, for this opinion I can cite distinguished authority. Dr. Nicholas Murray Butler in his commencement address at Columbia talked on The Insulated Life and said, "A liberal education is not to be confused with mere attendance at school or college or with the possession of a certificate to that effect." And later he added, "A liberal education is that which is worthy of a free man and which fits a man for intellectual and spiritual freedom."

It seems to me that no man can know life sufficiently to understand freedom until he has gone down into it—until, like a dog on a spring day, he has actually nozzled his way beneath the surface. William Bolitho had been newsboy, day laborer, student, soldier, writer, before he died. The last time I saw him he told me of his days as a mason's helper on a construction job in Cape Town.

Naturally it has been said that this brilliant journalist of thirty-nine had much of his finest potentialities still ahead of him. That's true, but still he had been all the way around the track before he died at Avignon.

61. A REPLY TO MY BOSS

Any working newspaperman is naturally pleased when the editor finds it necessary to sit down and write a piece.

My gratification was double because in this case it gave me one more day of vacation. But, naturally, I am grieved to find Roy W. Howard enmeshed in error. He objects to my running for Congress on the Socialist ticket in the Seventeenth District, New York, for four reasons:

1. No Scripps-Howard feature writer has ever gone to Congress.

2. The odds seem to be overwhelmingly against my election.

3. The profession of journalism is more important than that of politics.

4. Independence of thought precludes party membership.

One and two seem to square off pretty well from Mr. Howard's point of view, although I want to say a little more about the second later. In saying that journalism is more important than politics and that Broun could be "more constructive in a column than in Congress" Mr. Howard raises an issue which does not exist. The two things are not mutually exclusive. During the campaign this column will appear as usual. I don't expect to see it any better or any worse. When and if elected I should most certainly have daily opinions and the desire to see them in newsprint. There is no reason why a man or a woman could not be both columnist and Congressman. If Mr. Howard disagrees I suggest that he secure an option on the newspaper services of Mrs. Ruth Pratt to be exercised immediately after election day.

The real sticking point is party affiliation. I am quite sure that the fact of its being Socialist does not enter into the problem.

Surely it would be far more embarrassing for a liberal newspaper to have its columnist affiliated with the Tammany machine or the Republican organization of Sam Koenig than to be serving under the leadership of Norman Thomas.

Indeed, the *Telegram* supported Thomas for mayor, and I trust that it will also indorse him this year in his fight for Congress. But I don't know. Right here comes the weakness of an individual or an organization construing independence as meaning a permanent place on the sidelines. In order to have any coherence of policy it is necessary to make something more than annual alliances. At times the Scripps-Howard independence becomes little more than erratic whimsy. A liberal, for instance, may be pardoned if he rubs his eyes and asks querulously, "What is this liberal independence?" when he observes the *Telegram* supporting in one national election a La Follette and the next time around a Hoover. As the rowing experts say, the boat doesn't seem to run well between strokes.

I think it not in the least inconsistent for Mr. Howard to stop well short of complete acceptance of the Socialist program and, nevertheless, support Thomas for mayor, as was the case last year. It would be silly for a passenger to say, "I can't get on that Van Cortlandt Park express, because I want to go only as far as 72nd Street." Surely Thomas and the rest of us are going in the direction toward which the Scripps-Howard papers are heading. Why shouldn't they get on board? We'll let them off when they think they've reached their destination.

Independent liberals always get beaten in American elections because they reserve their commitments until a month or so before election. Sam Koenig and John F. Curry work three hundred and sixty-five days a year. Organization can't be beaten without organization. The Socialist Party offers the only existing machinery by which the Republican-Democratic alliance can be overthrown. It is hopeless to try to cleanse these parties from within. That's been tried. Mrs. Pratt herself made a gallant effort to free the local Republican organization of Koenigism.

She failed. My newspaper friends tell me that after election day she will be out of office. Sam won't.

My newspaper friends did not tell me that I would be elected. Herbert Bayard Swope, who used to be a newspaperman, said that I had a good chance. The rest were less encouraging. They felt that an enthusiastic Curry would do more for his candidate than a perfunctory Koenig. The Republican and Democratic organizations are not parties so much as marching clubs. For them this is no more than a drill or, more exactly, a game. When the final whistle has blown, the Tammany crowd huddles and gives three long cheers for Koenig and the Republicans do as much for Curry. The whole fight is carried on in a spirit of good, clean fun. Anybody caught slugging will be immediately sent to the locker room.

Mr. Howard knows this as well as and better than I do. He has fought the fight against Ewald and Vitale and Vause. And yet he says that I should stay on the sidelines with him and the rest of the Scripps-Howard executives joining in the long-drawn independent-liberal cheer of "Hold 'em, forces of reform and decency!" With all due respect for the cheering section the man who gets down onto the field and tries to spill a few of the trick plays is doing a great deal more. I'm going to do all I can.

Since when did it become a reproach to tackle a job with the odds vastly against you? It is not impossible to win. Twenty-one thousand votes out of the sixty thousand which Mr. Howard has mentioned would be enough. There should be that many people who are sick of Hoover's fake prosperity and Tammany's very real prosperity for Tammany officials. This could be Jim Dandy all over again even though I admit a certain slackness in any metaphor which links me to a race horse. And maybe the name isn't altogether suitable, either. But let it go.

In fact, I am afraid that it will be necessary for me to avoid any great insistence on the campaign in this column. Columnar modesty is against an overexploitation of the first person singular. Fair play forbids my using weapons against my opponents which they do not possess. If I attacked Brodsky in this column he would have every right to demand an equal amount of space for reply. I would have to print it. And as he is an amateur at the business maybe he wouldn't write a good column. That has been known to happen even in the case of regulars. And surely everybody can see how palpably improper it would be for me to solicit campaign contributions, through the medium of this column, to be sent to Morris L. Ernst, 285 Madison Avenue.

But I am tired of hearing all this talk about how the honest average citizen should get into politics and not leave it to the machine professionals. I am tired of hearing this, because I am average and honest and yet, when I do get in, my own boss tells me that this is no business for me. It's everybody's business and nobody's business.

But I am even more tired of standing with well-meaning liberals weaving a daisy chain of good intentions. I want to break that chain and enlist for duration. Here goes!

62. HEYWOOD COX BROUN

I had not intended to write anything about the death of my father, but I must. If I include many other fathers in this brief column, it may be possible to escape the charge of bad taste. But this has always been, by intent and instinct, a personal record. There is such a thing as leaning over too far.

On the day my father died I sat down and marked time by writing a column about the sea and cats and preoccupations which may move men to achieve a literary style. It was warmed-over stuff from half and three-quarters remembered columns written years ago.

But in any such painful effort to gain detachment from the thing actually in your mind there must be a very palpable in-

sincerity. That I came to realize. And the acuteness of the re-
alization was accented by the paragraphs in the newspapers
which marked the passing of a man of eighty.

And at this point it is fair enough to generalize. Save in the
case of the very great, and perhaps not even then, the news
notes must inevitably be inadequate. The reporter ascertains
when this man was born and where, with what business activities
he was affiliated, the list of his clubs and the names of surviving
relatives. Of this one it is said that for forty years he was en-
gaged in the cotton market. Of another it may be related that
he helped to found an athletic club or was a dignitary in some
fraternal organization. And through any such wide-meshed set
of facts the real man must slip through.

Every individual is more than his job, his social activities and
his span of years. It is a pity that when each one of us dies the
essence may not survive, whether the person be notable or not.

In the heart of everyone there is the desire to know what will
be said about him in the papers. I remember a story of two years
ago about a dying newspaperman who called his wife to his bed-
side when his end was near and with his remaining store of
strength and voice dictated to her what he would like to have
printed about himself. As he wrote it the paragraphs appeared
humble and modest enough. But at least the dying man was
assured that the facts were straight.

What I have in mind are things less tangible. Somebody
called me on the telephone the afternoon of my father's death
to ask for some little information about him. I failed, because
there was much I forgot in the matter of mere material detail
and even more I left out because it hardly fell within the tradi-
tion of what constitutes a conventional obituary.

Later it seemed to me unsatisfactory that a man of long life
should have his existence summed up to some extent as "the
father of the newspaper columnist." Such a report shifts the
emphasis. It makes the wrong man seem the debtor.

And yet there are practical difficulties in presenting any true and live picture within the confines of limited newspaper space. Once there was written a complete portrait of my father, but by a man who never knew him. And this adequate portrait required the full generosity of a two-volume novel. If you play the game of identifying your friends with famous folk of fiction I can explain my father to you by saying that he was to the life Thackeray's Colonel Newcome with just a dash of Major Pendennis.

The reporter at the other end of the telephone would have been surprised if, instead of saying that Heywood Cox Broun was the founder of a printing business and a member of the Racquet and Tennis Club, I had said, "The most important thing to mention is that Mr. Broun was just about the most charming man anybody had ever known."

And yet this report would have been more accurate and vital.

I have always been interested in problems of heredity and the curious manner in which people are conditioned by ricochet rather than direct fire. For instance, there is the fact that my father was an ardent National Guardsman and at one time among the four or five crack rifle shots in the entire country. When I was a child the house was filled with gold and silver medals as tokens of this prowess. And I, his son, am a fanatical pacifist and have never so much as fired a gun in my life.

Yet there is consistency in this. We were always told, as children, never to point a gun at anybody—not even a cap pistol— and it is not altogether strange that I grew up with a feeling that there is something almost inherently evil in firearms.

When I went to tell him that I was running for Congress on the Socialist ticket he was a little surprised and yet not displeased, though I was turning on a road which ran almost at right angles from his highway. We kept close through many episodes in which I followed philosophies quite foreign to his own. We kept close because of his wisdom. All he ever wanted to know was whether I believed honestly and sincerely in the path which I had chosen. If I could convince him of that the thing I did was all right, whether or not he grasped the detail of my emotion or my reasoning.

And in some respects I have tried to follow more closely the tradition which he set. I take pride in the fact that my father was a gay man. That he liked to give and receive parties. For many years after he was well past seventy we kept, with all the ardor of a religious rite, a cocktail hour.

I have always felt that truly kindly people, like my father, must be men who have themselves a flair for fun. Only from the exuberant is it possible to get an enlivening return in the execution of the commandment "Love thy neighbor as thyself." Nor could his tombstone have a better inscription than this: "He took and gave much joy in life."

63. GABRIEL

I find my mind goes back to Gabriel.

Naturally, everybody feels bad when a good actor dies, and Wesley Hill was such a special kind of good actor. He had been on the stage for forty years, but I never saw him until *The Green Pastures* was produced. As a matter of fact, most of his early career was with medicine shows and traveling "Uncle Tom" troupes. I believe he had only a few previous Broadway appearances.

Of all the angels in the play Gabriel was the darkest. In fact, it would be pretty hard to be much darker than Wesley Hill. Nobody will be able to come along in the patronizing way of the Nordic to say, "Oh, yes, he was quite good, but that was on account of his white blood."

I don't think I ever saw any actor enjoy a role so much. He moved around the stage of the Mansfield like a child in a pageant. He was terribly glad to be playing Gabriel. That's why he was such a good Gabriel.

After all, one expects angels to be joyous.

To me heaven seems a much more attractive place ever since I saw *The Green Pastures* and Wesley Hill. Very few writers have been able to present an acceptable abode for the blessed. Any fool can do a hell.

The trouble with heaven in literature is that the fabricator practically always leaves humor out of it. There's too much jasper and not enough jokes.

But here at last was a twinkling angel. The spheres rolled in their courses, and so did his eyes.

It must have been difficult for him of an evening to take off his wings of gold and his green robe and go home to Harlem. For a little space in a theater every night he stood as a symbol of power. After all, he carried, slung around his neck, the trumpet, and he only needed to blow a few notes upon it to send the world crashing and blazing into empty space.

It has been remarked that after an actor plays Lincoln or Napoleon for a while he begins to act like the character. He carries the delusions of grandeur with him even into the Lambs Club. But Wesley Hill was never an angel except in the best sense of the word.

I met him at a Harlem fish fry which was given in honor of the author, the producer and Richard Harrison, who plays the Lord. The Lord and Gabriel were great friends both onstage and off.

Gabriel, as I knew him, was a person of infinite jest. He could make the daily transition from heaven to Harlem without loss of dignity or kindliness. In his role there was that gorgeous combination of a humor approaching even the farcical and an ability to turn it off, to hold up his hand, as it were, to say, "Not funny any more."

To him and to Harrison fell the greatest and the most dangerous moment in *The Green Pastures*. I have said several times that Marc Connelly put the play to the test in almost the first few minutes of the second scene. The fish fry is funny and meant to be, although even before the entrance of the Lord I have always been a little annoyed at such patrons as put their heads back and howl as if they were viewing sheer extravaganza. It wasn't as funny as all that. After all, it is a humorous heaven and not a clownish one.

And then comes the moment when nobody must laugh if the audience is going to prove worthy of its chance to collaborate in a great play. It is a startling line which was committed to the Angel Gabriel. In fact, it is to me almost the finest single line in modern drama—"Gangway for the Lord God Jehovah!"

It may be that the audience fails upon occasion. I have never seen it do so. Always there came a great silence, and, better than that, a rigidity. It was as if Gabriel had actually put his lips to the trumpet. We were all called to judgment.

Much has been said and written about Richard Harrison and the impressive simplicity and dignity of his entrance. Not half enough has been said. The evolution of a veteran elocutionist into a wholly convincing and natural actor has always seemed to me an authentic miracle of the theater.

But now that Gabriel is gone I am reminded of how much he contributed to that particular scene. If he had read the line of introduction wrong by so much as half a tone the Lord could hardly command the rapt attention which the situation requires. David Garrick couldn't.

Gabriel was eternally right. The chief comedian of *The Green Pastures* came to be for that moment the everlasting straight man.

And so I hope that somewhere in space and time a trumpet blows for him and that along the Milky Way and back of the furthest stars a voice in all ways adequate cries out, "Gangway for Gabriel!"

PART FOUR

1931-1936

64. THE *WORLD* PASSES

I sat and watched a paper die. We waited in the home of a man who once had run it. A flash came over the phone. The *World* was ended.

F.P.A. looked eagerly at a bowl of fruit upon the table and said, "Mr. Swope, where have you been buying your apples?"

The *World* fired me, and the *Telegram* gave me a job. Now, the *Telegram* owns the *World*. This is a fantastic set of chances almost like those which might appear in somebody's dream of revenge. But I never thought much of revenge. I wouldn't give a nickel for this one. If I could, by raising my hand, bring dead papers back to life I'd do so.

Sometimes in this column I have opposed the theories of those who would break up mergers, end chain stores and try the trick of unscrambling large-scale production. I've said that this could not be done—that it wasn't even expedient. In the long run the happiness of all of us depends upon increased efficiency and a shorter sum of toil. That's true. I still believe it. I wouldn't weep about a shoe factory or a branch line railroad shutting down.

But newspapers are different. I am a newspaperman. There are many things to be said for this new combination. It is my sincere belief that the Scripps-Howard chain is qualified by its record and its potentialities to carry on the Pulitzer tradition of liberal journalism. In fact, I'll go further and say that, as far as my personal experience goes, the *Telegram* has been more alert and valiant in its independent attitude than the *World* papers.

Yet I hope, at least, that this may be the end of mergers. The economic pressure for consolidation still continues. A newspaper is, among other things, a business. And, even so, it must be more than that. A lawyer at the hearing before Surrogate Foley expressed amazement that a paper which had lost almost $2,000,000 within a year could command any of that intangible value known as "good will." He was reasoning from the basis upon which fish are canned and wire wheels turned out.

A newspaper is a rule unto itself. It has a soul for salvation or damnation. I was pleased to hear much said about intangibles in all the accounts of the preliminary negotiations leading up to the present merger. I was glad that for once the emphasis was taken away from mere machinery. The fact of presses and lino-type equipment was never stressed in the proceedings. This didn't count. The intangibles of a newspaper are the men and women who make it.

First in America, and now in a frenzied form in Russia, there grows a cult which bows and bangs its head upon the floor in worship of the machine. In some calculations man is no more than a device to pull upon a gadget. But here, at last, there was talk of millions, and checks in huge amounts were passed—not for apparatus, moving belts and intricate mechanism. This was a deal for a name and for some of the people who contributed to the making of the name.

Since my feeling is strong that a newspaper can neither rise nor fall beyond or below its staff, I was stirred by the notion— the dream—that *World* men might take over the *World*. I realize, as they do now, the difficulties which lay in the path of any such plan. I'll readily admit that 1,000 to 1 would be a gen-erous price against any such undertaking. But we are, or ought to be, lovers of long shots. There's nothing particularly stirring when the favorite coasts home in front. Although the newspaper crowd didn't put their project over, it isn't fair to call this miss plain failure.

For almost the first time in my life I watched reporters ani-mated by a group consciousness. Newspapermen are blandly and, I think, blindly individualistic. Once I was president of a press writers' union. There were four members. The three others were the secretary, the vice-president and the treasurer. The treasurer never had much responsibility. Nobody would join us, because the average reporter carried in his knapsack the baton of a managing editor, or even the dim hope of being some day a dramatic critic. What did he want with organization? He stood on two feet—a single unit.

But for a time down in the *World* office there was the excitement, the hip-hip-hooray—call it even the hysteria—of mob movement, of people rubbing shoulders and saying, "We are in this boat together."

One of the things which would have made the fruition of the plan extremely difficult is the fact that a paper lives or dies by personality. When forty or fifty are banded together they must select a single one to be the leader and articulate representative. Still, in any dream of a co-operative commonwealth I've always had the feeling that newspapers most of all were fit subjects for some sort of socialization. I've never known even the most obscure reporter who didn't think he knew more about running a paper than the man who owned it. I've always felt that way myself. And once I was right.

The curious thing concerning the death of the *World* was the manner in which it became animate just before the final rattle within its throat. Within the last two or three years there must have been times in which the morale of the staff was low. Last night I went late to see the men I knew and had worked with long ago—that is, two years, or maybe three years, which is a long span in the life of any roving and rebellious columnist. I never found the paper pounding and pulsing quite so much as it did now—when it was dead.

We sat together in a very vigorous sort of democracy. At first I felt I might be out of place as one who was an ex-*World* man. But by four in the morning we were all "ex." We had ex-managing editor, ex-city editor and dozens of ex-reporters. For the first time within many months it was possible for somebody who covered a district to point the finger of scorn or accusation at somebody who had been his boss and spill his whole mind and emotion. You didn't have to "sir" anybody or say "very good" or "yes" unless you wanted to. Out of a situation which was certainly tragic to many there was at least a glimpse of that heaven in which we may all walk and between harp tunes look up and say with impunity to any passing angel or archangel, "Oh, is that so!"

Naturally, I have both hope and confidence in the new paper. Like John Brown's body, the *World* goes marching on. To heights, I hope. But something is gone. They aren't all marching. Men have dropped out. For them there will be nothing more on any newspaper, and I think of these casualties. I think of a profession which grows efficient and overcrowded. And to those who can no longer make the grade and who stand under the indictment of being not good enough I bow low, I swing my hat, as if it bore a plume, and say:

"Good, bad or indifferent, you have been in it. You belong. Some part of stuff set down on paper was you, and ever will be."

65. MORE OR LESS

James Joseph Walker spoke to a group of social workers at the City Hall on Wednesday, and he said: "I will confess I have been more or less shocked by the reports of the framing of innocent women."

But in this duel between "less" and "more" the former has won the day, for the city's chief executive is about to take a vacation of three or four weeks at Palm Springs, Cal., since of late he has been more or less under the weather.

I have no doubt that James Joseph Walker is ailing. In fact, I am surprised that he feels as well as he does. Much has happened of late which is naturally disturbing to any sensitive city official.

We all hope he has a helpful vacation. We would like to watch him return refreshed and swinging his right. He will see bright skies, snow mountains and a blazing sun in the lovely land to which he goes. Even the name Palm Springs is glamorous. It suggests an oasis set within an arid country. And there, I trust, the palms will be straighter and itch less than those of Tammany. And if mere scenery and sloth and sleep begin to pall the delights of the race track and the casino at Agua Caliente are within easy motoring distance.

But, though I grant that James Joseph Walker is sick, it seems to me unlikely that his health can be as precarious as that of the City of New York at the present moment. It is a pity that the mayor cannot take the metropolis with him on the trip. New York stands in need of scathing sunlight, fresh air and a fine rousing wind to cleanse its lungs and vitals. It is feverish and haggard from the invasion of infectious disease. Oh, yes, I think New York is by much the sicker of the two.

Apparently Mayor Walker differs with this diagnosis. To the social workers at City Hall he suggested the possibility that "it is only another case of shell shock, and I guess the city will get over it."

Any man, including a mayor, is entitled to his guess. But shell shock itself is a serious ailment. Quite often it results in a complete paralysis. And yet I think it is not the shell but the very substance of corruption which has shocked the city into a feeling of helplessness. We have every right to be shocked and "more," not "less," when several judges are proved to be crooked and certain police professional perjurers.

"Some of these reports have been exaggerated," says the mayor. Suppose only one woman had been framed. And even suppose that lone case had concerned a notorious harlot. Even then I think we should expect from the mayor something much stronger than "more" or "less."

More or less! The dead at least are definitely dead. There can be no more-or-lessing them back to life.

But Palm Springs is a pleasant place in which to sit and dream and let the world go by. And possibly James Joseph Walker in his waking hours may find time to express the pious wish and the friendly prognostication that "the city will get over it." The hours will drift pleasantly while he is counting sheep and forgetting goats.

It is quite likely that the mayor stands in need of a tonic. Not, I think, a nerve tonic. But there is such a thing as sickness of the will. And the cure for that lies in getting down to cases, in putting a shoulder to the wheel, in being a real mayor and not just "more or less" Jimmy.

I seem to see a willingness upon Mayor Walker's part to shift responsibility. In the same pleasant speech to the social workers he expressed a grave concern over the failure of civic organizations and great newspapers. He said:

"While the reports are revolting, I am at a loss to understand why organizations like yours, why our great newspapers with reporters in every court, did not discover the situation until it broke out in headlines."

In other words, the press has held out on James Joseph Walker. Apparently no reporter took the trouble to tell the mayor the facts of life in a great city. Somebody should blurt out to him the news that there is no Santa Claus within the ranks of Tammany. At least, only for a very restricted set of good little boys and girls. And somebody should tell him of the birds and flowers and of the edge which the crane retains over his phonetic cousin in the district attorney's office.

The crane is mightier than the Crain and much more stalwart. The crane stands on at least one leg.

It may be that James Joseph Walker will sleep more abundantly and restfully under the palms, but if a parable could conceivably dissuade him from the trip I'd like to remind him of an ancient jest used by Charlie Case—a popular monologist dead and gone these many years.

This story had to do with a railroad journey which he took in the company of his brother Hank. "Somehow," Case used to say, "there happened to be forty or fifty sheep in the same car with us. And when the train stopped the brakeman pulled us out, and he began to beat my brother Hank. Now, Hank was always my favorite brother. I didn't want to stand there and see him abused. And so I crawled under the car to the other side of the track."

I don't think the mayor will really profit by his trip to Palm Springs. I don't believe James Joseph Walker can crawl under to the other side, though he go to the ends of the earth. No matter where he goes or what he says, he will still see. And he will hear.

66. THE AGITATOR

In recent years the word "agitator" is almost always used as a term of reproach. In fact, the imagination supplies the prefix "red."

And yet the most casual survey must show that all causes— conservative or otherwise—have been furthered by agitation. The chief complaint leveled against the agitator is that he takes people who are content with their lot and makes them dissatisfied. This is the charge hurled against labor leaders who organize strikes in districts where unionization was not heard of before. And the manufacturers like to say, as in the case of Gastonia, that everybody was peaceful and happy before the agitators came.

It may be true that even in certain industries where pay is low and living conditions severe a bovinity can exist until some outsider calls attention to the rigors and injustices of the situation. But this process of rousing men and women to a thought of something better, or at least different, is most certainly not confined to radicals.

Many wholly conservative people subscribe large sums of money for foreign missions.

Now, obviously, the missionary is always an agitator. He may go to a South Sea island where trousers are quite unknown and stir the savages into putting on garments by making them ashamed of their previous lack of attire. You may say that this is a harmful and busybody sort of proceeding. In the case of the South Sea missionary I agree, but my point is that the theory of "let well enough alone" has been constantly violated by many who hold the admiration of the conservative community.

Take the case of Woodrow Wilson. When he returned from Paris and began to preach his theory that salvation from international disturbance lay in the League of Nations he qualified as an agitator. I happened to be in favor of the agitation which he conducted. Nevertheless, it would be foolish to deny that he went into communities and endeavored to place in the hearts of men a dissatisfied feeling about foreign relations which had not been there before. These communities were content with the old order of national rivalries, or, rather, they gave small heed to them.

And so I deny that it is an intrusion to tell a socially maimed or wounded person that he labors under a disability. A striking case was much reported in the instance of a young man who had been blind from birth. The anti-agitation school, in all logic, should have been against the operation which gave him sight. Never having seen the passing show he could not have worried about it a great deal. And yet it was within his due that a window into the world should be opened up for him.

In somewhat similar fashion it seems to me an excellent thing that men should take occasion to tell workers in backward communities that $15 a week is a pitiful wage, even if it is the rate to which they have become accustomed.

And going back into historical precedent, it can easily be maintained that Jefferson, Washington, Franklin, Patrick Henry and the rest were agitators. It was not in the mind of every colonist to rebel under the slogan "No taxation without representation." In all truth, many of the inhabitants of the original thirteen States suffered no palpable burdens under British rule. They had to be aroused to their disabilities.

And it was entirely in accord with much of our modern editorial comment for the Tories to maintain that the revolutionists were spreading ill-will in places where content had grown.

And no one would deny the reasonableness of fastening the title of agitator to William Lloyd Garrison. In fact, in his case, the epithet was constantly employed by the slaveholders of the South. It was their argument that Negroes who had never even known a dream of freedom were merely rendered restless by the strong words of the man in Boston. And restless they did become as the tingle of the abolition movement began to prick against dead nerve centers.

Few would insist now that the fruition of a dream should have been denied forever to these men, even if the vision was carried to them by an outsider.

The agitator in all fields of human endeavor is the person who insists, sometimes with violence, that the world as it stands is not good enough. This insistence partakes of a very necessary quality of life. Contented organisms have already felt the touch of degeneration.

In man or beast or microbe life consists of the desire to push out wider borders, to grow and move and explore domains which have been barricaded. Posterity has picked practically all its heroes from the agitators. They are the saints and the holy men of our religions.

And since this process of honoring the despised and the criticized has become so universal, we might sharpen our wits enough to refrain from hasty condemnation of all who would shake us out of lethargy. They may be disturbing. They may be a nuisance. But they are the corpuscles of the corporate being through which the waste and the stagnation of the status quo is turned into living tissue.

67. MURDER IN THE FIRST DEGREE

The jury came in with a verdict of murder in the first degree. It so happens that I am thinking of a particular case, but it will serve as a text chiefly because it was a trial not animated by any touch of the unusual. There was no news in the conviction or the inevitable sentence. This was simply a run-of-the-mill sort of murder. A man with a bad record stabbed an enemy. Nobody could question the guilt of the defendant or the justice of the penalty. That is, nobody who believes in capital punishment.

But I saw the man stand up as he looked upon the jury and jurors looked upon him. I sat far back and could not tell with what twitch of the features he received the verdict. He had his hands clasped behind him, and all he did was to lock his fingers a little tighter as they told him that he was guilty. That could hardly have been a surprise.

He knew it all along. Nevertheless, the fingernails bit into his flesh. And as the fingers tightened it was possible to notice the play of muscles across his back.

"What a magnificent body!" I thought to myself. And then I remembered that those same muscles would flex and tighten once more as the community carried out its intention to flick him away like a burned-out stub. It seemed to me a pity. It still seems a pity.

A lot of energy and time and vegetative planning went into the creation of those shoulder blades and the delicate mechanism of nerve and tissue. I could not keep from thinking of this John Doe as some sort of flowering shrub, because his individuality and his personal quirks and whimsicalities were not discussed during the trial. He killed a man and therefore must die.

There is a nice shiny surface of logic in the rule which holds that repayment for an eye must be in kind. A life for a life. It sounds like an algebraic equation. There is a sense of perfect balance. But the fiber of the reasoning is marred by a flaw. It does not constitute a literal transcript of the circumstances.

"Why," people often ask, "is there always sympathy for the criminal and none for his victim?" The answer is easy. The dead lie beyond our pity. By quelling the heartbeat of the assassin we do not set up a rhythm in the breast of the one who was stabbed. And if we pluck out the eye of an offender there does not exist a socket into which it may fit with any utility.

And so what we are really saying is not "A life for a life," but "A death for a death." We deal in depreciated currency. Nobody profits either in a spiritual or a material sense by the transaction.

Sometimes the victim of the knife or the bullet leaves behind him sons and daughters destitute by reason of his death. The killer owes them something very specific. And it seems to me that no very material adjustment has been made when the community comes to the bereaved ones to say: "The man who killed your father has paid the price. He was electrocuted at six o'clock this morning."

In all reason just what has he paid which is in any way tangible? Far from paying, he has been allowed—even compelled —to welsh out of a settlement. His crime constitutes an offense against certain individuals and against the community, and by all means I would have him pay. But the payment will have to be by service. Instead of being made to die he should be compelled to sweat.

Some few exist whose potentialities for social conduct are dim, but this does not hold for the majority of criminals. There is stuff there, even in spite of flaws and marks which mar them. The human body itself is not so much kindling wood to be lightly tossed upon the slag pile. I can think of no one to whom I would deny the chance for regeneration.

Possibly I am a little romantic, but when the dramatic moment came in Cuba for the decisive yellow fever tests I think it would have been eminently fitting to pass the call for volunteers along the corridor of some death house. In that event the code of "A life for a life" would have had some meaning. Only under such circumstances can we justly say, "This man who killed another now has his chance to pay the price."

You see, the fault lies so close to our own home. The failure of the criminal is always a joint stock enterprise. We mark him as unfit to live among civilized human beings, but it follows logically that we were inept in fitting this cog into the machine we built. Repair shops have been built for motors, but we scrap men.

If it were compulsory for every citizen of New York State to attend an execution once a year we would be done with capital punishment. We—and I mean all of us—are content to be hangmen because we walk softly and do not talk of rope at our parties. We neither see nor hear nor feel, damn our eyes! And damn our hearts and heads and the life force within us, too!

Out of the all but eternal ages comes a human being delicately knit. Even though moronic, there is the wisdom of the centuries in his spinal column. God has joined together cell and muscle, and this we tear asunder. And I have come to think that perhaps I have at last identified that mysterious crime which worried me when I was a child. This supreme impudence of conduct may well be the sin against the Holy Ghost.

68. WILLIAM NUCKLES DOAK

Senators and Representatives in Congress are forever rising to their hind legs and hollering about entangling alliances. While they are on the matter I wish some one of the people's servants would take up a problem which both perplexes and grieves me. I refer to the power and the perquisites extended to Benito Mussolini by American officialdom.

He has but to crook a finger or raise an eyebrow when anything within our borders happens to displease him, and straightway somebody is called upon the carpet or sent to prison.

You probably have heard of Orlando Spartaco, who received a sentence of two years for raising a commotion during a visit of Grandi to Philadelphia. And yet, I doubt if you are familiar with the precise facts, since it was generally and erroneously reported that the young anti-Fascist had leaped upon the running board of Grandi's car. I have before me a transcript of the case as it was conducted before a jury and Judge Harry S. McDevitt.

Officer Richard E. West, being duly sworn, testified as follows:

"I saw the car entering Sansom, from 24th, and I also saw a lot of excitement on the north side of Sansom, about twenty feet ahead of the car, and a man was hollering something in Italian, I didn't understand. Then the fists started to fly; so I rode the horse down, and this man here was hollering. . . . So I got hold of this man here and drug him from the crowd."

"Mr. Levinson: 'I want to ask the officer one question. I understood you to say that the fists were flying; you mean they were flying against this man?'

"Officer West: 'Absolutely.'

"Mr. Levinson: 'And you went in to rescue him from the crowd?'

"Officer West: 'Absolutely.' "

That is the entire vital evidence on which a young man was sentenced in an American court to a term of two years in jail.

Contrast this procedure with what happened following another incident which also occurred in Philadelphia a few months before the visit of Grandi. This time the visitor was Herbert Clark Hoover, the President of the United States. He had come to witness a world series game between the Cardinals and the Athletics. As the President left Shibe Park, a number of people in the stands shouted "boo," and made other derogatory sounds. Nobody was arrested.

Now, I am not endeavoring to encourage the practice of booing the President. I yield to no one in my dislike for Mr. Hoover, but I much prefer to vote and work against him than to make vague vocal outcries. I am merely indicating that whether it is bad sportsmanship, poor taste or what not, the forces of law and order in Philadelphia were prepared to accept the right of the citizenry to indicate disapproval of our Chief Executive. Then why be so tender about the feeling of Grandi or Mussolini?

I have a special and personal feeling for Orlando Spartaco because I once figured in a somewhat similar incident and received nothing more than a black eye. Happening upon an anti-Free State meeting, I heard a speaker declare that Michael Collins sold out for British gold. Collins had been killed only the day before, and to me seemed a heroic figure in Irish history. Accordingly I hissed. That was, if you like, an incitement to riot, only I happened to be the riot. It was the biggest black eye I have ever received.

Personally I have no enthusiasm for organized jeering sections, but I hold that the spontaneous right of raspberry should be denied to no one in America. Far from being sentenced to jail for two years, Orlando Spartaco should have been protected in his privilege of shouting the equivalent for "To hell with Mussolini."

I think it is about time that somebody informed all those in authority that Benito Mussolini is not a dictator among us. If the snoot of King George can be punched in absentio in Chicago, there is no reason why Mussolini should not be razzed in Philadelphia.

And in particular I wish to have this fact called to the attention of Doak, the deporter. William Nuckles Doak he was inappropriately christened. N. D. Doak, or Nuckles Down Doak, would have been so much more fitting. He seems to be under the impression that dislike of Mussolini is a sort of sedition which makes a man liable to be sent back whence he came.

All I can say is get the transportation ready. I don't like Mussolini, even if that means that I must live in Brooklyn.

69. WE THE TINDER

"The Lord's going to set this world on fire—some of these days. You better git ready!"

The beat of the song has been with me for a week. It began in a room where people were dancing, but they danced to *Who Cares?* I can't remember the lyric, but it's something about "if banks fail in Yonkers" and "I love you."

"Who cares if the skies fall . . . tum, te, tum, te, tum." But the Lord is going to set this world on fire some of these days.

We are tinder for the coming of a great revival. We do care, even if we still seem sodden to every spark.

Of course we care, even though all the dervishes whirl to some variation of the theme. America first. No dole. Rugged individualism. We have followed the pipers down into the pit of the valley.

"The Lord's going to set this world on fire—some of these days."

My eye runs over a batch of morning papers, and I see: "Dies Game, Grins in Chair." "Manresa, Spain—A republic of Soviets is hereby declared. All acting against it will be shot immediately." "Woman of Seventy Holds Thirteen Spades." "Madrid, Spain—'I am going to give them back as good as they send!' declares Premier Azana." "Bombay Thousands Defy Police Staves." "Pittsburgh, Pa.—Unless immediate relief is provided 2,300 persons in nearby mining regions will starve." "Japanese Threaten Chinese in Shanghai." "Thugs Steal $349,-000 Gems." "Thuringian Villages Menaced by Starvation." "Trade Barriers Grow." "Calls on America to Arm."

Some of these days.

And so I turned to the brief paragraphs of Will Rogers. He has made himself famous because he sublimates American common sense. Here is what he says: "All Europe is looking for us to do all the debt canceling, so don't send delegates with hardened arteries, as usual, but get some with hardened hearts, for these people are even rehearsing their crying now."

Some of these days.

People in Germany starve, and in the streets of London huddle ragged men and women. It's all a device to bamboozle Hiram Johnson and Alfalfa Bill Murray. But it has served to give Will Rogers a quip. That ought to warn these scarecrows across the sea. There's nothing like a good joke.

Men with hardened hearts. Yes, that's the old formula. They have been the rulers of the world. Did Caesar scruple or Napoleon blanch at the sight of blood? The Old Guard dies but never surrenders. Don't fire till you see the whites of their eyes. We'll hang Jeff Davis to a sour apple tree. Remember the *Maine*, and make the world safe for democracy.

The Lord's going to set this world on fire—some of these days.

Some of these days there will sweep across the mountains and the plains a great wind which will stir the surface of the waters and the hearts of men. Even those with the hard hearts will feel the throb of the new day as if it were a pulse. Some of these days.

And I remember no thunder of the prophets, but by that curious twist of associated ideas a scene from an old melodrama by Augustus Thomas called *The Witching Hour*.

"You can't shoot that gun. You can't even hold it."

I saw them do just this at a Lambs' Gambol a few weeks ago, and I remember the startled look on the face of the villain as the revolver clattered to the floor.

And the men with the hard hearts will find, to their surprise, that they cannot hold the guns against the multitudes of marching men who come on and on from every corner of the globe. They will be invincible, for they bring with them no guns but the glory of brotherhood.

Some of these days.

It is said that such talk is fantastic and hysterical. There is a disposition to point out the hatreds of the world. An eye for an eye, a death for a death. And the deep abiding fear. Johnny, get your gun.

And the men of the hard hearts maintain that hatreds and fears can be eliminated by adjusting gunsights and sharpening the bayonet's edge. They would say that. They always have.

But some of these days—

70. GOVERNOR ROLPH SPEAKING

"Mooney was justly convicted," said Governor James Rolph, Jr., of California, in "a firm and measured voice."

But the voice was not firm enough or loud enough.

And what was the measure meted out to Mooney? It should have included a fair and honest answer to just one question. By every dictate of honor and justice Governor Rolph was under obligation to take to his heart this elementary problem—"Guilty or not guilty?"

It now turns out that this was the one phase of the case to which Governor Rolph paid no attention whatsoever. Almost five months have passed since the last formal application was made for a pardon. Governor Rolph would have the world believe that during all that interval he was "studying" the case, that he lay down with it at night and woke each morning to cogitate complexities.

This is sheer fiction. Much is made by Governor Rolph and his associates of the fact that no new testimony was introduced. That is correct. The last hearing was no more than the recital of an ancient wrong. A brave man, whether a rogue or an honest executive, could have given his decision in ten seconds. Governor James Rolph, Jr., of California, is not a brave man.

Even before he announced his surrender to big business, little business and apathy he indicated a lack of decent regard for the issue. His notion that injustice is a thing to be ruled upon at one's leisure indicated a bluntness of ethical sensitivity. And what came out of the silences into which the Governor traveled with Judge Matt I. Sullivan, former justice of the State Supreme Court?

In so far as the newspaper extracts go the learned jurist devoted himself not to a judicial finding but to an arrogant apology for a dirty deed. This man who sat upon the bench has the impudence to present the public with a mass of comment wholly irrelevant. I quote from the learned gentleman's report:

"For instance, Professor Einstein, the famous scientist, has joined the army of those protesting against the further imprisonment of Mooney and Billings. Unfortunately, this good man and great scientist knows as much about Mooney and Billings and the case against each as they know about Einstein's inexplicable theory of relativity."

So what? Guilty or not guilty? How can it conceivably be any part of the Honorable Matt Sullivan's job to discuss Einstein's mathematics or motives?

And again from the honorable one:

"The I.W.W. in practically every locality throughout the United States contributed liberally to the defense fund. Reds and radicals of every shade made their contributions. Workers in Russia and the United States likewise contributed. Anarchists, socialists, communists and syndicalists were in the list of donors."

But guilty or not guilty? Since when did it become a crime subject to life imprisonment for a worker to win the support of his fellows in his fight against injustice?

And just one more segment from the report of Matt the mighty:

"Mooney pleaders must be ignorant of the past life of Mooney, his record as dynamiter, his public and private utterances in favor of anarchy and revolution, his publication of the *Revolt*, his connection with the Blast and Blasters."

But, Your Honor, Mooney was not tried for the expression of radical opinions. He was not ostensibly tried on the charge that he was a militant labor leader who believed in direct action. He was sent to jail on the charge that he bombed a parade in San Francisco on July 22, 1916.

How say you? Guilty or not guilty as charged? Are you judge or herring tosser?

Mooney pleaders are not ignorant of the fact that Mooney is a radical agitator. He has made no secret of it at any time before his trial or since. We who demand his freedom know that, just as well as we know that Governor Rolph is a peanut politician and the Honorable Matt I. Sullivan is a convenient counsel for that same governor. And in these facts we find no adequate answer to the cry, "Guilty or not guilty?"

"Three of my predecessors," said Governor Rolph in extenuation—Governor William D. Stephens, Governor Friend W. Richardson and Governor C. C. Young—"to each of whom an application was made by Thomas J. Mooney for a pardon, denied such application."

And accordingly we are asked to accept injustice because it has been compounded by four timorous men instead of one. "This should end the agitation for once and all," says the New York *Sun*. Quoth the craven, "Nevermore."

"In a firm and measured voice." The governor had nothing to talk down but the whisper of conscience and the still, small voice of truth. He was louder for the moment. A breeze stirred the leaves. It was nothing. But the wind rises. Pin your ear to the ground, Governor. Listen to the rumble. It is not settled. It is not done. Truth can be and truth will be a tempest. Four little governors and a former judge will not be enough to stand before it. A lie may live and even wriggle after it has been spiked, but not beyond the sundown.

71. AL'S HOUR

Chicago, July 1 [1932]—I'd rather be right than Roosevelt. And if I just had to be a Democrat, why, then I'd be Al Smith.

If and when Al fails to get the nomination I know a young producer who would love to feature him in an intimate revue, for in spite of competition Alfred E. Smith has proved himself the greatest performer of all the troupe now playing in Chicago.

This might seem merely the reiteration of a well-known circumstance, but for the fact that there was doubt this time before Al came through. He didn't rehearse very well. The Huey Longs, Alfalfa Bills and other acts from the small time seemed to have caught the public eye before the big show went on.

Even some of Al's best friends went around before the first night shaking their heads and saying that the hop on the fast one wasn't there any more. He was a good fellow when he had it, was about the best that they could muster.

And then Senator Walsh said: "The chair recognizes the Hon. Alfred E. Smith, a delegate from the State of New York." And there was for a split second that curious humid hush which comes just before the wind sweeps over the valley and the lightning begins to shoot its fangs at chimneys and tall maples.

It was so in the Chicago Stadium, for the storm broke in the topmost gallery and swept down across the forest of delegates and up to the platform wall and over. Al stood there with the wind of popular acclaim beating around his head and shoulders. And he liked it.

I don't know how he felt about it, but any man would be a fool to swap those minutes for a term, for two terms, for an eternity in the White House. When did 20,000 people ever reach out in that way and pat a President between the shoulder blades and cry out to him, "Ataboy!"? No, we vote for Presidents; we pull the lever and put 'em away and forget about them.

The galleries cried "Al! Al!" as if their hearts would break. And the man from Fulton Market smiled for a while and then began to weep. Suddenly he broke through the din with that curious voice, half Caruso and half Tenth Avenue. When Al speaks the nose has it. It cuts like a sharp blade, a fish knife, through the uproar. Al carries his own gavel in his larynx.

He began to operate on Cordell Hull, who was already cut and bleeding. "The fact," rasped Smith, "that the Senator only found out in the last three days that there is sentiment for repeal is just too bad." With a right and a left, a left and right, Smith tore into the arguments of the Tennessee dry and the crowd stood up as if this were truly a main bout for a title and not merely a political convention.

Cordell Hull had quoted from a statement of Al's made during the 1928 campaign which was obviously far less dripping in its temper than the majority prohibition plank for which Smith was now speaking.

"That was four years ago," said Smith savagely. "Did the Senator agree with me then? He did not. And because I happened to be four years ahead of my time, look what happened to me."

I think it is true that Al does move, and I am for the men who know the difference between last year's little old camel and a present porcupine. And even so, I believe that the most progressive and radical of us should still adhere to some fixed point and tie the craft of our hopes to some ancient pier upon occasion, so that those who have been far away upon returning will know where to find us.

Al referred to the Republican Convention and said: "I promised myself to listen to it on the raddio." And the walls came tumbling down.

I suppose that, among the many reasons which induced millions to vote against Al Smith four years ago, not an inconsiderable number of thousands were alienated by the fact that he chose to call the instrument which brings crooners to our homes "the raddio." I did not sit in upon party councils, but it is inevitable that this fact was brought to his attention by friends and advisers. But Al is no man to swap a pronunciation while crossing a stream. He will change neither a "d" nor a devotion no matter how the vote may go. "Raddio" it was and "raddio" it shall remain though it splits the Solid South and tears untrammeled Democracy asunder.

Accordingly, when his name was placed in nomination I did a thing which is against the rules of the Convention Correspondents' Union and of other organizations to which I am committed. I joined the parade upon the floor and shouted: "Smith! Smith! Smith!"

My cold-blooded, or at least my fairly tepid, newspaper judgment assures me that he isn't going anywhere. And yet the 20,000 and one other never had a misgiving. We'd like to go along.

72. FRAU ZETKIN

In the parliaments of the world there have been many moments of great intensity. The very fact that legislative bodies are made up of conflicting forces affords the material for that clash of will which is the essential element in drama. But of all the shows put on by men and women gathered for the making of laws none can have surpassed the present opening of the Reichstag.

"I was born July 5, 1857. Is there anyone here older?"

This was the opening challenge of Frau Clara Zetkin as she stood at the speaker's desk, supported by two younger comrades of her party. It is the German rule that the session shall be called to order by the senior member of the Reichstag.

And so it fell to the grandmother of the German revolution to have the first word in a house in which the Communists constitute a bitter and a desperate minority. Frau Zetkin has been

ill, and her voice was criss-crossed with the ravages of time and
rebellious controversy.

And yet she hardly needed the strong arms of her supporters
as she flung out her challenge. For she looked to the Nazis—
row upon row of them, clad each in uniform for the first time
in any Reichstag. It was at these followers and disciples of the
mailed fist that she hurled all the strength of her seniority.
They sat silent, with arms folded, for her frailty was a power
which left them helpless.

"Is there anyone here older?" said the tiny, bent figure,
flaunting her years like a flag in the face of her foes. And, of
course, there was none. In 1857 the twilight of the czars was
not even a dream. Kings walked on earth which trembled, and
slaves tilled American fields.

But she did not come to tell them about the back of the book
or to call the roll of mighty dead men. She spoke of a new
world and a promised land this side of Jordan. And there was
in the small, strained voice the intensity and anxiety of one who
cannot wait.

The tradition of the chamber was broken when Frau Zetkin
utilized the formal occasion for a fiercely partisan attack upon
Von Hindenburg and called for his impeachment. The general
is more than eighty. Perhaps this is not yet a young man's
world.

It was too serious and stern for comedy, but surely there was
irony in this duel—a fight about tomorrow between those al-
ready weary with the years and days. It was as if two spent
hourglasses should lunge and lock in final combat.

And, though a gulf has always been spread between the mili-
tary chief and the violent revolutionary, there was evident a
forgotten and unacknowledged kinship. Hindenburg has many
times called on his countrymen to give force to the uttermost
and to fight and die for the Fatherland. And with a voice so
feeble that it could not reach to more than a few rows of the

silent house Frau Zetkin called upon her followers to take up arms and check the threat of war by shooting down all who believe in ruthlessness.

She lashed with her tongue as cowards all who would not seek peace by wading first in blood. Her hoarse voice broke, and she leaned back for a moment against the arms of the two women who stood beside her. Yet each time she straightened again and cried out for men to man the barricades and solve the economic crisis with proletarian bayonets. There was in her no more compromise than lies in a belt of machine gun bullets.

And yet it seems to me that there sounded above the head of Frau Zetkin a cry which dimmed her words. The thing she is became much louder than what she said. A little old woman told the members of the Reichstag that salvation lies only in the fierce thrust of steel to be taken up by oppressed and embattled workers.

And yet she herself was the living, flaming proof that force does not lie only in the gun racks. A puff of wind, a touch of the hand could have thrust her from her place upon the speaker's stand. But there was none dared raise that hand.

She was for her cause a regiment, a brigade, an army with banners. The Nazis in their uniforms seemed no more than sulky pupils kept in after school.

I wish Frau Zetkin could have sat a little apart from herself and listened to the speech she made. Then she might well have known the supreme truth which she created and spread out for the profit of mankind. There is no force which can stand against a fierce, a free and stalwart spirit. The voice of such a one is louder than the roll of guns. And though it sags down to a whisper, it will be heard around the world.

73. APES AND ELMS

New Haven should be gay and all agog after its striking football victory over Harvard. But Yale is gloomy, suspicious and furtive, and all because of a little rumor.

Several years ago a fund was left for the care and rearing of apes by the psychologists of Yale. At first there was a feeling that it might be necessary to lower the entrance requirements, but this scare soon blew over.

Every prospect was pleasing except the climate. The anthropoids could "Boola Boola" with the best of them, but they couldn't stand the chilling breezes from the Sound. Some three years ago the suggestion was made that the colony should be moved to Florida. In fact, an official announcement was made to this effect. There was some comment in the newspapers at the time, in which, as I remember, I joined, offering appropriate condolences to the football coaches.

According to the present rumor, the transfer never took place. The coaches and the psychologists sat down in secret conference, and one of the football men offered a way out of the difficulty. It was a practical suggestion, and the psychologists had never thought of it.

"Africa is a moist, warm country," began the coach.

"Yes," replied one of the professors testily, "and the American Great Lakes are the largest bodies of fresh water in the world. What about it?"

"Just this," said the coach; "when the wind blows free and cold what does a Yale man do?"

"He goes out for hockey," suggested an assistant professor, trying to get into the spirit of the proceedings.

"No, no," said the football mentor; "I mean what does he wear?"

Since the psychologists were all trained observers, it didn't take the head of the department long to answer, "A gray suit of clothes with a thin green stripe, a sweater with a large 'Y,' a purple necktie, pink and magenta woolen socks, occasionally underwear—except in Sheff, of course, and a raccoon coat."

"Now you've got it," said the coach.

"You mean that we should give 'Y's' to all the anthropoid apes in the Yale ape farm so that they can wear sweaters?" the assistant professor asked. He was a little duller than the rest, which was the reason why they made him an assistant professor.

"Not at all," exclaimed the athletic instructor; "that would cheapen the 'Y.' Let them earn it like everyone else. Under proper direction an undergraduate is just as good as the best anthropoid on the campus any day in the week. I mean give the apes raccoon coats and then who on earth will know the difference?"

"Done and done," cried the professors and clapped their hands in glee. They swore a mighty oath of secrecy, and the janitor of the building where they met was let in on the compact so that there should be no leak.

Yale athletic prowess boomed mightily, and it was not until last spring that any inkling of suspicion crept out. It was an unfortunate occurrence.

I am not referring to the slight unpleasantness which was created when it was discovered that a gorilla had been selected for Phi Beta Kappa. After all, that was known only to the few who watched the poor fellow cling to the chandelier and chatter when they approached him with a key. No, I mean the little scandal which marred the last tap day.

"Go to your room!" said a senior to a stalwart athlete, slapping him on the shoulder. He went, but to the horror of all beholders he reached it by swinging through the branches of an elm, and in transit he paused long enough to heave down a few coconuts.

The story never got out, and all the newspaper correspondents agreed to suppress it. But I think that sound journalism should not only permit but require some mention of the extraordinary episode which occurred in the Bowl immediately after the Harvard game. After all, some 50,000 people were present. And I for one will not keep silent.

As the final whistle blew, a substitute Yale tackle bounded from the bench and ran to the goal posts. Some thought that under the excitement of the victory he was intent on tearing down his own posts. But he did nothing of the sort. Leaping high in the air, he swung from the cross-beam. Even that could have been pardoned as a bit of youthful exuberance but for one little fact. He swung by his tail.

And so today there are gloom, suspicion, and furtiveness down at Yale. Indeed, it has grown to such an extent that whenever one undergraduate makes an offensive remark to another —be it in classroom, study or parlor—it is customary to answer, "Take off that raccoon coat!"

74. BRING ON THE ARTIST

New names seem effective in the promotion of new worlds.

Technocracy, for instance, is sweeping the country on account of a new label, in spite of the fact that most of the assertions which it makes are entirely familiar. And so I think I'll try to start a movement of my own. It will be called "artistocracy" and must inevitably be in violent conflict with the theories of Mr. Scott.

If I understand the new messiahs they believe that we can be saved only by handing over our lives and beings to the engineers. The Utopia which I have in mind would be not only willing but grateful in its reception of the statistics of the technocrats. But we would like a different sort of leadership.

We have had enough of engineers, great or otherwise. We want the world turned over to the artists as generalissimos. Nor is this still another subterfuge by which fascism may be introduced under some other name. The artist has never been a dictator, since he understands better than anybody else the variations in human personality.

But he has been kept on the sidelines far too long. In every age the artist has been the critic and the counselor of the prevailing social system. Yet always he has been called in after the event. His function has been to scourge the follies of his day as satirist or to bind up the wounds of a bleeding world in this role as a sort of sentimental Red Cross worker.

Even in the last ten minutes of play there has been no disposition to let him go on the field and actually take part in the play. And he has been held back because of the conception that he was visionary and impractical. Now, of course, he should immediately accept the impeachment and after pleading guilty say, "So what?"

His best argument is that the world has been run by realists, and look what they have done to it. I'm not quite sure that I would argue that Edna St. Vincent Millay should upon the instant become the president of the Chase National Bank. It might not be a bad idea, at that, and surely it would be less preposterous than life under the decisions of the little group of hard-boiled men who met after the great war to found a peace.

There was in that number one who had some fragmentary inspiration of the visionary. Woodrow Wilson, curiously enough, broke more trench lines than any general in the American army. He swept back resistance and dislodged gunners from concrete pillboxes by introducing a formula, by flashing before the world the dream of a new world.

It is palpable that he failed, and generally it is held that his defeat at Versailles was brought about by the fact that he was not sufficiently practical. The reverse is the case. Woodrow Wilson could not forget that he came up from Princeton to the Presidency.

He fancied himself as one who could meet the political bosses of the world on their own ground and conquer them, even as he got the better of the Democratic machine in New Jersey. He traded bits of his bright dream here and there for things which seemed at the moment practical. And whenever he bargained off some section of the rainbow he was hornswoggled.

The children of darkness are shrewder in their own generation than the children of light. A dream is so much more valuable than anything else that all who engage in such barter are sure to go away from the market place poorer than when they entered.

Woodrow Wilson needed a more clear-cut devotion to his vision. He was ruined and vanquished when certain European slickers paid him the dubious compliment of calling him a practical man.

I have said that there is a certain shrewdness in the children of darkness, but I would keep a strong string on that admission. The advantages which they gain either for themselves or their nations are largely fallacious. The time has come to shelve these men who cannot see more than twenty-four hours or even less beyond the end of their long noses. The world is now in a state where it should call upon the impractical for advice and counsel.

Many a crumbling civilization has been given force and meaning only through the contribution of its writers and painters and sculptors. One remembers both Greece and Rome not through their legislators but only because of the men who piled word upon word or marshaled marble blocks.

And so let us agree even before downfall that these are the important men in any community. Instead of having them mold memorials to something which is gone we should intrust them with a vital part in the plan of birth and growth.

The captain and the kings have departed. Call in the artists to make the bright new world out of their most shining visions.

75. WHERE MINK MEETS MINK

I have always been curious as to why Rome fell, and I have my own theory.

Very probably one of the causes of the decline of the empire was the fact that the patricians began to arrive late at the circuses.

Some commoner who was intent on watching a lion just about to devour a Christian suddenly had his view cut off by a dinner party which barged in half an hour after the beginning of the show. The usher came down the aisle and said: "Let me see your stubs. Are you sure you have the right seats?" And the people in the belated detachment couldn't seem to make up their minds whether Mildred should sit next to Jack or whether Betty should go in first.

By the time they decided that problem and allowed the poor commoner to have an unobstructed line of vision to the arena the Christian was gone, and nothing remained but a rather smug and satisfied lion.

It spoiled the commoner's fun for the whole evening, and when he got home he said to his family that the show was a flop and would be in cut rates within the week. He even spoke ill of the whole imperial system and ventured the opinion that Rome wasn't what it used to be.

You see, the patrician party insisted on carrying on a loud conversation all through the gladiatorial combats. The poor fellow was so distracted that he didn't have any clear conviction as to whether he should put his thumbs up or down. As a matter of fact, in his irritation he kept them down, which was a little unfair to the victim in the arena, because what the serious student of the sport really meant was that he wished the cackling crowd behind him were all Christians and suitable for casting in the next blue plate offering to the lions.

I have a strong feeling that something of the same sort is going on today. The most effective propagandists for the radical cause are the very rich. Of course, the cult of flagrant bad manners does not extend throughout the entire length of Park Avenue. Here and there any fair-minded revolutionist would mark a white cross. But he wouldn't need much chalk.

It seemed to me that the worst exhibition of boorishness I had ever seen in the theater occurred at the opening of *The Gay Divorcee*, but at that time I had not attended the first night of *Design for Living*.

There can be reasonable excuses for arriving late, but that is only a small portion of the indictment. Those who showed up anywhere from fifteen minutes to half an hour late came whooping into the lobby and down the aisles. The later they arrived the more noise they made as they swished down the aisle. One theater party, which occupied an entire row, swept in a full fifty minutes after the curtain had risen. And they behaved as if they were changing the guard at Buckingham Palace.

It seems to me that the ermined and sabled are under some illusion that they should be preceded by footmen with silver trumpets wherever they go. Nor does any signal to cease firing occur when Park Avenue is finally in its place and ready to see what the mimes have to offer. I want some day to see a Broadway opening without benefit of footnotes. I'd rather not be told by the lady just ahead that a line is "delicious" or "so quaint." I'd rather be surprised.

Indeed, since the play is hardly the thing, I suggest strongly to the leaders of New York society that they hire some one of the abandoned playhouses of the town and hold nightly receptions in the orchestra and the lobby, leaving the stage quite untenanted. As things stand now the later diners are under a sad disadvantage. At times when Mildred greets Mary a full four rows ahead the cheerful salutation is almost drowned by the hum of the actors' speaking lines. Some of our players have begun to forget the dictates of the recent realistic school and are actually audacious enough to try to make themselves heard.

And I would cite also the matter of intermission manners. It is quite true that many of New York's theaters are architecturally at fault. It is difficult under the best of circumstances to reach the outer air or lounge, and exit is hardly expedited by the current practice of those who reach the end of the aisle or a narrow doorway and there take up their stand, as if they were Spartans defending the pass at Thermopylae.

I wish that in my school days I had been a superb plunging fullback instead of a mediocre guard. Even so, when next I attend the theater I plan to equip myself with leather headgear, and when I get home I hope to find it all splotched with mangled ermine.

76. THEY WILL COME BACK

"And we are not coming back!" shouted a spokesman of Japan.

He was announcing the decision of his nation to leave the League and retain Manchuria. There came from the galleries some applause at this gesture of defiance.

But in spirit at least there was present an old gentleman full of dignity and years. He carried an hourglass and a scythe.

"And we are not coming back!" shouted the orator, filled with the fervor of aggression and the nascence of nationalism.

"Is that so?" said the old man under his breath. For he had seen the elephants of Hannibal go up to the Alps and over. He had watched the legions of Caesar tramp through the Druid groves of ancient Britain. He heard the tears of Alexander and saw the bloodstains on the snow in the retreat from Moscow.

And while the elders at Geneva talked the soldiers of Japan stormed Kailu and Chaoyang. They drew the ring more closely around Jehol, the golden city and the pleasant place of Emperors. And it was said in Tokio: "This is our destiny. Let the old men talk. We will act. History is on our side."

Of all inconstant allies history is fickle beyond the rest. It follows the call of a silver trumpet which may sound suddenly at night, and on that instant the forces of destiny, the horsemen and the footmen, gray as cats and big beyond belief, change sides, with banners flying.

Above the heads of this shadowy army on the march there flies the bird of victory, circling about and seeking some new standard upon which to perch.

Destiny never moves in straight lines but twists and turns, and, though the arc be great, it will return to its own citadel, which bears the curious name of Beginning of the End.

And in the great hall one may see the tattered banners of proud brigades and some other dim mementos of empires that once cluttered the earth with their majesty and might.

The light is thinly filtered in. The dust lies deep upon the floor, but all who pass by may read upon tablets of brass the names of the men and of the nations which once were things of sound and fury. And there is some strange enchantment in the place, for it is possible for no one to speak of these dead and forgotten expeditionary forces above a whisper. There is no echo.

"And we are not coming back."

Oh, yes, you will, Japan. There is a force, and the empire of which you dream will trickle down until it is one with the lost lands of Julius Caesar.

Not in Japan alone but in many other quarters it is held that the word of the wise men matters little and that destiny is on the side of the big guns and the tanks. "Read history!" cried Matsuoka to the League.

Look well, oh, men of Nippon. Read history. Read it and weep, for it tells in every chapter of the downfall of imperial adventure and the strong tides which set for human rights. A decent regard for the opinions of mankind is not a thing lightly to be thrown overboard.

It has been said of the League of Nations that it has proved impotent in the present crisis. I disagree. It seems to me that the reading of the roll, in which every nation except Japan and Siam voted for censure, marked a new manifestation of world solidarity.

I will grant that it did not on the instant check the armies as they moved over the frozen terrain toward Jehol. But it has put Japan upon the defensive in an important way. Even within the borders of the island empire doubt has been sown.

I do not expect to see the outside powers thrust Japan back from selfish adventure. I believe with all my heart that the better way will come from within the Japanese people themselves. Public opinion may seem to be no more than a fingertip laid upon the wrist in the beginning. But its force grows. It tightens. It is a mightier ring than that of men and machine guns which encircles the golden city.

They will come back.

77. THE TALE OF AN ANCIENT WRONG

A sailing ship came down the tide and cast her anchor over. She rode the long swell and waited for boats from the blazing coast to bear her black slaves. When they were below deck she picked up her pin and headed for America.

That was more than two hundred years ago. Yesterday in Decatur, Ala., a jury of twelve white men brought in a verdict of death against Haywood Patterson. The attorney general of the great sovereign state referred to him as "that thing."

They say it was a quiet courtroom and a gentle day down in Morgan County when the jury filed in after twenty-four hours of deliberation. But could none of them hear the wind in the rigging of the slave ship, the creaking of her timbers and the cries of the cargo?

That ghostly ship has steered her course around our coasts and even up into the backwaters times innumerable. She seeks in vain a final haven. We, the grandsons and the great-grandsons of the slaves of the slavers, are not appeased. We have not forgiven the Negro. It is less difficult to forgive your enemies, but the persecution of the Negro continues because we have wronged him so vastly and so vitally. We are bound to the wheel of our damnation and try to stave it off with silly postures and cruel antics. Fear grips us, and we sheer off even from an act of simple justice.

Attorney General Knight could not even bring himself to admit that he was in the presence of a man on trial for his life. He had to take refuge in such a phrase as "that thing." He was afraid of the facts. He had reason to fear.

There was much panicky talk in the speeches of the men who pressed the case. "Show them that Alabama justice cannot be bought and sold with Jew money from New York!" cried Solicitor Wright at one point in the trial. And the attorney general, after deploring the injection of prejudice by his associate in the summation, went on to say: "If you acquit this Negro put a garland of roses around his neck, give him a supper and send him to New York City. There let Dr. Harry Fosdick dress him up in a high hat and morning coat, gray striped trousers and spats."

And that was because Dr. Fosdick had told Ruby Bates to face the danger of return and go back to confess that she lied when first she accused the Negro boys. And that was because the attorney general was afraid.

If human life were not at stake this Scottsboro case might take rank with the most inspired of all extravaganzas, but the shadow of the chair falls across such ironic ribaldries as the conviction of a Negro field hand on the ground that Alabama does not like the modes and manners of New York City. Instead of a crown of thorns, Alabama rhetoric pressed down a high hat upon this poor laborer.

But the irony of the situation swings wide beyond the borders of the state where the trial was held. Does the learned counselor from the Southland actually believe that the song of the slave ship never floats above the roofs of Harlem? Instead of the fantastic festival outlined by the prosecutor, what would New York really have to offer any Haywood Patterson? Morning coats and garlands? Not exactly. The great and free city of New York would afford him an opportunity to share a three-room apartment with nine or ten of his fellows. And only with the best of luck would he be able to pay the rent.

The South imposes rather more lynchings, legal and otherwise; New York and Chicago take it out in tuberculosis.

We have no right to sit in the seats of the scornful. Nor is it the part of wisdom to think of the Scottsboro case as a local issue. We will get nowhere if comment merely takes the form of attacks upon the legal machinery of Alabama and charges that Decatur opinion is blinded by bigotry. That would merely be a matter of the mote calling the beam black.

As a matter of fact, some wise words were spoken during the trial. "The world at this time and in many lands is showing intolerance and showing hate. It seems sometimes that love has almost deserted the human bosom. It seems that hate has taken its place. . . . Wrong dies and truth forever lasts, and we should have faith in that."

That was said by the judge—James E. Horton. Well, Your Honor, when it comes time to pass sentence of death how are you going to plead? Remember that you and all the rest of us are on trial for our faith, our integrity and our lowest common decency. What say you? Guilty or not guilty?

Speak up, man! Let us all speak up and prove that we are not guilty of this monstrous thing. Let us scuttle the slave ship in forty fathoms and stop that whine of the wind in its rigging.

78. THE BURNING OF THE BOOKS

They burned the books, but there remains a red glow in the sky. The fuel of the foolish was curiously assorted. Upon the Nazi bonfire were piled the works of some who never glowed before. I had not thought to live into a day when sparks would fly from Morris Hillquit.

The names of the great, the near and never great came to the crucible along with the words of the lame, the halt and the blind. Side by side the magnificent and the feeble words of those who merely meant well ascended to heaven.

Unconsciously the Nazis paid a singular tribute of respect to certain authors of small fame and rather meager merit. What wouldn't I give to have some forgotten book of my own suddenly become fortuitously a part of a pillar of fire by night! I really must buckle down to work and write something which Hitler does not like in order to be in on the next illumination. Yes, and I will even consent to call it to his attention.

Remarque, Ludwig, Mann, Karl Marx, Jack London and Ben Lindsey! It sounds almost like what some of the book critics call "a balanced ration." But why Ben Lindsey? He seems to me one of God's noblemen and also among the most fearsomely bad writers who ever set an earnest pen to paper.

They burned the books of Dr. Sigmund Freud. One of the barkers at the bonfire explained that the little man from Vienna had put too much stress upon "the animal qualities of human nature."

I cannot understand at all the philosophy of these nascent Nazis. They seem to be engaged upon a rather pitiful attempt to combine the school of blood and iron with sweet violets. If I can make it out the accepted author must be a combination of Nietzsche and Harold Bell Wright. It's a swell trick if they can do it.

But most of all I was interested in the burning of Dr. Freud. Sigmund Freud, like Karl Marx, is a writer who has been vastly discussed by millions who never looked at a line he ever wrote. To paraphrase a familiar spiritual: "Everybody talking about Marx ain't gwine there. Revolution! Revolution! Gwine to walk all over Karl Marx's revolution!"

And in some respects Sigmund Freud is in an even better position than Karl Marx to get a pretty good chuckle for himself out of Nazi goings-on. The little man who led the first expedition into the darkest subconscious can afford to smile at the most amazing demonstration of national neuroticism the world has seen in our time.

An American correspondent who reported the address which Herr Gutjahr made as the books burned writes, "It was a boy's speech, and it was received with boyish enthusiasm."

I think Mr. Birchall might have gone a little further than that. It was, as a matter of sober fact, a child's set piece, and the whole enterprise represented a retreat from reality into infantilism. The I.Q. of the Hitler movement can hardly rate anything above six years of age. At that stage any one of us would like to dress up in a uniform and play with matches.

But somebody really ought to tell Adolf's adolescents that it isn't funny any more.

The first time I meet a Nazi fooling around writing things

with chalk on nice, clean walls and sticking his penknife into the furniture I purpose to fetch him a cuff over the side of the head and exclaim in a firm voice, "Naughty! Naughty!"

79. AN UNDELIVERED ADDRESS

I have not been asked in this year, or any other, to talk at a college commencement, but if I ever had the opportunity I think I would like to make an address about as follows:

"Seniors of Ooffus University, you are about to be graduated into an extremely lukewarm world. The chances are that not one of you will get any decent sort of job for the next two or three years. Now, what are you going to do about it?

"Two tragic things can happen to a young college graduate. He may come to utter failure before he is able to endure it or by some miracle he may strike sudden and unexpected success.

"Possibly I will be regarded as a little whimsical if I maintain that the latter is perhaps the greater tragedy. In support of my position I will seek solace in Scripture, which has often been quoted at commencements. I think it is true that it does not avail a man very much to gain the whole world and lose his own soul. And, after all, when I spoke of unexpected success I did not quite intend to include all that territory.

"What I have in mind is that the bright youngster of twenty-one or -two who immediately makes his mark is almost certain to be dependent upon luck, influence or some showy talent. None of these factors is to be enduringly prized. Genius, or even good second-rate ability, takes longer than that.

"The man who succeeds fortuitously is apt to become convinced that he lives in the best of all possible worlds, or something very close to it. He is likely to found generalizations upon happenings which are, after all, no more than a lucky turn of the dice.

"But perhaps it is not necessary to waste much time on these exceptions. The average college man will find himself on the wrong side of a wall of joblessness and indifference. Nobody, as far as I know, has any next Monday morning remedy to save him from discomfort and actual physical suffering. The best that any commencement orator can do is to urge him not to blame himself for conditions over which he has as yet no control.

"A few voluble people still go about the world saying that the unemployed are victims of their own folly and sloth and that they would easily find work if they only wanted to. This is an evil thing, but it is much more evil if any of the dispossessed can be induced to believe such nonsense even for a moment.

"I hope that college has taught you the undoubted truth that practically nobody fails without active collaboration. I would warn every one of you against the practice of self-examination and the recital of your own mistakes and shortcomings.

"Do not spend very much time in searching your own soul, but try instead to understand the psychology of the group or class in which you belong. By the help of this process you will probably find that the thing which you mistook for a personal weakness or ineptitude is characteristic of most of your fellows in like circumstances.

"College itself is a token of a new order of society. Though individual worth is recognized and encouraged, the rewards are not in terms of financial preferment. Every college or university is to a large extent a communal enterprise. In any educational institution worthy of its name and fame an effort is made to apply the rule of 'From each according to his ability; to each according to his needs.'

"It is right and very logical that the colleges of the world should be the places of inspiration for radicals and visionaries.

In a rough and inexact way the fellowship of colleges is a working experiment in the practical possibilities of brotherhood. There are few places where the student who flaunts wealth and special privileges is highly regarded.

"Even the overemphasis on sports has in it at least the saving grace that the individual does his best not for himself but for the team. And so it would seem to me that we might be much better off if alumni remained collegiate and sophomoric and did not swallow whole the standards of a world which is based upon a conception of human nature far more artificial than that which prevails in college.

"I would not have you seniors of Ooffus go out to learn from the world. It would be much better to make the world learn from you. You are going into a community which is illiterate. Some of them can read and write, but the vast majority of your fellow countrymen are wholly illiterate economically and politically. Keep your heads up. Do not be patient in that state of society to which it has pleased the depression to call you. Be skeptical of the authority of the wise men. Your professors, perhaps, were not so smart. The same will go for your bosses. You can't make mutton broth of your sheepskin, but keep it handy, just the same. Don't take the world as it is. This is no impregnable line of giants. Call your signals and shoot a play off tackle."

80. BACK TO BELLAMY

America's most authentic prophet died more than three decades ago and is not vigorously remembered for the moment in the land in which he lived.

I think there should be a great revival of interest in the work of Edward Bellamy, for notions which he expressed before the beginning of the century are just now coming into articulation and a few, indeed, into action.

The reasons for his decline are obvious enough. Bellamy was a Utopian. Radical thought is growing in this country, but the radicals themselves are impatient with men who seem to them visionary. The reproach is leveled at these idealists that they talk only of "pie in the sky."

Yet I think that the realists have slipped a cog in taking this attitude. It is false to assume that a visionary is a man who thinks only in terms of events beyond the horizon. In the strict sense of the word, anything which lies one-eighth of an inch beyond the end of your nose is visionary. For instance, if I say that it will rain hard at ten o'clock tomorrow morning I am a visionary. Yet if that rain comes I must be accepted as a lucky guesser or a blame good weather prophet.

Bellamy guessed right about such a variety of things that I think he must be accepted as a prophet. His major error lay in the time element. He foresaw a much faster movement toward co-operation than has occurred. He died in 1898, firm in the belief that the "new deal" was just around the corner and would begin early in the twentieth century.

The "new deal" of which he dreamed was, of course, a far more extensive economic upheaval than anything which has occurred during the Roosevelt administration, and yet there are observations set down in *Equality* in 1897 which have a striking pertinence to the present program. For instance, I opened the book at random yesterday afternoon in order to find some paragraph to prove the essential modernity of this last-century Utopian. Naturally I thought I would have to browse around a little to hit on anything available, but under my thumb lay a section which sounds precisely as if it had come from somebody's speech about the National Recovery Act in tomorrow morning's paper. Indeed, I recommend it to Donald Richberg for his next address.

Is there anything out of date in this observation by Bellamy?:

"I mean that under competition there was no free play whatever allowed for the capitalist's better feelings, even if he had any. He could not be better than the system. If he tried to be the system would crush him. He had to follow the pace set by his competitors or fail in business. Whatever rascality or cruelty his rivals might devise he must imitate or drop out of the struggle. The very wickedest, meanest and most rascally of the competitors—the one who ground his employees lowest, adulterated his goods most shamefully and lied about them most skillfully —set the pace for all the rest."

We are just beginning to accept this contention now, in 1933, and it has had its first expression in the set of codes which have been submitted or happen to be still in preparation.

But Bellamy would undoubtedly hold that, while all this marks a beginning, it doesn't commence to go far enough. Although a Utopian, Edward Bellamy was not an evolutionary socialist. Certainly not in the sense of either believing or desiring that the ideal state of which he dreamed might be built up slowly, one beam at a time. This frail son of a New England preacher was a revolutionist. Indeed, I think he was the first American revolutionist.

This claim would be disputed in various quarters. Some might hold that 1776 was actually a revolution. Obviously it vitally affected the political state of our nation, but it seems to me that it had almost no economic significance. And so Bellamy is still my candidate.

Even fiercer opposition might come from the sterner radicals. They would be inclined to dismiss Bellamy as a mere reformer because he believed in a "bloodless revolution." The phrase is an unfortunate one and also unfair. When a man says that he believes in a bloodless revolution he does not mean that nobody will get hurt in a vast upheaval. People who get in the way of any flood tide will be swept away. And when I say "swept," of course I mean shot.

But a good Bellamyite insists that force and violent action are a very minute part of an upheaval. "A great revolution," he wrote, "which is to profoundly change a form of society must accumulate a tremendous moral force, an overwhelming weight of justification, before it can start." And he added, "Revolutions which start too soon stop too soon."

In other words, heads which have been counted exert far greater force than heads which have been broken. A revolution founded upon the resolute will of a determined majority will never have to sit up nights to worry about counter-revolution.

81. A UNION OF REPORTERS

"You may have heard," writes Reporter Unemployed, "that, although the newspapers are carrying the bulk of NRA publicity, a number of the publishers themselves are planning to cheat NRA re-employment aims.

"The newspaper publishers are toying with the idea of classifying their editorial staffs as 'professional men.' Since NRA regulations do not cover professionals, newspapermen, therefore, would continue in many instances to work all hours of the day and any number of hours of the week.

"The average newspaperman probably works on an eight-hour-day and six-day-week basis. Obviously the publishers, by patting their fathead employees on the head and calling them 'professionals,' hope to maintain this working week scale. And they'll succeed, for the men who make up the editorial staffs of the country are peculiarly susceptible to such soothing classifications as 'professionals,' 'journalists,' 'members of the fourth estate,' 'gentlemen of the press' and other terms which have completely entranced them by falsely dignifying and glorifying them and their work.

"The men who make up the papers of this country would never look upon themselves as what they really are—hacks and white-collar slaves. Any attempt to unionize leg, re-write, desk or make-up men would be laughed to death by these editorial hacks themselves. Union? Why, that's all right for dopes like printers, not for smart guys like newspapermen!

"Yes, and those 'dopes,' the printers, because of their union, are getting on an average some 30 per cent better than the smart fourth estaters. And not only that, but the printers, because of their union and because they don't permit themselves to be called high-faluting names, will now benefit by the new NRA regulations and have a large number of their unemployed re-employed, while the 'smart' editorial department boys will continue to work forty-eight hours a week because they love to hear themselves referred to as 'professionals' and because they consider unionization as lowering their dignity."

I think Mr. Unemployed's point is well taken. I am not familiar with just what code newspaper publishers have adopted or may be about to adopt. But it will certainly be extremely damaging to the whole NRA movement if the hoopla and the ballyhoo (both very necessary functions) are to be carried on by agencies which have not lived up to the fullest spirit of the Recovery Act. Any such condition would poison the movement at its very roots.

I am not saying this from the point of view of self-interest. No matter how short they make the working day, it will still be a good deal longer than the time required to complete this stint. And as far as the minimum wage goes, I have been assured by everybody I know that in their opinion all columnists are grossly overpaid. They have almost persuaded me.

After some four or five years of holding down the easiest job in the world I hate to see other newspapermen working too hard. It makes me feel self-conscious. It embarrasses me even more to think of newspapermen who are not working at all.

Among this number are some of the best. I am not disposed to talk myself right out of a job, but if my boss does not know that he could get any one of forty or fifty men to pound out paragraphs at least as zippy and stimulating as these, then he is far less sagacious than I have occasionally assumed.

Fortunately columnists do not get fired very frequently. It has something to do with a certain inertia in most executives. They fall readily into the convenient conception that columnists are something like the weather. There they are, and nobody can do anything much about it. Of course, the editor keeps hoping that some day it will be fair and warmer, with brisk northerly gales. It never is, but the editor remains indulgent. And nothing happens to the columnist. At least, not up till now.

It is a little difficult for me, in spite of my radical leanings and training and yearnings, to accept wholeheartedly the conception of the boss and his wage slaves. All my very many bosses have been editors, and not a single Legree in the lot. Concerning every one of them it was possible to say, "Oh, well, after all, he used to be a newspaperman once himself."

But the fact that newspaper editors and owners are genial folk should hardly stand in the way of the organization of a newspaper writers' union. There should be one. Beginning at nine o'clock on the morning of October 1 I am going to do the best I can to help in getting one up. I think I could die happy on the opening day of the general strike if I had the privilege of watching Walter Lippmann heave half a brick through a *Tribune* window at a non-union operative who had been called in to write the current Today and Tomorrow column on the gold standard.

82. A ROOM WITH A VIEW

Good-by, Al; take care of yourself.

"I am too old now," writes Alfred Emanuel Smith, "to be regular just for the sake of regularity."

And to indicate the violence of his repugnance against things conventional, respectable and upholstered, Mr. Smith has written an open letter to the Chamber of Commerce of the State of New York denouncing experimentation.

Moreover, in order to pound home the full extent of his rebellious progressivism, Al Smith has come out lock and stock and barrel for Grover Cleveland.

I still want to feel that Al is more liberal than some of the other leaders and publicists. I try to console myself with the thought that, after all, Walter Lippmann has come out for both Hamilton and Jefferson, and that Carter Glass is probably grooming George Washington. Yet it isn't age but solitude which puts Al out of action. He has been living too long in that ivory tower. It's a long way from Oliver Street up to that mooring mast imbedded in the clouds.

From his office window Al can nod to any passing plane, but the noises of the street, the words of the people and even their cries come faintly to his casement.

For instance, we had but recently a city election of no little importance, and since Al Smith ventured no opinion I suppose it is charitable to assume that the matter was not called to his attention. If Mr. Smith had been informed that La Guardia, O'Brien and McKee were running, I haven't a doubt that he would have boldly declared himself for Peter Stuyvesant.

As one who no longer cares to be regular just for the sake of regularity, Alfred E. Smith would have delivered hammer blows to free the city from the grip of Tammany had he but known what was afoot.

In my heart there has been a deep devotion to Al Smith. The Happy Warrior was worthy of his title. I am not saying, even now, that he has let down people who believed in him. He has let down Alfred E. Smith. The governor used to say, "Look at the record." It was his battle cry in every argument. In those days Al could make a fact or a figure ring like a bugle note.

And there is no evidence whatsoever that Al looked at the record before he prepared his open letter to the Chamber of Commerce of the State of New York. He wrote that piece while he looked out his tower window and gazed at the setting sun.

"If I must choose between the leaders of the past," writes Al, "with all the errors they have made and all the selfishness they have been guilty of, and the inexperienced young college professors who hold no responsible public office but are willing to turn 130,000,000 Americans into guinea pigs for experimentation, I am going to be for the people who made the country what it is."

Now, the first person to say "baloney" to that would have been ex-Governor Alfred E. Smith. It might be well to remind the ex-governor of an appointment which he made to the State Labor Board. When he appointed Frances Perkins people said exactly the same thing which Al is saying now about "inexperienced young college professors." She was "a woman," "a radical," "a wife who kept her own name," "a visionary" and "a theorist."

Al and Miss Perkins worked together on some very experimental labor legislation. Chambers of Commerce hollered their heads off. The legislation was passed. It worked. By now it is accepted.

In a famous verbal duel with Cordell Hull at the last Democratic convention, Mr. Hull reminded Mr. Smith that the prohibition plank presented by the dry wing of the party was almost the same plan which Mr. Smith had espoused in 1928.

"Sure," said Al as nearly as I can remember, "but it took Cordell Hull four years to catch up with me."

Is this the same Al Smith who now wants to go back to Grover Cleveland? Indeed, Al seems minded to go even further back. "What the people need today is what the Bible centuries ago described as 'the shadow of a great rock in a weary land.'"

This is, indeed, a weary land, but the men and women grow weary of living in that deep shadow which is cast by the existing order.

Al should have his desk moved to a window with an eastern exposure. He has looked too long at skies in which the flaming red dulled down to green and purple and to darkness. And as the light faded he has thought of famous fights in which he dared the spears of giants. And does he think that with him died the impulse to take a crack at the forces of greed and error which he now nominates as preferable to the experimenters?

Look to the East, Al, and remember that the sun also rises.

83. "A FINE LESSON FOR THE WHOLE NATION"

Comment on the San Jose lynching constitutes an obligatory column.

In the beginning it seemed to me as if this thing were so monstrously and obviously evil that it would be enough to say calmly and simply, "Here is one more sadistic orgy carried on by a psycopathic mob under the patronage of the moronic governor of a backward state."

To my amazement I found not only condonation but actual

praise for the lynchers in no less than three New York newspapers. I read of "the vigilantes" and "the pioneer spirit" and so on.

Let us examine the evidence to see if there is any reason at all to ascribe the deed to the full-flowered resentment of an aroused public spirit.

Here is the story of the lynching as told by an eighteen-year-old ranch boy who asserted that he was leader of the movement:

"I was the first one of the gang to break into the jail. I came to town in the afternoon and saw the crowd around the jail. I decided to organize a 'necktie' party. Mostly I went to the speakeasies and rounded up the gang there. That is why so many of the mob were drunk. The word got spread around that it was going to be a Santa Clara University student lynching. But I'm not a Santa Clara student. I didn't go to college. I knew Brooke Hart by sight, but never had spoken to him. I thought that his terrible murder should be avenged. I found that several hundred others thought the same thing."

In other words, a farm boy who came into town for a spree managed to hit upon a drunken crowd which was willing to defend the American home and its institutions for the fun of it.

Governor Rolph has called it "a fine lesson to the whole nation." And a New York newspaper says in its leading editorial, "Nobody that we've heard of or talked to appears to disagree with the mob or disapprove of what Governor Rolph said."

All right; talk to me. Or better still read these selections from a United Press dispatch:

"Thurmond was unconscious, and probably dead, when the noose was placed around his neck. He had been beaten and kicked senseless. A boy, not more than sixteen, climbed to the top of a shed and shouted in a shrill voice, 'Come on, fellows!' He was the leader the mob had been waiting for. A new cry went up, 'Let's burn 'em!' Thurmond's body was cut down. It was drenched with gasoline. A match was touched to it, but only his torn clothing burned."

Governor James Rolph, Jr., has been quoted as saying that he would like to turn over all jail inmates serving sentences for kidnapping into the custody of "those fine, patriotic San Jose citizens, who know how to handle such a situation."

"Thousands of men, women and children looking on in carnival spirit cheered with a lustiness which could be heard for blocks."

"Both were dragged across the park, their bruised and torn bodies leaving trails of blood."

And so the fine old pioneer spirit of California, under the leadership of that fine old nature lover, Jim Rolph, has ended kidnapping in the great commonwealth of California. And what has it left in its wake? It has left an obscene, depraved and vile memory in the minds of thousands who stood about and cheered lustily.

"Some of the children were babies in their mothers' arms."

If it were possible to carry on a case history of every person in the mob who beat and kicked and hanged and burned two human beings I will make the prophecy that out of this heritage will come crimes and cruelties which are unnumbered. The price is too high.

Every mother and father of a son wants to have him protected against the danger of kidnapping. But how would you like it if it were your sixteen-year-old boy who climbed to the top of a shed and shouted in a shrill voice, "Come on, fellows!"?

Governor James Rolph, Jr., has said with audacious arrogance, "If anyone is arrested for the good job I'll pardon them all."

It does not lie within the power of the governor of California to pardon the men and boys and women and children who cried out, "Let's burn 'em!" For them there is no pardon this side of the Judgment Seat. To your knees, Governor, and pray that you and your commonwealth may be washed clean of this bath of bestiality into which a whole community has plunged.

You, James Rolph, Jr., stand naked in the eyes of the world.

"I'll pardon them all," you say. Is this to be the measure of justice in California? Men with blood and burnt flesh on their hands are to be set free. Mooney must remain in jail. Freedom for the guilty. Punishment for the innocent.

Governor, very frankly, I don't believe you can get away with it. There must be somewhere some power which just won't stand for it.

84. PAPER WORK

William James said that mankind must find a moral equivalent for war. Blow, bugles, blow, and let us put a ribbon with palms upon the breast of Travis Harvard Whitney. No soldier could have been more gallant than the man who crumpled at his desk in the Civil Works Administration. Before he would submit to being taken to the hospital where he died, Whitney insisted on giving directions to his assistants as to how the work should go on. He was torn with agony but it was his commitment to put two hundred thousand men and women back to work. This was just something which had to be done.

I saw him once, and in the light of his death I am not likely to forget. He called up to say that if the Newspaper Guild would furnish him a list of unemployed reporters he thought he could place some under the CWA.

"When do you want to see us?" I asked.

"Come down now," he answered.

We expected to find an office and an office boy and probably a couple of secretaries, but Whitney had a desk thrust right in the middle of a large and bustling room. He sat there and rode the tumult like a city editor. There were no preliminaries of any kind. The tall, gaunt man with deep-sunken eyes began by asking: "Now when do I get that list?"

I've heard so much about red tape and bureaucracy that I didn't suppose he meant immediately. "It will take a little time," I told him. "We haven't got a very big clerical force or much office space, and of course John Eddy will have to check up on the names for you. Let me see—this is Thursday—suppose we get you that list a week from Saturday and then on Monday we can really begin to get to work on it."

He indicated impatience. "That won't do at all," he said. "You don't understand. This is a rush job. Every day counts. Can't you let me have part of the list the day after tomorrow? This ought to be done right away. Can't you call me on the phone tonight?"

"Where can I get you after dinner?" I asked.

"Right here."

"How late?"

"I can't tell. I'll be here until I finish."

Travis Whitney made good that promise. He worked all day and he worked all night. He knew he was critically ill when he took the appointment. Doctors had told him of the necessity of rest and probably of an operation. "I think I can last," was his rejoinder.

And he set himself to win that race. Two hundred thousand jobs before the end came. I think it was Lord Nelson who had an ensign lash him to a mast at the battle of Trafalgar. Whitney's courage was better than that. He chained himself to his desk by a sheer act of will.

The people around could see him grow dead gray in the late hours. Almost you could hear the step of his adversary advancing. But all he said was, "We must hurry." He felt not only the pangs of his own physical torture but the bite of the wind upon the bodies of men who walked the streets without shelter.

I don't know what the economic philosophy of Travis Whitney may have been. He didn't have time to talk about it. "Some day" just couldn't fit into his scheme of things. His thought was of two hundred thousand jobs which must be made and handed out without delay. He had the harassed look of a flapjack cook in a lumber camp. "Right away" rang in his ears like a trumpet call. Maybe somebody came and said to him, "But don't you realize that you're not solving anything? This is just a temporary expedient. When the revolution comes—"

And I imagine Travis Whitney turned a deaf ear and only said, "Two hundred thousand jobs and this has got to be now."

He couldn't make the life force last until he had surged across the line. They put him on his shield and carried him away, and I hope that on his tomb will be written "Killed in action."

Unquestionably this shambling, thin man peering a little dubiously through glasses had a concern. It was a passion. I suppose it is a little difficult to make paper work seem as exciting or romantic as cavalry charges. But you see he had found his moral equivalent for war. And I rather think that when next I hear the word "heroism" my immediate mental association will not be that of any brass hat on a hill but of Travis Whitney bent over his desk. And maybe I will see him as a man against the sky. And I will hear him as he says, "More gently, death, come slower. Don't touch me till my job is done."

85. THE *TRIBUNE'S* GOBLIN EDITOR

Mark Sullivan suffers from insomnia. And when he drops off into fitful slumber by counting administration measures jumping over the Constitution he is tormented by bad dreams. The very milk wagons on Pennsylvania Avenue become tumbrils calling at the homes of those who refuse to accept the New Deal.

In the old days things were very different. Mark slept, Mellon slept and the President slept very well indeed. In the morning everybody but Mr. Mellon met on the White House lawn for exercise and when Mr. Sullivan threw the medicine ball at the President he was not called upon to aim at a moving target.

Herbert Hoover, there he stood the same on Monday as on Wednesday. He was no football quarterback like Franklin D. Roosevelt. No indeed, he was one of the goal posts merely waiting stolidly for somebody to tear him down.

I gather from the jeremiads of Mark Sullivan that most of the dirty work is done at night. It is then that Guy Tugwell sneaks out armed with chalk and writes "Capitalism Must Be Destroyed" upon the sidewalks of the town. Mr. Sullivan is convinced that the revolution is not only here but almost consummated. And as I understand it he has two major complaints. He maintains that the upheaval is being carried on secretly and that it is practically painless. When he shakes his head at night and finds that it doesn't roll on the floor you can bet that he is pretty sore about it.

"Is it unreasonable to ask," inquires Mr. Sullivan, "that we have an opportunity to debate the new system and that the outcome of this debate determine whether we adopt the new?"

And that reminds me that I should in all kindness suggest a remedy to Mark Sullivan for his insomnia. I think he ought to read himself to sleep. I fear that his wild words suggest an unfamiliarity with what is going on in the newspapers of America. No debate indeed! The careless Mr. Sullivan must have shaped endless columns of pros and cons within the last three or four months. It seems to me that every editorial page is filled with violent denunciation of Rexford Guy Tugwell signed "Intrepid Home Owner," "Original Settler" or "Indignant Member of the Sixth Grade."

To be specific, might I ask the Republican Revere whether or not he has familiarized himself with the writings of Mark Sullivan upon this very theme? I think that with a glass of warm milk and two Sullivan columns the sufferer will soon find his lids nodding as in the days when Pippa passed, and Hoover said, "I've got nothing either."

In all fairness to the *Herald Tribune*'s goblin editor I must admit that he has freshened his narrative from time to time. Only this week he introduced a new villain into the plot. It now seems that Professor Tugwell is not playing a lone hand in his effort to Sovietize America while Sullivan sleeps. Some of the blame falls on the head of Felix Frankfurter, who has recommended several young men who have received appointments under the administration. "Nearly all of them are graduates of Harvard Law School," adds Mark Sullivan ominously. It must be, I gather, that Roosevelt is a Red since he has allied himself with so many wearers of the Crimson.

"The country, I am sure," adds Mr. Sullivan, "would be instructed, and also, I suspect, amused by a joint debate staged with Professors Tugwell and Frankfurter on one side, and on the other, let me say, Senator Carter Glass, of Virginia, whose word for the New Deal is 'insanity,' and ex-Governor Alfred E. Smith, whose word for it is 'baloney.'"

Well, I won't promise to be amused unless they come a little funnier than that. I didn't even rock with merriment at Mark Sullivan's own contribution to the debate, which was to call Felix Frankfurter "the happy hot dog." The funeral baked meats of Herbert Hoover's administration did so coldly furnish forth the national weal that I'm afraid the gag may fall quite flat.

And yet I'm all for the debate. The American Newspaper Guild will be glad to arrange a proper scene for the discussion. Professor Frankfurter must be carrying on his machinations rather slyly, since he has been an exchange professor at Oxford for several months, but I don't see why Tugwell and Smith alone should not be sufficient to fill any hall. But before the New Deal is riddled as something lacking proper and sufficient clarity I would like to have some definition of "the familiar American philosophy" to which Mark Sullivan is so constantly referring. Who qualifies? Is it true that Mark Hanna and Theodore Roosevelt fit neatly into the same classification, or

Woodrow Wilson and Harry Daugherty? And what are we going to do about classifying Andy Mellon, who has always seemed to me the worst Secretary of the Treasury since Alexander Hamilton?

86. THE FIRST ROBIN

"YORK, PA.—With the temperature at ten degrees below zero the first robin of the year was seen in York today. It was found dead on Penn Common."

Call me an old sentimentalist if you will, but this seems to me the most tragic news note of the cold wave. I like people better than robins, and there has been widespread and agonizing suffering. But, you see, this was the first robin. He was by all odds the pioneer of his clan. He flew up from the South days, weeks and months before any reasonable robin weather was to be expected.

Without doubt the rest tried to discourage him. They spoke of the best recorded experience of birdkind. "Rome wasn't built in a day," some other robin told him. And no doubt he was advised that if he insisted on such precipitate action he would split the group and no good could come of it.

Somehow I seem to hear him saying: "If ten will follow me I'd call that an army. Are there two who'll join up? Or maybe one?"

But the robins all recoiled and clung to their little patches of sun under the Southern skies. "Later, maybe," they told him. "Not now. First there must be a campaign of education."

"Well," replied the robin who was all for going to York, Pa., without waiting for feathery reinforcements, "I know one who'll try it. I'm done with arguments, and here I go."

He was so full of high hopes and dedication that he rose almost with the roar of a partridge. For a few seconds he was a fast-moving speck up above the palm trees, and then you couldn't spot him even with field glasses. He was lost in the blue and flying for dear life.

"Impetuous, I call it," said one of the elder statesmen while someone took him a worm.

"He always did want to show off," announced another, and everybody agreed that no good would come of it.

As it turned out, maybe they were right. It's pretty hard to prove that anything has been gained when a robin freezes to death on Penn Common. However, I imagine that he died with a certain sense of elation. None of the rest thought he could get there. And he did. The break in weather turned out to be against him. He just guessed wrong in that one respect, and so I wouldn't think of calling him a complete failure.

When the news gets back home to the robins who didn't go I rather expect that they'll make him a hero. The elder statesmen will figure that since he is dead his ideas can't longer be dangerous, and they cannot deny the lift and the swing of his venture.

After all, he was the first robin. He looked for the Spring, and it failed him. Now he belongs to that noble army of first robins.

Many great names are included. The honors of office and public acclaim, of ribbons and medals, the keys of the city— these are seldom the perquisite of men or birds in the first flight. These go to fifth, sixth and even twentieth robins.

It is almost a rule that the first robin must die alone on some bleak common before mankind will agree that he was a hero. And sometimes it takes fifty years and often a hundred.

John Brown, Galileo and those who sought goals before the world was quite ready are all in good standing.

The man who says, "That would be swell, but, of course, you can't do it," is generally as right as rain; but who wants to get up and cheer for frustration? In the long haul the first robin is more right than any. It was his idea. He softened the way for the others. And with him even failure is its own kind of triumph.

He is not the victim of dry rot or caution or doomed eyestrain from too close an attention to ledgers.

"Here I go!" he cries, and I wouldn't be surprised to be told that the first minute of flight is reward enough, no matter what follows.

And so in a metaphorical way of speaking I bare my head and bow low in the general direction of the ice-covered plain which is known as Penn Common. And I think that the brief address should carry the statement: "You were the first, and after you will come others. They will inherit the grubs and the nests and the comfort. But yours is the glory. You are the first robin."

87. CHARLES A. LINDBERGH

The life of Charles A. Lindbergh ought to remain an American epic. He belongs truly among our pioneers. At the moment his fame is somewhat dimmed, but I feel certain that his countrymen will rediscover him. Under the heat of passion he was bitterly assailed by practically all the newspapers of the land, and even some of his friends and neighbors turned against him.

Even at the height of his success Lindbergh was never a national idol, for there was nothing romantic about the man. His associates were the farmers of his own community. Wall Street hated him, for he waged constant warfare against those big interests which tried to challenge the authority of the government. He was largely influential in forcing the appearance of Morgan before a congressional committee.

In his book Charles A. Lindbergh wrote: "Politics and business, we were told, should be kept separate. The wealth grabbers told us that. . . . But the wealth grabbers did not keep their business out of politics. We were the only ones that tried to keep business and politics separate, and the effect was that we kept out of politics altogether, except merely to vote to give politicians power. When we get down to 'brass tacks,' however, we will discover that business and politics should go hand in hand and should not be separated."

And Lindbergh was very definite in making a specific application of that principle in a memorandum which he wrote for the President of the United States. He said:

"1. The federal government must establish a financial system that is independent of private monopoly control.

"2. The federal government must own and operate the main lines in the telegraph and telephone systems.

"3. The federal government must own and operate all the transportation systems."

And Lindbergh amplified this third point in his brief platform by explaining: "Mr. President, no agency is more important than transportation, though it has not the controlling influence on commerce that finances have as finance is now regulated. The free interchange of commodities between the people is of the utmost importance, and travel as well. Therefore all transportation should be as near to actual cost as it is possible to have it. That being the case the government alone could handle it, and should do so."

"The postal system, to be sure," he added, "is successful when compared with privately owned business of any kind, but it would be pre-eminently more successful if the other services we designate were also operated by the government. It requires them all to make the success of any such as it should be."

A flier who testified in Washington on the question of government operation of the air mail said, "It is as contrary to American liberty as anything I have ever seen."

I doubt that Charles A. Lindbergh would have said that. It is true, of course, that he was not native-born, but he came from Sweden when only a year old and grew up and lived with American problems. Lindbergh was not a technical expert in aviation, but he made one memorable flight. He was piloted by his son, who later became the well-known flier.

Walter E. Quigley describes the incident in an introduction which he has written to a reissue of Lindbergh's book, which is called *Your Country at War*. The first edition was suppressed by federal agents in 1918. In 1923 Lindbergh decided to run for United States Senator from Minnesota. Knute Nelson had died suddenly, and a special election was necessary.

"Lindbergh telegraphed his son who was flying an Army Jenny plane in the South, to come to Minnesota and drive him in the plane so he could cover more territory and attract larger crowds. Finally one balmy May afternoon when we were conducting a meeting at the fair grounds in Marshall, we heard the drone of a motor in the sky and a few minutes later the future Colonel Lindbergh landed in a nearby field.

"I rode in the plane to Redwood Falls, our scheduled evening meeting, and distributed literature from the plane. Next day father and son flew to Glencoe—their first airplane ride together. That afternoon when the Colonel was going to take off he hit a concealed ditch on the Miley farm and cracked up, so the airplane method of campaigning came to an abrupt end."

I wish Mr. Quigley had described the incident in rather more detail. It would have been interesting to know what Charles A. Lindbergh, Jr., thought then of his father's fervid speeches in favor of government ownership. Possibly the young man was familiar with his passion for human rights. He may have heard him speaking when his father was in the House.

But this was the last campaign and Charles A. Lindbergh's last flight. He died the next Spring. And that was the end of his message. There was no one to take his place.

88. CHUMMY CHARLIE

Charles M. Schwab came back from Europe and expressed regret when he heard that the squatter colony of veterans along the Hudson opposite his Riverside Drive home had been ordered to move along. He said that they had been good neighbors.

"We visited back and forth," he explained. "They had been up to my house and very kindly assisted us around the grounds in getting rid of the heavy snows last winter. Mrs. Schwab frequently drove down to visit them in their homes. And I also called on them many times. When we had a surplus of produce from our farm at Loretto, Pa., we were happy to share it with them. They had looked forward to staying there, I know, until business improved. We shall miss them. They were not bad neighbors at all."

This I have no doubt was the sincere expression of a kindly old gentleman who worked himself up from the bottom to the top of the steel industry. He had a neighborly feeling for men living in plain sight of his turrets who just didn't have the good luck to get the breaks. The assistance which he rendered was quite in the American tradition that the more fortunately situated should help the stragglers in a casual and friendly fashion without any outside compulsion. After all, what are a couple of heads of lettuce and a bushel of potatoes between friends?

But in the long history of Bethlehem Steel I assume that it is entirely possible that there have been other shacks where Charles M. Schwab never got around to pay a visit. During the desperate days of the depression I venture to assert that thousands of jobless employees never saw so much as a leaf of the Loretto lettuce.

Does this mean that Mr. Schwab in his own person is some sort of exceptionally tight-fisted villain? In my opinion it means nothing of the sort. He is from all the accounts I ever heard kindly, genial and reasonable. The hitch is systemic and not individual. The American tradition that we can muddle through hard times by dint of private charity, individual benevolence and voluntary giving has broken down completely. And of course it deserved to break down.

When a man asks for bread and receives a stone he has a right to be indignant, but I hold that he should not be satisfied when he asks for bread and gets bread. It is quite true that in the life we know there do arise situations so desperate that private charity must be called upon in lieu of better devices and more rapid ones. But in the long run charity does desperate things to the donors. It makes smug prigs who go about saying that they would like to give but that they are afraid of pauperizing people.

I used to know, for my sins, a lady who went around on Easter, Christmas and Thanksgiving leaving baskets. Each basket contained one raw turkey, two cans baked beans, one jar cranberry jelly, two loaves whole wheat bread, one pound butter, one stick peppermint candy for the kiddies.

I suppose this generous woman was one of the most objectionable persons I have ever met. She would come back from her rounds on one of the three feast days all puffed up with righteousness.

"I know it is only a little," she used to say, "but one does the best they can." Her grammar was even worse than her personality.

One day a man at her house took her up on her favorite remark and answered, "You're damn tooting it is only a little. Did you ever stop to figure what any of those people lived on between turkeys? And did you ever stop to ask by what right you go around and get yourself into a glow of self-satisfaction by distributing a little occasional delicatessen?"

The young man was set down as a rude person and never was asked to lunch any more, but I think he was right. I have known people to stop and buy an apple on the corner and then walk away as if they had solved the whole unemployment problem. I think that people should make charitable gifts but only on their knees and with the deepest apologies. The fact that such things are in any way necessary constitutes an indictment of every one of us.

We have so snarled up the world with our rugged individualism and our insistence upon the preservation of initiative and our bleating that we won't stand for regimentation and compulsion that the whole blame planet is likely to fall right on our heads.

I can't understand how people can go on parroting stuff about taking care of the needy in our own good American way. The device of private charity is not working now, and it never has worked. The only dignified and decent way to attend to such matters until the doctor comes is to have the government say, "So much is needed, and this is your share."

Any reasonable system of taxation should be based on the theory of "Soak the rich." The rich aren't going to like it, but they should, because in the long run it is the only system which will preserve their souls from the decadence of donations.

89. THE STRIKE-BREAKER

To me it has always seemed not only illogical but improper that police or national guardsmen should be employed to protect the functioning of strike-breakers in any industry. In theory, at least, the police and the guard are supposed to be the servants of the majority of the citizens. Governors and mayors are elected by the masses. Why, then, should public forces be turned over to private individuals for their personal advantage, particularly when that advantage happens to be disadvantageous to the common weal?

Palpably the strike-breaker is an anti-social member of the community. As a rule he has no political or economic philosophy whatsoever, but in any case in which he became articulate he would be forced by the logic of the circumstances to assert that his temporary gain should be protected even at the expense of calamity among the many. Certainly whenever a strike is broken the city or town, as a whole, is worse off than it was before. Men and women are added to the list of unemployed and there will be an inevitable tendency to worse wages and working conditions all along the line.

In Toledo the head of a mercantile house told me that the strike in the Auto-Lite plant was costing his store a loss of 20 per cent of average business every week. I said to him: "That doesn't surprise me, but the thing which I can't understand is why the business men in this town or any other should take an attitude of opposition to the unions and get together at meetings to denounce 'outside agitators.' If I owned a business here I would be down on the picket line with a placard urging the employers to comply with the demands of the workers. The success of your store depends upon the purchasing power of the people of the city. Just out of self-interest you can't afford to have the men lose."

I think the same theory holds good in San Francisco. The guardsmen and the police are supported by the taxpayers, who will be assessed in order to win a victory for the owners of steamship lines and thereby lower the general standard of living and the general prosperity of all concerned with the exception of a few owners engaged in the industry now under fire.

I even doubt whether the immediate employers gain much from success in breaking a strike. Any such result must be among the most pyrrhic of victories. Strike-breakers are expensive, inefficient and unreliable. In the long run I'll wager that many a cost sheet will show that it would have been far more profitable for the stockholders to have granted the union demands at the beginning.

I have heard a few ill-informed and sentimental folk picture the strike-breaker as a rugged American who was fighting for the cause of individual liberty and the freedom of every man to work at whatever craft he may choose for his own. The strike-breaker is not like that. He sells his birthright for a few meager and immediate pieces of silver and heightens his own chances to be back on some breadline a few weeks or months after the event.

It seems to me that the average American is not very quick to realize the enormous benefits which even non-union workers have gained through the force of organization. The very people who will readily admit that prosperity can come only through the heightening and stabilization of purchasing power are the very ones who complain of the "tyranny of the unions." One of the familiar arguments is the citation of certain open shop employers who pay wages equal to the scale or even better. But people who mention Ford and other manufacturers as friends of labor lose sight of the fact that many a boss keeps wages up in a desperate fight to keep his employees from unionizing.

If there were no possible threat of organization all wages would drop to the intolerable levels established by the law of supply and demand. One does not need to be a complete technocrat to realize that with our present surplus of unemployed, wages would be next to nothing save in the case of a very small number of highly skilled individuals. And even they would suffer, since there are many jobs in which ten indifferent performers can approximate the efforts of one highly competent performer.

Much has been said about the American standard of living and the necessity of its preservation. That standard has been rather rudely battered about in the last few years, but where it still exists the credit must go to the unions, which have kept wages up and hours down. The non-union man is a person who reaps where he has not sown. He comes at the eleventh hour and receives his penny. He is willing to profit by the aggressive efforts of others to whom he has given no support. Worse than that, he stands ready to stab in the back the very people who have made it possible for him to command a competence.

And so I say that he is an anti-social force who decidedly does not deserve protection at public expense. I would not have him torn limb from limb by angry mobs. I think both the police and the guard have a proper function in strikes. I feel that they should in emergencies be called out by mayors or governors under the order, "It is your job to see that not a single strike-breaker enters this plant or so much as one wheel turns until the employers have made a fair settlement with their men."

90. I INTERVIEW A COLUMNIST

Early this morning I ran into a newspaper columnist who is a close friend of mine, and we were both complaining that neither of us had an idea for the next column. "Would you submit to an interview?" I asked. "What do you mean 'submit'?" he replied. "When did I ever run away from a chance to get into print?" But after a few seconds' consideration he added, "I think you had better not use my name or identify me in any way, because I have a vague feeling that I am walking along a road on which banana peels are being spread in my honor."

"Are you a labor agitator?" I asked.

"I hope so," he answered. "At any rate, I mean to be."

"How can you square that with the fact that you are reputed to have received a high salary for a number of years?"

"I have $125.70 in the bank right now," answered my fat friend gloomily.

"Please do not evade the issue," I insisted. "You could have saved your money. You've probably wasted it in gambling and riotous living." "Sure," he said, "I could have saved it up to buy Peruvian bonds. Or maybe I could have saved up enough to be in just the right state of mind to do columns about the cussedness of workers who demand their rights and forget to be polite to the boss."

"But you're still quibbling," I persisted. "Rumor has it, again, that you've signed a contract for a number of years, so that, no matter what happens, you at least have security."

The young man answered obscenely, and for at least a minute it seemed quite useless to take notes. After a final splutter he continued: "Once upon a time I worked in a large metropolis on a morning paper. It was a liberal paper. Up in Massachusetts two innocent men were being railroaded to the chair. As I remember, one was a shoemaker and the other a peddler. I got mad, I got so mad that the editor told me not to write on that subject any more. I got madder and went on a one-man strike for six or seven months. Then, like a fool, I went back, and in another couple of months I got fired. And during all that time I had a contract and what you call security."

The man annoyed me, and I broke in sharply. "Don't try any of those martyr airs on me," I told him. "You never went cold, and Heaven knows it's palpable you never went hungry a day in your life."

This time he grinned at me with that charm for which he is noted. "But I will, Heywood; I will," he answered. "In fact, I'm beginning to feel that I must. But mostly those are not decisions that you make arbitrarily. They are forced on you. If you are willing to wait until next pay before the money is put up I'll lay you $100 to $10 that I will die in abject poverty and spend my declining years in want."

"You needn't hold the pose on my account," I assured him.

"I've read the same amount of Freud as you have. I think we both recognize the Messiah complex which crops out in columnists at bars along about four in the morning. Quit weeping into your gin rickey."

I thought for a minute he was going to punch me, and, as we are both of a size, it might have been a good bout, though a short one.

"Look here, Broun," he said, growing more formal, "there's a point where all kidding ceases. You and I have known newspapermen better than either of us who were tossed on the scrap heap with charm for a coat and a 'so sorry, old fellow,' in lieu of an old-age pension."

I tried to mollify him. "Yes, I'd heard that you were one of a crowd that was working to try to improve conditions for editorial workers." But then I couldn't resist my traditional skepticism and suspicion of sham. "Still, they tell me," I added, "that in your case it's just a lark and that you go around making speeches and attending meetings just to show off."

Instead of getting angry he answered quite mildly, "Anybody who says that is a liar." And he quickly added: "That isn't fair. I ought to say he's mistaken. I had the same suspicion myself, because I am an old showoff. But I put myself on probation. A year has gone by, and so I know it isn't a lark. It's a job and the most thrilling enterprise to which a man can commit himself. In the labor movement I know which side I'm on. I'm for the workers. I hope you'll believe me."

And, as a matter of fact, I did.

91. HOW I GOT INTO THIS RACKET

I wish the world would calm down and go along for a week without any threats of war or violence or major disasters. I assume that this wish might well be shared by many. But I have a peculiar and personal reason for desiring an armistice in the matter of permanent crises.

You see, once upon a time I had an ambition to be a light essayist. As a matter of fact that was the way in which I got into this racket. At my own suggestion I was assigned to do three pieces a week on the most vital current books. In fact I believe it might be possible for me to establish the assertion that I was the father of the daily literary column. In those days I was indolent. There came a certain Thursday and I was at the office with no novel or travel tome under my belt. In desperation I dashed off a thousand words about my experiences in trying to buy a farm.

Nothing happened. The managing editor smiled pleasantly and issued no rebuke. One week later I was still behind on my reading and threw into my space, which appeared under the caption Books, an article concerning my infant son. This time the boss called me into his office. "Those casual pieces of yours are better than your book reviews," he said.

It was an ambiguous remark. You couldn't quite call it a compliment and yet it carried a certain amount of encouragement. As a matter of fact this somewhat vague statement from my immediate employer changed my whole life.

This was almost twenty years ago and I have read only two books all the way through since that time. A new vista opened up. To my astonishment I found that it was possible to get paid for the very simple task of writing about yourself and your own experiences. On many occasions since critical readers have sent me clippings in which the "I" was ringed around with a red pencil. The record, as I remember, was one hundred and twenty out of a possible nine hundred words. But the editor had said in effect, "go ahead" and I have always been a sucker for suggestion when its indicated path was easy and pleasant.

For almost two years I was supported by my infant son. His clever sayings and bright deeds made up the column which by this time had been retitled to read Books and Things. To be sure there were days when the kid did not come through. Some of the brightest things he ever did in print were sheer invention. Accordingly I have decided that when he comes to man's estate 10 per cent of the net ought to be a fair return. I mean 90 per cent for the agent and entrepreneur.

After he learned to read and write it was no longer possible to use him for copy. He made violent objection. Accordingly, I switched to the next best thing and began to write about myself. The outside world was almost a matter of complete indifference. Politics and international affairs were not touched upon more than once a month. I am a little surprised when some angry reader rebukes me for egocentricity. The only answer to that is:—"Boy, you should have caught me fifteen years ago and then you would really have had something to complain about."

The Sacco-Vanzetti case moved me to write the first violent newspaper pieces I had ever done. And pretty soon I was out of a job. Never since that time has it been possible to get back entirely into the mood of the kindly commentator on the less important phases of the passing show. Unlike Nero, I did most of my fiddling before Rome burned. I was left a tuneless minstrel in a world which proceeded to go into convulsions. Suddenly it was no longer possible to write about bullheads or crickets or the manner in which autumn comes to the maples of Hunting Ridge. It seemed a little silly to write about a fish and put it into a paper which was filled with assassinations, riots and revolutions.

In the old days I sat down ten or twelve hours in advance of the deadline and tried to imagine that I was Charles Lamb. Naturally I never made the grade, but presently it was no dice even if you did. Being whimsical or arch while Rome burns is even worse than meeting the fire with violin tunes.

I became a commentator because I was conscripted by the march of events. I do not regret the change in all ways. Of course, nobody got mad at me then. I was a little brother to all the world. It was not I but the world which asked for an annulment of the relationship.

Now I stay up till all hours to get the morning papers and find out who is dead and where the shooting is. On many occasions it is quite possible to get genuinely aroused about some snide performance by the captains and the kings.

I'm not kicking. All I want to know is would it be too much to ask for the privilege of writing once a month about cabbages and sealing wax or anything else which has nothing to do with the class struggle or the New Deal? Excuse it, please.

92. RUTH HALE

My best friend died yesterday. I would not mention this but for the fact that Ruth Hale was a valiant fighter in an important cause. Concerning her major contention we were in almost complete disagreement for seventeen years. Out of a thousand debates I lost a thousand. Nobody ever defeated Miss Hale in an argument. The dispute was about feminism. We both agreed that in law and art and industry and anything else you can think of men and women should be equal. Ruth Hale felt that this could be brought about only through the organization of women along sex lines. I think that this equality will always be an inevitable and essential part of any thoroughgoing economic upheaval. "Come on and be a radical," I used to say, but Miss Hale insisted on being a militant feminist—all that and nothing more and nothing less.

Deems Taylor once said to her: "Ruth, you have more capacity for emotion than anybody I ever knew. I wish I had it, because if I did I wouldn't waste it in such narrow channels."

Decidedly I was not unsympathetic with the Lucy Stone

League, of which Miss Hale was the president and prime mover. I agree thoroughly with the slogan of that association, which runs: "My name is the symbol of my identity, and must not be lost." Men as well as women live by symbols. But when I spoke of the brotherhood of mankind Miss Hale insisted on changing it into the sisterhood of womankind. "Mankind embraces womankind," I argued with due grammatical license. "It works just as well the other way," she responded, and the vigor of her drive moved me invariably to amend the familiar phrase and make it run, "Are we mice or women?"

I could hardly deny the assertion that the Western world is still stacked in favor of the male sex. I refer less to existing gross inequalities in law than to the force of custom and tradition. This came closely home to both of us. When we met we were reporters, and I have never denied that Ruth Hale was the better newspaperman of the two. I think the things which held her back were biological. Brisbanes don't have babies.

Vicarious expression was of no use to her. I may as well admit right off something which will soon be evident. A very considerable percentage of all newspaper columns, books and magazine articles which appeared under the name "Heywood Broun" were written by Ruth Hale. I mean, of course, the better columns. And even those which I felt I was writing on my own stemmed from her.

It was a curious collaboration, because Ruth Hale gave me out of the very best she had to equip me for the understanding of human problems. She gave this under protest, with many reservations, and a vast rancor. But she gave.

I understood then and will always understand the inevitable bitterness of the person who projects herself through another, even if that one is close. Of course, in regard to a few minor points I felt that I was standing on my own feet. Miss Hale could never quite convince me that she could keep a boxscore of a baseball game more accurately than I could. What she could not realize was the fact that she demonstrated to me, at any rate, the kind of equality which inches up to a decided superiority. Since it is true that very many of the ideas for which I seem to be sponsor are really hers, in the last analysis I am the utterly dependent person.

She was not my severest critic. Her tolerance was broad to the mass of mediocre stuff the newspaper hack is bound to produce in seventeen years. Nobody else, I suppose, ever gave me such warm support and approbation for those afternoons when I did my best. She made me feel ashamed when I faltered, and I suppose that for seventeen years practically every word I wrote was set down with the feeling that Ruth Hale was looking over my shoulder.

It would be a desperately lonely world if I did not feel that personality is of such tough fiber that in some manner it must survive and does survive. I still feel that she is looking over my shoulder.

93. THE MAN WHO CAME BACK

John Puckering, a market gardener of Arley, England, died the other day and came back to tell about it. On the whole he regretted his return. It seems to me fair to say that John Puckering was dead. He was pronounced dead by the doctors. He lay upon an operating table, and for 150 seconds there was not the slightest sign of a quiver in his heart. Dr. Mills massaged the heart, and after two minutes and a half it began to beat again. John Puckering is back among the quick and growing cabbages.

In all his fifty-eight years nobody paid very much attention to Mr. Puckering. "How are the carrots and the onions?" some customer may have inquired, but nobody was interested in his ideas about the empire and still less his conception of the cosmos.

I fear a little that John Puckering may have returned to a somewhat impaired artistry. From now on one can hardly expect him to suffer agonies over the life and death of eggplant or young radishes.

Even when he meets the select few of the world who have flown the broad Atlantic the market gardener of Arley has a right to smile in a superior way, for he has crossed over the vast expanse of Jordan River. Columbus was a recluse and Marco Polo no more than a hitch-hiker compared to Puckering.

It is true that the report which he gives of the life beyond is a trifle vague and shadowy. "It was," he says, "as though I were looking into a great place, something like a hall, though I cannot recall having seen either ceiling or walls. There was a good light, and I saw crowds of people. So many were there they seemed like a multitude at a football match."

It may be that heavens of infinite variety are provided for all the elect. The paradise of Puckering does not precisely suit my fancy. When I go to my just reward I do not wish to be a part of any football crowd and hear the cherubim and seraphim continually cry out that they are going back to Nassau Hall.

It would hardly be heaven for a Harvard man to find himself bound through all eternity to the gloomy prospect of watching his team furnish mincemeat for the Tigers. Nor is it soul-satisfying to contemplate the everlasting snake dance of the Princeton lads down through the jasper streets and up to the golden bar of heaven. Who wants to be a Cambridge angel and under compulsion to tread featly among the half-pint flasks of the victors?

But the rest of the testimony of John Puckering, of Arley and the Hereafter, is much more comforting.

"The people stood in a circle," he says, "and I noticed that there were no children among them. They looked natural, with healthy faces, and they appeared to be dressed as on earth."

All of that is swell by me. Existence would be more restful if I were not so constantly summoned from my work to the telephone to hear a piping and an eager voice say, "Papa, I want \$2 straight on Boom's Pal in the seventh race at Hialeah. A dollar on Our Mae at New Orleans in the fourth. That's on the nose, too. And 50 cents on Sweet Chariot to show in the eighth at Santa Anita."

"Dressed as on earth" also has its attractions. The blue suit and the brown which I have now are adequate, and to me the thought of wings and a long white robe has always been alienating. I would prefer, again, to walk all over God's heaven in the black shoes I now possess. I've broken them in. It would be a nuisance to have to ask some other angel to wear my sandals for the first two weeks.

"I was deeply impressed with the happiness which shone in their faces and which was so intense that I felt as though I should not have minded joining them."

Spoken, John Puckering, like an old Puritan and a true one. The most that the sight of joy could raise in him was a sense of acquiescence. Possibly, for the first time in his life, he was moved to feel that one could be both happy and respectable.

Perhaps somebody may ask whether I believe that John Puckering, of Arley, went to heaven for 150 seconds. I hope so, but how can I tell? All I know is that he was dead. Where was he? There must be somewhere the land of happy faces. At least there ought to be!

94. MR. JUSTICE HOLMES

Mr. Justice Holmes almost rounded out the century, and the circumstance of his great age was one of the factors which made him important to the modern world. He served as a constant reminder that most of the things called outlandish and newfangled had been a part of human thought in the years which were gone before.

Decidedly it was a healthy thing to have on the Supreme bench a man who touched the tradition of Thoreau and Emerson, at first hand. He was not one to be moved into sudden panic by the prospect of change, because in ninety-three years he had seen so much of it.

Had Oliver Wendell Holmes served on until that noon when Justice McReynolds announced in trembling tones the destruction of the Constitution I rather think that Justice Holmes might have been a shade amused. He would have regarded the diatribe of the Tennesseean as one of those groundless panics which often seize upon the young.

There was something a little strange in having a man thrice wounded in the Civil War passing upon the problems of utility corporations which rendered services unknown during the youth of Mr. Justice Holmes. The economic setup in which Holmes was born had been all but swept away by the time he began to render his great decisions and his great dissents.

And yet in some respects the march of events indicated no forward progress whatsoever. Certain aspects of American life moved merely in circles. The soldier of Fredericksburg retired only a little while before the Scottsboro case was up before the court. Mr. Justice Holmes saw the rise and the fall of populism and progressivism. He rendered judgment in such litigation which was hailed by many as making a new nation or wrecking an old one. And when neither thing happened it may well be that Oliver Wendell Holmes buried himself a little deeper in the Latin poets and arrived at the notion that the United States Supreme Court was set on a plane somewhat lower than the throne of God.

I do not mean to say that he was not concerned with the dignity, the honor and the integrity of the body on which he served, but in very many of his decisions he steered clear of the conception that a final legislative veto has been intrusted into the hands of nine wise men. Certainly he did not favor any strait-jacket conception of the Constitution. He supported only those denials in which he felt that some specific prohibition of the act in question could be found. The silence of the Constitution always seemed to him to imply consent.

Much has been made of the dissenting opinions of Mr. Justice Holmes, and I venture to say that an examination of these opinions will find the court just about catching up with his point of view. But Oliver Wendell Holmes was by no means habitually a deviationist. His mind kept a little ahead of the trend of the times, but, like the rest of humankind, he was motivated and touched by his own social background and by the temper of the land in which he lived. I have always felt that during the great war he lost touch for a time with his own liberal philosophy. The bugles and the drums stirred in him old memories and opened ancient wounds.

But in his seventies and eighties there was more elasticity in Holmes than was resident in younger men. He had made a fast recovery from the bullets of the Civil War. Just so the shrapnel fragments of the later conflict did not permanently affect him.

It would be foolish to say that Oliver Wendell Holmes was a radical at any stage of his career, but he did fight for the free field of complete human expression. And, curiously enough, it was in his latest years that he seemed most receptive to those ideas which some call dangerous.

Certainly his cronies in the last decade were recruited from the ranks of men upon whom much of the force of the vigilante drive has fallen. I have particularly in mind the close association of Felix Frankfurter and the Justice. Men were welcome in the house of Holmes who never appear in Hearst editorial pages, save grotesquely pictured as wearing whiskers and bearing bombs. Perhaps the Justice remembered back to the day when Thoreau rebuked Emerson for staying out of jail.

"The riders in a race do not stop short when they reach the

goal. There is a little finishing canter before coming to a stand-still."

This was part of the last public utterance of Oliver Wendell Holmes before he took his gear and went before the judges to weigh in. And since the racing metaphor is his own, I think it is not inappropriate to say that on the chart against the name of Holmes should run the familiar caption, "Closed fast."

95. NEW LAMPS FOR OLD

Place a rat within a maze and he will not remain forever fuddled. After he has scampered down blind alleys several times and come against dead ends he will begin to learn the lesson of the labyrinth and come at last into the way of freedom.

Man does not show a similar aptitude. With brazen stupidity he insists upon a lacerating journey through the wire and into trenches where the grass has hardly yet had time to heal the scars of shellfire. And he orchestrates his folly with a roll of drums, the blare of bands and patriotic speeches.

Senators, great editors and holy men who speak through radio pounce eagerly upon all existing international machinery for peace and cry that it should be scrapped because of its antiquity and ineffectiveness. And yet these same men continually do cry for the modernization of every implement of war.

I would not hold in my heart such bitterness for those who killed the League and later stabbed the Court to death if any one of them had mentioned a single substitute for the devices which they so wantonly destroyed.

To be sure, they brayed of "isolation," but that's an alley choked already with the dead of young America. And "pre-paredness" was mentioned even in the very shadow of the white crosses which bear testimony that here is one more dead end in the experience of the nations.

When we scrap a battleship we lay two keels to take its place, but the demolition of any machinery set up for making international peace is accompanied with no new sowing. In those fair fields we scatter the ashes of lost ideals and sterilize the earth with such salt cynicism as "Let them stew in their own juice."

And already the bitter broth begins to bubble and fills the corridors of the world with its deadly fumes. Oh, yes, "let them stew in their own juice," but that juice is the lifeblood of all mankind, and it is thicker than the mountains and deeper than the seas which are supposed to assure us a private prosperity and a separate peace.

We are the chosen of the Lord, and in our self-anointment we dream that by the simple device of never lifting a finger for fellowship we can remain secure upon our lofty plateau even though the watchfires dance upon the rim of our horizon. Moses smote the rock before the waters gushed forth, but we are to be safe and sanctified through inertia and the grumbling negation of a Cain rejecting the responsibility of brotherhood.

Look well, you Coughlins and you Hearsts, upon this world in which you ask us to disclaim all citizenship. Already the tramping of the millions across the sea sets up a tremor in the wheat fields of Nebraska. And we are to save the world from the great delusion by keeping our powder dry and training our youth in the art of war!

I am told that in a prison a single inmate sometimes begins to pound a spoon against his metal dish and that presently the whole tier and then the furthermost corridors of the jail will be engulfed in the din as all within the walls are drawn into the mad rite, not even knowing why. There is just such horrid magic in the beating of a drum.

The League of Nations was a poor thing, and the World Court represented little more than a feeble groping for some new way among the nations. It was easy to point out the flaws and even the dangers in this machinery of peace. Will Rogers was very comical and Father Coughlin very pious. We rejected foreign entanglements and pinned our faith again in Bethlehem, Pa.

Down the blind alley of preparedness and self-sufficiency we scamper once again. The old roads have failed tragically, and, even so, we have not yet set foot upon any new path of freedom. "New gas, new guns, new airplanes"—this is the inspiration of the statesmen.

But let us cry "No!" If the old League was bad, all the more we must set about the building of a new one. If the Court could not function, then we must create one which can. In time of war we must prepare for peace.

There must be some way, and it is not the way of the gunmaker or the manufacturer of munitions. Now, this very instant, we must join all the peoples of the world in raising a cry to build not ships or shells, but some giant plow to furrow under the teeth of all the dragons.

96. HARVARD INDIFFERENCE

Harvard should take something for its sense of humor. Indeed, it would not be too drastic if some of the undergraduates were to lose their kiddie-kar privileges for at least a month. According to the news reports, the peace demonstration at Cambridge was pretty much broken up by more than 2,000 members of the Michael Mullins Chowder and Marching Club.

"The Mullins group," says the *Herald Tribune* story, "paraded the yard and the purlieus of Cambridge in true imperial German style—goose-stepping, giving the straight-arm salute made popular by Adolf Hitler, and singing war songs. . . . All shouted 'Heil! Down with peace! We want cannon!' and other slogans until the university and Cambridge police put an end to the festivities.

"John Roosevelt, youngest son of the President, was among the supporters of the jokesters. He appeared amused at the vain efforts of the anti-war strikers to keep their meeting going in the face of such hilarious opposition."

I gather, therefore, that the object of the Mullins march was one of mockery, and that the cry of "Down with peace! We want cannon!" was intended to be awfully, awfully funny. But I would not call it hilarious. Rather, here was horror heaped on horror. It was as if the hangman's son were playing with a noose of thread. Not hilarity but hysteria was the note which was sounded by those voices. Two thousand strong they cried aloud: "It isn't true. It can't be so that anyone would mark and number our young bodies for the burning. That is the monstrous dream of an idiot and fair meat for a Hasty Pudding charade."

"Heil!" shouted the members of the Mullins Chowder and Marching Club, and there was, I suspect, almost a treble note of terror in the cry of "We want cannon!" They scoff at guns who never felt the earth tremble under the drum of a barrage.

"How heavy your guns are tonight, Mr. Mars. For what do you make preparation?"

"The better to bayonet you, my dears. You'll have to put your foot upon his chest before you draw that blade out right. That man behind you moans. He's still alive. Mop up, you fools, and leave not one behind you who, in his last agony, might toss a grenade."

Once I saw a soldier do a tap dance in front of his own wire until the machine gunners cut him down. He had mixed fear and brandy, and when he laughed it was not amusing.

There is, of course, the urge in all of us to delay the facing of reality. In our youth we cling to myths and legends in which the giants and the dragons of the world are pictured as push-overs for all little folk who live in the shadow of the beanstalk. And as we outgrow this fear we put on other armor of lighter metal and raise up to protect our hearts a certain shield called "the humorous approach." The device is a cap and bells set upon a field of motley. And you will find followers of this strange device even in the trenches of the front line. We who are about to die salute the zero hour with verse and chorus of *Hinkey Dinkey Parlez Vous*. If a man must tremble in the early dawn, let him pretend that he is rocked with laughter.

But it is well that the quality and inspiration for this mirth should always be sharply understood by all who hear its fearful cackle. I would have the men of the Mullins Marching Club take thought, now that their panicky jubilation has subsided. Eighteen years ago other undergraduates paraded through the Harvard yard gripped in the fervor of the coming war. They were perhaps a shade less larky than the present generation. To them there had been sold a last crusade which was to make all future conflict impossible.

Nor did they cry, "We want cannon!" They knew full well that the munitions makers of the world strove night and day to fulfill all the requirements in this respect.

The goose step of today under the elms was an echo of the tramping feet of eighteen years ago. And each humorist set his boot down where one had marched before. The rains and snows have obliterated the marks of Harvard, 1917. And of that band many have not and will not walk again past the entries of Hollis and Holworthy.

And so the Mullins march wasn't really very funny, after all. Even through the din there must have been some whisper of compelling voices from far off saying, "Weep for us. We are your comrades. We are the Harvard dead who died for a lost illusion."

97. REDDER THAN THE ROOSEVELTS

A kind client has sent to me my dossier from Mrs. Albert Dilling's *The Red Network*, which unfortunately I had not read at all. This single all-too-slender biography has sold the book to still another customer. I am fascinated not only by the subject matter but caught up with the manner of the telling. The style is terse and also free. Mrs. Dilling is, I suspect, own cousin to the Garble sisters whose dialogues are featured by Hi Phillips in his Sun Dial column.

But let me quote and try to show how completely an endearing revolutionary can be limned within the span of a couple of sticks. Had they been chafed together, think of the fire which might have been engendered. That is not the Dilling method. Dispassionately the author states her case and lets the reader soak it in. Here goes:

Broun, Heywood: New York *World-Telegram* newspaperman; resigned from Socialist Party recently, saying, it was reported, that it was not radical enough for him; Rand School; wife, Ruth Hale of Lucy Stone Lg., went to Boston to help stage last-minute Sacco-V. protest meeting (N. Y. *Post*, Aug. 10, 1927); ousted as columnist for N. Y. *World* because of friction over his abuse of the authorities in the Sacco-V. matter; at once engaged by radical *Nation*; principal speaker at Level Club, N. Y. C., blacklist party of speakers barred by D.A.R. as subversives, May 9, 1928. James Weldon Johnson, colored radical, was master of ceremonies and mock trial for revocation of D.A.R. charter was held, Norman Thomas being the judge and Arthur Garfield Hays one of the attorneys; nat. com. W.I.R., 1929; nat. com. W. R. Lg., 1930-31; L. I. D. (bd. dir., April, 1931); Recep. Com. Soviet Fliers; Fed. Unemp. Wkrs. Lgs. N. Y., 1933; contrib. *New Masses*, 1933; Nat. Scottsboro Com. of Action, 1933; Emer. Com. Strike Rel., 1933; Il Nuovo Mondo Nat. Com.;

supporter Rand Sch., 1933; nat. coun. Berger Nat. Found.; Nat. Com. to Aid Vic. G. Fascism; pres. and org. Am. Newspaper Guild, 1933; Conf. Prog. Pol. Act., 1933-4; Roosevelt appointee, Theatrical Code Authority, 1933.

It is true that I am the pres. but I am not the org. of the Am. Newspaper Guild and most bitterly do I wish to enter a denial of the last accusation hurled by Mrs. Dilling. President Roosevelt did not appoint me to the Theatrical Code Authority. In all fairness to Mrs. Dilling it must be admitted that she did not weave this serious charge out of whole cloth. I must admit that I sat at one hearing before the theatrical code administrator and that Mrs. Rumsey had informed me that I was there to represent the consuming public. But I was not alone in this reckless deed. Side by side with me sat Joseph Wood Krutch, who, as I later learned, is bd. of eds. and drm. ctc., and lit. ctc. of the *Nat*. At the end of the session, in which William A. Brady, thr. pd., made a long and eloquent speech, a Mr. Rosenblatt asked me if I wanted to say anything. I told him no. He then asked Joseph Wood Krutch, ed. radical *Nat.*, who was almost as eloquent. I was informed that I could get my expenses by turning in an account at the proper office but it happened to be at the far end of the Commerce Building on one of the uncharted corridors and so I said, "Oh, what the hl. I'll stake my country to the $6.15." And that, as Jvh. (Bibl. dty.) is my witness, is the only warrant for the charge that I was appointed to the Thl. Cd. Athy.

That was all the consuming or the theatrical public ever heard from me. And in justice to Mr. Rosenblatt it should be added that undoubtedly when he asked me if I had anything to say he was not cognizant of the fact that I was nat. com. W.I.R. In bringing this matter to light I'll freely confess that Mrs. Dilling has me worried. Indeed, this one revelation in *The Red Network* keeps me tossing and turning at night. Like the young lady in the song, I couldn't say yes and I couldn't say no. Nor is it sufficient to ask indulgence on account of the fact that this was way back in 1929 when I was a young man only nineteen years out of college. How on earth can I explain or justify my being nat. com. W.I.R. when I have not the slightest recollection of what the W.I.R. may be?

Of course, it could be World Institute Reds or Wabbling Into Republicanism. Or for that matter the When in Rome Society. The best I can do is to say that, whether I was a W.I.R. or not in the past, its purposes and its practices elude me now. I can truthfully say that I haven't been to any W.I.R. dance, banquet, or business meeting in the last five years. It must be that I was trying to forget and in this I have succeeded admirably. But there is just one tragic possibility. Perhaps Mrs. Dilling has also forgotten. Come on, Mrs. D., be a good scout and tell me what the W.I.R. is or was so that I can make amends and once more sleep peacefully at night.

Mrs. Dilling has fallen into an inaccuracy in stating that Broun, Heywood (with a little better detective work she might have dug out the "Campbell" for the middle) was "ousted as columnist for N. Y. *World* because of friction over his abuse of authorities in the Sacco-V. matter." My abuse of the authorities did lead to a situation during which I absented myself from the columns of the *World* for several months. That was of my own volition. I got fired by Ralph Pulitzer, almost a year later, after I had returned to the job. The offense was an article in the "radical *Nation*" attacking the editorial policy of the N. Y. *World* as administered largely by Walter Lippmann, p.s.b. Lest there be confusion I may state that p.s.b. is in no sense a radical organization. Some of the most respectable people in the American community belong to it. I appointed them myself. Nicholas Murray Butler is a member and William Randolph Hearst might very appropriately be the org. of this large and inclusive fraternal organization. Madison Square Garden being solidly booked for the season, the members of the p.s.b. have no clubhouse at the moment, although I believe guest privileges have been offered them by the S.N.S.S.—Society of Native Stuffed Shirts.

But to get back to Mrs. Dilling and her all-too-brief biography of Broun, Heywood. Much as I regret to say it, I feel that we have both failed. She has not made out her case and I do not deserve the accolade she has offered. As I read the account of the activities of this *"World-Telegram newspaperman"* I find, not the solid outlines of a red, but merely the portrait of a joiner. Better luck next time, Mrs. D.

98. BEST ALL AROUND

In the *Herald Tribune* my attention was attracted by the following item:

"South Hadley, Mass.—Miss Florence Dunbar, of Amherst, Mass., on the eve of her twentieth birthday, has been singled out at Mount Holyoke College as the most perfect example in the senior class of the classic ideal—a sound mind in a sound body."

A picture accompanied the story, and it showed a large young lady with a very pleasant countenance. I got pretty indignant.

"She looks like a darn nice girl," I said to myself. "They had no right to do a thing like that to her. Why should they make an example of a girl who seems to be having a good time with her studies and her athletics? Making her a symbol of the best potentialities of American womanhood! She ought to go over to the dean, or whoever did it, and punch him or her right in the nose. It's enough not only to ruin the rest of the college career of the hefty young lady but affect her later life as well."

I studied the story to see what material awards Mount Holyoke had conferred upon the luckless girl to make amends for the spiritual damage which might be wrought to her soul. All that she gets is her name inscribed on a silver bowl. She can keep the bowl until she quits college. Yes, it says on it, *Mens sana in corpore sano.*

I hope that's right. I copied it exactly from the paper. The motto was on a gate through which I used to go to college classes, but I never stopped to read it. At least I never digested it.

But if I speak with a good deal of feeling about the plight in which Miss Florence Dunbar finds herself it is because I went through a somewhat similar experience once myself and never have recovered. I was even younger than Miss Dunbar when this tragic thing befell me. The senior class of Horace Mann High School used to meet each year a little before graduation and vote the best this or that. I can't remember all the categories, but we had "the handsomest," of course, "the best dresser" and "the best all around."

When the totals of the votes were announced I was a little disappointed to find that I had not received a single vote as "the handsomest." The fact that I didn't receive any votes, either, for "the best dresser" made no difference. I wasn't running for that.

But then to my great surprise there came the announcement of "the best all around." The figures were read, and they ran Heywood Broun 103 votes, Carl Fernstrom 102. I'd won. I stood head and shoulders above everybody else in the class. It went straight to my head. It remained there. The size of the hat from that day forth has been 7⅞.

But my testimony is not based wholly on personal experience. I know a man who, through his talents, became a symbol of "the highest potentialities of the Negro race."

"How do you like it, Paul?" I asked him once.

He said he hated it. "Sometimes," he explained, "I'd like to take a cocktail or gamble or raise Cain, but there's always somebody around to look at me sternly and remark, 'Remember, you're a symbol.' "

In my own case I must admit that no such burden lies upon me now. Anybody who calls me a symbol of anything had better smile when he says it. Very many years ago I was graduated out of both a sound mind and a sound body. And so my heart bleeds for Miss Florence Dunbar, of Mount Holyoke College.

By dint of desperate work she may raise her blood pressure and lose her athletic figure, but it will take a lot of character for her to win her way through from 100 per cent health to the privilege of doing whatever she pleases.

In the course of time the general public will forget that she concurrently won a poetry prize and played on the field hockey team. Nevertheless, she will be compelled to work with desperate dedication to live down the official finding, "Of all the girls in the senior class she has the best combined record of health, posture, health habits and scholarship."

I do not like to be still one more uninvited interferer with the private life of a young lady who has every reason to be annoyed at the publicity which has been thrust upon her, but in all humility I would like to help. If Miss Florence Dunbar wants to learn how to get away from health habits I hope she will write to me.

99. NEW ORLEANS PLANTER

NEW ORLEANS, LA., Jan. 6 [1936].—"But," said my friend, "you don't understand them and you never will. None of you will. You try to apply white psychology and you miss the point that you are dealing with a people who cannot possibly comprehend our ideals.

"Fill up your glass, Yankee. I'm a round and a half ahead of you. I don't know whether it's the dinner or the drinks, but

I think it's a little stuffy in here. Do you mind if I open a window? Where was I? What was I saying?"

"It was something about our ideals," I suggested.

"Oh, yes, if I didn't have to get down to the plant at nine in the morning I could talk about that all night. Without ideals civilization perishes. And I mean practical ideals. I don't keep them separate from my business life. I take them right into the office with me.

"You might laugh at me, but thirty years ago I was going to be a poet. We all lived on a plantation up the river near Baton Rouge. But when I was twenty-six my father died, and I had to move into New Orleans and take over the business. There hasn't been much time for poetry since. Did you ever notice the little jingles we use in our ads—the one about our Christmas overcoat sale? I write those.

"Yes, I get up to the plantation sometimes now. Not as much as I'd like to. My cousin runs it for me. This isn't a show place. We grow cotton when the government will let us, and we sell it. The plantation has to pay for itself. That's one of my ideals. I've got fifty hands working the place. The amount of meat they eat would startle you. Help yourself and pass the bottle. I remember now what I was trying to tell you. Unless you've grown up with them you can't possibly understand them. They come to me with their troubles. I actually had to decide which girl Armistice Cable (that really is his name) ought to marry. They trust me because they know that I know.

"And yet even in my own case there are things which puzzle you. Maybe no white man, not even a Southern white man, can understand them completely. I'm thinking of a time last year. My cousin called me up and said that Carter had deserted his cotton patch and was walking up and down the roads crazy-like. It was the time for picking, and Carter's one of our best hands. It so happened that I was terribly busy at the store, but I wanted to see the old place and get the dust of the damn office out of my nose and the feel of the earth under my feet. So I shot up there. I can drive it in a couple of hours. The road is a thin white scar across a cypress swamp.

"I went straight to Carter's wife, Lucy, and she told me a curious story. Carter's always been on the place. He's big and strong and a good honest worker. But somehow or other when he was a child he got pellagra, and it's left him a little bit nervous. He can go hysterical and laugh and shout. Well, it seems that in the night he had a dream and a vision. The Lord God Jehovah appeared to him in person. Can you imagine that! And the Lord God told Carter that he had sinned and that he must walk the road along the bayou beyond his patch night and day and speak in the unknown tongues until he was forgiven.

"I called in Daingerfield, my foreman. He isn't a white man, but he's very light. 'I want you to go to Carter,' I told him, 'and point out to him that while he's mumbling I'm losing ten acres of cotton, and that means money. I can't let those ten acres go. Tell him if he doesn't get back to work right away there'll be no meat coming to him next winter.'

"But the strangest part of it all was that Daingerfield wouldn't do it. I grew very angry, and he was frightened. But he kept saying, 'None of us can.' And when I finally asked him the reason he said, 'We don't dare interfere with no man when the spirit is on him.'

"And so for another twenty-four hours Carter walked the banks of the bayou under the sun and the stars and besought God in the unknown tongues to restore peace to his soul. And then he came home.

"And speaking of home, how about just one more drink? I've got to be at the office early. I'm doing some jingles for our crockery festival."

100. MAJORITY OPINION

WASHINGTON, D. C., Jan. 10 [1936].—They say that the voice of Justice Roberts dripped with honey as he said that the high court was always loath to set aside an act of Congress on the ground of unconstitutionality. But at this point his tone grew sharper as he uttered the words, "We naturally require a showing beyond the possibility of a doubt."

And at this precise point I think that Justices Stone, Cardozo and Brandeis might well have risen to their feet to inquire, "And do you think that our dissent casts upon the majority opinion no shadow of a doubt?"

As a matter of fact, if even a single member of the Supreme Court failed to detect any unconstitutionality, that might well constitute a reasonable doubt, for surely there should be no one on the high bench incapable of casting a shadow.

But if the Constitution is to be conserved from the wild and reckless attacks made upon it by the sabotaging six it will probably be necessary to pass an amendment. Essentially this will be a matter of restoration and not of change.

The people of America are rather tardy in realizing the fact that the structure of the basic document has been very radically altered by the ruling majority of the Court. If there were any true sincerity behind the announced purposes of the Liberty League, its first activity would necessarily be an attempt to keep the Supreme Court from kicking the Constitution around. The warning of Mr. Justice Stone on this particular point, in his dissenting opinion on the AAA decision, went unheeded by a little willful group which seems intent upon destroying the traditional balance of power by obliterating the legislative function of Congress.

On Wednesday Representative Marcantonio, of New York, dropped into the hopper at the House a proposal for constitutional revision. Its purport can adequately be summed up in the opening sentence, "The Congress shall have power to establish uniform laws throughout the United States to regulate agriculture and industry."

Mr. Marcantonio is a Republican, although in some quarters he is considered slightly more radical than that label would imply. But there is nothing in his suggestion of a revolutionary nature. In fact, he is merely urging that a clause be put back into the Constitution which the present hell-bent Court has stricken out.

It is well to remember that the decision read by Mr. Justice Roberts merely used triple A as a springboard to write the most sweeping pronouncement ever handed down from the high bench. Three times the original Constitutional Convention went on record against the right of the Supreme Court to invalidate the acts of the national legislature. Marshall made a bold stroke when he overrode this expressed intention of the founders, and he chose a case in which the issue at stake was trivial. Otherwise there might have been an outcry.

But even Mr. Chief Justice Marshall might well have been inclined to join with Stone, Cardozo and Brandeis in saying to a rampant majority, "Boys, aren't you going just a bit too far? Remember that, after all, you are not the exclusive owners of this Constitution. In theory, at any rate, it does belong to the people, and their interpretation must be the final one."

As yet there has been no way to check the reckless six marauders from laying hands upon traditions considered sacred. They are behaving a little like old grads back at a class reunion, and their theme song seems to be *Hail, Hail, the Gang's All Here*. And when they come to the rousing chorus of "What the hell do we care!" it is almost possible to see and hear Sutherland and Pierce Butler smacking their steins on the table and marking time with their feet.

Nothing but a slight excess of school spirit can serve to explain the cavalier way in which Mr. Justice Roberts and his mob removed the general welfare clause from the Constitution. Certainly there can be no legal or rational support for the contention that the welfare of agricultural workers is not a matter of general concern. In the earlier decision against the Railway Pensions Act Mr. Justice Roberts again wrote the opinion which said that labor was a local issue.

It is inspiriting, then, to find emerging from the Republican ranks a man like Representative Marcantonio who wants to get away from these newfangled notions of the Supreme Court majority and go back to the clearly indicated intentions of our forefathers. There ought to be united and enthusiastic support for his back-to-earth proposal that "the Congress shall have power to establish uniform laws throughout the United States to regulate agriculture and industry."

101. RUDYARD KIPLING

I never saw Kipling but for several years I lived in an apartment which he had occupied during an American visit. Indeed it was in those rooms that he lay gravely ill with pneumonia for many weeks. Even when he recovered, he probably did little writing, for he was here to lecture. And for that matter almost all his best work was already behind him although he had not yet turned thirty-five.

However, I liked to pretend that his desk had stood in the very spot where I was sitting engaged in my daily stint. It pleased me to hope and imagine that some emanation of the man still remained in the room. Unfortunately no evidence accrued to make good the theory. Nobody ever said of any column produced during that period, or any other for that matter, "How Kiplingesque." Although extremely lenient in such matters, I could not even see any resemblance myself.

And yet, I suppose, almost everyone who has set down one little word after another in the last thirty years pays unconsciously, whether it is palpable or not, some tribute of imitation to the man who most unquestionably was king. Nobody escaped the spell if Kipling caught him young enough. Many pretend that they had completely recovered. It was popular and also eminently correct to say that Kipling's native imperialism grew upon him with the years. He became the world's worst Tory. Indeed after the war he became a sort of imperialist scold. He was no longer a dangerous propagandist because the old magic and eloquence were gone.

Perhaps it isn't quite true that all great story-tellers have been persons of a low order of intelligence. I hear that Shakespeare was quite smart. But on the whole, popular tales are composed by those who believe everything they see and hear. Or even what they think they see. Kiplings are easy marks for tailors who can fashion a robe for the king out of thin air.

The man believed utterly in the divine right of English rule. Where others saw only a tax gatherer, he visioned a crusading knight in shining armor. Indeed he was so credulous that it seemed to him that even the black panthers and the wolves of the jungle spoke to each other, saying, "The empire is mighty and must prevail."

But if Kipling had not been sufficiently simple to believe in the white man's burden, and that the white man was actually toting it, he might never have written *The Man Who Would Be King*.

In the beginning there were many Englishmen in India who failed to realize how great a propaganda service Kipling was doing for king and country. Indeed the charge was current that he had gone native. The whole thing, of course, was a typographical error. He went naïve.

Yet what wouldn't any one of us give to be twelve again and

meeting Mowgli for the first time in the pages of *St. Nicholas*.
I believe that Rudyard Kipling will live although there may
well be a curious irony in the decision of posterity. I think that
almost everything he wrote concerning the captains and the
kings and the might and majesty of England will go down the
wind along with yesterday's stray paper. He will be remem-
bered because he knew elephants and tigers.

I have not been much for the conversations between carniv-
orous animals in very recent fiction. And the chatter of the
smaller beasties like Willie the Woodchuck and Goofus the
Squirrel have been distinctly appalling. Kipling had a feeling
for the dignity of our four-footed foes. He endowed his ani-
mals with speech but he never subjected them to using baby
talk.

At twelve I was more idolatrous than I am now, but it re-
mains no small thing to have created Kim and Mulvaney and
Ortheris, not forgetting that disturber of traffic who saw the
streaked lines in the water beneath his lighthouse. And it would
be easy to suggest precisely the satisfactory heaven for Kipling.
If the Creator can arrange it, the celestial city need only be
some little corner of the British Empire.

102. AMONG THOSE PRESENT

WASHINGTON, Jan. 27 [1936].—Clara was crying. The rest of
the Liberty Leaguers were either laughing or applauding. Al
was discussing the issues of the day and he had just said, "I
have five children and I have ten grandchildren." Or possibly
it was at a later point where he attacked demagogues and cried
out in a stirring voice, "There can be only one Capital—Wash-
ington or Moscow." At any rate, Clara was crying all over what
Jouett Shouse described as "our simple, modest $5 dinner."

"What's the matter, Clara?" asked the gentleman who brought her, "aren't you having a good time?" She lifted her tear-stained face and said, "He's saving the republic."

If I had not been at the party and had merely read the oration it might have been enough to say, "An old man from a tall tower vented an ancient grudge." But, strangely enough, Al Smith did not dominate the evening. At times he seemed no more than some lightning-change artist who had come out from behind the potted palms to amuse the guests.

The whole thing seemed unreal. Certainly it was surprising to hear Al Smith begin a speech with a reference to his wife and end it with the Bible and the American flag. Almost any moment you expected to hear somebody interrupt to say, "This program comes to you through the courtesy of—." Yes, that was the mood, and the announcement might have run, "This program comes through the courtesy of the shade of Mark Hanna and the ghost of Thomas Platt."

As I looked about I almost expected to see Boise Penrose with a crowd at a table just below the speaker's spot on the dais. Of course, I didn't. John W. Davis had that table. And even so one did not feel that we were dining in the land of the living. Practically all the guests seemed to have stepped from a page of Art Young caricatures done during the gay '90s.

It is true Al Smith stopped just this side of attacking the popular election of Senators, but here seemed to be men who saved us from Populism in 1896. This was the guard which dies but never surrenders, the legion dedicated to the theory that the status quo shall not perish from this earth. And they laughed so long and so loud and clapped their hands so heartily that the sound of masses marching was scarcely audible.

"I talked to my workers, 900 of them," said the gray-haired man behind me, "and I told them just what Al is saying tonight. I told them that they'd have to work their fingers off for every last nickel they ever earned, that it always had been so and it always would be so and, by gad, sir, I made them like it."

But now Al was swinging into the question of taxation, and you could have heard a diamond bar pin drop.

"There are three classes of people in this country," said Al, "there are the poor and the rich and in between the two is what has often been referred to as the great backbone of America—that is, the plain fellow. That is the fellow that makes from $100 a month up to the man that draws down $5,000 or $6,000 a year. Now, there is a great big army. Forget the rich; they can't pay this debt. If you took everything they have away from them they couldn't pay it; they ain't got enough."

And the big ballroom of the Mayflower rang with the happy applause of the diners who sat there trying to hide their proud poverty behind brave laughter.

The speaker spoke of those who believe in a liberal interpretation of the Constitution and said, "What I have held all during my public life is that Almighty God is with this country and He didn't give us that kind of Supreme Court."

The Liberty League paid a generous tribute of applause to the Almighty in recognition of His sound principles.

The man introduced as Al Smith hurried on to compare the Constitution with the Bible and finished with a tribute to our National Anthem and our National Emblem. Everybody jumped up and cheered except Clara and myself. I had joined her in weeping. I wept because the Happy Warrior was dead.

Among those present were Felix A. du Pont, Jr.; A. V. du Pont, Mrs. A. V. du Pont, Emile F. du Pont, Eugene E. du Pont, Henry B. du Pont, Mrs. H. B. du Pont, Irenee du Pont, Mrs. Irenee du Pont, Miss Octavia du Pont, Pierre S. du Pont and Mrs. Pierre S. du Pont.

103. MR. MENCKEN'S CANDIDATE

Henry Mencken says that the Republicans can beat Roosevelt with a Chinaman. Mr. Mencken and his Tory associates must be suffering from delusions of grandeur. What earthly reason have they for believing that any Chinaman would accept the Republican nomination?

Moreover, H. L. Mencken, the Main Street sage, must be familiar with the fact that the Chinese cannot pronounce the letter "r." In the days when he was an editor of international fame he must have received many holiday cablegrams from his Shanghai subscribers beginning, "Melly Chlistmas to you and the Melculy." Now, wouldn't it be silly to have a man dashing around the country appealing for "Lepublican votes"?

As a matter of fact, in an effort to aid Mencken and the G.O.P. I made a short tour of the city yesterday in an effort to find a Chinese who would help the conservatives out of their dilemma by consenting to run. Ah Wing Fongh, laundryman, when interviewed replied, "Velly solly, me no leactionaly. Lepublicans catchee no ticket no shirtee."

Chinn Lee, restaurant man, merely answered, "No wantchee," and followed with some obscure Pell St. joke about Bill Borah and a native delicacy known as century eggs.

Wong Fah, who is a junior at Columbia and speaks as excellent English as any Liberty League orator, replied, "Not on your celestial life. Apparently the only relief the Republicans are prepared to offer is low comedy. They may want a change in dialect, but we will furnish no pidgin to put in every pot. One of our philosophers of the Ming dynasty remarked, 'In time of distress the rich and respectable will do anything for a poor man except get off his neck.'"

But if it proves impossible to get a Chinese to accept the Republican nomination I have another suggestion which I trust will not be lightly discarded. Why not run Mencken? It may be argued that Henry does not write with quite the snap and verve of Herbert Hoover. His style is more ponderous and less illumined by epigram, but it should suffice. The point of view is the thing which matters, and Henry L. Mencken can provide both the horse and the buggy, not to mention the carriage whip.

Why be content to go back merely to 1929? Why not return all the way to the age of Mencken when the *Mercury* was a magazine and little boys went around behind the barn to smoke cornsilk and read the dramatic reviews of George Jean Nathan?

Al Smith has indicated that the campaign should consist of an attempt to win the great middle class of the United States. And who but Henry completely typifies that group? Mencken represented precisely what Babbitt wished to be when he grew up. He was the village slicker who stayed away from prayer meeting, and it was even said that he went to mad revels where people drank beer and played the trombone. He was always a full year ahead of the Rotary Club.

Republican leaders have racked their brains to find another Calvin Coolidge. They have even gone as far away as Kansas to find his equivalent. And all the time, much nearer home, Henry Mencken has been sitting in the ashes in Baltimore waiting for Prince Charming to come along with the glass slipper.

There need be no doubt that the shoe fits. Mencken is Coolidge—that is, Coolidge with one cocktail. His political and economic ideas are precisely those of the late Republican President. Farmers and workers are in distress, according to the Mencken-Coolidge school of thought, because they didn't put their salaries in the savings bank every Saturday. If people go hungry the thrifty should not be called upon to aid them. Why don't they pay their bills and go to work?

"Instead of safeguarding the hard-earned money of the people," Mencken writes of Roosevelt, "and relieving them from their appalling burden of taxation, he has thrown away billions to no useful end or purpose and has piled up a debt that will take generations to discharge."

That is typically Coolidge—the insistence that "the people" means men of substance and men of property, the feeling that the unemployed are in some way wasters and sinners. To be sure, "A camorra of quarreling crackpots" is a somewhat unsuccessful attempt to imitate Herbert Hoover in his new manner, but the same man who taught Herbert might put in a little time brushing up the style of Henry.

By all means let them run Mencken, and I offer him gratis the slogan "Let 'em eat pumpernickel."

104. MRS. HEYWOOD COX BROUN

Maybe my mother won't like this column, but at least it seemed to me that she suggested it herself. Every once and so often there appears in the letter department of my home town paper a very violent communication about me signed Mrs. Heywood Cox Broun. Mrs. Heywood Cox Broun is my mother, and, unlike her younger son, she never pulls her punches or sneaks up on an adversary.

Although her economic point of view is highly conservative, she expresses it with all the flaming ardor of a revolutionist. I know some radicals who, by dint of hard practice, can actually hiss the words "Wall Street." My mother can do that with "labor union."

If she actually met a labor union face to face I believe her hostility would evaporate. You see, most of her contacts have been made through the editorial page of the New York *Herald Tribune*. I have lent her a few copies of the *New Masses*, but they only served to madden her. I imagine it would have been shrewder tactics to have started with the *New Republic*.

In the beginning Mrs. Heywood Cox Broun did not take "my views" very seriously, but I am happy to say that she no longer tries to dispose of me as a posing pink. Only the other day she admitted in all seriousness that she regarded me as a menace, and I was very proud.

"The trouble with you, Heywood," she told me, "is that you have never been an employer."

To be sure, that is not entirely accurate. For one year I was a minor newspaper executive, and theoretically I had the power to hire and fire. I never fired anybody, but the one writer whom I engaged turned out to be top man in his division. Not only did I pick and choose Bill McGeehan for the sport page of the *Tribune* but I exploited him.

The bargaining base on which I was empowered to operate was very slim. The managing editor said I could have him if he would come for $50 a week, and if he wouldn't take that I could go as high as $55. Bill was a very shy man all the days of his life, and I was pretty shy myself back in 1916. Besides, I never had hired anybody before. The conference was carried on with each of us looking out the opposite window.

"Mr. McGeehan," I said, "I am empowered to offer you either $50 or $55 a week to come to work. Which would you rather have?"

Bill chose $55, and in a few months he was the best-known sports writer in New York. There is, then, no blot on my escutcheon as an employer. Still, it is probably true that my talents do not lie in that direction, and I have no ambtion to try again. The strain of waiting to see which salary he would accept taught me my lesson.

My mother thinks I am a "phony," although I am pretty certain she did not use that word, in the matter of parading and picketing. "It might teach you a good lesson and you would get to bed earlier if somebody did send you to jail for a couple of months," is her dictum.

However, if anything of the martyr complex lurks in me I have a right to assert that it is hereditary. For one afternoon there was no elevator service in the apartment building in which my mother lives, and now it has been restored, which makes my mother pretty indignant. The service came back because the landlord signed up with the union. My mother is considering walking up and down the five flights of stairs as a protest.

Individually the elevator boys are all right by her. She furnishes ice cream on Sundays and takes up the Christmas collection from the tenants. I forgot to say that my mother is very executive. She would make an excellent agitator herself, but she doesn't like to see anybody else agitate. I can easily imagine a situation in which she would picket for Eddie and George and Caleb. But they mustn't do it themselves. In some way that isn't fair to Mr. Pease and Mr. Elliman.

I am using them as symbols. She has another landlord. Mrs. Heywood Cox Broun has been in the same building for twenty-five years, and to my certain knowledge she has called that landlord every conceivable name, short of profanity and obscenity, which my mother does not employ, that a gentlewoman can lay her tongue to. But when it's a union fight my mother switches sides. She does not think that anybody else should employ violence.

When the revolution comes it's going to be a tough problem what to do with her. We will either have to shoot her or make her a commissar. In the meantime we still dine together.

105. POPUP JOHN

Spring and the baseball season are here again and I'm going to root for Brooklyn. This has nothing to do with my being born on Pineapple St. In fact the people on Pineapple St. say it was at least a couple of blocks away. Those people are going to be very sorry when the memorial tower goes up.

But getting back to the Dodgers, I'm for Casey Stengel's club because he seems to be giving an opportunity to a couple of groups which are underprivileged in the world today. According to the sports writers, the Brooklyn infield is composed of striplings and the outfielders are all old men. Thus Casey provides a haven for Miltons who are mute and Miltons who are shopworn.

All projects for the easement of the aged are right down my alley. In recent seasons I have remained away from baseball parks because they serve so poignantly to remind a man of his lost youth. They recall the days when it actually caused me anguish to watch the Yankees lose a ball game. Indeed, they weren't even called the Yankees in the days to which I refer. We knew them as the Highlanders, and their ball park was a skimpy affair perched precariously on the front lawn of a deaf and dumb asylum. I can't remember now the name of the first manager, but his hardest job was to distinguish between his players and the inmates.

Since the Highlanders were a new club, the other teams in the league helped them out by sending them one or two players from their surplus material. As a result of this antique shower the Highlanders boasted the finest collection of grandfather clucks ever seen on any diamond.

How well do I remember old Popup John at first. Some of

the most poignant tragedies of my early youth are associated with this same John Ganzel. My youth wasn't so very early at that. Already I was a full-fledged baseball reporter hired for a meager sum to give a dispassionate account of 154 games a year.

Unfortunately, I was wholly unable to attain objectivity, and veterans such as Damon Runyon and Sid Mercer were shocked each afternoon as I broke all traditions of the craft by rooting violently in the pressbox. It was John Ganzel, old Popup John, who eventually induced me to conform to the custom of my confreres and maintain an aloof demeanor.

The teams which played against the Highlanders generally amassed a lead of six or seven runs in the first couple of innings, but presently the Hilltop team would rally. Before you knew it the bases were full, nobody was out and John Ganzel was walking to the plate.

At such times the air was rent with my loud cries of encouragement. I would implore John to hit the ball over the fence, which was not much more than a long putt in that particular park. But Popup John was mashie-minded. What a wizard he would have been in getting out of sandtraps. Ganzel was a little ahead of his time. He was a pioneer in the movement for the industrial or vertical setup. That man could take a full swing at a fast one and meet the ball in such a way as to drive it straight into the air.

Longitudinally, few of his drives carried much more than five or six feet, but it was a fine sight to see the baseball climb and climb as if to meet the setting sun. Indeed, the bleacherites would join in a long-drawn "Ah" as if they watched the flight of rockets.

Ganzel having been disposed of, Jack Kleinow, the catcher, would come up and hit into a double play, and that was the inevitable ending of the Highland fling. Jack was a sixteen-second man, which made the task of the opposition a little easier. I hope and believe that I was the sports commentator

who wrote, "Jack Kleinow goes down to first as if he were pull-
ing Big Bill Taft in a ricksha."

And yet in spite of this brief lapse into cynicism I remained
sentimental about the ball club. Hope did not die that some
day John Ganzel would hit for distance and not for height. I
believe one afternoon he did bounce a single over second. But
the Highlanders continued to lose with a high degree of regu-
larity, and since these were my formative years it had quite an
effect upon my social philosophy. I used to laugh scornfully
when patriotic orators said that any man in America could be
President. I knew that it was not within the range of Popup
John's capacity ever to make it.

Indeed, to this very day I trust no leader utterly and keep
my fingers crossed because I fear that in the pinch he may have
the Ganzel touch. Nevertheless, I mean to haunt the Brooklyn
ball park and, particularly, the seats abutting on the outfield.
I want to see baseball again and in the company of men of my
own age.

106. MY MOTHER'S BRIDGE GAME

I see the police are making raids on contract bridge games
and, naturally, I'm worried about my mother. She was not sym-
pathetic when I was arrested in Milwaukee, even though I
pointed out that I was a first offender and also a "political pris-
oner." But now if the campaign against contract continues she
runs the risk of being apprehended as a common gambler.

Indeed, from my observation, her bridge is even a little
worse than that, and so if her apartment is raided I suppose I
could stand aside and say grimly, "Retribution," and let it go
at that. But I would do nothing of the sort. If the worst occurs
I will stand shoulder to shoulder with her in court. Maybe I

could arrange to get arrested for picketing on the same day as a sort of tactful gesture to lessen her sense of shame.

She leads away from aces and neglects to keep jump bids alive. But she is still my mother.

I never thought to see her part of a crime wave. Probably it could all be traced to something in her early environment, and I have retained Leibowitz just to be on the safe side. If he was able to win an acquittal for Vera Stretz I have every reason to feel that he could get my mother off with a small fine.

It ought to be quite possible to procure witnesses to testify that she seemed to be under the impression that she was playing parchesi.

Of course, my mother doesn't actually run a bridge club. She plays only with her friends. Still, some of the strangest people do drop in. It would be a quibbling defense to say that the stakes are small.

If the prosecution summoned me I would have to break down under cross-examination and admit that the usual fortieth of a cent is sometimes abandoned. Along about two or three in the morning I have known my mother to say recklessly, "Let's play two more rubbers and make it a twentieth." I know she always seems offended when midnight comes and I point out that as a working man it is necessary for me to retire early.

But the phase of the case which would give Leibowitz the greatest trouble would be the undoubted fact that sometimes my mother sallies forth and plays contract for a good deal more than a twentieth of a cent a point. I have wired to her that if the cops put the lug on her and she faces a rap the best thing to do will be to come clean and throw herself on the mercy of the court. Of course, I wouldn't like to see her snitch on Marc Connelly's mother, who generally takes her to these tournaments, but she might as well admit that sometimes she plays for prizes.

These so-called tournaments are always advertised as being for the benefit of something or other. My mother has been so faithful in this sort of charitable work that I don't quite see how a single American can still be starving. Indeed, in spite of my mother's highly conservative political and economic philosophy, I wouldn't put it past her to play for the benefit of the *Daily Worker* if only there was a signed photograph of Earl Browder as the first prize.

Somehow it doesn't seem to matter just who or what is named as the object of the drive. The tournament always turns out to be a benefit for my mother. Maybe she plays under wraps at home, for put her in with a hundred other women and it is ten to one that she will come home with the hand-painted vase, the ash tray or the silk umbrella.

You can't move around the apartment at all without tripping over an umbrella. A casual visitor who did not know the secret passion of the hostess might well get the impression that she was about to embark for Ethiopia to spend the rainy season. I wonder whether the rest of us should be indicted as accessories after the fact. We all have umbrellas and ash trays gleaned from my mother's rich store of loot.

Ours has not always been a united family. We were split into three sections by the elevator strike, the Guffey coal bill and the fact that my mother once belonged to the D.A.R. and was thinking of running for third vice president.

I have always felt that contract bridge came along just in time to save her from a fate worse than death. At present I think I ought to say, in all fairness to her, that she wouldn't go across the street to hear a patriotic address unless it was in the hope of getting a fourth for bridge.

Ironically enough, some of my activities of which she has strongly disapproved may now prove useful to her. I am in a position to give her good advice. When the police come go quietly. Insist on your one telephone call before they lock you in the cell and don't give your right name or my record will be used against you.

107. KITTREDGE'S FAREWELL

Once I wrote that no man ever knows just when to stop. Human beings time themselves badly in the matter of making exits. We all stay on too long. So it must be admitted that Professor Kittredge did rather well. For my taste his farewell to Harvard University was a shade too theatrical, but it was effective, and, after all, he had taught Shakespeare for forty or fifty years.

He did not dramatize himself in the manner of Lear or Mercutio or Macbeth. I wish I knew more about Shakespeare, but that can't be blamed on Kittredge. He did his best, or, if not that, at least he put no obstacles in my way. However, I have a vague recollection that somewhere in *Julius Caesar* Brutus and Cassius sit down in a tent and talk together very quietly. Perhaps that's the thing called "the quarrel scene." In any case I refer to the part before they get to fighting.

That would be the mood of Professor Kittredge's farewell. The high and florid tradition of Shakespeare was revised into the swaggering underemphasis of New England.

Professor Kittredge has a long white beard but insufficient showmanship to swing it, and so when he came to the river's brink he made no oration but set up his tent and placed upon it the sign "Business as Usual." In addition to the pupils in his course some three hundred other students had gathered to hear "Kitty" take off.

If any expected him to weep or sing *The Last Round-Up* they were disappointed. He did fetch Shakespeare out and saddle the old word painter for a final foray, but it was done without benefit of bugle calls. The absent-minded professor gave no indication of noticing the studio audience. He addressed his remarks solely to those enrolled in English 2.

The class was at work on Gene Tunney's old favorite, *A Winter's Tale*. Where they had left off on the previous occasion they took up again. No hint was given by the preceptor that this was an occasion having anything of unusual significance. It was just a segment of that same old course—a course, I might add, in which the bones of many luckless Harvard seekers after knowledge lie moldering. But it's too late now. There is no spot this side of Judgment Day where I can argue to have my D minus raised to a simple D.

A little before his hour was up he informed the class that he would not be able to finish the play at that morning session. He suggested that they might use the printed notes in the book, although he added that they were hardly as good as he could furnish. And then quite casually, too casually I fear, he said, "We'll stop here."

From now on Harvard will have to find Shakespeare without the aid of George Lyman Kittredge, the last of the Old Guard of distinguished scholars at Cambridge. And since he had taught his subject in the same place and the same room for very nearly fifty years, perhaps he may be pardoned for departing at the end a little from the honored tradition of Harvard. He did not, as he might have done, step directly toward the door and so out into the yard and through the gate and home from Harvard. He blew himself for a full minute to the privilege of behaving like a leading man or a Yale professor in the department of English. He stood poised at the edge of the platform and took his full sixty seconds of applause from the three hundred.

George Lyman Kittredge did not bow or blow kisses to the crowd or in any way acknowledge the plaudits of the undergraduates. No flashlight photographers had been bidden to be present. He kept clearly in his mind that this was not New Haven.

Nor is there any reason to be captious about the way things are done among the Elis. "Each man to his taste," as the Yale senior said when he signed up to take the course on Robert Browning with William ("Billy") Lyon Phelps. To be sure, Kittredge might have stood his ground indefinitely and run no risk that any one of Harvard's sons would dare to call him "Kitty." But precisely at the end of a minute the Professor indicated with his hand that he wanted the aisle cleared.

It used to be a cloak he wore, if I remember. But in any case he threw something over his shoulders and without another word he left fifty years of teaching behind him. And as he walked under the elms in the direction of his house it may be that like Christian he felt relieved of his burden. It is even possible that he went straight to his library and, taking down a copy of *Hamlet*, said, "Now for the first time in fifty years I can read this for fun and find out if it really is any good."

108. G.O.P. TO G.Y.P.

CLEVELAND, June 11 [1936].—They ask for bread and they receive a slogan. There is a clamor for advice and counsel, and it is met with a keynote wisecrack, something such as Steiwer's nifty about "bookworms and hookworms." Under the hoopla and the hippodroming there actually exists an eagerness to come to grips with those problems which afflict the nation, but whenever a serious note is sounded the band breaks in with *Three Blind Mice* and all the clowns go crazy, or at least as crazy as they can.

This is written before the speech of Herbert Hoover. As yet it has been a dull convention. No bird, with the exception of the mythical roc, has ever laid so large an egg as that which the gentleman from Oregon contributed to the audience in his speech as temporary chairman.

The Hon. Bertrand H. Snell did little better in his extended remarks as permanent chairman at yesterday's forenoon session.

This convention may still prove magnificently interesting and inspiring, although I'll let somebody else do the betting on that prospect.

Wherever two or ten thousand are gathered together there exists a field of interest. Here is tinder. They wait the coming of the word, and before the eyes of the jaded and the cynical there might sweep a flame dancing from one shoulder to another across the vast expanse of the public auditorium. The Republican leaders seem to have regimented against any such happening. "No miracles, if you please," seems to be the policy of the management.

The second day session began more than an hour late with a prayer forbidding in length and alienating in context. For one I wish to protest against being asked to stand up while a gentleman of the cloth addresses God in the calm assumption the Ruler of the Universe never has and never will give sanction to anything but the straight Republican ticket. The preacher failed to get a hand and seemed disappointed.

The band played *Trees*, and a trio sang a swing song, and Bertrand H. Snell made a speech. "We will win in November if we prove to the masses we deserve to win." What could be fairer than that? And, even so, I doubt that Snell, sandwiched between *Trees* and *Three Blind Mice*, is good enough to set the pace for a political upset.

War looms in Europe, and a man with a guitar steps in front of the microphone to sing *Ickey-Ickey-Oo*.

Ten million men are out of work, and Bertrand H. Snell raises a pudgy fist against "The spirit of class conflict among us."

Our whole relationship in a changing world is up for the consideration of duly chosen delegates, but while the keynoter cools his heels and dulls his points Reinald Werrenrath, in a melodious baritone, informs the convention that "The dawn comes up like thunder out of China 'cross the bay."

The Cleveland *News*, a little impulsively I am afraid, suggests changing the familiar designation of the Grand Old Party to the Grand Young Party. But just what has the G.Y.P. to give to the youth of America? As yet its offer has been limited to the poems of Kipling and the protective tariff. To me, of course, this convention of young Republicans makes great appeal. Chauncey Depew has passed on, but the rest of us are all here. *The Road to Mandalay*—what memories it conjures up! (Twice around the park, driver, and then up to Jack's for breakfast. I'll try to get tickets for the matinee at Weber and Fields').

"The flying fishes play." Well, why wouldn't they? Here today and gone tomorrow, and that old devil dawn coming up out of China 'cross the bay. Can you see it, Steiwer? Do you sense it, Snell? Put away your rattles and all childish things and look. Any minute now it will be upon you, that great red ball of fire which proclaims the coming of a new day.

I tell you the convention has an inkling in spite of your dreary words of cold comfort. Just once there ran through the delegates a wave of excitement. There was tension. Werrenrath sang an old song. He sang "Mine eyes have seen the glory of the coming of the Lord," and when he came to the chorus there was that coalition which has been mentioned. Thousands of voices joined in, "As we go marching on."

But they were not animated by the sour vintage of petty partisanship. Theirs was the wine trampled out of the grapes of wrath, and they marched toward a new world of which there has been no whisper. They cannot hear the paddles chunking. The old order is lost in the thunder of the dawn.

109. HOOVER SPEAKS

CLEVELAND, June 12 [1936].—As one who does not like Herbert Hoover I must admit that at least he went down swinging. Indeed, he hit a couple over the fence which were not foul by more than a couple of hundred feet. But I do not wish to be too fulsome in my flattery. I think that the address which Herbert Hoover made to the Republican convention was one of the most dangerous and vicious utterances ever made by a public man in this country before an open assembly. Under the thin disguise of defending "liberty" Herbert Clark Hoover gave aid and encouragement to every Kluxer, every Black Legionary and every Vigilante in America.

Mr. Hoover is a gentleman who pretends to be able to see around corners. Once, through his extraordinary gift of oblique vision, he professed to see prosperity lurking just behind the bend of the street line. And now he says that he sees red revolution.

The evening did not belong wholly to Hoover. He must share the credit for his gospel with William Randolph Hearst. Like the Lord of San Simeon, the Sage of Palo Alto cries "Communism" whenever three or four liberals are gathered together.

Early in his speech he accused the New Deal of having loosed "the propaganda of hate." He then proceeded for more than forty minutes to heap invectives on all who will not agree to let the issue of patriotism and liberty be decided by a vote of five to four. Under the stipulations laid down by Herbert Hoover, Chief Justice Hughes becomes a soapbox agitator.

"The American people should thank Almighty God for the Constitution and the Supreme Court." Working women in the

State of New York who have added hours piled upon their backs for smaller pay should get down on their knees and give thanks to those surrogates of Hoover's heaven who have assured them of their right of contract.

"Lead the attack, retake, recapture and reman the citadels of liberty."

Herbert Hoover would bring comfort to those who are crippled and maimed by a reckless economic system. To such he would say, "Take up your bed and run," for even those who are without arms or legs are not denied a right to the pursuit of happiness in Hoover's generous dispensation. The small children in the mills and factories are to be guaranteed their liberty. Freedom to starve quietly and without any outside interference whatsoever will be assured to all under the clarion call of Herbert Hoover.

The voice of Butler, Van Devanter, Roberts, McReynolds and Sutherland is the voice of God. When those five have spoken you know precisely what crumbs you will be permitted to scramble for. These are your liberties. Take them and cherish them, for if you have any idea that there may be a better way you have been poisoned by the ideas of Europe.

By a curious coincidence I followed Mr. Hoover's speech through a proof furnished by the Cleveland *Plain Dealer*, which carries at its masthead the name "Paul Bellamy—Editor." I rather hoped that Bellamy might rise in defense of his New England father and say, "The gospel of brotherhood is rooted in our native soil, and Edward Bellamy, who first gave to America a vision of a co-operative state, was neither muddled nor murderous. When you seek to identify the merchants of venom look to your own lips."

Paul Bellamy, as it turned out, did not get up to say anything during the tirade, but, at least, his conservative paper made the comment the next day:—"If some world power were ready within a few hours to bombard half a dozen American cities, if Communists in arms were encircling Washington and proposing on the morrow to sack and destroy the capital, if the British army were on the point of crossing the lake to thrust a spearhead into the heart of the republic—such a speech as Herbert Hoover delivered to the convention would be completely justified. By no less absurd hypothesis can some parts of it be excused."

The glorification of war was decidedly such a part. In speaking of American ideals of liberty Herbert Hoover said, "Less than twenty years ago we accepted those ideals as the air we breathe. We fought a great war for their protection."

And has the mind of America become poisoned, Mr. Hoover, if many of us are opposed to sending once again our boys and men to make the world safe for your conception of democracy? Your kindly suggestion that another little conflict might be a tonic for national ideals comes strangely from the mouth of the Great Humanitarian. Nor does it fit altogether with your attack upon the gospel of hate.

When Hoover raised the fiery cross and leaped into the saddle, logic did not ride beside him. He canonized five members of the Supreme Court, and the convention sang "As we go marching on." The delegates had forgotten, perhaps, that this song was not dedicated to Chief Justice Taney but to an American radical named John Brown.

110. NEWS FOR KNOX

Frank Knox has not yet been notified officially of the fact that he is running for the Vice Presidency. That ceremony occurs some time in August, I believe. At the moment the workers on his paper must have a hard time to keep the news from their boss. They do not allow him to read his own publication without first clipping out his photograph and scissoring the news section. Nobody wants to spoil his fun at the August party so far in advance.

The present plan is to have all the reporters and rewrite men leap to their feet and cry "Surprise! Surprise!" when he walks into the office on the appointed day. But there are certain dangers in keeping Frank in the dark. Too much of the running news has been withheld from him. For instance, the good gray publisher seems to be unacquainted with the fact that he has been drafted for the Youth Movement. He did not see in the classified department of his own paper a little ad which read, "Will exchange elderly elephant for kiddie-kar in reasonably good repair. Communicate with G.O.P., General Delivery, Topeka, Kan."

If the Colonel were abreast of events he would surely understand that this is no time for him to be reminiscing about the good old days. Take, for instance, his communication to Alf Mossman Landon in which he said:—"Both political and economic conditions call for a display of the same great qualities which endeared us both to Theodore Roosevelt. I know that we have them."

And the whole world just knows that Frank wears them. For that very reason I think it would have been better if the Colonel had been content to wait for someone else to bring the matter up. In pointing with pride the finger should always be extended out as in drinking coffee. The Colonel should have waited in silence until somebody came up and said, "Frank, I've got a trade last for you."

But even beyond the matter of the technique of getting compliments upon the record I think Frank Knox made a mistake in recalling the Bull Moose years of 1912. That was almost a quarter of a century ago and might tend to disqualify the Colonel from membership in the Children's Crusade to save the Constitution. Even worse is the tactless insistence of his friends in saying, "Frank Knox followed Teddy Roosevelt up San Juan Hill." Come to think of it, that was a full thirty-eight years ago. Knox's name should never be mentioned in connection with such ancient history unless it is distinctly mentioned that he did not run up the hill but merely toddled, lisping in a childish treble, "Good gracious! Wait for baby."

There are a great many voters who no longer remember the *Maine,* and they will have to be reminded all over again that we were called upon to fight in the middle of a tough summer when the Spaniards were about to land upon our shores and snatch away our traditional liberties. Old George Morris, of this newspaper, says that he also was at San Juan. He didn't happen to see either Colonel Roosevelt or Colonel Knox, but he admits that it was a pretty big hill and that there was plenty of room at the top. His own recollection is less romantic than that of his two comrades in arms. George Morris remembers San Juan Hill because he was fined $25 for losing his rifle. At that he didn't exactly lose the gun but threw it into the bushes for safe-keeping. It seems that every time he fired the weapon a great cloud of black smoke arose and left him eligible for the sniping of the Spanish sharpshooters. Mr. Morris would not be here today but for the low academic standards of the enemy's riflemen.

Indeed, the whole maneuver might very well have resulted in a glorious annihilation of the Rough Riders but for the arrival of the colored soldiers composing the Tenth Cavalry. In addition, the rumor persists that Teddy Roosevelt chose the wrong hill to ascend. He was supposed to charge up San Juan, but when the dust had cleared away he found himself on top of Kettle. But that, I am told, is a good hill, too.

As far as immediate political strategy goes, it might seem the part of wisdom for Frank Knox to forget the entire San Juan episode. In the next few months the Colonel will be called upon to do a good deal of charging on his own account, and it would not do at all to have the impression get out that the first assistant candidate of the Republican party is addicted to climbing up any hill which meets his fancy whether it is the right one or not. When politicians begin to rush up the wrong hill they are likely to find that this is a form of exercise calculated to keep them out in the open, and permanently at that.

Again, if the Spanish-American War really gets to be the critical issue of the race somebody may thumb back among his old documents and start the story of Hearst's famous wire to Frederic Remington. Whether or not he actually did send such a message, it has gained an enduring place in national folk tales. Mr. Hearst is supposed to have cabled to his impatient artist, who feared arbitration. "You furnish the pictures and I'll furnish the war."

If I were Colonel Knox I would put the rusty musket in the attic, hide away all decorations and swear off mountain climbing. More than that, I'd get myself a calendar plainly labeled 1936 and under the caption "Things to do today" I would write in a legible hand, "Don't forget to run for the Vice Presidency of the United States."

iii. AT FRANKLIN FIELD

Franklin Delano Roosevelt saved the show. Even the best friend of the Democrats would be obliged to tell them that their convention was dreary, dull and exuberant only under artificial stimulation. The lone exception was the genuine tribute to Governor Lehman.

The reason why the delegates sought to drown their apathy in Brighton punches is easily explained. A very great number of the persons bearing badges do not really like their candidate. At times they spoke rapturously of the New Deal, but it is not in their hearts. The Democratic party as such is just as conservative as it was four years ago. People like Joe Robinson and

Pat Harrison and even the Vice Presidential candidate are not enthusiastic about the more abundant life.

And yet I came away convinced that Roosevelt is going to slay the dragons, including the copperheads which lie close at hand.

The Copelands, the Smiths and the Colbys cannot hurt him, nor even those more dangerous foes who follow with their fingers crossed. Al is but a single Smith. On Saturday night at Franklin Field and throughout the nation Roosevelt spoke to millions of Smiths and Browns and Cohens and Kellys. And they are walking in a mighty army close behind him.

The President is a good trouper. He gives his best performances in the tight spots. As a piece of effective oratory his Franklin Field talk was second only to his inaugural address. There was no question that he completely captured the huge audience. Most of the delegates and the fringe folk had been poured onto trains before he arrived. This was a new crowd. Thousands of tickets had been distributed to the big unions. This was very largely a working-class audience. Roosevelt was talking to Al the coal miner and Colby the cutter.

From where the President stood he could not possibly see the far edge of the multitude, which seemed to stretch back endlessly behind the furthest sweep of the floodlights. This might have been the army which a chieftain of Israel summoned from behind the rim of the hills and from the bowels of the earth, and, like him, Mr. Roosevelt could cry, "I will call to my side one hundred to take the place of every one who quits me."

These were the people of warmth and passion to whom he talked. There were men sitting at the Liberty League dinner who could have bought and sold the entire 100,000 who sat under the skimpy moon and a few stars as Roosevelt attacked the Industrial Royalists. Nor need it be limited to "they could." They are doing just that.

I did not see the Prince of Pay-Cuts at Franklin Field nor the Lord of Speed-Up nor the Count of Company Unions.

Even though they walk with all the pace and dignity of a terrapin on the way to the tureen, they never, never will be missed or much regarded.

In the days to come it may be used against me that I was deeply moved by Franklin Roosevelt speaking to the many in Philadelphia. His limitations as a leader of labor are too obvious to need recapitulation. But here in a rough yet exact way was the nucleus of the great third party of the people's front. And I think that few men have spoken with more complete sincerity than Franklin Delano Roosevelt when he said, "Governments can err—Presidents do make mistakes—but the immortal Dante tells us that Divine justice weighs the sins of the cold-blooded and the sins of the warm-hearted in different scales."

In the days to come, when the almost perfect state has been established, there will be, I suppose, some sort of inferno for all who gave any sort of aid and comfort to the perpetuation of the old order, even through modification. But I hope that in that region there may range a proletarian Gunga Din to give a swig to a lad who did not altogether let Groton get him.

As a matter of fact, Dante got one of the biggest cheers of the night. Perhaps he controls more votes than Al.

Vocally, Franklin Delano Roosevelt was magnificent. The overly genial tones which had begun to creep into the fireside chats were all gone. Now he was out in the open and fighting. Of course, there were many places where he let connotations carry him well beyond his actual words. But when he cried out, "This generation of Americans has a rendezvous with destiny," I know one man who tingled and who felt, "The New World is really on the march." And it seemed to him that he could hear the thunder of its steps.

112. REV. COUGHLIN AND REV. SMITH

It was a cowboy who called one of his associates a so-and-so. Under pressure by his fellows he agreed to apologize and said, "You're no so-and-so. Oh, no!" Father Coughlin seems to have followed a similar technique in regard to his burnt-toast letter to the White House. It was a somewhat grudging retraction of an epithet at best and now the prelate has taken to the stump again. According to a United Press dispatch from Buffalo: "The Reverend Charles E. Coughlin told 10,000 followers today, 'I have no apologies to offer the gentleman in the White House who lives on the rotten meat of broken promises.'"

But just how good are Coughlin's promises? It took him scarcely more than a week to break the pledge he took to abstain from intemperate speeches. And the President is only one man out of a multitude to whom the reverend ranter owes an explanation. It seems to me, for instance, that he owes a distinct apology to Old Doc Townsend and all the physician's followers. Booming "Priest" Charlie (since the lid seems to be off on the free coinage of epithets) went to Cleveland as one of the feature spellbinders. He certainly not only permitted but persuaded the revolving pensioners that he was heart and soul with them in their cause. His handpicked candidate, William Lemke, flatly announced himself as a convert to the Townsend plan, making only the slight and probably unnoticed reservation that the precise details would have to be ironed out by a congress composed of Union Party members and the Townsendite leaders themselves. When Gomer Smith told the delegates that the good father had previously referred to the Townsend scheme as "economic lunacy" he was shouted down as a prevaricator and a bearer of false tidings.

But in Buffalo, according to the same dispatch, Charlie under some pressure was forced to admit that he still believed the revolving pension plan to be "economic lunacy." His justification for his misrepresentations in Cleveland was simply that he and Dr. Townsend must fight together "to oust the New Deal from office." It may be that Charles E. Coughlin also deceived Gerald L. K. Smith. But even if that is so I would urge no apology upon the gentleman who is temporarily absent from his parish. If the priest can live by taking in the preacher, or vice-versa, I am quite satisfied provided the existence is a meager one.

Father Coughlin has mentioned Landon once or twice and even directed a mild and wholly polite rebuke toward Hearst, but it grows increasingly evident that during such passages Charlie winks the other eye. The radio ranter is most palpably playing politics. He is not sufficiently naïve to believe that Lemke can make a showing for himself. His whole intention in 1936 is to prove his nuisance value. It is entirely probable that Father Coughlin has no liking for Landon, even though he is trying his best to bring about his election. It would not surprise me to be told that Coughlin regards Townsend as a fool and Smith as a knave. Indeed I am quite ready to believe that he has a certain contempt for his own fuzzy followers and sees them as so much fascist fodder.

Coughlin has one faith and one alone. He has one favorite candidate and no other. He is pushing as rapidly as he can the political fortunes of a single individual. I may be wrong and so I should be reticent in bandying about the name of any good man. The most I am prepared to do is to hint in a sneaking way. My idea is that the proprietor of the Union Party is first and last and all the time for C--rl-s E. C---hl-n. If any considerable pressure comes from the Vatican I will wager $10 against an autographed photograph of William Lemke that Coughlin will shed his collar and coat as readily as he did at the Cleveland conclave. Although he pays occasional lip service to the creed and the customs of his church it is merely a coincidence that Coughlin is a priest. He most certainly is not functioning in this campaign as a Catholic. If he were there could hardly be so complete a tie-up between him and the Reverend Mr. Smith, the bullfrog kleagle from Louisiana's mud flats.

Gentle Gerald told a *Herald Tribune* reporter: "There have been rumors lately of a break between Dr. Townsend, Father Coughlin, and me. I want to tell you that after Father Coughlin spoke at the Cleveland convention, I took his hand and said, 'Reverend Coughlin, though we die, we are going on until our people have been freed,' and he replied, 'Though we die.'"

"Now I telephoned this afternoon," he continued, "and told him about these rumors of division of councils and he replied to me, 'Gerald, though we die.' That was enough for me."

And I think it's enough, too. In fact, I think it's too much. To Gerald L. K. Smith he may be "Reverend Coughlin." To Lemke he stands as, "Yes, boss, anything you say." But there is no reason why the average voter should make any allowance for the cloth of either Charlie or Gerald. Their function as clerics is merely an afterthought. In verbal encounters they should be prepared to be treated with the same consideration shown to the President of the United States—and no more. And so I say without any intention of any apology at any time that Booming Charlie is not garbed in holy orders, that he is not in any true sense a cleric of the Catholic church, and that he is solely a fascist faker using whatever means come to his hand to lend dignity and cover to his effort to achieve literal dictatorship in the United States.

What Charles E. Coughlin is really looking for is a large white horse and somebody to give him a boost into the saddle. When he clasped hands and said, "Gerald, though we die," he was moving quite close to one of his objectives. However, it is generally considered the wrong way to approach a horse.

113. THE 1936 ELECTION

Subject to last-minute changes of mind, this will be the final column touching on the election of 1936. Of course, there ought to be at least one after the ballots have been counted. In what seems to me the highly improbable event of Landon's election there may be a whole shower of columns pointing out the sinister forces which brought about his triumph.

My first plan had been to hire a cave in the event of a triumph for the Kansan. However, it was easy to see what a mistake such an isolation policy would be.

If my opinions were governed wholly by personal interest I would necessarily be in favor of Landon's election. From a columnist's point of view he would be a honey in the White House. People have said very often, "Your stuff is no good at all except on the days when you get mad." With Landon as President I could readily be mad six days a week and really make something of myself as a commentator.

In supporting Roosevelt I am putting the country's welfare above my own. Naturally I do not expect to be in any kind of continual agreement with Franklin D. Roosevelt. There have been plenty of things in his first administration to warm up a columnist and a few to make him boil. There will be more. All of us will have to wait to see which way Mr. Roosevelt goes when a second mandate has been put into his hands.

It is my belief that his margin of victory will be greater than in 1932. Alf M. Landon has not come up to the standard of Herbert Hoover as a campaigner. But whether the majority be large or small, a second mandate to Roosevelt would be more binding than the first.

Some commentators, including the astute Arthur Krock, of

the *Times,* think that the day of the so-called "Roosevelt radicals" has ended and that in a second term the President would cling most tenaciously to the middle of the road. I trust this is not true.

If it turns out that way the labor groups can console themselves a little by saying, "Landon would have been worse," but it will afford them much greater comfort if they proceed to build their own party on the foundations which have been established now.

It would be silly for me to deny that at the moment I am a Roosevelt enthusiast. But I have recovered from other fervors, and I could do so again if asked to take bitter medicine. But to one statement I will stand committed, no matter what happens —Franklin D. Roosevelt is the political genius of our age.

To me there is something ironical in protests by Republicans that Franklin is not Theodore. For that matter, Tad Lincoln was never Abraham.

My own notion is that the fifth cousin of the President of the United States was a somewhat dim and vague figure in comparison with his relative. Teddy never had one-tenth the force and driving power of Franklin. He moved too much with his own gang ever to get any very lively conception of Americans as a whole. It is well to remember that even in his days as a Progressive his chief associates were men like Amos Pinchot and Frank Munsey.

Colonel Roosevelt had not even a smattering of understanding of the labor movement. It should stand to his credit that for a little while he favored the recall of Supreme Court decisions, but he did not have the nerve to stand by it.

Teddy, according to my estimate, was a dude rancher and a parlor Progressive. He paid so much attention to being strenuous that he had little time for important things. He seemed to live in constant dread that somebody was going to call him a mollycoddle, and in order to protect himself from this feeling of inferiority he had to hold boxing bouts in the White House and go to Africa to shoot lions.

No matter what Franklin D. Roosevelt may do in the days to come, he is of higher caliber than that. I certainly believe that in history Colonel Roosevelt will be set down as Roosevelt, minor. Roosevelt, major, will be his fifth cousin.

114. YOUNG RANDOLPH CHURCHILL

Randolph Churchill, England's Ambassador of ill will, has gone home breathing maledictions upon our native press. I have known Randy, cub and boy, for fifteen years, and as he approaches maturity he grows more annoying with every birthday. It is an art with him, and since I recognize it as such, he cannot get my goat any more.

When first we met, young Churchill was about sixteen. He was engaged on a lecture tour and went about the country telling women's clubs what was wrong with American politics, customs and cookery. He was even then a journalistic delight, because if any ship news reporter asked him what he thought of our skyline or the American woman Randy would tell him in no uncertain terms. I rather gather that young Churchill thought the American woman looked best in a heavy fog. But, of course, it was seldom if ever necessary to ask Randy. He was the first to volunteer.

At the age of sixteen I observed him in drawing rooms interrupting his elders and telling them where they got off. But it came to be so magnificent that you could hardly call it bad manners. It was Promethean, and one could almost hear the flapping of the vultures on their way home to peck at little Mr. Churchill's liver.

Distinctly I remember a historic occasion in the home of Herbert Bayard Swope. At that time I was in the employ of Mr. Swope and regarded him with great awe. In fact, I still regard Mr. Swope with great awe. Only for a space of some five minutes did he seem to me neither a god nor a devil, but a man. This brief deliverance from the thralldom of hero worship I owed to Randolph Churchill. He sawed through one bar in the window of my cell, and I tried to slip out but got stuck in the middle.

At the time Mr. Churchill had just turned seventeen. Mr. Swope and I were somewhat older. I forgot what the argument was about, but as a trusted employee I took no part in it. Suddenly the chill English voice of the young visitor smote upon my ear saying, "Herbie, you talk like an utter idiot." I could hardly believe my ears, and I turned my eyes. Mr. Swope was slowly and gracefully growing a little purple.

The room was bathed in that silence which comes before the crack of doom. Only on one other occasion have I experienced such a stifling stillness. It was during a hurricane in Florida, and it is called a lull. For the space of fully a minute Mr. Churchill and Mr. Swope sat without saying a word. This in itself constituted a new world's record, and has since been accepted by the A.A.U.

Naturally I held my peace and gripped the arms of my chair. I averted my face. At any second the lightning would come through the roof and strike Randy dead or Mr. Swope would rise quietly and strangle him. I did not want to be struck or held as a material witness.

Instead I gazed out the window, and to my great surprise pedestrians were going about their business as usual and trying to get into a speakeasy just across the street.

A well-remembered voice shouted, "Heywood!" Indeed, the voice said, "Heywood!" a second time before I jumped and replied, "Yes, Mr. Swope." And that was another world's record.

"Heywood," said Mr. Swope. "I've been wanting to talk to

you about your review of *Processional* for some time. The
trouble with you as a dramatic critic, Heywood, is that you are
always reviewing the play the dramatist intended to write but
didn't get around to doing. I might add while we're on the sub-
ject that your column isn't holding up very well, and I didn't
like your last couple of baseball stories. Besides, your book re-
views are getting a little dull. I wonder if maybe you are doing
too much work. I think perhaps you're staying up too late. Come
down to my office around midnight tomorrow and we'll go out
to lunch and have a nice friendly chat about what's wrong with
your work."

"Yes, Mr. Swope," I answered, but for a fraction of a second
I was almost inclined to give him a slightly more contentious
reply, because Randolph Churchill had made him change the
subject.

A good many years elapsed before I saw Randy again. This
time we were on a train following Franklin Delano Roosevelt
through New England. We were sitting in the dining car, and
several other newspapermen joined the party. I introduced
Randy as a visiting British journalist to the group of White
House correspondents, all of whom were pretty much fans for
the President. Randolph Churchill acknowledged the introduc-
tion and started to lay down the law. Perhaps somebody had
dropped a hat, although Randy never needed any such encour-
agement.

"I think," he said, "your American press is most peculiar.
Your greatest journalist, of course, is William Randolph Hearst,
and yet his conduct in this campaign amazes me."

Several of us nodded in agreement.

"Yes," said Randy, "it amazes me to observe the way in
which Mr. Hearst leans over backward in order to be fair to
Mr. Roosevelt."

That broke up the debate. We had to shout for the porter to
bring spirits of ammonia. Three Hearst men had fainted.

115. THE BABY SLEEPETH

"And she brought forth her first-born son, and wrapped him in swaddling clothes, and laid him in a manger, because there was no room for them in the inn."

From near at hand and from distant lands there came visitors to Bethlehem. There were kings and there were shepherds. They followed the same star. Somewhere in the streets of the little town these columns met, and there was talk between the wise men and the shepherds as to the nature of their mission. They exchanged such information as they had about the birth of the King of kings and where He was to be found.

One of the royal party leaned down from his camel to listen to a shepherd who said, "We were in the field watching our flock and suddenly an angel appeared. We were very much frightened. And the angel said to us, 'Fear not, for, behold, I bring you good tidings of great joy, which shall be to all people. For unto you is born this day in the city of David a Saviour, which is Christ the Lord. And this shall be a sign unto you; ye shall find the babe wrapped in swaddling clothes, lying in a manger.' And then suddenly the sky was filled with a great light and voices sang, 'Glory to God in the highest and on earth peace, good will toward men.'

"And the light faded and we began to talk to each other and we decided to leave just one man with the flock and we went up to Bethlehem to see this thing which is come to pass and which the Lord has made known to us. And we were in great haste."

And the king who sat high above the shepherd got down from the back of his camel to hear the story more clearly, and the shepherds clustered around him to learn what signs he and his party had received which brought them from far countries to Bethlehem.

And the eldest of the wise men explained, "For us it was a star, a new star in the heavens, and it seemed to us that the star beckoned, and we gathered together treasures of gold and frankincense and myrrh." And he pointed to the great retinue behind him and the camels heavily laden with bales and bundles of precious stuffs.

And the shepherds seemed ashamed and said, "We have brought nothing. We came straight from the field when the angel spoke to us. And we were in great haste."

And all the shepherds were abashed in the presence of the three kings and their servants and their camels bearing the burden of rich gifts. They could see and detect the place of their destination at the end of the street. The star shone directly on the stable. And because it was only a small place and the party of the kings was large the shepherds made as if to step aside so that these great men from a distant land might go first with their precious gifts for the King of kings. But the eldest of the wise men waved to the shepherds to join his servants and not to humble themselves.

"Whether it be from far or near," he said, "we are on the same mission. We should enter into the house together."

But the shepherds were still reluctant, and one of them answered, "First must come your servants with your precious gifts of gold and frankincense and myrrh. We have told you we bring nothing. We came straight from the fields, and even if we had not come in great haste there is nothing we possess fit to bring as a gift to the King of kings. We will linger and tarry here until you have given over your treasure."

The city was dark and still, but in this street there was a babble of voices and the sound of camel drivers calling to the great beasts to kneel so that they might dismount and unfasten the thongs which held in place the treasure chests and the sacks of incense. And the cavalcade drew up before the door with clatter, noise and tumult. The shepherds were silent, for they had seen many wonders in a single evening, and not the least of these were the kings of the East and their camel train.

And in the street the servants opened cedar chests and revealed great bars of gold heavier than the stones which lay in the meadow where the flocks had been left to graze. And the eyes of the shepherds opened wide again as when they saw the light of angels and heard the voices from the heavens.

Through the narrow door and up to the manger itself strode the kings and great bearded men bearing treasure. The timid shepherds followed and ranged themselves in the back of the room against the walls of the stable, for they were affrighted to be in the presence of princes and of the King of kings.

The eldest of the wise men said, "Where is He that is born King of the Jews? For we have seen His star in the east and are come to worship Him. And we bring with us rich treasures of gold and frankincense and myrrh."

And Mary, the mother, looked up at the great throng and paid no heed to the gifts of gold and incense but placed her finger upon her lips and said to the shepherds and to the kings, "The baby sleepeth."

PART FIVE

1937-1939

116. CHILD LABOR DEFEAT: 1

In the eighteenth chapter of the Gospel According to St. Matthew it is written of anyone who offends against a child that "it were better for him that a millstone were hanged about his neck, and that he were drowned in the depth of the sea."

To Albany should go 102 millstones to the Assemblymen who killed the Child Labor Amendment.

It goes without saying that these members of the Assembly should be set in the memory books of the voters and blotted out of public life when next they show their heads. But that is too long to wait. Right now they should be belled so that all shall know them by their comings and their goings. And quite properly some distinguishing mark might be set upon the door of their abodes.

Shameful days have been known before in the Assembly in Albany, but now the lower house of the Empire State becomes the lowest in all the land. At times, I understand, men have gone to the Legislature who were not above sharing in illicit profits, but even such might recoil at the thought of trafficking in the toil of children.

This is our Legislature—yours and mine—and we must share some part of the blame. Many of us in election years have been so intent upon some major candidate that we have swept down a line of levers hardly knowing or caring about the fact that we are also expressing a decision as to the Assembly. The name of the man escaped us—if, indeed, we ever knew it. But we must know and we must care, for these people have put New York within the ranks of backward States.

And if we chance to see the regimentation of children in a mill in any part of this broad country we must bow our heads and say, "That is our concern. This deed was done in Albany."

It is not often that a simple member of the Assembly gets an opportunity to export his stupidity into every State of the Union. And if anybody says that some few acted out of a high sincerity it need only be answered that sincerity will hardly serve as a shelter for children who struggle through torturing hours in the sugar-beet fields of the West.

We know the names of the men who did this thing, and we know the forces and agencies which cracked the whip, and these men and things will be remembered.

In the ranks of this legion places should be reserved for all who pretended to be wholly against child labor but— There are few foes so dangerous as those who proffer aid but insist that the goal must be obtained in some other way. They are the painted clowns who assist in laying down the circus mat.

And surely there must be one section of this parade of philanthropists, public men and prelates devoted to a representative of those publishers who brought the tragedy into being. There ought to be a special award for smugness.

I do not see how it will be possible to top the *Herald Tribune*, which even twisted its news columns and made "youth control" the mandatory phrase in describing the Child Labor Amendment. When the knife had been driven home out popped an editorial entitled Now End Child Labor.

The friends of exploitation have won a temporary victory. But now we know all our foes and their names. At least none of them can stab us in the back next time. Let the cry go up, "When do we fight again?"

117. CHILD LABOR DEFEAT: 2

When 102 members of the Assembly of the State of New York voted against the Child Labor Amendment, I wrote what

I hoped was a bitter column concerning their action. In order to back this up, I sent a letter to each member of the legion of infamy. And in that letter I said among several other things, "In voting against the Child Labor Amendment you have participated in the dirtiest day's work ever done in the New York State Assembly. That is saying a good deal. But let it stand."

This, I thought, was provocative, and I have been waiting for replies, but only a few have come in. For instance, here is one from Charles R. McConnell, 5th District, Kings County. Mr. McConnell writes: "Thanks for your letter of March 10. Sorry I am unable to agree with you in the remarks set forth in the first sentence of your letter. As far as I am concerned, you'll receive no noterity [sic] in connection therewith. I take the remark from whence it came."

Mr. Charles R. McConnell, of the 5th District, Kings County, need not worry about the "noterity." I will attend to that myself. I am not going to forget Mr. McConnell or the additional 101. He will be up for re-election fairly soon, and at that time I purpose to go over the same ground all over again.

But in campaigns against unfaithful public servants the difficulty is that their misdeeds are so soon forgotten. The voter has a good deal of difficulty in carrying in his head just how his representative voted on various vital issues. As a man with a newspaper job it is my intention to keep alive the names of those men who voted to maintain the toil of children.

Some members of the Assembly do not seem to be quite bright in their answers to a challenging letter.

May I quote from the reply of James J. Wadsworth, chairman of the Public Relief and Welfare Committee? Mr. Wadsworth writes to me: "You convict yourself when you say that the organized newspapermen of this country are against the use of immature newsboys and carriers and all other forms of exploitation of child labor. You know perfectly well that you need no legislation whatever to change the situation as far as newsboys are concerned. All you have to do is to stop hiring them if you don't want them to work."

I informed Mr. Wadsworth about the opinion of organized newspapermen. I was not speaking for owners, editors and publishers.

Mr. Wadsworth must have a very hazy idea of the function of a reporter or a columnist. We have no opportunity to hire or fire anybody. Like the "little merchants," we are people on the payroll. It is not within our scope to dictate the editorial, news or business policy of the great organs which keep alive the glorious tradition of the freedom of the press.

And now let us come to Ernest J. Lonis, who writes: "If I were in the habit of resenting vicious attacks of individuals and groups, I might have reason to resent your letter of March 10, referring to my participation 'in the dirtiest day's work ever done in the New York State Assembly.'

"If I cared to be vindictive I might refer to your letter as being the dirtiest insinuating letter ever coming to my hand during my service as a representative of the people of New York State. I take no personal affront to your letter, but, as a member of the State Assembly doing my duty as a conscientious representative of my constituents, I think you owe the members of this Assembly who received this letter an apology."

Go ahead and wait, Mr. Ernest J. Lonis. And wait! You are not going to get any apology from me, and you will receive additional letters. I do not mean to let this issue languish and die.

You say you are a conscientious representative of your constituents. Have you got the nerve to go back into your own district and ask the men and women who sent you to Albany whether they approve of your stand in favor of the maintenance of child labor in this country?

You ask for an apology. I will give you nothing of the sort. But I will give you a challenge. Beginning next Monday, or the Monday after that, I dare you to debate this issue with me on every street corner and hall in the limits of your own constituency.

This case is not going to die. Your name—I believe it is Ernest J. Lonis—will not be forgotten. Not as long as I have any space in which to set one word after another.

118. WILLIAM GILLETTE

I was sorry to hear of the death of William Gillette, because he was the first serious actor I ever saw. My first play was a musical show about a French maid. Father seemed to like it all right, but I didn't quite get the drift of the plot, and so I asked for something weightier.

Accordingly, we went next week to *Secret Service*. That would have been about forty years ago, but then, and to his dying day, William Gillette was the complete master of what is known as modern acting.

In later years they told me that no one would ever realize what naturalism on the stage could be without seeing Duse. I saw Duse. She was old, and I was a not so young dramatic critic who spoke no Italian. But granted these handicaps, it seemed to me that the famous hands of Duse waved like those of a musical maestro and that she orchestrated each line.

No, for my taste Gillette was the least actory person who ever backed away from the footlights. Of course, he appeared for the most part in highly theatrical vehicles. Probably *Secret Service* would be laughed at today, but certainly it gripped the attention of my father and me.

Fortunately, I never saw it in any revival. It remains in memory as the almost perfect play. I don't even have to close my eyes to recreate the scene in which Gillette, as the Northern spy, is trapped at a telegraph instrument by a Confederate officer.

Mr. Gillette, as I remember, was sending information about Lee's army straight to Grant's headquarters, and the rebel villain raised objections. Very possibly this was my first sight of censorship. It was violent and drastic. The officer in gray fired through the window and nicked Gillette, or rather Captain Thorne, in his sending arm.

Not content with this violation of free press, the fellow stalked into the room and said to Captain Thorne, "Do you know why you're not lying dead with a bullet through your head?"

Gillette used to throw in a very long stage wait right there. Of course, he held your attention with the business of binding up his wounded arm with a handkerchief. I watched him fascinated.

"That's red ink," my father whispered. I waved him away, for I knew better. It must be blood. The hero had just been wounded.

Gillette adjusted the bandage and then looked at his foe with scorn. "Because you're such a damn bad shot," he said.

Since then I have been told that "The rest is silence," from *Hamlet*, is the finest line in English drama. I prefer "I choose the weaker," from *Candida*, or possibly "I never saw a woman burned," from *Saint Joan*.

Forty years ago I would have backed Gillette's rejoinder against all others. It was, of course, that famous still, small voice.

Gillette always gave the impression that he hadn't quite learned his part and that he was ad-libbing as he went along. I believe it is called "the illusion of the first performance."

It is quite possible that he purposely chose ranters when he was assembling a melodrama cast, for he was always the quiet one in the midst of tumult. Even when they had him trapped in the death chamber in *Sherlock Holmes* he hardly spoke above a whisper.

It was, of course, a triumphant whisper, for they followed

his lighted cigar which he had stuck in the far corner of the room while he corporeally slipped out the door.

And I remember the night he opened in Barrie's *Dear Brutus*, bringing out with him for each curtain call a little girl who was brilliant in her performance.

And now Helen Hayes is playing Victoria and William Gillette is dead and time flies, but I think I can still see the red glow of a cigar even though Sherlock Holmes has slipped out the door.

119. THAT SPRING OF 1909

STAMFORD, CONN., May 19.—As a reward for five days of practically perfect conduct Connie allowed me to take a night off and go into town for a business meeting. At least, that is what I told her. It turned out to be a very gay party. We sang college songs such as *Choo! Choo! Rah! Rah! for Holy Cross* and all the verses of *Hinky Dinky Parlay Voo* which seemed meet and proper for mixed company. I met a blond girl who said, "Why, Mr. B., you look fifty years younger since your week-end in the country," and we danced twice around the floor.

When I got to Grand Central Station I found that I had just time to catch the last train, which goes at 11:50. It would be midnight and more before I got home. But in spite of the lateness of the hour I didn't feel in any way tired. On the contrary, there was a spring in my step and my eyes were bright, and somewhere back of the New Haven ticket windows the birds seemed to be singing. I fumbled in my pockets and found that I had lost my mileage book, but I still had the slip of paper with the telephone number. There's nothing so useful to revive your youth as getting around with young people. I must do it more often.

Seated in the smoking car, I lit a big black cigar and started to relax with the editorial page of the *Times*. Presently the conductor was shaking me and asking if I wanted to get off at Stamford or New Haven. He said he couldn't quite make up his mind whether I was a commuter or a Yale sophomore off for an evening's entertainment. Bill, the station taxi man, knows where I live, but I had to stay awake in order to make up my story about the business meeting. As I piled convincing detail upon detail I smiled to myself. Wasn't I the devil and what was it she had said about her lithographs? Well, after all, you're young only once.

Arrived at the Ridge, I took my shoes off and walked in boldly through the back kitchen door. A telegram was lying on the table. I'm long past night letter fears, for mostly they are nothing more than an inquiry as to when you can address the Women's Study Club in Spokane and what a pity it is that the organization has no funds. I opened the envelope idly, but then I blanched, for suddenly all the weight of my years came tumbling down upon my head like a rockslide on the Kensico Highway. The message was from a small college town in Pennsylvania, and it read: "Owing to liberal spring spending policy have run through May money Stop Please advance June stipend Stop Am also doing well in my studies Stop Love."

That conductor on the New Haven train must have been fooling when he said he thought I might be a Yale boy out on a spree. I was no boy but a man, and an old man at that, the head of the household and the good provider. I took the slip of paper with the telephone number and threw it into the fireplace. Sitting down at my work bench, I started to compose a reply beginning, "You may be doing well in your studies, but you will have to learn that Pompoon cannot beat War Admiral and that money doesn't grow on trees. Father has to work very hard to make both ends meet."

But then I remembered a spring day during the Taft administration when I wired for $100. It turned out to be Blue Tues-

day or Ferocious Friday or some other catastrophic day in the
market, and I got only $25, and so I wrote a simple little note
explaining that Walter Lippmann and I had been in the same
class and had had the same opportunities, only Lippmann at-
tended the lectures of Professor Carver, while I kept cutting
classes to watch Tris Speaker play with the Red Sox. If only the
Boston outfield had not been so good that year I might under-
stand a lot more about the sanctity of the gold standard. How-
ever, just thinking about that spring of 1909 made me feel
young all over again, and it turned out that there wasn't any
fire in the fireplace.

120. COURT BILL DEFEAT

In chortling over the setback suffered by the plan to liberalize
the court the *Herald Tribune* captions its comment "Never
Again!" "Never" is a long word. It is well to remember that
the progressive forces of America not infrequently lose every
battle but the last one. They have just begun to fight.

The issue is broader than ever before. No longer does it lie
as some quarrel between Franklin Roosevelt and the Senate.
Clearly the struggle lies between those who would go forward
and those who are determined to go back. Many of the false
fronts have been stripped away. In the beginning there were
those who said that they were wholeheartedly in favor of end-
ing judicial oligarchy but that the proper method was to present
an amendment. Nothing has been heard about any amendment
in many weeks. Such moves were all obstructionist.

Moreover, Mr. Roosevelt has proved his point about the
practical difficulty of such a movement because of the probability
that powerful interests could seize upon the smaller States. Sen-
ator Gerry's dinner parties indicate that there is a bottle neck,

and it is significant that the Senators from the "rotten boroughs" have been the ones to perform a sudden right-about.

Most of the self-called liberals have now dropped the mask. Senator Burke, of Nebraska, who opposed the fight against the Supreme Court oligarchy from the beginning, always insisted that he did so because the proposal did not conform with his progressive principles. But at a dinner of the American Defense Society, hardly known as a liberal organization, he declared blandly that the people are "willing to proceed with less haste" and that "the pressing need for speed is no longer essential."

On the same day that Senator Burke expressed this opinion Representative Hoffman sent a telegram labeled "Official Business" in which he offered to raise a force of one hundred vigilantes to end peaceful picketing in Michigan. And on that same day George C. Chandler, secretary of the Ohio Chamber of Commerce, told the Black-Connery Wage and Hour Committee, "South Carolina fired on Fort Sumter for a far less pretext than this bill affords."

Walter Lippmann (not a radical) has spoken of "the reactionary steel companies," and Hugh S. Johnson (not a progressive) has said that there are only two answers—"statutory intervention or war." And Senator Burke says there is no need for haste.

The issue is industrial slavery. The record of the Supreme Court on slavery is not a pretty one. More than half a century ago a reactionary Supreme Court precipitated a civil war, and there are those now who would like to see this same body, which has fallen out of balance, do so again.

Once upon a time there was an army of the Lord which was trapped in a narrow valley by the Hittites, the Canaanites, the Ishmaelites and other reactionaries of the day. The army of the Lord was sore beset, and some of its ostensible members deserted and sought caves in the hills and holes in the ground, which did not make it any easier for the army of the Lord. But at that moment there began to appear, coming over the top of the mountains, the hosts of heaven, horsemen and footmen without number. And they routed the Hittites and the Canaanites and all the forces of reaction.

And now the armies of labor can be seen along the peaks, and answer can be made to those who skulk or run or turncoat. The answer will be, "Seek caverns in the hills or holes in the ground if you will, since for every one who quits the good fight we can get ten, twenty or a thousand to take your place."

121. THE IMPERFECT REPORTER

When I was fourteen I decided that I would like to be a good newspaperman, but in spite of a fairly hard try over a considerable number of years I am afraid that I will never make it. There are other failings, but one of the chief difficulties is connected with the circumstance that there are almost no situations in which I am neutral by the widest stretch of the imagination.

It has been said that the perfect reporter ought to be patterned more or less along the physical and chemical lines of a plate glass window. It is not his function to take the light from the sun and shade into blue, green, yellow or even red. He is an associate member of the light brigade, and when cannon roar from the right or left his mission is to keep precisely in the middle of the road in the hope that he will find the truth, which is always said to lie between the two.

I am not altogether certain whether these entrance requirements are wise and shrewd in every detail. But my skepticism may be based upon a doubt as to my own ability to pass the entrance examinations. I fear I am not glass, either clear or opaque. When hit the result is something other than "Tinkle! Tinkle!"

Although an inveterate joiner, my disability does not depend upon the fact that I am devoted to the Elks and Rotarians. Even in my youth when I was a baseball reporter and attached to no organization save the New York Giants I could not help taking sides. When Fred Merkle sent two runs home with a timely single to left field it was my wont to stand up in the press box and holler, "Ataboy!" These peculiar performances embittered my colleagues who had not slapped one palm against another for fifty years.

Profanely they would implore me to remember my age and my assignment and to sit down and keep my yap shut. I tried. The old malady of partisan enthusiasm still remains. As a visiting fireman I sat at the press table when the Post Office Committee of the United States Senate undertook what was advertised as an examination of Tom Mercer Girdler, chairman of the board of Republic Steel. But that situation can be taken up in another column.

Indeed, it is my hope that I may have an opportunity of mentioning Mr. Girdler from time to time. Although he has made no effort to engage me, I would like to do rather extensive publicity in his behalf.

At the Girdler hearing in Washington I took an emotional commitment from the beginning. I didn't like Tom before he opened his mouth, and I liked him less when he did. As the hearing got hotter and hotter I suddenly had a sense that the ranks of the spectators were closing in tighter and tighter upon the devoted ranks of the working press. I began to feel as if I were in the same spot as General Custer just before the Sioux started to shoot it out in the Battle of the Little Big Horn. And so I turned to the stout lady who had her hand on the back of my chair and expostulated.

She had laughed at Girdler's road company wisecracks, and applauded just behind my left ear when Tom Girdler wrapped himself in the American flag and did bugle calls. And so I said in the most icy tones of pure politeness which I could muster,

"May I ask, madam, whether you are connected with any newspaper?"

The large lady replied, "I am not, although I ought to be."

"That," I answered, "is an interesting technical point but, until it has been solved after due deliberation, will you please move your chair away from this table? And if I hear another cackle after some second-hand crack by this man now on the stand I'll call the cops."

And that's why I will never be a good reporter. I never feel minded to call for a bowl of water and ask, "What is truth?"

122. MERCUTIO NO NEUTRAL

I am fearful lest I be picketed by some Shakespearean ghost bearing the sign "This column is unfair to Mercutio." I grant that I have erred, and the only excuse which can be offered is that President Roosevelt tore a single phrase out of a scene when he allowed a press conference to quote, "A plague on both your houses."

To be sure, it appears in most texts as "A plague o' both your houses!" However, one should not quarrel with a Chief Executive over the mere matter of an apostrophe. And yet there should be some defense of the gallant "kinsman to the prince and friend to Romeo." Mercutio was not, as his famous phrase might indicate, a tired liberal. It is tragic that a warrior's life should end upon a defeatist note.

However, a recapitulation of the incidents leading up to his death should serve to show that he was not cut down as an innocent bystander preaching a peevish neutrality. In Scene 1 of Act III Mercutio enters a public place in the City of Verona accompanied by Benvolio, page and servant. The two principals josh back and forth about the quarrelsome nature of each other.

Mercutio professes no eagerness to engage in any altercation upon that particular occasion. But then there enters Tybalt, who seems to have been conceived by Shakespeare as a sort of Veronese Tom Girdler.

At any rate, Tybalt is full of sound and fury, and Mercutio menaces him upon the instant. "I will not budge for no man's pleasure," says Mercutio, not only ready but eager to fight it out immediately rather than go up an alley as Benvolio suggests. Indeed, Benvolio goes to the length of arguing for compulsory arbitration, which Mercutio indignantly rejects.

Before swords can be drawn Romeo comes in and complicates the situation. With the possible exception of Hamlet, this stripling Romeo is one of the most inept and unlikable heroes ever put upon the stage. In all critical situations Romeo has a most unfortunate habit of thinking with his thumbs.

Tybalt is much more bold and insulting in his treatment of Romeo than he dared to be with Mercutio. He knows the young lover is a sap. Tybalt hails him to his face as a villain. Romeo offers mediation much to the disgust of Mercutio, who knows that the Tybalts of all times and ages regard reasonableness as a weakness. Indeed, the inopportune pacifism of his friend Romeo moves Mercutio to such a rage that he himself draws, crying, "Tybalt, you rat catcher, will you talk?"

Facing a firm purpose and a sharp sword, Tybalt begins to take a softer tone, and inquires wistfully, "What wouldst thou have with me?" But Mercutio is just as adamant against the fellow's charm as he was before his bluster.

"Good king of cats," snarls Mercutio, "nothing but one of your nine lives. . . . Will you pluck your sword out of his pilcher by the ears? Make haste lest mine be about your ears ere it be out."

They fight, and Mercutio is at least ten to one to win by a knockout before blundering Romeo steps between them and gets in the way. Tybalt takes advantage of Romeo's clumsiness and sneaks in a fatal thrust. "Why the devil came you between us? I was hurt under your arm," complains Mercutio. At this point Romeo adds insult to injury by taking an attitude dear to blundering liberals ever since. "I thought all for the best." It is at this point that Mercutio in his dying agony gasps, "A plague o' both your houses."

Mercutio was not a neutral, and sooner or later all the Shakespeare courses in college will have to be turned over to the Department of Political Science, so that the student will understand the lessons which Mr. Roosevelt and Mr. Lewis really wish to convey. It might even be expedient to combine Bible study with this particular course, so that the words of William Green may be properly interpreted in case anybody cares.

123. THE DEMOCRACY OF DEATH

The President of the United States placed a wreath of white flowers on the Tomb of the Unknown Soldier in Arlington Cemetery, and officers and men stood at attention. The bugles blew.

But all that is known of the national hero is the fact that he was in the American army. The outfit to which he belonged is not known. His nativity and race are matters of conjecture. Indeed, the inscription reads, "Here rests in honored glory an American soldier known but to God."

There were eight coffins in the beginning, and Sergeant Younger walked around them several times before he placed a sprig of white roses on the one he chose at random. It happened to be the third from the left. From birth to death to final fame this man who lies in Arlington was the creature of chance.

We do not know what was in his heart when he died. It is entirely possible that he was a fearful man. He may even have gone unwillingly into the fight. That does not matter now. The personality of one who lived and breathed has been obliterated not only by death but by the fact that here lies a symbol. One man has come to represent the memory of many.

He was drawn from a far edge of the world by the war, and in it he lost even his identity. Joe or Jim or Charlie he may have been, but now he is Everyman. The Unknown Soldier stands for us as a symbol of the blind and far-reaching fury of modern conflict, but his death was in vain unless it helps us to understand that the whole world must be the concern of the whole world.

No one is too great to take his place in the affairs of mankind and none too humble. Indeed, those who refuse to make a choice and set up ivory towers will inevitably find that the affairs of the world are thrust upon them.

War and sudden death are tragic things, but it would be even more ironic and bitter if the Unknown Soldier were also one of the unknowing.

He was, we may assume, a typical American, and it is probable that once upon a time he used to speak of faraway folk as "those foreigners." He thought they were no kin of his, but he died in one of the distant lands. His blood and the blood of all the world mingled in a common stream.

The body of the Unknown Soldier has come home, but his spirit will wander with that of his brothers. There will be no rest for his soul until the great democracy of death has been translated into the unity of life. Isolation ends at the edge of the grave. Whatever the estate of the dead, they are not divided by prejudice of race or nationality. To them, at least, all things are common.

But that is not good enough. If there are to be no more wars the men and women of the world must put their hearts and minds to the task of bringing us all into comradeship this side of Jordan. There is need of some living symbol of unity. Blow, bugles; blow—not for the unknown dead, but for the plain and palpable brotherhood of life.

124. CARVER TO SPEAKER TO BROUN

"Tell me, Mr. Broun," said the young lady to my right, "how did you happen to become a Red?"

Assuming that her question was sincere, I proceeded to tell her in my own words which, by a fortunate coincidence, happened to be just sufficient to fill one page of the *New Republic* when printed in this type.

The first person to tempt me to the left was a Vermont Republican named John Spargo who wrote mildly Marxian tracts years ago when I was very young. Had there been more violence in his views or in his presentation I might have scurried home, but he was as soft-spoken as any curate and he succeeded in sneaking up on me. Later, in college, Lippmann asked me to join the Socialist Club and, as I had failed to make either Gas House or Fly, I yielded to his blandishments.

But commitment was not yet complete. The way of retreat still lay open. It was Professor Carver of the Harvard faculty and Tris Speaker, centerfielder of the Boston Red Sox, who closed the door and left me locked in the hall of heresy. Possibly an assist should be scored for a particularly salubrious Spring which came to New England in 1908. The good bald economist gave a course which might be roughly described as "radical panaceas and their underlying fallacies." Professor Carver introduced these crack-brained notions in the Fall and Winter semesters and then proceeded to demolish them in the Spring and early Summer.

Faithful to the Harvard tradition of fair play, the Professor gave the revolutionaries an ample amount of rope. Indeed, he did not undertake to state the case himself for the various aberrant philosophies, but invited a leader of each school of thought to tell all from his particular point of view. The soap boxes were carried openly into the classroom and mounted by the orators. Men with burning causes are generally more eloquent than cloistered dons and there was not a single visitor who could not talk rings around Professor Carver.

We had an anarchist, a socialist, a syndicalist, a single-taxer and a few other theorists whose special lines escape me now with the passing of the years. The single-taxer was a little on the dull side, but all the others sparkled. It may be that I was more susceptible than my fellow students, for I must report that I hit the sawdust trail at each and every lecture in the creation of a united front against the capitalist system.

In other courses it was my custom to draw starfish in my notebook and jot down reminders such as: "Be sure and get Osmond Fraenkel for the poker game tonight." But under Carver I took notes as long as the cavalcade of visiting firemen was on. Later I would peruse the book and find entries such as "Born 1839—died 1897," "unearned increase in land values," "P. J. Proudhon," "Five dollars ($5) with Horseface McCarthy Dartmouth doesn't beat us by two touchdowns." And I used to wonder what some of the notations could possibly mean. But I paid closer attention than ever until the last galoot had reached the shore and Carver went up into the pilot house.

At this point Spring broke through. It had been a tough Winter. Dartmouth did beat us by two touchdowns and Osmond Fraenkel, who was a mathematical shark, had just become wise to the fact that it doesn't pay to draw to inside straights. I had failed to make the *Harvard Crimson* after my third try.

But gone was the Winter of our discontent and now it was Professor Carver's turn to haul us back from the pie counter of the sky and put our feet again upon the good earth and the law of supply and demand.

Carver was at bat but, as luck would have it, so was Tris Speaker. Spring can come up like thunder in Massachusetts. One day all the elms of the yard may be cased in ice and the next you read that the Boston Red Sox are opening the season against the Athletics. Tris Speaker, just up from Texas league, was the particular star of the greatest outfield trio that has ever been gathered together.

Speaker and Duffy Lewis and Harry Hooper—that was a united front. For a little while I tried to give Professor Carver an even break. Naturally I missed his first blast for the cause of conservatism, because that particular lecture conflicted with the opening game. Still I did ask a fellow scholar what went on and he lent me his notebook. He seemed to have boiled the discourse down to the bone because all he had written was, "Adam Smith was Scotch and died before the industrial revolution—look this up in the library. He approached economics from the side of ethics and believed in laissez-faire, which means 'anything goes.' Has anybody here seen Kelly?"

I decided that in all fairness to my parents, who were paying for my education, I should attend some of the lectures myself and so in the beginning I made it a rigorous rule to give only three afternoons a week to the Red Sox and the other three to Professor Carver. But on a certain Wednesday, which was a baseball afternoon, Tris Speaker made a home run, two triples and a double. In addition he went all the way back to the flagpole in center field and speared a drive with his gloved hand while still on the dead run. Two innings later he charged in for a low liner and made the catch by sliding the last twenty feet on his stomach. Professor Carver couldn't do that. I had seen him stand on his head in the classroom but never did he slide on his stomach. Even at such times as he got to base it was my impression that he had profited by an error or made a lucky-handle hit. Tris Speaker was batting .348 and Carver wasn't hitting the size of his hat. At times he did dig his toes in and take his full cut at the ball, but never when I was around did he succeed in knocking socialism over the fence.

Adam Smith had died in 1790 and Professor Carver wasn't getting any younger. I got hold of *The Wealth of Nations* and learned that to Smith laissez-faire meant "the obvious and simple system of natural liberty." And so in the books I read no more then, and not very much later.

I just went completely laissez-faire and never missed any of the remaining games. The arguments for the radical theories I had heard, but I never got around to hearing the answers. Tris Speaker had thrown Carver out at the plate because the Professor forgot to slide. And I went out into the world the fervent follower of all things red, including the Boston Red Sox.

125. COLUMNIST AS LUMBERJACK

STAMFORD, CONN., Nov. 20 [1937].—I worked at least thirty-five minutes this morning cutting up a tree for firewood, and this makes the first full day I have ever put in at manual labor. Although proud of myself, the man whom I will envy from this day forth is that fellow in the circus who saws a woman in two.

There's your true lumberjack. After all, in addition to the saw I had an ax, an iron crowbar and an old mashie niblick. Moreover, I was working on a maple, which is nothing as tough as a circus performer.

To be sure, if the man saws the same woman in two at every matinee I assume that in time he becomes familiar with the grain. It was George Kaufman who said that this particular performer was the first ever to use the phrase, "Shall we join the ladies?"

Still we are getting off the point which concerns my ordeal and not the job of the man in the circus. The first ten minutes were easy enough. Indeed, I sang at my work as I raised the ax and let fly. I did the *Anvil Chorus*. It's from *Trovatore*, isn't it? At any rate, it's the one that begins, "Ring, ring, ring," and goes along for quite a while in about the same vein.

But presently I could no longer continue as the singing woodsman. I couldn't remember the rest of the words, and there was no air in my lungs. Indeed, I felt as I had in the last two and a half minutes of the game against the Yale freshman basketball team which we played thirty-one years ago. And so I engaged in the fantasy of pretending that the tree was the Yale (Yule, i.e.) log and I was the alert Harvard aggregation. Every time I slammed the maple with the crowbar I would cry, "So you're the great Clint Frank, are you?"

But, even so, defeatist thoughts crept in. "Columns are made by fools like me," I mused, "but only Paul Bunyan can demolish a tree." And as I thought of the terrific labor of the loggers who strip the forests to make a newspaper piece possible my face grew very red.

But at this point help loomed up over the horizon in the form of a friend. Along the Ridge came driving good old Ten Per Cent Bye, the literary agent, in his new high-powered car.

"What are you doing, Heywood?" he asked. I eyed him coldly and, answering with more bitterness than wit, replied, "Manicuring my fingernails." This struck him as funny for several reasons, but even as he laughed he leered. "Don't you know," he said, "that just down at the foot of the hill there's a little store where you can get a whole armful of logs like that for a quarter? I'll take you down. In fact, I'll lend you the quarter."

I'll grant I was tempted, but I felt that I stood as a symbol for all men and that the time must come for us to make up our minds whether we are lice or loggers.

And so I answered with deeds rather than words. Raising the ax above my head, I took a full swing before I let drive at the tree. I didn't miss it by much, but it's lucky I wasn't wearing sneakers. The doctor thinks he can save the big toe and the little one and that with proper nursing I'll be walking around again in a month.

126. CHINESE POKER

The news that the Japanese have held a victory parade through the streets of the International Settlement brings back old memories to me, for once I was familiar with the City of Shanghai. Its political and economic problems are not within the scope of my researches. The year was 1911, and I was on a leave of absence from the lobster trick on the copy desk of the New York *Tribune*. That means I quit work at 4 A.M. But now the nights belong to me and the Bubbling Well Road.

War was rumbling in the north, and when I got to Peiping later I found machine guns and sandbag barricades upon the wall of the legation quarter. But it did not seem to me that turmoil had touched Shanghai. I have never been in a city in which it was so easy to find people to sit up all night with you. The Germans still had a concession and a real Culmbacher.

A couple of United States marines introduced me to a poker game which we played with a group of Chinese merchants. Only one of them could speak English, but they all thought they knew the value of the hands. It turned out that I had made a good bargain for myself by agreeing to go to China without salary and simply on an expense account. Although I looked, I never was able to find that place later celebrated in *The Shanghai Gesture*.

If you remember the play, young women were put on the auction block. Perhaps it's just as well I didn't run it down. Auctions excite me and I'm always bidding for things I don't particularly want. If I had come away with a blonde I really wouldn't know what to do with her now. However, there was no lack of co-education in the cafés of Shanghai.

Young ladies from every corner of the globe seemed to have

assembled there under some urge or other. And as a good American I was struck by the fact that each spoke sufficient English. Anglo-Saxon enterprise girdles the globe. I did not see a great deal of the ancient walled city. It smelled to heaven, and I was not a customer for jade or ivory. Still I went occasionally to study the gambling situation, which seemed to be loose and pleasant.

There was some sort of dice game which was played on alternate corners. I watched a Chinese boy risking coppers, and when he was broke I lent him some more. It did not change his luck. "Make way for a real shooter." I said, and used pantomime to carry my point. I won the first toss, but then the clever dealer discovered that I had not the slightest conception of the rules of the game.

It was not craps or Indian dice. That day I won no more. The transit situation was less than satisfactory. None of the rickshaw men wanted me as a customer. Eventually I learned to hold up two fingers to indicate that I would pay double for the tonnage and then I got a few volunteers.

"Chop chop," I'd cry, since somebody told me that meant to run fast, and we would go roaring down the Bubbling Well Road into the night life of Shanghai. And now many of those gilded houses are splintered, and the singsong girls have fled, and bad luck has continued to pursue the boy to whom I lent copper coins.

Never was there such a noisy town. In narrow streets you could hardly hear the screech of the fiddles. The Chinese are a great lot for laughing. In those days Shanghai rocked itself to sleep. All is gone. The sound of the guns has moved to the north. The gay city is silent. Pray God that the Bubbling Well shall know again the touch of Spring.

127. MEETING THE N.A.M. HALFWAY

I went to a meeting a good many years ago of Irish repub-
licans. The chief speaker was Jim Redmond. According to the
announcement, it was his intention to conciliate the forces of
Ulster. He began his speech by declaring, "I have never said
an unfriendly word against the Orangemen, misguided, bigoted
and besotted though they may be."

In much the same spirit the National Association of Manu-
facturers has invited the government and labor to sit down in
fraternal conference to iron out the ills of America. I have read
all the many-pointed programs of the leaders of industry and
listened attentively to the speech of Colby Chester, but as I get
it, the captains of business are saying nothing more than, "We
are eager to co-operate if you will meet us wholly on our own
terms."

As far as I could gather, the offer to Mr. Roosevelt was
simply that he could take a chair on the fringe of any confer-
ence if he would consent to metamorphize himself immediately
into Mr. Hoover.

Labor was told that it could obtain standing room tickets on
the basis of consenting to play dead and keep its mouth shut.

Most of the deliberations of the manufacturers went on in
secret sessions. It is possible that the views expressed in camera
were more liberal than those given forth in public sessions. But
that would hardly seem the way to bet. The lineup of orators,
both in the front window and the back room, was not reassuring
to the aspirations of labor.

Practically all the orators, either for sotto voce or national
hookup, are notorious as baiters of trades unionism. A billing
which included Girdler, Weir, General Johnson and Dorothy

Thompson was hardly one to encourage labor into a feeling that here was a haven where its rights would be respected. How on earth did the manufacturers happen to omit Pegler?

Mr. Chester's speech boiled down to an offer that Franklin Delano Roosevelt would be welcome as a consultant of big business if he would forswear all the objectives to which he is committed. Even the C.I.O. would not be denied admission to the gathering for brotherly love if only all its representatives would agree to check their hats and cut their throats before entering the conference room.

Possibly the high point in unconscious irony was achieved by poor Miss Thompson, who spoke against "smearing," after a session which had been largely devoted to calling John L. Lewis everything from racketeer to potential dictator. It then expressed a pious hope he would co-operate.

Tom Girdler had the privilege of introducing Dr. George B. Cutten, president of Colgate, which did not have as good a football team as usual. The executive of the Red Raiders put Thomas Jefferson in his place by declaring that equality is "a dismal failure."

Mr. Chester's dinner address, which came after Miss Thompson's pep talk, was entitled How Liberal Is Business? No vote was taken.

One listener got the impression that business is still back in the days of Mark Hanna and William McKinley. It is just too bad about child labor, but the States will have to attend to it. It is unfortunate that anyone should have to work through punishing hours for tragic underpay, but, again, the federal government must not interfere with the right of local communities to allow people to starve to death quietly and in good order.

Indeed, as far as I could judge, the liberalism of the Manufacturers' Assn. lay in saying, "Bring me the regular dinner."

There was need of a Paul Revere to ride through the diners and make the startling announcement, "You didn't win the last election."

At the moment the generous offer of these business men is simply, "If you will consent to do it in our way we will be quite willing to compromise with any man."

Weir is wisdom and Girdler is God. Take it or leave it. I hope I know the answer the millions of America will make to this proposition.

128. "JAM-TOMORROW" PROGRESSIVES

A technical objection is the first refuge of a scoundrel. Having indulged in a generalization I must proceed at once to take part of it back. Obviously a good purpose may be ill served by a bad law and it is not unreasonable for legislators to try and frame measures that will work effectively.

However, I do not agree with the notion that all progressive action must be suspended until the one-hundred-per-cent statute has been found. And there are publicists and politicians who are always voicing their support for certain objectives in theory but never in fact. The most damaging opposition to the abolition of child labor has come from those who insist that they bleed for the suffering of young toilers but that the method of relief suggested is not the right way.

Sincerity has never seemed to me one of the most vital virtues. It all depends on what you are sincere about. And so I will readily grant that some members of this group may mean well. But many don't mean well at all. Ten thousand different measures for the abolition of child labor could be brought up and they would pick flaws in each and every one of them.

Continued delay and complete opposition are twins not to be distinguished save by the ribbons in their hair. Progressives will do well to take Luke XI, 23, for a text: "He that is not with me is against me."

The same sort of negative support obstructs any kind of anti-lynching legislation, or wages-and-hours bill. Of course, all those who oppose present available measures deplore lynching and long hours and low pay, but they insist upon solutions which are arduous and nebulous and not even in the present picture. These are the jam-tomorrow progressives and they will never agree with any remedy which is timed for today.

In so far as these spokesmen consent to become definite and articulate as to the sort of thing they would support, it boils down to some watchful sort of waiting for the backward states to catch up with those which have made greater advances. It is always easier to be patient when the rope is not around your own neck.

Nor will these advocates of a slow evolutionary development admit the palpable fact that the reluctant communities do more than slow up progress. They actually inspire rapid retreats. Communities which bid for cheap labor and assure employers that they will see that it remains cheap tear down the whole structure. We know that far from winning the fight against child labor, the present set-up has encouraged a retrogressive movement.

The good will of certain individuals is less than enough against the pressure of economic advantage. And anyhow I doubt damnably the honest intent of those who are all against evils but carry in the palm of the right hand a nullifying "But."

I deny that most of these men and women have a right to assert that they are actuated by good will, for I believe that true humanitarianism has been unjustly discounted and that the one who can prove he has a burning concern should not be scorned even though he cannot produce a pat program for every problem.

By now it is probably too late to insist that the word "liberal" should be something other than an insult. The true liberals who find themselves living under a label which has lost repute must blame themselves in part. They made the entrance requirements too low.

But I still feel that something should be done for the word "humanitarian" before it goes down the drain. A man whose first animating influence toward progressive action is a genuine sympathy for the underprivileged should not be made to feel ashamed.

If he never gets beyond the stage of running around in circles and saying, "Something must be done," I am ready to grant that his usefulness in the social scheme will never be very great. But even a muddled emotion may bring a recruit into an understanding of practical programs. There ought to be more than one entrance to any church.

In the beginning the radicals themselves were pretty toplofty in saying, "Oh, he's just a sentimental Socialist." Surely it is better to be an emotional radical than a sentimental Fascist. Jack Reed did not come into the fight for a new world wholly on any program of required reading. He felt the need of change in his very bones. Eugene V. Debs had his romantic side as a labor leader and John L. Lewis has been known to quote Shakespearean verse with a great emotion when it suits his purpose and his mood.

Unless I am much mistaken, radical groups are now far more friendly than they used to be toward those whose only qualification as recruits is that they are men and women of good intent. Indeed by now it is the conservative forces that have switched tactics.

Once I used to read that they fought all radical ideas because they were conceived in hate. But now I find stern-visaged practical persons complaining that their enemies are feeble folk actuated wholly by visionary ideas built around impossible concepts of human brotherhood.

The reactionary will be just as hostile to the missionary who approaches him with a smile and a tract as he is to those who frankly offer to punch him in the nose. There seems to be no pleasing these people.

Thus I find Sinclair Lewis quoting with great gusto the statement of Fred Beal that Mike Gold "is a sentimental revolutionist." It has never seemed to me that Gold was particularly sentimental, but even if the accusation could be driven home one hundred per cent I would still feel that any avenue of escape from Bourbonism was better than remaining mired in heartless indifference.

Theologians still quarrel as to the respective merits of faith and works. I never could quite understand how any sharp dividing line was possible. Work without faith is all but impossible and when a faith grows confident enough it inevitably transfers itself into deeds.

If mankind is to march to better things I see no reason why there could be complaint if happy warriors walk arm in arm with those who wear a fighting face. That is as long as both boys "are members of this club" and heading in a common direction.

129. ARE WE APES OR MEN?

The circus winters here in Sarasota and its pride and joy is the largest gorilla now living in captivity. His name, reasonably enough, is "Gargantua the Great" and he is plenty tough. "Gargantua" is only just cutting his second teeth and weighs four hundred and fifty pounds. He will do better as the years roll by.

Until quite recently the largest gorilla was in the Berlin Zoo. He was a six-hundred-pound specimen and I am told that when he died the Germans regarded it as a national catastrophe. Their feeling of sorrow was logical enough, for even more than the swastika, a gorilla could well stand as the symbol of Nazi philosophy.

But I am afraid that possibly the largest of the anthropoids typifies the whole spirit of the modern world. Frequently the question is asked, "Are we mice or men?" and the connotation in the query seems to be that there is something rodential and mean in peacefulness. I think it would be more pertinent for rational human beings to debate the problem, "Are we apes or men?"

In looking at "Gargantua" in his cage I felt that a strong circumstantial case had been made for the theory of evolution. I can hardly doubt that we stem from some such animal. And what worried me was the feeling that whatever blood stream goes up can also go down. If we have ascended from the gorilla, there may be at least a chance that we will return to our fathers. Since force seems to be the desired goal of all the peoples of the earth, the gorilla might well demand the logical right to be nominated as the fittest. There is a chimpanzee here which can drive an automobile around a track if only someone else will work the gear shift. And that of course is intricate. I have never been able to master it, but if that gorilla can be taught to shoot a gun, which is easy enough, he and his kind may inherit the earth. Indeed, if the good soldier is to be the noblest work of man, the differentiation between men and monkeys may be small enough. I do not think the day of despair is here. It seems to me that we can and that we will work our way out of international madness. Yet if we are to do that there must be more respect for verbal contacts. It angers me when people scorn all sorts of international conferences by saying, "Nothing comes out of such affairs but talk."

What's wrong with talk? If civilized man has worked his way out of the primeval slime, it has been by the exchange of ideas. It is wholly unfair to speak of "talk" as the negation of "action." Words have sent more walls tumbling down than any shells or shrapnel. It is quite true that disarmament conferences and other international meetings have frequently been disappointing. They have even been failures, if you like. But not one of them has been so bloody a failure as each and every war.

It seems to me that the last laugh, and a grim one at that, lies in the grave with Woodrow Wilson. Borah, Johnson and all the other die-hards who still survive, preen themselves upon the fact that they killed American participation in the League of Nations and thus saved America from dangerous foreign entanglements. And now we are about to build the greatest navy in the world to prove that we are happily situated between two oceans and need not bother our heads about the strife in Europe or Asia. Woodrow Wilson erred in many matters. But I believe that history will acquit him of all his sins of judgment because he fundamentally had the right idea about collective security.

There is no room for argument about the Treaty of Versailles. It was a mess of tragic greed and stupidity. It is also true that the League was handicapped from the start by the circumstance that it was built up on a crooked cornerstone. Nor would I like to deny that today the League is dead. And so I say, "Long live the League of Nations." If this one does not function—and it does not—then we must create forthwith another. Certainly the right to criticize international co-operation does not belong to those who first stabbed the effort and then exultantly exclaimed, "We told you from the start that the thing was sickly."

Are we apes or men? There isn't too much time for the world of human beings to come to a decision. Some man and some nation must take the lead. I am all for collective security, but I want permission to define that phrase in my own terms. As a last defense I am in favor of the combination of democratic lands against the Fascist adventurers. But that should not be the starting point. It is well enough to say that we stand at Armageddon, but even a battle in which the issues are clearly drawn is not so good as no battle at all. There should be at least one more try. The nations of the world, right, left and center, piratical or puritanical, should sit down around a table and ponder the question of how the world is to be saved.

Not long ago a flaming body in the sky missed the earth by a mere four hundred thousand miles. I assume that if some astronomer of repute should tell us all tomorrow that within forty-eight hours an asteroid was about to strike our planet and shake us from stem to stern, there would be a mitigation of national altercations. We might then come together and make plans or methods by which we could meet the shock. But in cold reason the flying particle which sailed outside the corner of the plate was no such threat to human security as the possibility of general conflict. Some man and some nation must lead the way.

To be specific, I think that Franklin Roosevelt ought to use the naval program as a hole card, but seek world accord before a single rivet is driven home. It can easily be said that such a gesture would be futile and that Germany, Japan and Italy would refuse any invitation. That is probable, and yet if the effort met with failure it would not leave millions of maimed bodies strewn across the meadows. Another approach might well be an international congress of all the trade unionists in all the lands, even including representatives of nations where trade unionism as we know it does not exist. The difficulties of such a conference are palpable. But again I say that rational human beings owe it to themselves to make the effort. I think that we are men, not apes, and before we fly at one another's throats we must exhaust every effort to preserve civilization through civilized methods. Only when such risks for peace have been made and such experiments been carried through will it be reasonable for even the most righteous leader to take up the sword and cry out, "God help me, I can do no other."

130. COLUMNS WILL OUT

They are trying to streamline William Green. The engineer in charge of the project is Phil Pearl, a former Washington newspaperman, who has taken over the job of public-relations man for the veteran president of the A. F. of L. Mr. Pearl's diagnosis of the complaint seems to be that Mr. Green has been too austere and stand-offish for the good of the organization. Accordingly, the work of reconditioning has begun. One can hear the sound of rivets being driven home. They are changing William Green from stem to stern.

Naturally he has a new speech. The old one was a rapt auto-biographical portrait of William Green which began in effect, "I was born of poor but God-fearing parents," and went on in the same manner for the full two hours. Now the Green state-ments contain wisecracks and even literary allusions. In the duel with John L. Lewis, William Green is preparing to fight Shake-speare with Shakespeare and Virgil with Virgil.

But Phil Pearl is attempting to do something more ambitious than giving Green a background in belles-lettres. He is trying to change his personal habits for the worse. Mr. Green was a Baptist lay preacher before he was a labor leader and he has always kept on the weather side of the fleshpots. Now he takes one cocktail every day.

Phil Pearl told him it would be extremely helpful if he would show up in some public place each evening, preferably in the presence of newspapermen, and casually call for a drink. In a self-sacrificing spirit, Green consented.

His mentor got a menu and showed him a list of the names of all the conventional mixed drinks. Choosing at random, Mr. Green decided that an old-fashioned would be the bitter pill which he would choose for his own. Pearl vetoed that. He thought the name itself might be bad propaganda for the American Federation of Labor.

And so they compromised on a Martini as the daily drink. I have never seen the rite performed, but they tell me it is both thrilling and tragic. Phil Pearl gives the signal when the zero hour has come and William Green, with a roguish twinkle in his eye, or the nearest he can muster, says, "Waiter, you might bring me a Martini."

The publicity man is disappointed because as yet he has been unable to prevent his chief from closing both eyes as he takes up the fearful tonic and making a fearful face as the dreadful draught goes down.

But the counselor is still filled with high hopes and aspirations because he succeeded here in Miami in breaking down an age-old precedent in the life of William Green. He induced him not only to go to the horse races at Hialeah Park but to place a couple of bets. Mr. Pearl was quite a picker in the days before he was saved. Mr. Pearl, indeed, was the finest handicapper among all the Washington correspondents. Naturally he got Green out to the horse park on the plea it would be a humanizing gesture. But I suspect that the reformed newspaperman was, on his own account, mixing love and duty.

Installed in a box at Hialeah, Green refused to act on the first-class tips of his guide. He insisted on playing hunches. His first choice was a colt called "Dignitary," which was a logical selection for the leader of labor's most exclusive club. "Dignitary" did not win.

Next, Green bet on "Mine Boy," which ran fifth. Mr. Green used to be a worker once himself. It is even possible that he got that bet down just in time, for the United Mine Workers would have ousted Green but for his resignation. That may be embarrassing, for the only card Green holds now is his solid-gold badge in the musicians' union.

William Green is not a musician, although Phil Pearl is

making frantic efforts to teach him to render *Bei Mir Bist du Schön* upon the trombone. Phil has done a good job, but just the same he runs the risk of getting Green fired not only out of the labor movement but out of the Baptist Church as well. Indeed Mr. Pearl may be personally in peril. Somebody might hale him into court on the charge of impairing the morals of a miner (retired).

At this point I would like to explain that the foregoing essay was sufficient to get me barred from the local press conference of William Green. I had written it as a column for a New York newspaper and points west, but one of the head men tossed it out. However, a carbon copy had been shipped to a local paper and so the piece was called to the attention of Mr. Pearl. He responded with a great indignation and added that if I attempted to crash the press conference I would be barred because he said that I was not a newspaperman. I do not know whether the issue is "the freedom of the press" or the debatable problem "Are columnists people?"

At any rate I went to the press conference equipped with a press card, a Newspaper Guild card and a telegram addressed to myself so that I could establish my identity. I also took along a stooge. Mr. Quentin Reynolds, Jeremiah Mahoney's nephew, is an acquaintance of mine. Indeed at dawn on the day of the conference we were at the Hialeah race track, where Mr. Reynolds had a date to interview "War Admiral," his jockey and his trainer. And so I said, "Quent, this has been most interesting and I want to make some return in kind. You have been kind enough to show me 'War Admiral,' which, at the moment, seems to be America's finest horse. Now if you will come with me to the A. F. of L. press conference I would like to show you William Green."

But first of all we had to fool the watchful public-relations man—Mr. Philip Pearl, a press agent of great price. And so though we rode from Coral Gables in the same taxi we behaved as strangers when we got to the Everglades Hotel and started up the stairway toward the shrine. Mr. Pearl barred me as he had promised. And on the grounds that I was not a newspaperman. I've only been in the business thirty years. Quentin Reynolds did his act just as we had rehearsed it. He introduced himself as a writer from *Collier's Weekly* and said that he would like to get in to see the chief in action. But twice he stressed the point: "Of course, I'm not a newspaperman." Pearl welcomed him for all that, and said, "You must come in. I think I can arrange to have you shake hands with President Green."

But by this time I was out in the bar, or rather the "cocktail lounge," ruminating. I found it difficult to whip up any considerable amount of indignation. A private citizen has an undoubted legal right to see all reporters, some or none. And as the afternoon wore on my irritation grew less and less. Since I was not permitted to go into the press conference and get Mr. Green in person, I decided that there was no point in hanging around for an hour or so waiting for the pithy statement. I went back to the race track. And by a fortunate coincidence I got there just in time to buy a ticket on the daily double. It won and paid ninety-seven dollars. William Green is a good old soul.

131. MY BROTHER'S KEEPER

Scripture offers small support to those who would close their eyes and thank God that the rest of the world is well lost. I have just been reading the brief and eloquent account of the greatest isolationist of all, who lived many years before Borah or Neville Chamberlain. The story can be found in the ninth and tenth verses of the fourth chapter of the Book of Genesis. And it runs:—

"And the Lord said unto Cain, Where is Abel, thy brother? And he said, I know not. Am I my brother's keeper?

"And He said, What hast thou done? The voice of thy brother's blood crieth unto me from the ground."

It seems to me that Cain's heresy was the crisis of his crime. Other men in Israel were violent and killed in anger those near and dear to them. But it was Cain who first voiced and set the philosophy of isolation and rugged individualism.

And it is recorded that God said, "Now art thou cursed from the earth which hath opened her mouth to receive thy brother's blood from thy hand."

How, then, will it fare with those who say, "It's none of our business"? And will there be praise in the long eternity of posterity for those statesmen and leaders who take delight in declaring, "Nobody can touch us for years and years. What do we care about the rest of mankind?"

I think that upon the brow of such there will be placed a mark, the circle of complete indifference, which should make them known to their fellows. The blood of our brothers does cry out from the ground. It cries out from Spain and China and from the concentration camps of Nazi Germany. Will it be well for us to wash our hands and say with the cynicism of Cain, "Am I my brother's keeper?"

Until this clinging and continuous heresy can be eradicated from the earth there will not be peace. It is the solace of the smug in all the nations of the world. It affects both domestic economy and international relations. The contemptuous cry of Cain has been coined over and over again in a thousand current expressions:—"Let them worry," "What's it to me?" "Ishka bibble," "Let George do it," and "I've got to think about myself."

There are scabs and finks among nations as well as among individuals. The theory that each man is sufficient unto himself is the core of industrial conflict, just as the theory of complete nationalism has been the cornerstone of war. Peace through co-operation is a difficult task, but it is not an idle and fantastic dream. Men who call themselves realists stabbed it to death. Neville Chamberlain cannot be questioned as to accuracy when he says that the League of Nations is impotent. And Hiram Johnson is correct when he makes the same assertion.

But I wonder whether these two men are just the persons who should take pride in putting over the point. It is a little as if Cassius and Brutus should join in a report declaring, "Caesar is not fit to function because he's dead as a doornail."

The League of Nations was not conceived under the most auspicious circumstances. It was delivered bunglingly by diplomats. And now it lies bleeding like the body of Abel. And the earth has opened her mouth to receive the blood. But that red stream is articulate. The people of the world must organize again. The toilers should take the lead. Agreements with Fascists are feeble things. Such arrangements are the indorsement of war and not its negation.

What have we done? We cannot pass by on the other side when the cry comes from blood brothers. The peace and freedom of the world can be preserved only by free men. And each of us is his brother's keeper.

132. *THE CRADLE WILL ROCK*

This is getting around to the season during which the Pulitzer Prize Committee makes its awards, and also the Critics' Circle. It seems to me that the award of the Circle carries more weight than the judgment of the elderly gentlemen of Columbia. After all, the reviewers who face the ordeal of seeing every show are in a better position to decide than any group which merely makes a short sightseeing trip along the surface of the cream. No one can appreciate a good show as much as a man who has sat in the blinds along the aisle and watched the wild turkeys flutter by.

But since I am neither a Pulitzerian nor a newspaper critic, I will have to play a lone hand. Maybe my choice will find no official support. But at least I can get in the first word. And so without either plaque or palms I nominate *The Cradle Will Rock* as the best play of the present season.

And I like it so much better than anything else that I would not compromise on any second choice. I like it both for its substance and its shadow. Marc Blitzstein's play with music (which is really a slightly longer way of saying "opera") strikes the only optimistic note of the serious shows along Broadway.

This is a better season than usual, and the writing men have been less disposed to turn their backs on reality. The antic attitude, the cute stuff and the whimsy-whimsy have gone somewhat out of fashion.

Just the same, there are many sprinters among the dramatists. They have chosen a new direction, but the creative artists of the American stage still show too keen a disposition to run for their lives. This year the finishing line for the annual marathon has been the local cemetery. The popular slogan celebrated in the show shops is the contention that it is better to be dead than alive.

Without any disposition to pose as a final authority on that moot question, I vote "No," and if my side loses I am prepared to bring in a minority report.

The Cradle Will Rock is not wholly a series of humorous interludes. It does deal with things somber and sad. But its final note and its continuing philosophy appear to be the conception that even a bitter and a muddled world still remains putty in the hands of those who are disposed to get together in organized effort.

The world is not your oyster or that of your neighbor, but with a little lemon juice and a dash of tabasco it can be made not only palatable but wholly desirable.

It shocks me to find so many men and women who are professedly idealists rushing around and shouting, "All is lost!" For instance, most of the announcements that war is just around the corner come from pacifists. And I think the answer ought to be, "Stuff and nonsense." This is no time for Pollyannas, and there never has been an era in which they were of any use. Just the same, it is well within the possibility of man to change a tragically imperfect world from stem to stern.

Such plays as *Our Town* and *On Borrowed Time* suggest a placid surrender to the reaper upon the theory that he is not nearly as grim as he has been painted. But even if he has a smiling face I still think it is a mistake to court his attention. There is no sense in arranging appointments in Samarra by long-distance telephone calls.

And so I urge again preferment for *The Cradle Will Rock*, because it shouts and sings that this earth can be made to glow and glisten if working men and women will only decide forthwith to kindle flame by rubbing together souls and shoulders.

133. HOW DO YOU SLEEP, FRANCO?

Francisco Franco, Generalissimo, how do you sleep of nights? Possibly you are not sensitive to sounds. But a scream can be distracting. Even a moan may murder sleep. To some there is a nightmare quality in the curious rhythm made by the feet of hundreds running for their lives. And the cry of a child in anguish seems poignant to many people.

And so, Francisco Franco, your lot is not a happy one. You must live on until the day of your death with this savage symphony ringing in your ears. Even a Generalissimo may discover that it is impossible to stay the thing he has begun. Bombs loosed in the night may set up a succession of waves as pebbles tossed into a pond. Franco, you cannot evermore issue an effective order for firing to cease. You are doomed to carry to the grave the din of bombardment and those noises which men and women and children make when they die.

Our own Mr. Ellery Sedgwick, an ornament to that New England culture which gave us Lowell and Thayer and Grant, has bestowed a blessing upon you. He has written that after you have prevailed by "peremptory methods" you will "work out Spanish salvation in a thoroughly Spanish way." I assume that Editor Sedgwick, in his impulsive Puritan way, intends to compliment you. Poking about among the ruins, he seems to say, "Neat work, old fellow."

But, Francisco Franco, you will err if you take the Brahmin blessing too closely to your heart. I trust I labor under no misapprehension. Before salvation can be attained there must be absolution. Ellery Sedgwick is a thoroughly respectable member of a highly respectable community, and I do not mean to belittle him when I say that the *Atlantic Monthly* is neither broad nor deep enough to wash all your sins away.

Indeed, it seems to me that there is no one this side of the Judgment Seat who could possibly say, "Francisco Franco, Generalissimo, you may walk forth into God's sunlight a man pure of heart and stainless."

It has been said of those who injure children that it were better to have a millstone hung about your neck. Have you noticed, Franco, that you can no longer hold up your head? And so it is and will be.

Some have bestowed the title, "Defender of the Faith." What faith can that possibly be? Surely there is no coherent connection between the raids on Barcelona and the Church of Christ. The song of the herald angels cannot be scored in such a way as to admit the dissonances of those who cry out in agony.

But it has been said that you are a liberator who took to the sword only because Spain was Red. It is redder now. Barcelona is drenched in the blood of men, women and subversive babies.

Francisco Franco, Generalissimo, how do you sleep of nights?

134. THE WATERS OF THE JORDAN

The text is from the Second Book of Kings, the fifth chapter and the tenth verse. It reads, "Go and wash in Jordan seven times, and thy flesh shall come again to thee, and thou shalt be clean."

The words are those of the prophet Elisha, and they were sent to Naaman, captain of the host of the King of Syria. The Bible says, "He was also a mighty man in valor, but he was a leper."

Naaman's wife had a little serving maid who had been brought away captive out of the land of Israel. In those days Israel was sore oppressed and feeble in the face of the great power and military force of Syria. Still it was the little captive maid who said, "Would God my Lord were with the prophet that is in Samaria, for he would recover him of his leprosy." And Naaman, the mighty, "came with his horses and his chariot and stood at the door of the house of Elisha."

And this Bible story came vividly into my mind when I read that Hitler had come to Vienna with his storm troopers and made a speech in the public square. Like the other captain of the host he would have been wiser if he had stood humbly at the door of the prophet. He should have sought out Sigmund Freud, the healer.

Freud is now an old man of more than 80, and I think he will be numbered among the great of Israel and of the world. Today he is a captive of the Nazis, and the soldiers of this new

Syria have invaded his home to scatter and ransack his papers.

The healer lies within the mailed fist of the conqueror. It is as if death were condemning life. And yet Sigmund Freud has within his hands the power to perform again the miracle which came to Naaman.

"Then went he down, and dipped himself seven times in Jordan, according to the saying of the man of God: and his flesh came again like unto the flesh of a little child, and he was clean."

In the beginning Naaman, captain of the host, was loath to accept the advice of Elisha. It seemed an oversimple thing to the Syrian commander, and he cried out, "Are not Abana and Pharpar, rivers of Damascus, better than all the waters of Israel?" Indeed, "He turned and went away in a rage." But finally he did come to Jordan River and was made clean.

Fascism is a grotesque philosophy. It is the mechanism of a mentality which has become maladjusted. Anyone who has lost his own soul feels that he must gain the whole world.

Little men hag-ridden by their inhibitions strike out with cruelty and with violence to soothe the ache which lies within them. It is neither far-fetched nor facetious to theorize that perhaps a paperhanger is the very one who would be bidden by his unconscious to paste the swastika across the map of Europe.

Surely Hitler's anti-Semitism rises from some inward uneasiness. A series of symptoms have been translated into a career. Der Fuehrer is literally the sick man of the Reich. And, as the case history stands, he can never find peace through any sort of conquest. Alexander wept.

Hitler should know that the goal which he is seeking lies buried somewhere in the secret springs of his own mind. Not all his guns or troops or tanks will ever suffice to lead him to integration.

The Bible says that Naaman was valorous and mighty, but he found his personal salvation only when he stood humbly at the door of Elisha. And Hitler, too, must seek the voice of the prophet and wash away his hate and fears and prejudices in the life-giving waters of the Jordan.

135. NUMBER 31921

Coming back from the city of sleep, one passes through a little death of dreams before reaching reality. And this time the dust of the dream was heavy upon me. I could not shake it off.

In the fantasy I was to speak at a meeting in Madison Square Garden. The chairman began his introduction in complimentary fashion, but then he proceeded to take me apart. He spoke of sloth and failure and frivolity. It was as searching a survey as if I had done it myself. Which, of course, I did.

Whole phrases from the dream came along with me. The old man who lives on the further side of consciousness said, "Broun once spoke and wrote with fire and fervor about Sacco and Vanzetti. Sacco and Vanzetti are dead. Why has he no word for one who fights from a tomb for the right to live?"

All this is literally true, and I sat, shaken, on the edge of the bed for several minutes. "Hello," I thought to myself, "has someone nudged me as I traveled along the road to Damascus?"

But presently it was easy enough to put aside the miraculous and supernatural. This was an assignment from my conscience. I remembered that for almost a week I had been carrying in my pocket a letter from Tom Mooney.

The letter from San Quentin said, "The case represents things bigger than any one individual, and certainly the case has greater and more far-reaching significance than my own welfare as one man." It was signed, "Tom Mooney—31921."

Number 31921 was right.

But it is also true that Mooney remains an individual as well as a symbol. They have pinned a number upon him, but he is still a man.

I choose to discuss things which may not be relevant. There is a school of thought which seeks to justify a great injustice by the use of the angler's apology. Spokesmen for this side admit that the prisoner is not guilty, but they add that he has been in jail so long that he really doesn't mind it. So why worry about the whole affair?

He has now served twenty-two years, and it has been said, with what seems to me a perverted pride, that the old man is no longer set at hard labor. And, again, an effort has been made to celebrate the generosity of American justice by asserting that special privileges are accorded to him in the prison. Sometimes he is allowed to leave his cell and walk the entire length of the corridor.

It may even be that his feet have worn a pathway in the stone. And so, if I understand this theory, while justice has not been done, it has been approximated and everything is fine and dandy.

The only trouble with this doctrine lies in the fact that it simply is not true. Mooney has flung himself against the bars for twenty-two years. All sorts and conditions of men have fought for his freedom. As conservative a gentleman as George Wickersham drew up an eloquent plea in his defense. Radicals, liberals, progressives and phonies have had their say. But the leadership of the fight for Mooney always has been in the hands of Tom Mooney. They have not caged his spirit.

No man is more passionate for freedom. Here is a general who has kept at the head of his forces although locked in a cell. To the authorities of San Quentin he may be 31921, but no American is better known to the workers of the world. And they know him as Tom Mooney.

People who think he should have accepted the boon of parole do not understand the quality of this man. When he comes out of jail it will not be on his hands and knees. He has kept his head up. Twenty-two years have gone under the bridge, and there is no power on earth which can give them back. And so if any shred of justice is to be done the time is here and now. And if Tom turns at the gate to cry out, "Damn your eyes!" what living man has a greater right to say it?

136. A CHEER FOR THE MELTING POT

One of the most heartening things that has happened in our international relations is the present move to find havens for political refugees and oppressed peoples. We are going back to one of the finest of American traditions. And it is a tradition from which we have strayed in recent years. It was not a small thing that America was known once throughout the world as the homeland of the homeless.

At the moment it would not be wise to discuss our entire policy toward the immigrant. In an age of crash and recession certain arguments might be presented against unlimited hospitality. But I can see no reason that could be advanced against a policy of shelter for the men and women and children who live under a terror.

Too much, I think, has been said about the debt which the immigrant, the alien if you please, owes to America. And too little has been said concerning our debt to the stranger within our gates.

And when that familiar cry, "Why don't you go back where you came from?" is raised, it seems to me that the person under pressure might well reply, "Yes, but let me state the stipulations. I will go back where I came from, but in all fairness I have a right to ask the privilege of taking with me the things which I have created. I will take the railroads which I and my fellow foreigners have set down across your prairies. And I will take the ditches which we have dug and the towers reared against the skies. Even more than that, if I depart you must permit me to retain within my baggage the hopes and aspirations and the ideals which I took with me when I came to you from across the sea. It was said that here was the melting pot and in this crucible men and women of many countries have poured not only their sinews but their souls. If I go back in company with my fellows, give us that flesh and blood which we dared to risk in the great experiment."

And whoever says this will be quite correct, because if America goes completely Aryan and nationalistic it will betray the bright dream of the founding fathers. Most of the tough and dirty work which has made us a great and wealthy nation has been performed by aliens. Even beyond the taking of naturalization papers they became part of this continent through the foot-pound energy of their arms and shoulders. A compact that is signed in blood and sweat should be, in all logic, more binding than a signature by pen and ink.

The Pilgrim fathers, and they, too, were immigrants and aliens, may have cut a thin bite into the wooded shores of New England, but the wilderness and the desert were conquered by Italians, Irish, Slovaks and that vast undefined group known in our colloquial speech as "hunkies."

The hunky is probably the most typical American of all. We are, for what it's worth, a land made up economically and culturally of contributions. The hundred-per-cent American is an Indian in a blanket. And at the moment he does not seem to be a person of much consequence. There is an American culture. We should be proud of it. There is no reason why we should be ashamed to face the English critics or the visiting lecturers. Here novels have been created and short stories and music; and paint has been set down on canvas in a way to be remembered. But no single race or national strain can legitimately claim all the credit. This has been a synthesis of far-flung cultures. I think it is good. It seems to me that America has made its mark and that "X" may forever mark the spot of one of the greatest experiments in human brotherhood. And so we would be both vain and cruel if we departed from the old standard and made any declaration such as, "Nobody can join, nobody can help, nobody can hang around."

Of course the immediate problem is the establishment of a free land for the Jews of the world. We ought to know the contribution which they have made to our civilization. There would be a very meager amount of American music if it were not for the Jewish composers and the Jewish performers. Our theater has been largely developed by our Jewish citizens. It will be said and has been said that the net result has been a vulgarization of the arts. But this can be maintained only by those who look most casually upon the enterprises concerned. In the first place there is no such thing as "the Jew." There can be such a thing as a model T in the field of automobiles, but men and women cannot be grouped under any single hood. Among Jews as well as among Pilgrims and Scandinavians there is a gap between the topmost flight and the bottom. But here increasingly, because of the drive of fascism, we identify by race the person whom we dislike. In a restaurant I have heard it said, "Look at that loud Jew over there in the corner." We seem to forget that there are also loud Lithuanians and graduates of Groton. In fact some of the most flamboyant public exhibitions of bad taste which I have ever seen have been put on by Harvard men. I say this with regret but, I think, with entire accuracy.

One of the criticisms raised against the immigrant within our gates is that he sends some of his money back to his homeland. From the point of view of the economic experts, such a complaint is silly. After all, the man who digs a ditch and gives some part of his hard-earned stipend to parents in Italy, Rumania, or Russia is not in any true sense diminishing our national wealth. There is still such a thing as international trade, and if no money were ever sent abroad to Europe we should have no customers beyond the boundaries of our country. But above that, there is the certain truth that the laborer is worthy of his hire and that he produces more than he gains. Surely it is unfair to deny the underpaid and hard-pressed manual worker the right to do what he pleases with his paltry pay.

One of my favorite orations is a speech which B. Charney Vladeck has delivered several times. Mr. Vladeck was a revolutionist in Russia in the days of the Tzar and so, of course, he was sent to Siberia. And while he was in prison he got out of the library a copy of Charnwood's *Life of Lincoln,* which had been translated into Russian. And as Vladeck read this story of the Great Emancipator he thought to himself, "When I am released from this cell I want to go to the land of Lincoln."

And finally he was free and he came to America. He came to the slums of New York City and he was both puzzled and shocked as he looked about him, for this was not the land of Lincoln. And later he got a job which sent him traveling through the Middle West. But he ran constantly into the fierce rivalry and cutthroat contact of our competitive economic system. And every city to which he came had slums not unlike those of New York. He had despaired, but one night in Indianapolis he saw a poster announcing that Eugene Debs would speak. He went. Debs spoke. And as this American with a Hoosier twang preached his gospel of brotherhood, Vladeck suddenly sat up in his seat and said to himself, "I've made no mistake. This can be the land of Lincoln."

And let us make no mistake. We will and can make our country true to the ideals of the Emancipator, and that means we must resolve to leave the door ajar for all those who suffer under oppression.

137. THE EASTER STORY

"And they said among themselves, 'Who shall roll us away the stone from the door of the sepulchre?'" To me the most vivid account of the Easter morning is in the sixteenth chapter of St. Mark. It contains as lovely a verse as any in the Bible.

"And very early in the morning, the first day of the week, they came unto the sepulchre at the rising of the sun." I am not thinking of the strictly theological significance of the Gospel account, but of other connotations. The Easter story is the story of the fundamental fight between life and death, between hope and despair. I think it is fair to note that those who came to the rising of the sun did not come in the spirit of surrender. They knew the stone was very great, but the query, "Who shall roll us away the stone?", was no mere rhetorical question. It was in the minds of these devoted believers that the task could be accomplished.

They sought a means and a method, "and when they looked they saw that the stone was rolled away." That faith which can move a mountain is sufficient to roll away a mighty rock. But I like to think that if the Angel of the Lord had not intervened the women themselves would have set their hands against the stone which barred their way. The idea of defeat or frustration never entered their minds. They came very early in the morning not to celebrate a lost cause but to perform a practical task. Indeed, they had "brought sweet spices, that they might come and anoint Him."

Of course, they knew that the tomb was sealed, but their faith was lively that a way could be found to break through that wall of death. They talked it over among themselves. Their very normal instinct was to co-operate in solving the problem. As far as precedent and tradition went they may well have seemed visionaries.

Mark names those who came to the tomb at the rising of the sun as "Mary Magdalen, and Mary the mother of James, and Salome." It might have seemed utterly impractical for three women to bear spices to a tomb which was guarded by a huge and heavy stone. And probably there were those among the disciples who turned their love of the crucified leader into nothing more than loud lamentations. All they could contribute was grief and despair. They may even have told the three women that their mission was a fruitless one, and that all hope lay buried behind a rock too mighty to be moved.

But the Easter story has been repeated again and again in the history of the world. Those who follow the course of the sun have found that every morning may mark a miracle in the life of man. Life is greater than death. And the true realist is not the person who is content to look at the stone and sigh. There are those who look about the world today and declare that civilization is done. Men who profess to be of good intent say that war is inevitable. In our own land the head-shakers and the nay-sayers are always with us. They even condemn as cynical and destructive people who suggest that peace can be won and the woes of the world solved by taking thought and action and quitting the dead modes of the past.

To some, history itself is a sort of hard rock. What has been must forever endure. If man has always turned to battle, so it must be until the end of time. Poverty has been set as the lasting lot of humankind. There were days in America when we had pioneers. They were not crippled by precedent. They went out and created it. It is true that we no longer possess unlimited forests to be cut down or rich land to be taken over by the hardy and the adventurous. We must pioneer along new lines of endeavor. We must make the adjustment between man and the machine. A world more great and gay awaits us when the problem of distribution is solved.

To pioneer is to experiment. Let us leave by the roadside those who simply sit and say, "Isn't everything terrible?" and here and now at the rising of the sun it is for us to answer it.

138. F.D.R. AND THE D.A.R.

Franklin D. Roosevelt is extremely skillful in impromptu remarks, and I think that he has seldom been more felicitous than in his brief discourse to the Daughters of the American Revolution. I hope the text he furnished is graven in the heart of every lady who heard him.

"Remember always that all of us, and you and I especially," said the President, "are descended from immigrants and revolutionists."

It was well put, but one may doubt that the Daughters will remember. The organization has spent a great many years in teaching its members to forget their radical and humble forebears. By now they seem to believe that there were plush carpets at Valley Forge, and that the embattled farmers of Concord rose to protest against the New Deal. Indeed, whenever there is reactionary work to be done somebody takes the name of Paul Revere in vain.

And from under the sod where the distinguished silversmith is buried comes a muttering. They say that Paul Revere stirs in his long sleep and calls out, "Whoa, Bess. Let's turn around and go back to the stable. Some of this crowd aren't worth the saving."

I have always had a great interest in the D.A.R., because as a manly lad of nine or ten I used to sit outside the door and eavesdrop on the discussions of the New York Chapter. The Daughters met at our house once a year. Practically everybody met at our house. It was the headquarters of the Silent Nine, the grammar school fraternity, of which I was secretary and treasurer, and there were weekly gatherings of the Anti-Bug Society, a group formed by my brother to discourage the rising tide of feminism. My father belonged to a club called the Forty-third Street Farmers, which met almost every night in the week, but their rendezvous was a saloon way down town.

And so the great day at home was the annual gathering of the Daughters to elect local officers. My mother invariably ran for first vice president, but unfortunately she never made it. Progressively she put more effort into her campaign and for two days before the conclave all of us children had to help Kate, the cook, squeeze oranges and lemons. I was too frail to be of much assistance to my brother in getting the gin up out of the cellar.

I do not think the Daughters had anything personal against my mother. As an amateur reporter I snooped around and never unearthed any whispering campaign. The trouble was with the ancestor through whom we qualified for admission. There seems to be no doubt that he was a wrong guy, although a general. Smug little vice presidents slid into office with no claim higher than that of a corporal or quartermaster with which to bless themselves. But when my mother's name was placed in nomination and she was identified as the great granddaughter of General Stirling, the silence was so intense that you could hear an eyebrow lift.

It seems that General Stirling, whose proud blood courses, or rather ambles, through my veins, led the most famous retreat in American history. He was on a horse and had every six-furlong record shattered when he ran into George Washington, who bawled him out good and proper. That incident has led to what is known to psychiatrists as the Broun inferiority complex.

But my mother took her defeats in good part. She may have been down but she was never out. Addressing herself to the successful rival, she would ask sweetly, "Will you have cream or lemon, dear?" And whatever the newly elected vice president said, she got a good strong shot of lemon.

I wish I could have been of some help to my mother in her D.A.R. aspirations, but I was too young, and she was too naïve. In those days neither of us had ever heard of a mickey finn.

139. THE WALLS OF NAZI TYRANNY

An official Nazi newspaper in Vienna has attempted to set down the future, and says that Czechoslovakia has but a year to live. A physician told something like that to a friend of mine and he replied, "As long as that, Doc?" for it seemed to him that so many things could happen within the year. There would be spring, perhaps, and summer and autumn, and with the winter would come an ending. And he lived with danger as if it were a season. But the years rolled by and the doctor is dead and my friend goes on and on.

It is not safe to be precise as to the longevity of men or nations. Doom can be delayed, and again it may come suddenly, almost between the tick and tock of a grandfather clock. Who knows now what the year holds in store for the Nazis? Emperors and kings have ridden at dawn surrounded by mighty armies only to see all their hopes and aspirations swept into dust by nightfall. Marathon marked the death of a nation. Napoleon had victory in his grasp at Waterloo, and yet he lived his last on the little island of St. Helena. And the proud ones who boast and threaten and lust for power must watch the split seconds on the stopwatch of time.

Often some mysterious and moving finger has written its compelling message on the wall, even at the feast of triumph. And there is no appeal. The forces against tyranny may gather slowly, but they can strike with the speed and fury of the hurricane.

Jericho was a mighty city, and from its battlements the warriors watched the forces of Joshua and the men of the great King laughed, because for six days no spear was leveled at them. According to the command of Joshua, the Ark of the Lord was carried around the walls of the city. And seven priests bearing seven trumpets of rams' horns marched and blew upon these trumpets. Before them and after came the armed men, but they were forbidden to shout. That was the strict injunction of Joshua.

"Ye shall not shout, nor make any noise with your voice, neither shall any word proceed out of your mouth, until the day I bid you shout; then shall ye shout."

And it seemed to the warriors of Jericho as if the armed men of Israel were meek, and that in them there could be no threat to the might and majesty of great Jericho. They merely marched with sword in hand and said no mumbling word. But for the blare of the trumpets this might have been an army of the dead, so softly did they walk while they bided their time.

But on the morning of the seventh day the ghostly host marched seven times around the city, all misty in the dusk of dawn. Then Joshua commanded the children to shout.

"And it came to pass when the people heard the sound of the trumpets and the people shouted with a great shout that the wall fell down flat, so that the people went up into the city, every man straight before him, and they took the city."

So it shall be again. History has ordained it. When the people shout in unison and every man walks straight before him, the walls of tyranny will come tumbling down. Already the trumpets begin to sound. And throughout the world free men wait for that final piercing note and the command, "Shout, for the Lord hath given you the city."

Books have been burned, and yet they live. Nor can fire or flame, humiliation or torture make an end of liberty. The wall of Nazi tyranny is tall; upon it floats its sinister emblem. But the voice of peoples of the world will and must be heard. That wall shall fall down flat.

140. COLUMNIST'S PROGRESS

I got a kick when I picked up last week's issue of the *New Republic* and saw the caption "Brickbats for Broun." And there they were—a full half-dozen, all edged and jagged with anger and with irritation. I like to boast, but I refrain occasionally through fear of being caught crawling out on some insufficient limb. But this week I propose to sun myself and gloat.

Presently I will be fifty years old, which is practically halfway home, and it seems to me that I have progressed considerably during the Indian Summer of what I call facetiously my career. Until I was forty, or a little beyond, my small circle of readers and acquaintances were inclined to refer to me as "good old Broun." If my name was mentioned somebody would say, "Good old Broun, he never said an unkind word about anybody in his life."

That is a pretty nasty reputation, but I'm afraid I deserved it. Save for deficiencies in prose style and intellectual capacity I was a sort of road-company Chesterton in my early youth. If I had been able to do jingles I might almost have been a bush-league Eddie Guest. Good old Broun—the fat friend of all the world!

No natural juices of benevolence swept me into this low estate. It was timidity pure and simple. If I said, "Yes, Mr. Swope," to my employer I merely followed the form observed by those about me. But I even lacked the gumption to maximate my ego by bawling out office boys and waiters. Frequently I am forced to blush when ex-office boys of the *Morning World* happen to alight from their limousines at the precise corner where I am walking. Most of them are high-powered scenario writers, although a few have gone into banking and the arts. But each and every one greets me with well-simulated enthusiasm. The greeting generally runs, "Come and have a drink, Heywood. I owe you something."

My first faint hope is that some fugitive dollar cast upon the waters a quarter of a century ago is about to return with compound interest. It doesn't work out that way.

"I want to thank you," says the tycoon, "because in the days when you were a columnist and I was a humble copy boy you were always pleasant and even-tempered. That meant a lot to me then. In those days I actually thought that columnists were important. You remember those little cubbyholes down that corridor off Herbie Swope's office? When Swopie bellowed you can bet we all came running. He scared the life out of us. F.P.A. was just about as tough, and on a mean day Alec Woollcott would bite your head off. But you were different, Heywood. We used to laugh about it."

And in these meetings I wince and drink the wine of remorse gingerly because I realize that of all the early worms in the newspaper craft I must have been the most abject. Many years ago a well-known actress, who was a little tight at the time, got me in a corner during a party and said, "Mr. Broun, promise me just one thing."

"Anything your little heart desires, Mrs. Siddons."

"Promise me that you will never lose your wistfulness," said the lovely lady. And I promised. It was as if a man with a malformed foot vowed never to cease limping.

The first faint glow of release came out of a fugitive and minor comic column. At least the intent was one of very mild mockery. It so happened that a particularly bulldoggish son of Eli had written a sentimental novel about life under the New Haven elms. The hero was a halfback and in the big scene he rescued a newsboy who doubled as mascot of the mighty Yale eleven. According to the story, the dashing undergraduate scooped him up as if he were a fumble and saved him from the advancing rush of the trolley line which skirted the campus.

Commenting on the story, I observed that there had been a somewhat similar incident just outside the yard in Cambridge. One of our own newsboys stood stupefied upon the tracks as the midnight car from Scolly Square swept down upon him. But I added that the rescue was accomplished in a way more dashing than in the Yale legend. The nearest undergraduate was not a star halfback. He was only a second substitute end upon the Crimson's scrub eleven. And instead of picking up the newsboy he tackled the trolley car and threw it for a ten-yard loss. I believe there were a few further rambling comments about the decline in Yale virility since Professor Billy Phelps managed to teach the Boola boys to read and turned them loose on Shakespeare and other lyric poets.

To my intense surprise I received the next day the first unfriendly letter I had ever had in twenty years of journalism. The writer said that I was evidently a Harvard snob and a stiff and that if I would furnish him with my home address he would be glad to call any morning and give me a good poke right in the nose. The next day I had four more missives written in similar vein. This was pretty heady stuff for me. It was the first testimony ever to bring home personally the power of the press. In a startled way I said to myself, "How long has this been going on? I can make people mad if I want to." And so, emboldened by my triumph, I wrote a snooty piece about Princeton and got two dozen outraged letters. In fact the managing editor called me in and said, "Broun, don't you think that you are making a mistake in raising controversial issues? Better stick to your old charm and let it go at that." But I had tasted beef tea, if not blood, by this time and there was no holding me.

"I will be bold," I cried, "I will be forthright and nobody can check my utterances." I would like to make this autobiographical note a tale of a steady upward climb. It didn't work out in that way. The trouble was that I had nothing much to utter. I had been "good old Broun" for so long that I had no passionate convictions. All I did was snipe at sitting birds. It took a major national tragedy to animate me to any major purpose. But I trust that I am not being conceited in saying that by now a considerable number of people regard me as one of the most offensive persons engaged in newspaper work. I have almost a complete set of enemies who detest me with a very convincing sincerity. I mean to fill the shelf. I am never going to be "good old Broun" again. In fact, if anybody tries that upon me, my lip will curl in anger as I advance menacingly and say, "When you call me that, smile, damn you."

141. YOU, FRANK HAGUE

Of course, it wouldn't be feasible or constitutional or popular, but I wish there was a law providing that nobody could carry an American flag without a permit. And before an applicant received permission he should be required to show a rudimentary knowledge of what the flag symbolizes. No man has a right to go around flaunting the flag unless he has comprehension of the general purpose and spirit of the Constitution and the Declaration of Independence.

In the hands of hoodlums the flag can be a dangerous weapon. It stands for too much to be sullied by the itching palms of political plug-uglies and morons. Hague has no more right to distribute the star-spangled banner to his dupes and henchmen than he has to supply them with machine guns. It goes deeper than mere irony that thugs with flags should assemble to throttle the most essential of democratic rights.

The mob which was regimented into Journal Square in Jersey City constituted the most dangerous Nazi demonstration which this nation has yet known. I think there is small doubt that there would have been bloodshed if Representatives O'Connell and Barnard had attempted to hold their meeting.

But Hague was able to lay his powder train into more remote places. Just what have the various clerics who indorsed his plan to say for themselves? And what excuse can be made for the labor fakers who ordered their members to support the Mafia? It is not true that one who wears a Legion cap has the special privilege of taking the law into his own hands. Men who fought for their country should be the last to take up arms against it.

A good deal of disillusion has gathered around the phase "To make the world safe for democracy." And, even so, it is a better slogan than "To make liberty impossible in the United States."

Fortunately, Hague can hardly afford to win another such victory. Members of the system which made him and preserved him are beginning to feel that perhaps he has gone just a shade too far. At the eleventh hour some of the most reactionary commentators are beginning to shake a warning finger at the boss and say, "Have a heart, Frankie."

You can't sow dragon's teeth and then complain because you get no lilacs. And what has happened in one society can happen in five or ten and in time sweep across a nation. It has probably been a mistake for foes of Fascism to concentrate so much attention on the personality of Hague himself.

Lincoln Steffens, after a long life of crusading, decided that he had wasted time in going after individual bosses. This was just hydra hunting. He felt before he died that salvation could be found only in getting down to the roots of the man in power and discovering the soil and sources which made him possible.

Who pulls the strings to make Hague strut? Why do Church dignitaries sit on the platform behind him when he speaks? And will associations of industrial leaders ever declare against him at their conventions?

But most pertinent of all is the question as to just how long the President of the United States is going to refrain from declaring for freedom and against the bully who holds a high post in the Democratic organization.

America must speak out and speak out soon. The nation should say, "You, Frank Hague, lurking over there, take your hands off our flag."

142. FREUD'S EXILE

The most famous man in Austria has left Vienna and entered into exile. At the age of eighty-two Dr. Sigmund Freud tears up his roots, but he is taking with him his notes and manuscripts so that he may go on with his work. The Nazi press did not deign to mention his name in reporting his departure, but merely spoke of his school of therapy as "A Pornographic Jewish Specialty."

He has gone to London and it is said that later he may come to New York. There is no civilized country where Freud will be forlorn, for he is truly a citizen of the world.

It is quite true that medical men still quarrel as to the lasting value of his theories. Possibly the technique he devised is on the wane or will survive only in modified form. Still, it seems to me that psychiatrists who reject his teachings at the same time take on some of his phrases and borrow, unconsciously if you like, a little of his approach.

Some of these phrases which were once considered a kind of jargon now are commonplace in the American language. Leaving the medical contribution of Freud out of the picture, his philosophy has touched all writing men and women, boxers and baseball players, advertising copy writers and a few wrestlers.

It is quite possible that Dr. Freud himself may be both puzzled and perturbed by the fact that while he wrote for doctors, his most fervent acceptance has been at the hands of the lay public. And most of those whose way of thought and habit of speech have been affected by the great physician have never read a line he wrote and never will. Topsy (I refer to Little Eva's friend) had a somewhat similar experience. As I remember, both her genesis and development were by word of mouth.

Within the month I was talking to a big league baseball manager, and inquired with solicitude just what was wrong with his shortstop. The manager shifted his tobacco before he answered, "There's just one thing wrong with him. He ought to be the greatest infielder in the game. He can hit and throw, and go to his right or left. The only trouble is that he's got an inferiority complex."

I doubt gravely whether the manager had any knowledge of the source of his inspiration. When Bucky Harris was first managing the Senators a good many seasons back he assured me that when one of his pitchers began to go sour he always tried to find out whether the player's home life was pleasant, and just what kind of trouble he was having with his wife. Some will say that such considerations were always part of good common sense, and that Freud did no more than invent a terminology, and some high-falutin' theories. But as far as baseball managers go that isn't true, and I assert that a little man in Vienna who didn't know the difference between a base hit and a fielder's choice wrote finis to the school of McGraw and made the Vitts, McKechnies and Cochranes possible.

This, like many of the researches of Freud himself, may not be susceptible to laboratory proof, but verse and chapter can be cited to demonstrate that the modern novel, and to an even greater extent, the modern biography stem directly from the consulting room of the exile.

The Nazis burned the books of Dr. Sigmund Freud in Germany back in May, 1933, and a man who was present told me it was queer to see what long shadows were cast by the dancing flames. The fire could not consume the ideas. They spread out to the world.

There are those who find the concepts of Freud degrading. To me they seem to constitute an eagerness for that deeper comprehension which is the death of prejudice. And when a man of eighty-two takes up his notes and papers and leaves his home for a free land in which to go on with his work it seems to me that in his own person that man proves the integrity of his philosophy.

143. I'LL SHOW YOU THE CITY

I have a letter from Miss L. K. G., who lives in Great Falls, Montana, and the burden of her letter is that Great Falls is dull and humdrum and that she would like to be in and of New York. "How can it be accomplished?" Miss G. would like to know. And she adds, "I am a competent stenographer and I think that I am more metropolitan-minded than most the girls out here because I read Walter Winchell and the *New Republic* religiously. Tell me something about New York."

That is a large order, Miss G., and may I make a guess and call you by your first name? Is it the world of Broadway, Lucinda, or the intellectual approach of this particular sanctum which enlists your curiosity? To be sure, these are not always mutually exclusive. Mr. Winchell begins to emerge from political isolation, while the *New Republic* runs a paragraph column and serves Scotch or rye to favored contributors on Friday.

The chances are all against your getting a job here, Lucinda, for the town is filled with stenographers who assert that they are competent. I will not be presumptuous enough to say that you are better off in Great Falls (where you can vote for O'Connell instead of O'Connor) but New York is not the ideal place for the perpetuation of the comfortable life. If you plan no more than a visit of forty or fifty years, that is all right, but

I would advise no man or woman to take up permanent residence in Manhattan. As soon as parole is possible I would suggest Stamford, Connecticut.

The late O. O. McIntyre used to tell his country customers that in their own Main Street all the joys and treasures of the metropolis could be found. But that just isn't true, save for the materially minded. I have no doubt that in either Great Falls or Ashtabula one may find love, loyalty, T-bone steaks and iced beverages. But the esthetic and spiritual values of New York are not to be had in the smaller cities.

In all the United States man has made with his own hands no such beauty as exists in New York City. The name Great Falls suggests to me that in your immediate neighborhood, Lucinda, there is some kind of mill race and that the tumbling water may be pretty under the moonlight. But I have found that a week with a waterfall, even a large one, is plenty for any man. Twice I have looked upon Niagara and it is not graven upon my heart. The song it sings is repetitious and I shall not return until I hear that the wall of water has begun to hesitate upon the brink, adding some element of dramatic suspense like the famed choice of Candida. The river does fall quite a distance, but what else can it do? What else has it ever done?

And if other natural wonders are to be brought forward for contemplation, I must admit that I would much rather crane my neck to look up at the Empire State Building than stoop to survey the bottom of the Grand Canyon. The making of towers is a more noble endeavor than the digging of ditches.

Works of nature often leave one chilled because they offer no vicarious satisfaction to the tourist by enabling him to say, "I might have a shot at that myself some rainy afternoon."

It is true that the odds are all against my ever painting a Rembrandt or your capturing the flight of a skylark in some spare poetic moment. Still these are achievements of the race and not the fortuitous product of a slow geologic cataclysm. And so I would turn off the moon and toss aside even a successful sunset as being nothing more than a chance hit. Beauty without plan is also beauty without meaning.

Your Great Falls, Lucinda, is near some one of the National Parks, if I remember, and I assume you have a vast expanse of forest, hot springs which smoke and roar and mountains lumbering toward the sky. But believe no one who tells you that any one of these set pieces can produce the same wonder as the spidery span of a bridge across the Hudson. That leap of steel broad-jumping into space makes even the rapids of a troubled stream seem slow-paced and indecisive.

If you can keep body and soul apart, come rushing to the magical city, Lucinda, whether a job waits or not. But remember that Manhattan is also the place of sacrifice. It is only for those who can subsist on locusts and wild honey. In many respects it is an American equivalent of Ceylon's Isle and there be those who have been borne down by too much beauty and who walk through the canyons of the city as impervious to visual excitement as any pack mule. The plain fact of the matter is that New York is much too good for New Yorkers. Complete appreciation will come only when some Vesuvius has laid it low and posterity is forced to dig down into the dust to bring to light the buried treasure. If you have patience, Lucinda, it might not be a bad idea to postpone your trip to some such time when the guide, pausing in his patter to speak with deep emotion, may say, "And now beneath your foot, lady, is a crumbled stone which is all that is left to remind us that here the *New Republic* once functioned in offices which were considered very modern."

But, Miss L. K. G., you have every right to ask why I have put beauty behind me and fled to the drab landscape of the Connecticut countryside. It is not so much from a fear of impending doom but rather because the wine of loveliness comes to be too heady a draught after protracted maturity. I shall not look much again upon the George Washington Memorial Bridge at dawn or Brooklyn Bridge in twilight. My arteries grow too precarious to watch the Chrysler needle grow dim and lost in fog as if it had been thrust into a specter haystack.

We have tame flowers and wild ones, too, here on Hunting Ridge and a bit of greenery. But everything is under control. A local stock company is going to do *The Jest*, but I shall see no Barrymores nor watch the rain sweep down the street of hits. I have begun to taper.

And you, young lady, I think you said Lucinda, may come from Great Falls to Manhattan if that is your pleasure. But as you value your return-trip ticket, bring a mirror and never dare to look Medusa in the eye.

144. JAMES WELDON JOHNSON

The Negroes of America quite naturally take pride and joy in the victories of Joe Louis and Henry Armstrong. The race has almost a monopoly of the ring titles. And in track athletics, leadership in the dashes and the jumps has gone very largely to the darker-hued competitors. When Joe smacked Max, great crowds came cheering into the streets in many cities. And why not?

But Negroes should join again in a mass demonstration for one of their own who could not fight with his fists or sprint or leap. But this man did more for his race than any athlete, however great, could possibly accomplish. James Weldon Johnson died on Sunday in the State of Maine. He was killed in an automobile accident. He was slight in stature, but here was the greatest fighter of them all. And when public tribute is paid to Jim all groups should join in the mourning.

You know him, although perhaps his name escapes you. At the moment this broad appeal rests largely on his lesser work. The songs which he and his brother, J. Rosamond Johnson, wrote, in collaboration with Robert Cole, are on your radio almost every night. Most of them go all the way back to the days of the Klaw and Erlanger extravaganzas.

But of late they have had a second blooming. Once again *Under the Bamboo Tree, Congo Love Song* and *In My Castle on the River Nile* are heard in the land. One of Anna Held's most successful songs, *The Maiden with the Dreamy Eyes,* was written for her by Cole and Johnson. They were the song-writing kings of Broadway at the turn of the century.

J. Weldon Johnson was the lyricist and later on he published serious poetry of high merit. I have particularly in mind a lovely long poem called *God's Trombones.* Jim finally left off song writing to crusade for his people as secretary for the National Association for the Advancement of the Colored People.

When Jim was a Broadway song writer he never let success go to his head, and when he crusaded for the National Association he still kept his feet on the ground. There was a time when both Jim and his successor, Walter White, were under bitter criticism as compromisers. I think that in both cases this was unfair. Mistakes in tactics may have been made, but Jim was at his best in making flank rather than frontal attacks on prejudice. He did do both, but he was most useful in doing his work in his own way. He never surrendered anything of his high aspirations and ideals.

He had charm and humor, and in his own personality and life he did a great deal to brush aside the words and thoughts of those who would minimize the achievements and the potentialities of the Negro race.

Under his smile there was often the substance of iron. I felt that when he once told me laughingly of an incident which occurred during a rehearsal of a big Klaw and Erlanger show. A young white girl from Mississippi had a song to sing, and a hardboiled director was bawling her out. Jim Johnson tapped him on the shoulder and said, "You can't talk like that." "Who says so?" Jim answered, "I do, and Rosamond and Cole and I are your show." James Weldon Johnson told me, "It was sort of funny. Down where that singer came from I was an inferior person. But in that theater I wasn't. We were the show and what we said went."

"Did she thank you, Jim?" I asked. "Yes," he said, and grinned again. "She told me that on her grandfather's plantation before the war the slaves were treated almost like members of the family."

And so let *God's Trombones* sound for James Weldon Johnson, a small man with a smile who was a great and true heavyweight champion in fighting for his people.

145. THE PROCURATOR WRITES

Of course I remember Jesus Christ. I crucified him.

It is strange that any should speak of Him now, for His teachings died with Him. They might have been momentous if I had not taken action. It was an important issue but it was fought out in an obscure corner of the world and settled for all time.

Still, as I sit now to write the story of a long and varied life the figure of Jesus looms so large that everything else is blotted out.

We exchanged no more than a dozen words. I was finished with Him in less than an hour, but that morning tested everything that I was or had ever hoped to be. Judgment was passed on me as well as on Jesus in that short span.

I knew then as I know now that it was my hour of trial. And I triumphed over great temptation because all my life had been a period of preparation for that crisis. I stood as lonely as a sentry.

It is easy to say that I represented the might and majesty of the Roman Empire while He was a disinherited fanatic. He was of the stuff by which kingdoms fall. With words He might have destroyed that authority which legions protect precariously.

He never called Himself the King of the Jews. His mind went far beyond that goal. He knew and I knew that the Eastern world of mystics and dreamers could be aroused to march on Rome.

March, I say, and I mean it, for an idea can cut through shields which javelins would never pierce.

Civilization as we know it faced the threat of going down under the feet of the mob. The weak were to overthrow the strong through weight of numbers. The meek, of whom He spoke, would walk through streets where once the proud held up their heads. And in plain sight there was a possible world in which the meanest slave could pluck a Roman by the sleeve and call him brother.

I was a provincial governor, but no Caesar was ever called upon to render so momentous a decision. With a wave of my hand I might have swept the surface of the known world and left a clean tablet upon which Jesus might write a new one. If I had allowed Him to live we could have done that.

And let no man think that my decision was in any way affected by the clamor of the High Priest who was wholly without honor in his own community. Jesus was the leader of the people. The High Priest served my purposes as a blind.

My choice lay between Rome and the new empire to which Jesus had given the name of Heaven. I had to decide whether to save that tangible civilization built upon the exploits of our far-flung armies, or to make out of the mist a new city towering to the skies. I had to choose reality or a dream world.

It is true I hesitated. I stood in the presence of a great man. We were alone, for I had drawn Him into a room away from the noisy riffraff of the High Priest. Jesus was not afraid. And in the supreme moment of which I have written neither of us spoke.

I stared intently into His eyes to catch even a glint of that fear which comes to men who are in the shadow of death. It was not there.

He smiled. It was a friendly smile, almost as if He were saying, "Make either choice, I will understand."

And as I looked at Him it seemed as if my spirit left my body and I was carried up to a high place from which I could see the Kingdoms of the world. But though I looked to the far horizon, Rome was not of them. Gone, blotted out was the Eternal City.

An old wound in my left shoulder began to throb. I remembered how our thin ranks stood up against a charge in defense of our homes and firesides. It was an early campaign. For the moment I have forgotten in what distant land we fought it. But when we beat them off we raised our swords high in the air and cried out, "Rome! Rome! Rome!" Once again our eagles had conquered.

And suddenly I found myself back in a little room in Jerusalem staring into the eyes of Jesus Christ, and I knew I had come to my answer. In a voice so low that we could hardly hear it I said, "Crucify Him," for I was still shaken. But then, lest there be any mistake, I threw back my head and I cried loud enough for the guard at the door to hear, "Crucify Him."

The incident was over. Rome had spoken.

146. SACCO-VANZETTI ANNIVERSARY

This is written on the anniversary of the death of Sacco and Vanzetti. "The Good Shoemaker and the Poor Fish Peddler" were tried and sentenced eleven years ago.

In an old column I found this: "A woman in the courtroom said with terror, 'It is death condemning life,' " and for eleven years I have not written about Sacco and Vanzetti nor even talked much about the case. There have been meetings for commemoration, but it seemed to me that there was small point in turning back the page. For all its ill the episode had ended.

Now I know that I was wrong, for in Washington I saw the shadow of the dead hand dance upon the wall. And the fingers wrote in air, "They shall not pass." J. B. Matthews exorcised demons for a House committee. His voice became shrill and fervent as he attacked the Youth Congress. And then upon a note of almost sheer hysteria he thrust out a thin arm and screamed that Shirley Temple was a "stooge" of the "reds." The chairman of the House committee leaned forward eagerly and said, "Go on, professor."

The name of the chairman is Martin Dies, and it is pronounced as if it rhymed with cries or tries, or whatever else comes to your imagination. It might have been very funny, but I can assure you that it was not. Mr. Matthews is not a conscious humorist. Before he became a business man he was a missionary to Java, and I wouldn't be a bit surprised if he touched at Pago Pago. Almost I could hear the rain machine of that old familiar show, and once again the Rev. Davidson hammered home the gospel of frustration and surrender. Dies and his post-meridian confreres thanked Mr. Matthews and promised him a national hook-up with some thirty stations.

Even in a modern age there are fair rewards for those who preach and peach. But I was not amused. It was death condemning life. And before I came to the witch hunt in the caucus room of the old House Office Building I had stopped at the bar of the National Press Club to compose a statement. There I met a newspaper reporter who had been covering the primary battles in Georgia and South Carolina. He reports that Fort Sumter is being heavily shelled and that the civil war is raging furiously along the entire front.

Cotton Ed Smith, of South Carolina, did not list his natal year in the *Congressional Directory;* however, he admits that after finishing his freshman year at the University of South Carolina he transferred to a smaller institution of learning called Wofford College and was graduated in 1889. Since that was almost half a century ago, it is generally believed that Ellison Durant Smith is in his seventies. And yet he has never been more active along the hustings.

"It is quite remarkable to watch him," said my informant. "He keeps his hands high over his head for more than an hour at a time, and he calls upon the name of God and Jesus in almost every other sentence. Naturally he is using 'The Speech' almost exclusively." I have heard "The Speech." It is not pleasant. And it is certainly not within the spirit of the Sermon on the Mount.

"The Speech" is an account of the ravishment of a relative of Cotton Ed's which he says occurred during the period of re-construction. In the course of the years graphic details have been added. It is not pleasant, because it is done with gusto and a trace of froth.

The "scholarly" Walter Franklin George is putting up a bitter resistance against Sherman's march to the sea. Gene Tal-madge is telling the up-country farmers that the WPA is teach-ing toe dancing to boys and girls "who come from good Chris-tian homes." But it isn't funny. Fingers of bone clutch at the bridle of progress. It is death condemning life.

147. A GOOD LAUGH

One approaches the news of the day with apprehension. Nor is it so much tragedy which the reader dreads as having to face the fact of international insanity. And to those who sit in an outward room the most terrifying sound of all may be the noise of empty laughter drifting across the courtyard or down the corridors where the attendants walk softly in felt slippers.

Death comes in these afternoons bereft of dignity as well as all other human attributes. I have heard it said that in time of trial and tribulation there is nothing like a good laugh. That's right.

There is nothing like it to freeze the marrow of the bones. Let's not have it.

There is, of course, a transcendental kind of mirth which can be tonic against despair, but it bears no kinship to those didoes which are generously included under the label of "good clean fun." No attempt should be made to extend the silly season into the days of bleak and bitter storm. Man's hope is not dead, and there will be spring again and resurrection, but this dawn cannot be brought into being by any kind of barnyard cackling.

It seems to me that there should be a moratorium on all things cute and antic. I would not have been much amused if I had been privileged to watch Bruce Barton led blindfolded to the dais as he played the part of "Fall Guy" at an initiation dinner of the Circus Saints and Sinners. "As the blindfold was removed 'Jolly Bill' Steinke, in the role of a sideshow barker, nominated the Representative for President of Maine and Vermont, blank cartridges were fired and the gathering broke into noisy applause." That "Jolly Bill" must be a card, and the blank cartridges were most appropriate. I'm glad I missed that.

But it was even better to have missed the demonstration in West Fortieth Street on Wednesday, where "five debutantes and socially prominent young matrons picketed briefly the headquarters of Kenneth Simpson, Republican county leader." The debutantes took up direct action because Mr. Simpson has not given aid to the Sutton Place rebellion to save the nation by indorsing John J. O'Connor, of Tammany, for the House. Mr. O'Connor says that there should be no "yes" men in Washington.

An interesting current biography in the [New York] *Mirror,* which supports O'Connor, relates that his first intimation that he was to be a Representative came when Charles F. Murphy received him in his private office and said, "John O'Connor, you're going to Washington." Mr. Murphy fixed it just as he had promised, and so John J. is running today on the platform of "Let the people rule." And all the daring debutantes just know from their civic studies that Tammany is the champion of liberty and a bulwark against one-man rule. Charley Murphy practically devoted his life to that cause.

The debutante of today is not the empty-headed miss of a previous generation. If she feels that it is her duty to picket she will not shirk the sacrifice, even though it breaks up her whole morning and makes her late for lunch. The ladies were not on the picket line very long, as it happened.

"As soon as they had been photographed and interviewed they signaled a taxi."

All the same, there they were, as brave as lionesses, carrying signs up and down just like the grownups.

One of the debbies had a bright idea. She brought along her Dachshund, whose name is Romeo. She carried a sign urging voters to support O'Connor, but the dog had a smaller placard urging support for Allen W. Dulles, the opponent of O'Connor. This was side-splitting, of course, but I should think that this conflict in opinion between the dog and the debbie might serve to confuse the voters. Dachshunds are said to be very intelligent.

148. DAMN THEIR EYES

I hate hunting. And in particular I wish that the regulations in Connecticut were far more strict. There isn't much game here in the hills north of Stamford. When I first came to the

Ridge which is named for the sport of meager men, partridge and pheasant were plentiful in the woods. They have been shot down. Only the rabbits remain.

It was exciting once to walk along a path and have the birds rise up almost from underfoot. The noise of that partridge whirr was far more pleasant than the sound of guns. Although I have never shot at anything I can't pretend to be a transcendental fanatic. Rabbit stew is excellent and partridge makes a dainty dish. Still, though I live on Hunting Ridge, it seems to me that all the shotgun crew take life for rewards which are insufficient to justify the killing.

Sports are designed to maximate the human ego. When a man breaks a hundred for the first time on a golf course he has a thrill denied to champions. He will bore the life out of everyone in the locker room or at home as he gives the play-by-play account of the manner in which he achieved his triumph. But I would rather listen to him than hear the hunter's story. Colonel Bogey is a foeman worthy of any man's mettle. Rabbits and squirrels are slight creatures.

People who go after lions and tigers and leopards are better equipped than their quarry. But sometimes the jungle strikes back and one has the pleasure of reading a news item about how a hunter had his head mashed in. But even the cornered rabbit cannot strike. It would seem to me as if a large man with a shotgun would feel a little as if he were the Notre Dame quarterback calling a play against an eleven from an academy for backward children.

In the hunting of the squirrel there can be no such thing as a reversal in form. The biter runs the risk of being bit only if he trips across his own fowling piece. The barking of the guns in our peaceful autumn woods creates a dissonance. Already the leaves turn red and they should not be further incarnadined by human cruelty.

Sometimes they miss—these gentlemen with the guns. Damn their eyes. But they return to their sport and even after dusk one realizes that back in the thicket hell's a-popping. Out comes the moon with little stars attendant. There's frost and the smell of wood smoke from the chimney. One could almost take a spoon and dip it in the air as if it were a pudding. This is the sweet time of the year. On such a night in creation week God looked down upon his handiwork and called it good. But in the brambles stands some goof or lout blazing away to draw blood from the feeble folk of the forest.

In the wilderness one lives through the death of others but now that we have touched and taken domain over from nature we should establish a state of amity with our neighbors. I trust that those of us who have come barging into these hills from the island of Manhattan do not wish to set up a smug suburbia. Only a little of wild life remains and we should shelter it for our soul's salvation. Certainly it is a bad bargain for a man to sell his birthright in the soil for a mess of mangled chipmunk.

And in protecting the lives of other weak creatures we would protect our own. It isn't reasonable that a harmless householder should expose his hide to buckshot the moment he strays twenty feet from his back porch. Of late I have felt constrained to get myself up like a masquerader before taking a constitutional. And when branches obscure immediate vision I make a practice of yodeling lest some nearsighted nimrod mistake me for a squirrel. For two weeks I wore the same red shirt every day until George Bye advised to desist.

"I don't want anybody to take me for a deer," I said.

"But you're taking a greater risk than that in this particular country," he assured me. "You won't get shot as a deer but have a swell chance to get plugged as a New Dealer."

And so I say let's be done with musketry. Cease firing. None of us is here forever and the span of the little animals is even less than that which is our portion. Let them alone. We ought to feel fidelity to our cause. We belong to the army of life and we are enlisted for duration. Who crosses over and takes up arms for death is a traitor to all the living.

149. MODERN NEBUCHADNEZZAR

In the seventh verse of the third chapter of the Book of Daniel it is written:

"Therefore at that time, when all the people heard the sound of the cornet, flute, harp, sackbut, psaltery, and all kinds of musick, all the people, the nations, and the languages, fell down and worshipped the golden image that Nebuchadnezzar the King had set up."

The nations and the peoples did not bow down to the image set up by Nebuchadnezzar because they had faith in it. On the contrary there were many who wanted to have none of it. But they were terrified.

The mighty king had said, "And whoso falleth not down and worshippeth shall the same hour be cast into the midst of a burning fiery furnace."

It was a conquest by threat. The rulers of the nations roundabout stifled all ardor which their peoples possessed for their own ways and their own liberties. They feared to burn. And so they talked of "peace with honor" and "breathing spells" and "making terms with the dictators." They did bow down.

And today many instruments and tunes call the men and nations of the world to worship the great image which has been set up by another Nebuchadnezzar. Some follow the pipe of pacificism. Others say that the lute which summons them sounds the true note of liberalism. Even the psaltery of what Norman Thomas calls "Socialism" is taken by some as a reason to join in at least a semblance of worship. There are "all kinds of musick" and from "the people, the nations and the languages" come many protestations that they are yielding to the command of Nebuchadnezzar only for the moment. But they do bow down.

In the days of the great king there were three who stood out. They could have yielded with the rest, but Shadrach, Meshach and Abednego made their position perfectly clear. They were unwilling to make any gesture of assent whatsoever. "O Nebuchadnezzar," they said, "we are not careful to answer thee in this matter."

They closed their ears to the seduction of soft music or the brazen command of the trumpets. "Be it known unto thee, O King," said Shadrach, Meshach and Abednego, "that we will not serve thy gods, nor worship the golden image which thou hast set up."

They knew the nature of the doom which threatened. They knew that in every age men of firm heart must put themselves to the test of the fiery furnace. Faith can be proven in no other fashion. And they came through the ordeal for these men "upon whose bodies the fire had no power."

They made their protest and they made it on the instant. They knew that true faith could not be consumed by fire. They knew that it could rot away through delay and compromise and accommodation. Neither threats nor pacts nor blandishments could move them. The fight for liberty is something which cannot be relegated to yesterday or put off until tomorrow. Now is the time. The answer must be as strong and as clear as the challenge.

"Be it known unto thee, O King, that we will not serve thy gods, nor worship the golden image which thou hast set up."

Thus spake Shadrach, Meshach and Abednego. Who will follow in their train?

150. NOT GOOD ENOUGH

One of the most important elections held in the last few weeks came a little before our own and was held in a suburb of London. But it was a contest of far more than local significance. Dartford returned a Laborite in a by-election. The district was not precisely a Tory stronghold, although a Conservative had been the incumbent, but here was a straight out-and-out test of the Chamberlain policy of collaboration with Hitler. The Munich Pact itself was the issue upon which the men and women voted.

And the strategic advantage lay with the government. Dartford is a community of little clerks and small shopkeepers. It is filled with the kind of people whom H. G. Wells used formerly as the characters in his novels. I rather imagine that it would be possible to find in Dartford an English equivalent for Webster's Mr. Milquetoast. Certainly it is not a warlike district.

The villas do not stand shoulder to shoulder, but for the most part, are semi-detached. Between the houses run little alleys in which on a clear day it might be possible to swing a kitten. And here the very average Englishman lives in his castle with a few flowers in front and radishes abaft his dwelling.

The Thames winds its way through Dartford, and the villas cluster close to the river bank. On a bright night one might easily imagine enemy planes following the course of that silver ribbon and dropping bombs upon the slow curve of that shining silver stream.

Dartford sent its men and boys to the war in 1914, and its women folk huddled in shallow cellars when the Zeppelins came over. Those who came back from France bore with them their share of decorations for bravery under fire. They were a stubby lot, but also stubborn. Yet, though they had acquitted themselves well, the warriors of Dartford took no great joy in the adventure. They were glad to stand behind counters again rather than up to the neck in mud and blood. And in the long English twilight there is time for a tradesman or a clerk, even after long hours, to mess about with the flowers or the vegetables.

Dartford is bourgeois and somewhat insulated and isolated from the rest of the world. They have a saying in Dartford which runs, "Thank God for the British Channel." Although Chamberlain sits in the seat of the mighty and comes from a line of monocled Parliamentary leaders, his origins are in the Dartford set. Cliveden came later.

The Prime Minister spoke out of a knowledge of middleclass psychology when he said that Czechoslovakia was a faraway land and a tiny country. He realized that in the little houses of Dartford a man might stand up and touch a roof which was all that stood between him and an enemy bomb.

And so he made the peace which passes understanding, firm in the belief that the small and humble of the placid villas along the Thames would agree that even temporary safety of life and limb was of more importance than abstract things called liberty and justice. And in the vigorous campaign Chamberlain's men spoke of just one thing when they argued for the Tory cause. They pushed aside all other issues and said, "He kept us out of war."

But when the peace came the men and women of Dartford found it was no peace at all. They could still hear the voice of Hitler. There was no cessation in the tramp of marching men. The fires of Fascism burned more brightly. And to the hearts of clerks and small tradesmen of Dartford came a consuming decision. Among them were those whose ancestors pulled a good bow at Hastings. And louder than the roar of any bomb there came the inner voice to say, "Justice and liberty are not just words. These are the very soil in which our flowers grow."

They turned the Tories out. They spurned the Pact of Munich. And to the world they said, "This thing is not good enough for British freemen."

151. DEATH ON A SIDE STREET

A neighbor agreed to drive me to Darien the other day but he said that he would have to stop for a little while at a house where an old friend had died—and where he had been born. I waited in his car outside. Across the road a carpenter was shingling a roof. A boy three houses away was throwing a ball against the wall of the garage. A little girl rode her bike. And once a bus passed the door where the white and purple flowers were festooned.

A few had gathered to pay their respects. This was a man who had been loved and respected in the community. But none stood at the edge of the lawn gaping at the freshly painted cottage. The last coat was scarcely a week old. That had been his request just before he was taken ill. "Let's make the house look as if it were new."

And each on the quiet street went about his usual occupations in an orderly way. It seemed strange to a man who spent his boyhood in Manhattan. The street of my childhood was not one of closely packed families. We were brownstone folk except at the corners where apartments stood. Indeed it was customary to ask the boy with whom you played, "Do you live in a house or a flat?" It was better to live in a house.

But that estate could hardly be called exclusive, for there must have been at least a hundred dwellings. The undertaker's men were not strangers to us. And even so we made much of death. There would be a buzzing crowd around the house of the dead waiting for the Lord knows what. We stared at those who went in or came out, particularly anybody in black. That would be "a member of the family." And at such times some boy in the crowd would shout to a playmate down the street to come on over.

There was neither cruelty nor pity in the prying. Perhaps we were all anxious to look upon the face of grief so that we might recognize it if we encountered it ourselves in later life.

Much went on in the block between Amsterdam and Columbus Avenues and we felt that every happening was properly part of a public performance.

This did not seem to be the mood of the quiet street. It may be that in small towns where farms begin around the bend in the road there is more familiarity with birth and death. These are things which can be learned from the fields and the barnyards where the animals come into life and go out of it with slight articulate protest.

The folk in quiet country streets follow this tradition. On our block the upstairs bell, or the one in the basement, jangled loudly even on the most solemn occasion. Hereabouts doors are opened with less reluctance. It almost seems as if the strange visitor were some guest who had been long expected. And when he calls he will find that all things are in readiness.

152. HINTS TO THE EPICURE

It is well enough for Mr. Roosevelt to eschew "grilled millionaire" as a breakfast dish, but it is disappointing to learn that he prefers scrambled eggs. Hardboiled ones are better. The reference, naturally, is to eggs rather than millionaires. A gourmet of my acquaintance says that a one-minute millionaire is not so bad, but that any boiling beyond that point is as useless as bleaching the lily. Still, one need not be an ogre or an epicure to find a millionaire quite tasty upon occasion.

For instance, did President Roosevelt ever try roasting one over a national hookup for fifteen minutes? But if you like game the best culinary approach to a millionaire is to fricassee him. Of course, you must first catch your millionaire, and it is best to get him young.

Experienced hunters go down to the blinds long before daybreak carrying an elephant gun and a set of decoys which are arranged alphabetically in a receptacle known to sportsmen as a sucker list. These decoys are cleverly carved and painted to look like innocent investors. A bright green seems to be the favorite color, and the design should resemble either a young sheep, a widow or an orphan.

After they have been placed at convenient points in some open meadow the hunter goes into hiding and bides his time. In an earlier generation the guide would try to summon millionaires by imitating a margin call. This was done under the theory that the big birds would always flock together to save the market, but scientific experiments made in the hard winter of 1929 proved that this was merely an old woodsman's legend without validity. The easiest way to spot a millionaire is to remember that he is the precise opposite of a poet or a pheasant. He flies high, and it would do you no good to dust him.

In order to bring a millionaire to earth it is necessary to score a direct hit in the pocketbook. Retrievers of any sort can be left in the kennels, because there never will be any doubt as to whether or not the millionaire has been hit. As he flutters down he emits loud squawks of protest which are very piteous. Humane hunters make it a practice to put the quarry out of its misery by clubbing the wounded bird over the head with an income tax, but even this requires almost surgical skill, because the blows must be delivered in the higher brackets.

However, even at this point the job is scarcely begun. You've got your millionaire, but before he can even be considered as potentially edible you've got to skin him. This may take days or even weeks. Some hunters can never learn the trick at all. But once the tough hide has been removed the lucky sportsman can bring the millionaire back to the cook in triumph. At that, it is likely that the chef will give the hunter a dirty look, for the fricasseeing still presents an elaborate problem.

One time-tried formula is to soak the millionaire overnight or longer in brine in proportion of sixteen to one. Then he should be baked to eliminate the water and the paper profits. After that you may add salt in generous quantities, pepper, Scotch whisky, port, one-half pint sloe gin, truffles, mushrooms and a pousse-café. Then turn the heat on and allow the whole thing to simmer over a slow fire while a group of cooks, known as an investigating committee, stirs the whole mess continuously.

If anything is left of the millionaire at the end of that time go to the nearest telephone and order a hamburger steak from your neighborhood butcher.

Maybe Mr. Roosevelt is right, after all. At least he has chosen the safer method. Any journeyman can run up a dish of scrambled eggs, but only an expert can do a millionaire.

153. WE, TOO, ARE BIDDEN

The angel of the Lord said to the shepherds, "And this shall be a sign unto you: Ye shall find the babe wrapped in swaddling clothes, lying in a manger."

They made haste to go to Bethlehem to see the thing which had come to pass. "For unto you," the angel said, "is born this day in the city of David a Saviour, which is Christ the Lord."

But as they journeyed to Bethlehem they fell into a discussion as to just how they should find the place where the infant lay. The shepherds were not folk familiar with the town, even though it lay a short journey from the fields in which they tended their flocks. Besides, they knew that many from the country roundabout had gone to Bethlehem in compliance with the decree of Caesar Augustus that all the world should be taxed. Indeed, one of the group grumbled, "In Bethlehem there be many mangers, and how are we to find the one?"

And the youngest shepherd said, "It will be made known to us."

The night was bright with stars and the way more easy than they had expected. In spite of the late hour many walked in the narrow streets of Bethlehem, and fom all the houses there came a clatter. The shepherds stood for a moment in some perplexity as to the appointed place. The noises of the town were confusing to men who had been standing silent under starlight.

And suddenly the volume of voices increased, and down the street there came a caravan of camels. Upon the backs of the beasts sat great bearded men, and with them they brought sacks of precious stuffs and huge treasure chests from distant kingdoms. The air was filled with the pungent tang of spice and perfume.

The startled shepherds stood against the wall to let the cavalcade of the mighty pass by. And these wise men and kings seemed to have no doubt as to their destination. They swept past the inn and dismounted at the door of a stable. Servants took the burdens from the backs of the camels, and the kings and the wise men stooped and went in through the low door of the stable.

"It is there the child lies in the manger," said one of the shepherds and made as if to follow, but his fellows were abashed and said among themselves, "It is not meet that we should crowd in upon the heels of the mighty."

"We, too, are bidden," insisted the youngest shepherd. "For us, as well, there was the voice of the angel of the Lord."

And timidly the men from the fields followed after and found places near the door. They watched as the men from distant countries came and silently placed their gifts at the foot of the manger where the child lay sleeping. And the shepherds stood aside and let the great of the earth go out into the night to take up again their long journey.

Presently they were alone, but as they had no gifts to lay beside the gold and frankincense they turned to go back to their flocks. But Mary, the mother, made a sign to the youngest shepherd to come closer. And he said, "We are shepherds, and we have come suddenly from the fields whence an angel summoned us. There is naught which we could add to the gifts of wise men and of kings."

Mary replied, "Before the throne of God, who is a king and who is a wise man, you have brought with you a gift more precious than all the others. It lies within your heart."

And suddenly it was made known to the shepherd the meaning of the words of Mary. He knelt at the foot of the manger and gave to the child his prayer of joy and of devotion.

154. I LIKED IT FINE

A friend of mine from the *World-Telegram* called me up last year on Christmas Eve and said, "I thought you might be interested to know that President Roosevelt is going to read a piece of yours over the radio for his annual Christmas tree broadcast."

"You're kidding me, Carl," I told him in some surprise but he insisted it was on the level. "I don't happen to read your stuff myself," he explained, "but they've got the story at the desk to be released as soon as the President begins to talk. It's some piece you wrote about Judas and an old clergyman."

That sounded like my story, but I was still incredulous. If the advance information were correct I thought my mother might like to listen in, but I didn't want to sell her out on some office practical joke. And so just to confirm things I called up the paper and asked for the city editor. I had quite a tough time getting him. The girl at the switchboard said of the chief, "I believe Bo is upstairs in the darkroom shooting craps. We're getting out a kind of good-will-to-men edition. I'll try and dislodge him for you."

A somewhat impatient city editor did finally come to the phone to say, "Carl wasn't kidding you. The President's going to read your piece. The one we printed yesterday."

I called up my mother and turned on my own radio in the big living room in the farmhouse. As the zero hour of five-thirty drew closer, I got more and more nervous. I still suspected that there was something screwy about the whole business and even if the tip were authentic I began to worry as to what sort of performance Mr. Roosevelt would put on. The thing I'd written was very simple and, in that excessive egoism which afflicts even minor writers, I had a feeling that I didn't want to have the finest voice now known on the air to take my brief story and turn it into an elocutionary exercise. Besides, by this time there was a sort of split feeling in my subconscious. It was almost as if I were going to stand up and do my stuff for potential millions of listeners.

Naturally, I took a drink. Then I grabbed three more very hurriedly. There was no one with me but Connie and my son and daughter. Even so I could hardly endure it to sit in a room with anybody else when the ordeal began. I mean the ordeal for me and the President. Would he get by without stumbling or coughing? It so happens that I have a sort of phobia which makes me hideously unhappy if I have to sit and watch anybody read something of my own, aloud or to himself, when I am present. And I feel it even more strongly if I think that the piece is all right. You keep watching the other fellow to notice whether he will grin at the appropriate places or look grave when the stage directions call for such expression.

And so I strolled up and down sipping my whiskey until Mr. Roosevelt began, "We were sitting in a high room above the chapel . . ." I knew then that it was mine and I rushed out into the hall and began to weep and listen, even though I kept walking.

Frank Roosevelt really did it very well and when he was finished I sent a telegram to Steve Early saying, "Please convey to the President my appreciation for the fact that he read my story. And tell him, also, that he did it even better than I could have done it myself."

The story never had a name but I suppose *Even to Judas* would do for a title. Here it is, along with Mr. Roosevelt's brief introduction.

155. EVEN TO JUDAS

"Last night before I went to sleep, I chanced to read in an evening paper a story by a columnist which appealed to me so much as a Christmas sermon that I am going to read to you from it. Here is his parable."

We were sitting in a high room above the chapel and although it was Christmas Eve my good friend the dominie seemed curiously troubled. And that was strange, for he was a man extremely sensitive to the festivities of his faith.

The joys and sorrows of Jesus were not to him events of a remote past but more current and living happenings than the headlines in the newspapers. At Christmas he seems actually to hear the voice of the herald angels.

My friend is an old man, and I have known him for many years, but this was the first time the Nativity failed to rouse him to an ecstasy. He admitted to me something was wrong.

"Tomorrow," he said, "I must go down into that chapel and preach a Christmas sermon. And I must speak of peace and good-will toward men. I know you think of me as a man too cloistered to be of any use to my community. And I know that our world is one of war and hate and enmity. And you, my young friend, and others keep insisting that before there can be brotherhood there must be the bashing of heads. You are all for good-will to men, but you want to note very many exceptions. And I am still hoping and praying that in the great love of God the final seal of interdiction must not be put on even one. You may laugh at me, but right now I am wondering about how Christmas came to Judas Iscariot."

It is the habit of my friend, when he is troubled by doubts, to reach for the Book, and he did so now. He smiled and said, "Will you assist me in a little experiment? I will close my eyes and you hold out the Bible to me. I will open it at random and run my fingers down a page. You read me the text which I blindly select."

I did as he told me and he happened on the twenty-sixth chapter of St. Matthew and the twenty-fourth verse. I felt sorry for him, for this was no part of the story of the birth of Christ but instead an account of the great betrayal.

"Read what it says," commanded the dominie. And I read: "Then Judas, which betrayed Him, answered and said, 'Master, is it I?' He said unto him, 'Thou hast said.'"

My friend frowned, but then he looked at me in triumph. "My hand is not as steady as it used to be. You should have taken the lower part of my finger and not the top. Read the twenty-seventh verse. It is not an eighth of an inch away. Read what it says." And I read, "And He took the cup and gave thanks and gave it to them, saying, 'Drink ye all of it.'"

"Mark that," cried the old man exultantly. "Not even to Judas, the betrayer, was the wine of life denied. I can preach my Christmas sermon now, and my text will be 'Drink ye all of it.' Good-will toward men means good-will to every last son of God. Peace on earth means peace to Pilate, peace to the thieves on the cross, and peace to poor Iscariot."

I was glad, for he had found Christmas and I saw by his face that once more he heard the voice of the herald angels.

156. A TEXAS SLUM

SAN ANTONIO, TEXAS, Feb. 6 [1939].—"It may be dangerous if you go with me," said Father Tranchese, "for there are many who have made threats because I am in favor of the housing project."

One in the group whispered, "It would be very curious if I were killed fighting in the same cause with a padre." And then he raised his voice and called, "Let's go."

The Church of Guadalupe stands upon the fringe of what had been described to me as the most fearful slum in all America. It covers four square miles. At first I thought that the extreme description might have been dictated by local pride. It was my notion to protest and say, "Why, we in New York City know worse than that." But after we had gone up the third back alley I had to confess defeat gracefully.

You can see shacks as bad as these in several States, but I do not know of any place where they have been so ingeniously huddled together. This is flat, sprawling country, and there is much of it, and so it seems devilish that one crazy combination of old lumber and stray tin should be set as a flap upon the side of another equally discreditable. I did not quite comprehend the character of the alley until I discovered that what I took to be a toolhouse was a residence for a family of eleven people.

And these are not squatter dwellings. People pay rent for them, just as if a few rickety boards and a leaky roof constituted a house. They even have evictions and go through the solemn and obscene farce of removing a bed and a frying pan as indication that the landlord's two-dollars-and-a-half rent has not been forthcoming. However, the Sheriff's men cannot very well put the belongings on the sidewalk, for a pool of stagnant water generally serves as the pedestrians' right of way in any alley.

I am not going to discuss the sanitary arrangements.

The district which I visited is the home of the Mexicans. There are in San Antonio some ninety thousand. I wanted to look, because I had read that Americans are being badly treated in Mexico. It seemed to me pertinent to inquire how Mexicans are treated here. And now I am convinced that there is something to be said on both sides of the border.

It will not suffice to say that if the Mexicans do not like it here they should go back where they came from. Some of them, at least, were here before ever a Texas Democrat pioneered into this territory. This was their land until American civilization crashed through.

There is in San Antonio an old Spanish mission which is perhaps the most beautiful building within our borders. It was set up before the Texans came. And it is by no means impossible that descendants of those workers who did miracles in masonry and carving are now housed in bristol board and rotted pine.

I could not go all the way through the four square miles, because we came upon a most hideous, diseased and malformed dog. Nobody had thought to put him out of his misery. The Mexicans didn't notice it. They weren't getting along too well themselves.

Back at the Church of Guadalupe, the priest said, "I have other letters from those who fight federal housing because they like their rents." He tossed over an anonymous message, which read, "I could start a story that there is a priest who writes love letters to young girls and gives jewels to women of his congregation."

"Doesn't this worry you?" one of us asked.

"No," said the priest, "last month we buried thirty-nine persons, mostly children, from this little church alone.

"I am worried," he said, "about people starving to death."

157. ARTIST UNKNOWN

The ragged man eased himself over to the fat customer who sat alone in a far corner of the bar.

"Charlie, the barkeep, tells me you're a newspaperman," he began in a wheedling way.

"So what?"

"I was just wondering whether you'd buy a fellow a couple of drinks if he told you a story that maybe you could write up for a paper or something."

"Let's hear the story."

"Oh," said the ragged man who by this time had eased himself into a chair, "I couldn't do that unless you bought me one of the drinks right now to get started on."

"Bring him a whiskey," called the fat reporter without much enthusiasm.

The interloper reached eagerly for the drink when it was set before him. It was a thin hand with long tapering fingers. It was a fine hand but that might have passed unnoticed because it trembled so violently. The drink being done, the man with a story began, "I used to be an etcher and a drypoint man."

"You mean you were an artist?"

"I guess that's what you'd call it. And I was a good one. I studied in Paris and in Rome before I came here and in those days I only got drunk once and so often. Nobody in particular knew anything about me, but take it from me I was good. If you're a lefthanded pitcher somebody'll discover you, but there's nobody scouting around for etchers. Maybe that's why

I got drunk. And this time I was good and drunk. It started on Easter Sunday and finally it was Monday morning and somehow or other I was in a cell in the West Forty-seventh Street police station with a cut over my left eye. When I woke up, the sun was streaming into that first cell. It only gets the light early in the morning.

"I should have had the shakes and the jitters but, for some reason, I felt fine. There was an energy in me. Sometime during the night I'd dreamed of a picture. The whole thing was complete in my mind. All I had to do was to find a surface and set it down. In my pocket there was an etcher's needle. I looked at the wall of the cell. It was steel and just recently they'd put a coat of dark green paint on it. The surface was soft but not gummy. It was all right. Something like wax. The steel underneath was bright like silver. If you know anything about etching you understand that you don't try to cut into the metal with your needle. That's left for the acid.

"With the bright metal underneath and the dark paint my fine lines showed up sharp and clear. I never worked so fast or intently in my life. I did the crucifixion.

"You wouldn't understand about composition, I suppose, but the idea was this. Although there was a lot of detail—Roman soldiers and servants of the High Priest and all that and not skimped at all—the emphasis went on two faces. You wouldn't be interested in the technical details, but it's as simple as this. Everything in the composition led the eye to the Man on the cross and his mother Mary who watched afar off. And I made the face of Jesus serene, exalted. There was no suggestion of agony in his expression. Already he felt the surge of resurrection. It was his mother's face which mirrored the agony. It was as if the nails pierced her hands and feet and as if she bore Him again. Do you get what I'm driving at?"

The fat man nodded slowly.

"I worked fast and full of fever but I hadn't quite finished when I heard a cop coming down the hall to take us off to court.

I slipped the etching tool into my pocket and the cop didn't even come into the cell. He simply called, 'Get a move on, bum, the wagon's waiting.' In court the Magistrate said, 'Learn to hold your liquor like a gentleman,' and turned me loose a free man.

"By now I did have the jitters and it was almost a week before I thought of the picture again. Then I tried to do it in the regular way on a zinc plate. It was no good. Something was gone. I destroyed the plate. In the last six months I've tried a dozen times, copper as well as zinc. No go any time. I can't get what I put on the wall of that cell Easter Monday morning.

"And then one day about a month ago I picked up an evening paper and saw what I guess you call a feature story—a two column head. It said, MIRACLE IN WEST 47TH ST. POLICE STATION. And the story went on to say that for a long time the cops have been wondering about a marvelous picture scratched in the paint of cell No. 1. According to this newspaper story, there's no record of anybody having been in the cell the night they think the picture must have been made. Of course, the truth is that it may have been there for weeks before any cop noticed it. Lots of people scratch things on the walls of cells. All sorts of things, but not like my picture. And the newspaper story goes on to say that several great artists have looked at the picture in cell No. 1 and that they all say it's a work of genius. And then, to nail down the miracle theory, the police say that the cell has a curious influence on prisoners. They put the worst drunks in there and in the morning they come out sane, sober and exalted."

The reporter interrupted. "Why don't you go down to the station and explain that you did the picture and get the credit? After all they've got your name on the blotter and in the police record."

"Who would believe me? And it isn't my name. I can't even remember what name I did give or what address. You see this was all of six months ago and at that time I thought I might be disgraced if anybody knew I'd been picked up as drunk and disorderly. It wouldn't matter now."

"Well," said the reporter, "even if you have got the shakes you could draw something like the picture. That would prove you did it. How would you know otherwise?"

"That's too late, too. That feature story has a reproduction of the picture. Anybody could copy that. Anybody can copy that, but drunk or sober I'm the only man who can finish it. My name wouldn't matter. I could sign myself with every one of those last missing lines. Drunk or sober. That was the scheme.

"Two weeks ago I tried it. I would be the first and the worst drunk of the night and they would put me in the cell which brings sanity and exaltation to even the lowest bum. I took no chances. I put what was left of my pride in my pocket and also my etcher's needle. I got myself roaring. And I chose a saloon just around the corner from the West Forty-seventh Street Station. At that I miscalculated the time. It slipped by on me and so, although I was probably the worst drunk in the precinct, I wasn't the first. The sun was already up when I staggered around and lay me down on the steps of the police station. I didn't have long to wait. In a few minutes a couple of cops came swinging down the street heading for the station. They seemed a little surprised to find me there on the steps and one of them clubbed me on the soles of the feet. 'Come along, bum,' he said. 'This is the shortest haul I've ever had in my fifteen years on the force.' They jerked me to my feet and started to rough me up a little and out from the station came a young cop with his face all aglow. 'Boys,' he called out to them, 'let that poor old bum alone.'

" 'What's biting you?' asked the one who clubbed me.

" 'It's like this, Mike,' answered the young cop. 'I'm just after putting a drunk in cell No. 1 and I saw that picture. I never saw it like this before. The sun is shining on those faces. It is a miracle.'

" 'Here,' he said, taking a dollar out of his pocket, 'give me fifty cents, Mike, and let me have what you've got, Tom.'

"It amounted to a dollar and ninety-five cents. The young cop called a taxi from in front of the bail bond office across the street and said to the man, 'Take this poor fellow and drive him around till he sobers up. See that he gets a good breakfast and then turn him loose in God's bright sunshine.'

"And so," said the ragged man, "I remain mute, sodden and inglorious and there's nothing can be done about it."

"Well," said the fat reporter, "you can have that other drink."

158. PASSION IN THE ANDES

Some few years ago I went on a spring cruise. The steamer touched the northern tip of South America and paused for a day at the port so that passengers might travel up the mountain to Caracas. When we reached Venezuela word came that Gomez, the old dictator, lay dying in the capital. And as we went up the winding road, which drops a sheer two or three thousand feet at convenient corners, I noticed that all those who walked along the highway were clad in black or purple. Young and old all seemed to be hurrying to some central point. And, naturally, it was my notion that they were hurrying to the palace to learn the fate of Gomez.

Of course, we went faster than the pedestrians, much faster than was my will and pleasure. I remember mountains above me and hills leaping like waterfalls to meet the sea. Sky and sea and chasm pin-wheeled across my vision. And all because an old dictator drew close to his appointed hour.

In the great square of the city these signs of mourning and of tribulation became banked into moving masses of people. And

I thought to myself, "Perhaps the potentate is already dead, and it is for that reason that the garb of grief is everywhere."

But at the door of the cathedral the driver stopped and said something to my companion. My friend translated and explained, "The driver says this is the service to mark the three hours of agony on the cross."

And it came to me that they mourned not for Gomez but for the Son of God. Out of bright sunlight I came into cool darkness flecked, but not wholly broken, by the light of many hundred candles. And all about the walls and statues and across the shoulders of the worshipers I saw the badge of purple. Holy Week had come to the foothills of the Andes.

I have seen church services in far and near places, and many were impressive, but here for the first time I saw a people who seemed to feel that the Passion of the Lord was actually occurring once again.

Pilate was not a famous dead procurator of Judea who washed his hands in an ancient city long ago. It was but yesterday that Jesus stood before the Romans on trial for His life and was condemned. And at the very moment the living Christ hung on the cross.

An Indian woman, older than any being I had ever seen before, lifted her head from the floor as she prayed that death should not achieve its victory. Children in their purple smocks looked at the dancing lights and wondered. But they were silent.

It was as if someone of their own lay dying in a room at home. And all of them lived in a world in which each year Jesus again walked the earth and Judas brought betrayal in a pleasant garden. Many stood outside upon the steps under the hot sun and peered through the doors and down the dark aisles. They waited for some word from the mourners. Almost they seemed to say, "What is the news? How fares our Lord on Calvary?"

The faith of the faithful burns high along that mountain

shelf. Some part of the agony is theirs, but the joy of resurrection bursts in their heart like an apple tree suddenly come to bloom. To them the miracle is without question. They have lived through it, and rebirth becomes a part of their own experience.

Only one sleepy sentry stood outside the palace of Gomez. My friend spoke to him. "Gomez is very old," said the soldier, "and, like you and me and the beggar in the street, he must die some day. But he is of strong will. He will breathe until he has seen another Easter morning." I suppose that before death the old man wanted once again to dip his hands in life.

159. THE FEDERAL THEATER

In the face of a war crisis in the world and economic pressure at home there is the chance that efforts will be made to cut some of the most vital and important projects in which our government is engaged. I refer to the Federal Art Project. To me it seems that these activities are a vital part of the struggle between democracy and dictatorship. It is by constantly raising and nurturing the cultural standards of our country that we justify our way of life and our form of government. We reaffirm faith at home in American institutions and give tangible evidence to the world that here are the atmosphere and the incitement toward the search for truth and beauty. This search is certainly part of the pursuit of happiness.

Possibly the gravest mistake which Goebbels ever made in his propagandistic endeavors was to release the little list of jokes and wisecracks which he proudly presented as the flower of Nazi humor. In a wholly serious sense, I think, they testified eloquently to the sterility of mind which Fascism has engendered. Germany once led the world in its superb comic papers and sprightly draftsmen. All have been crushed under the heel of Hitler.

It is just as important to prove that democracy can foster good plays and short stories and mural paintings as to prove our ability to build airplanes. Indeed, I think *The Swing Mikado*, in its display and development of Negro talent, is a great force for national unity and integration. It serves at least as useful a purpose as a battle cruiser.

After all, when we say that we believe in democracy we are not merely expressing faith in an abstract principle. Democracy naturally must be judged by its fruits. Few, I suppose, would contend that all phases of American life are without flaw or error. In fact, the most useful and lively proponent of democracy is the person who points out things which are amiss. Under our system that is not only his privilege but his bounden duty. He points them out because he feels that it is well within the national capacity to correct them.

The more joy which can be brought into the life of all increases the stake which each of us has in protecting and amplifying our liberties. Happiness should be the chief cornerstone in national defense. In praising the Federal Art Project I am, of course, not contending that the government would be the sole custodian of American culture. No such attempt has been made, nor is there any indication that it ever will be attempted.

My own feeling is that federal plays and pictures and books have been of benefit to commercial managers and to private publishers. A swing and hot "Mikado" are both thriving now along Broadway, and there would have been no venture of this sort at all but for federal enterprise. I think the government might almost claim an assist in the matter of the magnificent performance of Bill Robinson in *The Hot Mikado*, even though that is a commercial venture. In many cases federal activity inspires private enterprise to put its best foot forward. In the case of Mr. Robinson it so happens that two divinely dedicated feet are set in motion.

And, although it is slightly irrelevant to the matter of federal art, I think that Marian Anderson's great triumph at the foot of the Lincoln Memorial is still another factor which gives a democratic and devastating answer to the Fascist creed of Aryanism.

We live in a troubled world, and we must help to solve its problems. But do not let us dedicate ourselves to this task in sackcloth. We should accept our responsibilities with no sullen mien. We uphold democracy because it is the way by which the hearts of men are lifted up toward the high reach of human aspiration.

160. REPORTER'S RECESS

"Bleeck's," also known as the Artists' and Writers', seems to be the spot the Broadway columnists forgot, although it is situated directly below the New York *Herald Tribune,* one of Manhattan's most eminent dailies. Indeed, on many occasions the paper is practically laid out in Bleeck's back room between match games. Some years ago, Stanley Walker wrote eloquently about the establishment but that was for a magazine. Once, rather briefly, the place got in the news but only under the rather unusual stimulus that at its bar a dramatist endeavored to bite a critic.

Things which would go out to all the world if they occurred at the Stork, or "21," or El Morocco linger in the limbo of private gossip if put on display at the Artists' and Writers'. Seemingly there is no surer way to keep a story quiet than to dangle it under the accumulated noses of a number of reporters on recess.

A young man, of social prominence or news interest, may woo and win a lady at Bleeck's and nobody will be the wiser save possibly the parents of the bride. Indeed the twain may be welded, go on to one or more blessed events, and into ultimate reno-vation, without one single section of the saga making the public prints.

It is quite possible that in some quiet corner of the middle room where the light is dim Judge Crater sits wholly safe in self-chosen disappearance, since he is entirely surrounded by newspapermen. And if their majesties of Britain wish an incognito afternoon they can get it by taking the table by the overcoat rack and asking Charlie for a couple of whisky sours.

It may be that through some sort of gentlemen's agreement Bleeck's is regarded as out of bounds as a news source save in the event of the better sort of murder or mayhem of a kind too picturesque to be ignored. As far as office discipline goes, the restaurant does offer sanctuary and if a city editor meets an errant reporter coming through the rye, neither body is allowed to cry.

Indeed, it was in Bleeck's that Lucius Beebe once regaled practically the entire bar with savage criticism of an immediate superior who might as well be known as John Q. Doe. Nor did he desist until the tactful bartender remarked, "Would you mind lifting your elbow, Mr. Beebe, it's resting on the head of Mr. Doe."

Possibly the man who bore the brunt of Beebe's weight and phrases did not remember the incident the next day. His official capacity was exalted and he could easily have broken a butterfly upon the wheel. But he tempered his wrath toward the well-dressed lamb. Lucius went on to fame and fortune. Misconduct in Bleeck's is punishable only through the full vote of the House Committee.

And yet, perhaps, I do exaggerate in suggesting that every single inmate wears a literary reputation on his sleeve and carries in his knapsack the boutonniere of Richard Harding Davis. Whenever newspapermen find a better mousetrap the world is sure to beat them to the door.

So it was with Joel's which once stood within a block of Bleeck's. Mr. Rinaldo, the proprietor, was himself a writer and the author of *Joel's Polygeneric Theory of Life* which was mentioned on the menu just under the chili. But though of a scientific turn, Joel had his sentimental side and the banner at the top of the bill of fare read, "Joel's is the home of newspapermen, artists and actors—the most lovable folk in the world. I will take care of your money while you are on the road."

During at least one bitter winter the boast was in a measure true and you could run into Charlie Hand practically every night. But when trade slackened the profit motive nudged Mr. Rinaldo out of his passion for the arts and he shut off credit and put in a floor show. The most lovable folk in the world folded their tents and advertising men rushed in to take the chairs where once the dreamers sat.

And so in the days to come it could be with Bleeck's. Mayhap a debutante will advance to the microphone to entertain the customers and on Sunday nights gift hundred-dollar bills will shower from the ceiling *pour le sport*.

But when money rains from the skies the reporters will go away. To them it will be a sure and certain sign that the place no longer belongs to them and that once again they must give ground to the rush of the Philistines.

161. THE HAPPY DAYS OF BASEBALL

In the smoking compartment of a New Haven train recently I struck up a conversation with the man next to me and after we had dismissed the weather we started to discuss baseball. It wasn't so much a discussion as a sort of dialogue in free association. His first question, after the fact that three strikes are out had been established, was, "Do you remember Josh Devore?"

I said I did and that I also remember Eddie Plank who fanned him five times in a World Series game.

After that we just swapped names. I'd say "Sandow Mertes" and my new-found friend would answer "Dan McGann." We jumped around the lot a good deal and often our chronology was imperfect but most of the men mentioned were at one time or another Giants. Possibly it is just the enchantment of distance but "Red Ames, Red Murray, Mike Donlin, and Dummy Taylor," do stir up more romantic images than anybody now playing for Terry.

When we got back as far as Pink Hawley I declared myself and said that I was hardly more than a tot when I saw that particular athlete perform. But I recall that he wore a pad on the right leg of his pants because he always went down to one knee when he threw a fast one. My friend coopered me by declaring that he was just a babe in arms when he first went to the old, old Polo Grounds.

But we agreed that we had been brought up properly. At an early age we took the home team very seriously. The outside agitators from Brooklyn or Philadelphia were villains of the deepest hue and there was none of that nonsense about applauding a good play by either side. The perfect game was eighteen to nothing with the home team on the heavy end.

I'm afraid the tolerance of New York has done much to impair baseball as a spectacle. At both the Yankee Stadium and the Polo Grounds there is so much tolerance that the Man from Mars would be wholly unable to tell which were the Phillies and which the Giants. And this season he could hardly make a distinction by looking at the standing of the clubs.

Fortunately they do things very differently in Brooklyn. This is one of the few bright spots in the entire circuit. There is no sportsmanship among the Flatbush fans. They do not cheer even the most spectacular play by any invader and they do throw pop bottles. Of such stuff is the greatness of baseball made and the proof of it is that Brooklyn draws excellent crowds even though it hasn't been going anywhere for many seasons.

Once upon a time, St. Louis fairly bubbled with local pride and baseball enthusiasm. A man's life was hardly worth the price of admission if he dared defame the Cardinals or the Browns while sitting in the bleachers. Even in the grandstand he would be lucky to escape with no more than a black eye. St. Louis doesn't give a blame who wins and who loses. In fact the fans stay away from baseball in droves.

Curiously enough, Washington is second only to Brooklyn in the intense partisanship of its rooters. This city made up of men and women from all the states of our country and harboring many foreign representatives can boil about its baseball. Sober citizens acted like college boys and pinched signs along the thoroughfare during the two years in which the Senators got into the World Series. The explanation probably lies in the fact that residents in Washington are disenfranchised. They cannot vote and so they need some emotional release. This they get by yelling "Kill the umpire."

One of the reasons for the diminution of baseball fervor is the development of the low-priced automobile. I am not referring to the fact that many a fan would rather be caught in a traffic jam than watch the St. Louis Browns, but to a more immediate effect in the matter of staging the pastime. Even the rookie in the big leagues buys himself a car and he uses it going to and from the park in his home city. Sometimes he can get permission of the manager to drive to the next engagement if the jump's a short one. And even when he is compelled to leave his limousine in the garage the modern ballplayer takes a taxi to his place of employment.

McGraw, when on the road, would make all members of his club dress in the hotel where the team was resident. He would then escort them to the top of a bus and they would proceed slowly through the main street like circus elephants on exhibition. The ballplayers would leer from the top of their lofty perch at the hostile fans and the rooters would leer back, throw eggs and tomatoes and grow maniacal. If a crucial series were in progress it was frequently necessary to call out the reserves in order to limit the number of killed and injured. Those were the happy days of baseball. Those days are gone forever.

162. THE PASSING OF MARTIN D.

I miss the rooster. Although we called him Martin Dies, his shrill call is heard no more.

The first intimation that a voice was gone came to me at breakfast. Connie, in her crude way, tried to break it to me gently. As I looked up from my hardboiled egg she said, "Martin's gone."

"Somebody stole him or he flew away?" I asked excitedly.

"No," answered Connie, "I've sent the rooster to your mother."

Impatiently I asked, "What on earth is my mother going to do with a live chicken in a small city apartment?"

"I've been trying to tell you," said Connie in her low voice which can hardly be heard a block away, "that Martin isn't a live chicken any more." She made the grim gesture of drawing her right hand across her lovely throat.

Horror seized me. It was as if my coffee had been served to me by Lizzie Borden. "Who has done this fearful thing?" I wanted to know. The hardboiled egg I pushed away. From this time on neither the flesh nor the fruit of fowl would have much appeal to me.

"I didn't do it personally," Connie explained. "I told Quent to do it. He said it was quick. He used that ax you chopped trees with three years ago when you were exercising. And that old stump where you paint."

And so even the arts were profaned to do away with Martin. No more can I set my brush to limn green landscapes or the white spray of tumultuous brooks. The red shadow of the rooster will intrude.

"When did all this happen? I did not hear the sound of any struggle."

"It was early before you woke. He's been plucked and dressed already."

"Do not," I said with dignity, "ever attempt to serve that bird to me. Even as croquettes or fricassee it would be impossible. Too many mornings I have heard him sing for the sun and in the yard I watched him with his harem of hens picking out fat worms for himself. No, let us dine on peas and spinach with possibly a mutton chop to sustain life. Martin must not come to my table either in flesh or spirit."

"I told you already," Connie replied, "that I sent him to your mother. She never knew him personally and she won't mind. I told her to hang him up a day or so because Philip said he seemed a little tough. He needs maturing."

Since I am not wholly vegetarian I realized that perhaps my early morning qualms were too romantic. A chicken can be palatable when roasted and also when he's fried. I tried to put the best face possible on the matter of Martin.

"He was a large bird," I reminisced, "and probably my mother will invite all the neighbors to share in the repast."

"Martin won't go that far," said Connie. "Philip says that when he plucked him there wasn't much meat. He stripped down rather scrawny."

"But that's impossible. Martin was the largest rooster on Hunting Ridge and he could outcrow any three or four birds in all of Fairfield County. There was no Rhode Island Red in the whole state which could stand comparison with him as he preened himself and strutted."

"Yes," said Connie, "that was the trouble. When he was plucked and cleaned we found that pretty much all of Martin was just fuss and feathers."

163. GENERAL MOSELEY

I have never met Major General George Van Horn Moseley. In fact, as far as I can remember, it has not even been my privilege to gaze upon his picture. Sight unseen, I conjure him up as an old gentleman with a long, white mustache who fairly bristles with military pomp, patriotism and excellent intentions. Certainly no charge hurled at any man by the Dies Committee should be accepted in whole or substantial part without check and double-check. The General has a right to his day in court, and he has already announced that, far from being a Fascist, he merely seeks to lead true Americans in defense of traditional democratic principles.

And so it is in a friendly spirit that I would like to offer a word of caution and advice to the retired soldier. General, in spite of the intensity of your devotion to the American way, your place is in the ranks and not in the pivotal position of staff officer behind the lines. Time is a great leveler, and age lays its finger upon the brass hats as well as the corporals and sergeants. You and I, and two or three others, are not as young as we used to be. It is well to face the fact frankly. Our mental and nervous reactions are less rapid than in those fine old days when we were fifty.

You say that it should be the privilege of a patriot to discuss national problems openly and frankly. What rogue will dare deny that? But I think, if you will pardon my glove, General, that you bite off more territory than you can chew at present when you declare that it's your intention to save America from itself. It seems to me that now, and at all times, the United States is rather larger than any single major general. You ask too much in suggesting that the millions should stand stiffly at attention and wait until you have made up your mind just what our marching orders are to be. Has it slipped your mind, Major General Moseley, that you are not in the army now?

If the news-gathering organizations are correct, you announced in El Centro, Cal., "My attention has just been called to press reports to the effect that I am a Fascist." No man may reach the higher brackets in the military service of the United States until he has demonstrated his ability to both read and write the short and simple words of our mother tongue. And when your name was flung into the news the story was not printed obscurely in some remote quarter of the real estate section. No, indeed, General, you had your day on the front page.

The story, on the average, rated a two-column head, and in some journals it commanded an eight-column streamer. And yet you noticed none of this until some old friend or orderly nudged you with the news, "George, did you see the piece in the paper in which your name is mentioned?" With what pursuit were you occupied to the extent of needing an attention-caller to rub your nose in the obvious and make you acquainted with the palpable? The man who undertakes to save America from itself, preserve our democratic institutions from all attacks, cannot afford to be a cloistered recluse to whom the noises of the street come feebly, like bees in swarm around the turning of the road. The man who sees himself as another Washington or Lincoln must sound a trumpet call.

Blow, bugles, blow! No matter how pure his patriotism, it will not suffice if he waves aloft an ear-trumpet and shrills out, "Follow me!" The age of retirement is clearly indicated when the services of an attention-caller become imperative. And so, General, I think you should lean back and take it easy. Avoid starchy foods and too much excitement. A little chess and some debate about Grant's strategy in the Wilderness are indicated.

Can you hear me, General? I was trying to say that this is 1939, and that your mustache is on fire. I hope you won't mind if I call your attention to it. Sooner or later you've just got to learn.

164. THERE IS A SHIP

There is a ship. It is called the *St. Louis*. If suddenly the vessel flashed an S O S to indicate that the crew and the 900 passengers were in danger every other steamer within call would go hurrying to the rescue. That is the rule of the sea.

And no vessel which got the flash would pause to inquire the economic, political, religious or national position of those in distress. It would want no more than the position of the ship.

And the captain on the bridge, according to the prevailing tradition, would ask the engineer to put on all speed so that the work of rescue could be completed as expeditiously as possible. And this would be true of the skipper of a totalitarian merchant-man, one from a democratic nation or a ship flying under the flag of a monarchy, liberal or otherwise.

But there is a ship. It carries 900 passengers—men, women and small children. This is a group of God-fearing people guilty of no crime whatsoever. And they are in peril.

They are in peril which threatens not only their lives but their very souls and spiritual freedom. It would be better for them by far if the *St. Louis* had ripped its plates in a collision with some other craft, or if an impersonal iceberg had slashed the hull below the water line.

Then there would be not the slightest hesitation in a movement of all the allied fleets to save these members of the human race in deep and immediate distress.

But this is not an iceberg or a plate which has been ripped away. The passengers—men, women and children—are Jewish.

It is not an accident of nature but an inhuman equation which has put them in deadly peril. It is quite true that when the *St. Louis* gets back to Hamburg these 900, with possibly a few exceptions, will not die immediately. They will starve slowly, since they have already spent their all. Or they will linger in concentration camps—I refer to the men and women. God knows what will happen to the children.

And so the whole world stuffs its ears and pays no attention to any wireless.

There is a ship. And almost two thousand years have elapsed since the message of universal brotherhood was brought to earth.

What have we done with that message? After so many years we have not yet put into practice those principles to which we pay lip service. Nine hundred are to suffer a crucifixion while the world passes by on the other side.

At any luncheon, banquet or public meeting the orator of the occasion can draw cheers if he raises his right hand in the air and pledges himself, his heart and soul to the declaration that he is for peace and amity and that all men are brothers. He means it, generally, and so do the diners who pound the table until the coffee cups and the cream dishes rattle into a symphony of good feeling and international sympathy.

But there is a ship. If one were to look upon it with cold logic it would be better for every one of the 900 if the vessel suddenly buckled and went down in forty fathoms. That would be more merciful.

Against the palpable threat of death we can muster brotherhood. But against the even more plain sentence of life in death we pretend to be helpless.

Our answer is, "We must look after ourselves. What can we do about it? Life is greater than death." We agree. Here is our test. What price civilization? There is a ship. Who will take up an oar to save 900 men, women and children?

165. A TALK WITH A FRIEND

Recently I was talking with a close friend of mine who has been received into the Catholic Church. We are associated in the trades-union movement as members of the C.I.O.

"I thought," said my friend, "that Americans held that a man's religion should be his own business, but it seems that I have been mistaken. In particular I was surprised to find how many bitter letters I received from persons wholly unknown to me who identified themselves as 'free thinkers.' Seemingly it is a freedom which they assign wholly to themselves. They are passionate about the right of disbelief but censorious of affirmation.

"And silliest of all was the accusation of a number of persons that in joining the Church I must be preparing to desert trades-unionism. Such a thing could be said only by those who are ignorant of the fact that a very heavy proportion of both the membership and the leadership of C.I.O. is Catholic.

"Indeed it seems to me that the fraternity which one seeks and finds among his brothers in a union is a sort of stepping stone to the ultimate and all-embracing brotherhood of the church. The Mass itself is co-operative worship. And though I may put it crudely I certainly am not minded to irreverence when I say there should be collective bargaining even at Final Judgment.

"One learns the limitations of the individual in the labor movement. One must always find his refreshment and strength in contact with his fellows. And from that fraternity none may be barred. When I was eight years old I started a club in school called the Silent Nine. We wore a padlock as a pin and met once a week, usually in the cellar of my father's house because we made so much noise. We were seeking fraternity.

"The wholly useless years of my life were spent in a not particularly ivory tower functioning as a feeble individualist. The Newspaper Guild lifted me out of this slough.

"But even that is not all-sufficient. I wanted the brotherhood of man. I have found it now because its full fruition can come only under the fatherhood of God. And, in spite of the delays and doubts, it seems to me that there is in every living being the Word and the Seed.

"Before we find complete fraternity, we must find Christ complete and manifold. No matter from what quarter we begin the journey, here is our home."

166. SQUARE PEG

Westbrook Pegler is the man who chiseled down the word "enough" from a granite boulder into a watch fob. When Mooney was in San Quentin prison Peg complained that the prisoner took no interest in the wrongs of Billings. Now that Mooney is speaking throughout the country in behalf of his associate, Mr. Pegler complains that he ought to be engaged in some gainful occupation.

If a man went around forever crying out, "Observe how my heart beats for humanity," he would undoubtedly be set down as a fool or a hypocrite. And he could be both. But how about the fellow who encases himself in triple brass in the pretense that he has no heart at all? His would be the deeper folly. It may be a good idea for a columnist to keep his shirt on, but that is no reason why he should insulate himself like a telephone wire.

The tragedy of J. Westbrook Pegler consists of the fact that by nature he is not the man he pretends to be. His native sympathies are wide and deep. When he is aroused about some ancient wrong he can be more eloquent than any newspaperman I know. The most understanding and sensitive column I can remember was written by Peg in Germany about the peculiar persecution visited upon Jewish children. And recently he broke through a long string of his regular higher-bracket moans to cry out passionately against the fearful housing visited upon one-third of the nation. And yet upon all too frequent occasions he writes as if he has taken over the role of light heavyweight champion of the upperdog and game warden for the preserves of the over-privileged. Some day somebody should take the hide off Peg because the stuff inside is so much better than the varnished surface which blinks in the sunlight of popular approval.

How has it come about that so much of the best of Peg is mislaid? I blame it on his technique and his talent for fictional creation. Peg has created a character called Westbrook Pegler and, except when he forgets himself, he tries to live up to the role. The fictional fellow is hardboiled, querulous and materialistic. But the man who assumes this part morning after morning is actually shy, sensitive and sentimental. A tip-off may lie in the kidding title which our hero chose for his last clip book. He called it *The Dissenting Opinions of Mr. Westbrook Pegler* as a mild burlesque of the name under which the legal papers of the late Oliver Wendell Holmes were published. But here Peg mistakes the nature of his performance. He isn't playing Mr. Justice Holmes. He is playing Mr. Justice McReynolds.

In my opinion Peg is much more the creative artist than the reporter and this has led to his undoing. The personality with which he has endowed himself in print has been developed with so much skill and loving care that the author thinks of this thing of shreds and patches as a living, breathing person. Frankenstein fashioned a rough guy who destroyed him. Peg's monster didn't have to go to that slight trouble. When the last clay tonsil was modeled by this syndicated sculptor he said in high artistic pride, "Why, this is me to the life," and proceeded to cut his own throat under the theory that in a troubled world one Westbrook Pegler might be sufficient.

I have said that Pegler's worth as a newspaperman has been compromised by his increasing felicity as a writer. When a commentator's chief concern is finding the right word rather than the just cause he isn't a reporter any more. He has gone around the corner and become one of posterity's children.

Peg told me once that he sometimes spent as much as four or five hours in the creation of a column. This seemed to me a shocking confession for any man who came up from a city room. It is too much time for Peg to put in with himself. It is too much time for anybody to waste upon the works of Westbrook Pegler. The daily commentator who takes too much pains with his writing has insufficient energy left to get out and find something to write about. A column ought to be something more than hem-stitching a pattern around the phrase "the second Louisiana Purchase." It may be all very well for Shakespeare and the musical glasses to tinkle sweetly but a newspaperman ought to go clanging down the street along with the hook and ladder. He will seldom be lucky enough to have a four-alarm fire come dropping down his own chimney.

I am aware that Pegler's column appears under such widely separated date lines as Miami, San Francisco, and Paris, France, but in recent years the copy has taken on small color from the point of its origin. Of late Peg seems to carry with him wherever he goes not only his portable tyepwriter but also his collapsible ivory tower. He can go to a flood and come up with nothing more than another of those columns about the income pains of men with yachts. One suspects that he must have been bitten by a tax.

It does not seem to me that Westbrook Pegler has much background of factual knowledge. But of course the answer to that might be "Aren't we all?" Moreover, there are certain advantages in seeing things with naïve eyes. Pegler himself proved that in the justly famous articles he wrote from Germany during the winter Olympic Games. He had heard of Hitler in headlines, but to him "Fascist" was just a fancy word to be encountered in "the butcher's paper magazines." And then he went to Germany and suddenly with all the exciting shock impact of something new he saw the Nazis and their work with his own eyes.

His cry of "How long has this been going on?" rang with all the arresting force of one who felt the knife in his own skin.

But time goes on and Peg's heart stays home in Poundridge. Only rarely does he send it out now. He did break down at *Snow White* and Disney has done a lovely thing. But it is not the right of any man who lives in this generation to choose for himself a dwelling in the magical forest. None may enter unless like Grumpy he chooses to scale himself down into the expression of single point of view.

Newspapermen must come back from the city of dreams. I wish Peg had the same energy which possessed him in the days when he covered the beat from Gondrecourt to Chaumont. I wish he would stop writing out of the side of his mouth and quit the effort to be a Damon Runyon version of Peter Pan.

This job of being a professional clay-foot shooter may be a worthy one. But the gun should not be handled by a lad who can't seem to distinguish between plaster and solid bronze at twenty paces.

167. RED CAPS

I was talking yesterday with four Red Caps of New York. They were explaining the problems and difficulties which confront all new labor unions and their drive for fair and equitable conditions. I promised to try to set down some of the things which make the job tough and the returns meager.

But it will be easier to start by trying to discuss the relation between the man with a bundle and the porter who carries it. Recently I saw somewhere a picture of a Fair tourist to New York who was consulting her guide book to find out what is said about tipping, while the Red Cap waited in trepidation. The four men with whom I talked drew up a set of rules for the traveling public which I shall attempt to interpret.

First of all, the word "tip" is less than exact as a description of the quarter or more which you give in the station. It is not a tip; it is part of a wage. There is a general delusion that Red Caps get some basic salary; they do not. Indeed, they start from behind scratch, since they have to pay for their uniforms, both summer and winter. The cap itself costs $2.50, and may represent more than is earned in any given day.

Under the wage and hour law the Red Cap who earns less than $2 in any given day may put in a claim upon the company to make good the deficiency. But experience has taught most of the workers that it is not a very good idea to stand upon this right.

Accordingly, the passenger should bear in mind that he is handing no gratuity, but that in actual fact he is one of the employers of those he calls upon to take him to a train or taxi. And establishing a fair return, the member of the traveling public should use the same logical appraisement that he takes into mind in paying the taxi driver. It is a question of time and distance. The bane of the Red Cap is the man or woman who gets to the station thirty or forty minutes early and immediately hails a porter. If this occurs during the middle of a rush period the man assigned to a bag may lose two or three potential jobs. So if you hold a Red Cap up remember that part of your tip ought to include his waiting time.

And, again, it makes a difference whether he takes you into

the last car on the train or whether you want him to go all the way to some smoker up front. Indeed, it would perhaps be just if he wore upon his sleeve a clock to measure mileage. In getting off a train let the porter put you in a taxi if that is to be the means of conveyance. He knows the nearest exit and the quickest way to hail a driver. Twenty-five cents should be the standard payment, although you can get under the wire with fifteen on a short, swift haul. But remember that twenty-five cents is not enough if you are requiring extra time or extra service. And extra bags, of course, ought to mean extra payment. Pay no attention to the popular delusion that Red Caps roll in wealth. There are only three good months in the year, and three or four dollars a day is par. Anything beyond that is an eagle.

On the whole, men tip more generously than women, although my four friends made an exception of dowagers. Old ladies are the best of all. Homely women tip better than pretty ones, who seem to be accustomed to accepting favors. College boys are a dead loss. No matter how much luggage encumbers them, they are inclined to carry it themselves as proof of virility. The same thing goes for college girls, although the committee which I met made a mild exception in favor of Smith and Wellesley. Among the men's colleges Dartmouth is at the top of the heap, with Harvard and Princeton in a camera finish for dead last. As far as national traits go, Italians are the best tippers among the visitors to this city and the English the worst.

The World's Fair has not helped much, and it has brought in a flock of visitors suspicious of city ways. They are intent on asking the number of the porter, and often say when checking a bag, "I guess maybe it will be a good idea for me to go with you."

That's our next to last rule: "Trust the porter." Nobody ever loses a bag. And the final rule should be, "Mind your manners." If you get hot and angry you are taking an unfair advantage of the Red Cap. He can't answer back. All railroads go upon the principle that the customer is always right. That gives him about 70 per cent more than he honestly deserves.

168. THE *NEW YORKER*
AND THE KIDDIES

The *New Yorker*, a magazine, is so self-assured and Winchellwise—a little word run up on the machine—that it is comforting to find it has a heel. Indeed, I had suspected as much. In a recent issue the weekly took a fling with a short piece on child psychology and fell upon its nose. If the old lady from Dubuque were only a reader, the last laugh would have been hers.

Granting the wit and wisdom of Manhattan's smart gazette, I sometimes find it not quite up to its usual standard at such times as it attempts to discuss labor, politics or the radical movement. But it ventures forth with even less impedimenta of information when it attempts to discuss babies—just babies.

The average writer for the *New Yorker* marries only sporadically and leaves few hostages to fortune. Indeed, the latest statistics show that there is something less than one-third of one per cent of child per contributor, which leaves the sheet trailing somewhat behind the recorded fertility of old Bostonians and graduates of Vassar.

Imagine, then, my surprise at finding the leading item in a recent issue to be a purported transcript of a free verse poem made up entirely out of the head of a four-year-old boy. The mood of rebellion against parental authority is familiar enough and undoubtedly authentic. But I strongly suspect that the child's original chant has been vastly touched up by the doting mother—a literary lady, I assume—before she made a fair copy and sent it to the editor. Of course, it may be that the infant in question is a prodigy or that he has been brought up wholly on "leaves of grass" instead of spinach.

However, I ask leave to offer in evidence the first half of the poem as Exhibit A:

> He will just do nothing at all.
> He will just sit there in the noonday sun.
> And when they speak to him he will not answer them.
> Because he does not care to.
> He will stick them with spears and put them in the garbage.
> When they tell him to eat his dinner he will just laugh at them.
> And he will not take his nap, because he does not care to.
> He will not talk to them; he will not say nothing.
> He will just sit there in the noonday sun.

Upon this evidence I will rest my case that the *New Yorker* has been hornswoggled and done to a turn. One of the great giveaways is the sudden introduction of the double negative in the eighth line. Up to that point, young Walt Whitman has been grammatical to the point of prissiness. You get "will not" instead of "won't" and "does not" instead of "doesn't" or the much more natural "don't."

Moreover, "sitting in the noonday sun" is decidedly a literary phrase, even though it did once appear in the lyric of a popular song called *Lazy Bones*. And here the error is not only one of expression but even more tragically and fundamentally a misconception of the behavior pattern of male infants. There is no rebellion in the announcement of a desire to sit in the sun and do nothing at all. Any parent on the face of God's green footstool would gladly compromise with a child on that sort of conduct.

When a four-year-old child wants to sit quietly and do nothing the time has come to call the family physician. At that age he wants to beat his blame drum, eat popcorn, stick pebbles up his nose or ask fool questions. Children are not escapists. Never does a boy pine to live in an ivory tower until he gets old enough to be a *New Yorker* editor.

And before the magazine prints any other bright sayings of tiny tots I think it will be well advised first to submit the material to Papa Dionne or the old lady from Dubuque for comment and criticism.

169. A WOMAN'S JOB

There is logic in the fact that the same women who fought for the vote are now defending their sex against job discrimination. And I think that Carrie Chapman Catt was quite correct in her assertion that any move to make the home compulsory would be a step toward Fascism. The notion that unemployment would be largely removed by eliminating all married women from work is a fallacy in the first place. In a vast majority of cases the combined salary of husband and wife is just about enough to provide a decent home. Barriers of any kind against the wife in business would actually constitute an effort to lower the living standards of our country. But even more important than the economic factor is the spiritual one.

Surely there is no sanity in trying to make the honorable state of marriage a handicap, if not a disgrace, for the lady involved. In perpetuating itself the race will be wise to encourage the best and the brightest women to reproduce themselves. And if there were a rule that no woman could have both a husband and a job I gravely fear that many men would get some terrific turndowns. It seems to me that the woman who knows how to run an office is the very person with more than an average chance to succeed in the still more difficult task of running a home.

Some of the familiar objections to the dual role of wife and worker are less pertinent than they were once upon a time, and if our civilization is to be arranged upon intelligent lines the argument that marriage should include a resignation from each wife and mother will grow even weaker. I mean, of course, that labor-saving devices should literally be a means to shorten the working day and halve the toil of the producers rather than demons of destruction which put millions on relief or breadlines.

Of course, I will agree that a good mother should have close contact with her children, but that does not mean that her association with her brood should be on a 24-hour time shift. The most likely children whom I've seen lately are those who get enough time with the mother to think of her as a grand person without entering into that field of diminishing returns which must afflict anybody who is handy and on call every second of the day.

To put it bluntly, I think a mother can become, through no fault of her own, a bore as well as a blessing. There comes a time, particularly during the summer, in which even the best little woman in the world begins to scream at Eric and Patricia and maybe Eloise and Tony. And that isn't good for either the screamer or the screamed at.

My own mother didn't have a job, but she was a great gad-about, and it was a treat to us boys half a century ago when she turned up in the home. She would bring exciting stories about what she did in the woman's suffrage parade or give us as much fill-in as she thought discreet about the high jinks at the Café Martin.

We thought she was a grand and exciting person, and now that a number of years have passed we still think so. My mother had sense enough not to wear out her welcome in the nursery. The fact that at times we knew her only as a sort of week-end guest made her all the more glamorous.

If by any chance she sees this column she will probably write an indignant letter to the paper, in which she will assert that, as usual, I am romancing. But I will continue to be right, and I think that Mrs. Heywood Cox Broun should agree with me in principle as she certainly did in practice.

The ideal mother is a woman who is also expert at some other occupation. She should not be under the feet of her family. A brood does best when it is directed from the top and not the bottom of the living scale.

170. NOT IN THIS ISSUE

I have received a number of letters and a few have been printed elsewhere in which I am asked to write an explanation of the reasons why I have become a Catholic. I have no intention of complying in this issue.

In part it is my feeling that no man should discuss those things which are closest to him without taking great care to express himself as well as his best potentialities permit. And again I bridle, for the moment at least, because most of the missives appear to come from those who seem quite ready to condemn with an answer or without. Indeed they seem to ask not so much a statement of belief as an immediate apology.

Very many begin, "Of course a man's religion is his own business, but—" And the conjunction is used as a dull blunt instrument with which to club me on the head.

As I understand it, I must answer on call because I am "a public figure." That description seems to me a little strained and stretched. I have passed no civil service test nor received any position of trust through the mandate of the people.

It is true that up till now I have written a vast number of words on various subjects in various places and that for the most part they have been set down in haste. But surely the world would hardly suffer if I wrote much less and weighed my thoughts and emotions with a greater deliberation.

It is a little illogical for the same correspondent to complain that all newspaper columnists are too ready to be dogmatic on the international situation and at the same time demand that one of the most slapdash commentators of the crowd should forthwith put in type his own most intimate feelings about Catholicism and the cosmos.

And so I will not do it now. Some morning there will come to me a feeling that the time has come and the words will spring up in such a way that what I want to say will be done with some measure of eloquence and dignity. A merely peevish answer to a peevish communication would be of little service. I did not make any impulsive decision. I will not make any impulsive answer.

But aside from the question of religion, I would like to discuss and defend the newspaper columnist from the responsibility of having to assume the burden of being "a public figure." If he is so regarded, it cannot be denied that the fault is in part his own. For instance, I would be compelled to admit that I have been snapped in almost as many preposterous poses as the late President Calvin Coolidge. But here at least I can put in some measure of defense.

The fact does not rest wholly on my being rapacious about publicity, and some of the pictures themselves should be convincing evidence that I do not stand hitched for cameramen out of any personal vanity. All news photographers, whether they work for weeklies or dailies, proceed upon the principle of Joseph in Egypt and store away in the granaries more negatives than can conceivably be called for under the present demand.

This goes for the great, of course, the near great and also for persons of no importance. There used to be a rule that newspapers never mentioned newspapermen. One of the first rules of journalism which was dinned into me was, "Don't write about yourself or the other reporters. Who cares?"

That principle has fallen into some disrespect, and columnists in particular sometimes fill up their space by taking in each others' washing and particularly the dirty linen.

But even today the cameramen appreciate the fact that no-body would stop the presses on the New York *News* if a photographer rushed in to say, "I've got a swell shot of the head of Walter Winchell." It would have to be on a pike or a platter before the managing editor could be expected to display much interest.

And yet somewhat after the manner in which big leaguers take batting practice before a ball game, the cameramen will click at almost anybody in those intervals before the siege guns come into action. My own photograph has been snapped at public gatherings at least one thousand times and about one-tenth of one per cent of these have been used. If there ever is any occasion, some person with a savage turn of mind goes to the art department and snatches out the most punishing profile which can be found.

Still, I have nothing against cameramen, and since most of the best ones are members of the American Newspaper Guild, I would cut a pretty silly figure if I ever said, "Men, please stand back and do not annoy me with your flashlight bulbs. They make me nervous and today I will consent to no photography."

As a matter of fact, flashlight bulbs don't make me nervous. Often they are a most convenient aid to an orator. Every now and then a bulb explodes and scatters the speaker of the evening with glass, which is enough to assure him of one good hearty laugh and burst of applause during his address.

But aside from pictorial representation in the press the average columnist does mention himself on many occasions. He is nothing if not autobiographical. And, of course, he may be both.

But it should be remembered that these snatches of home life and little visits for a restricted number of tourists to the secret springs of the columnist's heart and mind are largely fictional in content and intention. The author of a daily stint may choose to paint himself as a craven or a crusader according to his necessities as a writing man. Although as dry in his own habits as Mr. Bryan, he may find copy in the pretense that he is a Falstaffian swaggerer.

To be sure if he is a reasonably honest man, and that goes for practically all columnists, he does not intentionally bear false witness against his neighbors. He draws a long bow in discussing the incidents of his own life, and even this does not give him license to applaud the things he hates or speak with anything less than fervor of his faith.

But under the obligation of a daily or a weekly deadline it is not always easy to put down with simple dignity your feelings about something which is dear to you. And so neither now nor possibly at any time have I an intention of discussing my own relation to my church in the hurly-burly of the *New Republic* under the standing head of Shoot the Works.

171. MORAL RE-ARMAMENT

SAN FRANCISCO, Aug. 9 [1939].—I'm up to my neck in Moral Re-Armament. Dr. Buchman himself and hundreds of his followers buzz about the hotel lobby. All the young men look precisely like Bunny Austin, and the outsider has a fear and a foreboding that the whole lot may suddenly appear in shorts and begin to volley. The Oxford accent is extremely thick, and it is difficult to get past the desk without a punt or a canoe. I must admit that the sight of the dedicated young men has no way improved my own morals. On the contrary, I am much tempted to rush out and do something horrendous to make my protest against the smuggest aggregation with which I've ever come into casual contact.

Of course, it would be an excellent thing if all the peoples of the world were to become men and women of good will. I would be for spiritual and religious revival, but it is a little tough to take morals from men who wear them across their stomachs like gold watch chains. I am for the good and true in this world, but do they need to clank as they pass by with the feeble tinkle of fabricated cymbals? It will do the world good to get on its knees and pray, but these prayers should not be addressed to pompous men whose only claim to divinity is that they happen to be well-heeled in financial or business positions.

Down in Los Angeles they told me a story about a prominent motion picture producer. He has gone in for Moral Re-Armament. Indeed, he made a speech in which he said that his company had been haggling for weeks with a famous screen star about the renewal of her contract. "And then," he said, "both of us suddenly went into Moral Re-Armament and the contract was signed within five minutes." I'll warrant the arrangement was not altogether to the advantage of the young lady in question.

A young man went up to the show window of the M.R.A. group here in the hotel and said, "I have a wife and two children. I get $18 a week. We can hardly survive on this. Is there anything in Moral Re-Armament which would help me?" And the bright and beaming young man at the window answered, "If you join M.R.A. you will be much better off, because you will cease to worry."

As I see it, the whole fantastic enterprise is an endeavor to prove that a camel can pass through the eye of a needle if only he is sufficiently buttered. And heaven knows the oil of sanctity and the grease of phony pretension flow through the hotel lobby with all the volume of the waters which run in past the Golden Gate.

It seems to me that essentially M.R.A. is attempting to re-write the famous story of a certain rich young man who went to a great Teacher almost two thousand years ago. Dr. Buchman's precept seems to be that the poor should give their goods to the rich and let them be administered by the benevolent.

I have a certain amount of respect for various aberrant forms of spiritual enthusiasm, even when the fervor leads to absurd and curious antics. But I prefer to take my Holy Rollers straight rather than in the streamline form which has been set by the Oxford Movement. The adage that confession is good for the soul has been accepted by men and women of various beliefs, and there may be a certain profit in self-criticism, even aside from the religious angle. And yet I cannot be convinced that the house party method of the Buchmanites, in which experiences are swapped within the group, can be a healthful process.

Every starry-eyed young man I see about the lobby seems intent upon finding six or seven others so that he may say, "And now let me tell you all that happened to me." Certainly there must be some line between confession and sheer exhibitionism. The flanneled fervents seem ready to tell all at the drop of Dr. Buchman's right eyebrow. They can tell me nothing. I know what it's all about. This is just a slick device to corrupt and undermine the labor movement.

172. THE SUBVERSIVE PRIMITIVE

A formidable lady in San Francisco is leading a fight for what she chooses to call "Sanity in Art." The Hearst papers are helping her. Now they have brought the gospel here. When mixed with red-baiting cartoons and an anti-labor editorial one of these ukases to painters can give a page quite a Goebbels look.

By some process of mind which is difficult to follow the lady in San Francisco seems to labor under the impression that unless art is photographic it must be subversive. Indeed, I rather imagine that she would like to bring back the studio picture of Grandpa with the pink cheeks which used to hang on the wall of the parlor. You could tell it was Grandpa by the earspread alone. Just why an experimental canvas or a photograph definitely and purposely out of focus should be taken as an indication of economic or political aberration I have never been able to understand. Hitler has held that modernism is treachery to the state, but in Italy the artist may still put a wild oat in the foreground. To me there is no connection between Marxism and Matisse. Indeed, a professional friend of mine paints purple cows and votes the straight Republican ticket.

On a recent Hearst editorial page an article against modern art was twinned with an attack on Harry Bridges, although Mr. Bridges, as it happens, greatly admires the work of Maxfield Parrish and likes Landseer. And the explanatory article makes things no clearer as far as I can see. "It is a noteworthy fact," the editorial in question says, "that all children love to draw and paint and that as they learn to observe and better handle their tools their drawings tend to acquire precision and objectivity, to correspond with natural shapes, forms and arrangements."

It seems to me unfair for Mr. Hearst to demand objectivity from painters, since he does not always require it from his editorial commentators. But let us allow the enemy of modern art to continue upon his impartial way.

"The so-called modern school of painting," he says, "proceeds in the opposite direction until we see adult and presumably skillful 'artists' carefully cultivating infantilism. In other words, instead of cultivating maturity of thought and workmanship they go back to the meaningless and fantastic scribbling of fumbling babies."

I think the gentleman who writes in this manner should go back to the galleries of the world, and even more particularly to the great cathedrals, for there, if he has eyes to see, he may observe both in sculpture and painting much that is primitive and lovely.

The lady in San Francisco will never live to see an adequate literal representation of God set down in any mural. It has been said that we shall not enter the Kingdom of Heaven unless we become as little children. I rather think that the same spiritual truth obtains in the kingdom of art.

Mr. Hearst's authority on art is misinformed in his contention that the juvenile painter invariably improves with practice and instruction. Very often the reverse is true. A child may get extraordinary effects through the very fact that he is ignorant of technical problems and therefore unafraid. Many an academician should go back to his earliest adventures with pigment, and I believe that there are those who might well say, "At ten I had something which now eludes me."

The critic who espouses sanity in art speaks contemptuously of "the hasty smears from a child's brush" and assails grown-ups who exhibit and sell work done in primitive tradition. Such painters, he says, are obtaining money under false pretenses, and the editorial ends with the startling suggestion, "They should be prosecuted like anyone else who commits that offense."

And so one of the great champions of "free press" now commits himself to the Hitler theory that art should be regulated. And in concentration camps we may find prisoners whose sole offense is the fact that a tree trunk may seem to them a bright magenta.

173. SARATOGA FADES

"There's nothing turning tonight," said the man. "Tomorrow, maybe. And maybe not."

The latter seems the more likely selection. Chips cease to fall on Saratoga. And very much I fear this is no passing frost but the beginning of the Ice Age and the coming of the long, dark night.

Certainly the twilight of gambling is upon us. Naturally, I'm not counting horse racing, because that is something you do in the daytime. As a belated Victorian with a strong sense of proprieties, I regret the passing of the green baize era. Man was not at his noblest when he sat and watched an ivory ball go popping past his numbers. He might easily have been engaged in pursuits of a more worthy nature. But I ask the reformers, man to man, whether the world is really any better for their efforts. Sweetness and light have not rushed in to fill the void created by the frustration of the gambling instinct.

The sucker snarls when anybody steps in to save him from the loss of money. He knows of things more valuable than the dross within his pocket. He would rather have the friendly "Hello!" once accorded him than be condemned to a thriftiness to which he is not accustomed.

The wolves of the gambling casinos howl dismally at night in Saratoga because they are forbidden to fleece their victims. But the sheep themselves are even more mournful and morose because they may not bare their throats to the friendly fangs of the predatory. Hell hath no fury like that of an unshorn lamb.

The goose that laid the golden egg is by no means dead, but she is so discouraged that she has quit production. Eggs of that sort were meant to squander. For hatching they are no better than a door knob.

Insiders say the present situation is a local issue, but they are very much mistaken. The tides of the age have set against them. An angry and cruel asceticism begins to befog the world. It is no mere accident that Adolf Hitler neither drinks nor spins. In the materialistic setup of the Fascists there is no room for the dreamer who lives to take a fling at hitting numbers on the nose. The man under such a machine is ever at attention from the moment a gun is first put into his chubby hands until he marches to the grave. Show me a community or a country where all the minor vices are discouraged and I will show you one bereft of major virtues.

Naturally, when I speak in kindly fashion about gambling I mean gambling in moderation. They tell me the thing can be overdone. Years ago in Mexico I frequented a casino which opened at noon and did not close its doors until the following dawn. Such a schedule may be excessive, although at the time I did not find the hours taxing.

However, not even the most ardent advocate of an open Saratoga is asking for anything like that. It is generally agreed that in the morning everybody should take the waters. But unless relief of some sort comes I shudder to think of the fate of this fair village. Not only grass but giant redwoods will grow in the streets if the lid is a permanent adjustment. To be sure, the town will still have its excellent mineral waters, but no man ever beat a path through the trackless forest merely to get a better bath. There is a tonic in gambling which far surpasses the power of any medicinal spring, no matter how frequently its product bubbles.

When first I came to Saratoga I used to observe with envy the clear eyes and brisk tread of all those who passed by. And naturally I assumed that these were the result of clean living and sparkling water. Later I discovered, among the bright-eyed, many who had not been to bed at all, but had, instead, refreshed themselves by sitting up all night at some one of the casinos. In a wrestling match with chance even the loser comes away all rosy and limber as a result of his exertions.

Clean living is the order of the day in Saratoga right now, and the tread of the natives isn't the least bit springy. The townsfolk are full of acid. Only at the peril of your life is it possible to ask a taxi driver, "How is business?"

Joy does not rule supreme. In fact, it's hardly worth a bet for place. Zero has come up for Saratoga.

174. TO SAVE A FACE

It has been said by some defenders of Adolf Hitler, "He had to save his face." And this same excuse has been put forward by other war lords who plunged the world into misery and bloodshed. "I have to save my face." Occasionally the phrase is changed to read, "This is a matter of national honor, which cannot be discussed."

But what is this face which has launched the greater part of Europe into the lunacy of slaughter? It is the strangely drawn face of a man possessed by the devils of delusion. Before the world he identified himself as "the first soldier of the Reich." But he is not the last. To save the face of Hitler millions must die, be maimed and mutilated. Bodies will be dismembered to the end that one single individual may lie down at night wrapped in his pride.

In all warlike addresses Hitler takes pains to stress his own personal bravery. "I am putting on the uniform, and I shall take it off only in victory or death. Just as I fought in the last war, so I will fight now." In other words, "I'll win or die," says Hitler. And so, apparently, he thinks of himself not only as a tribal leader but as a tribal god. Wotan is himself again, and in Valhalla the bearded warriors drink deep from the skulls of slain heroes. But this is the legend of mythology and not the fact of modern conflict.

In the great halls of the dead there pass today not the huge flagons fashioned out of the bone of men of iron but chalices more slight and small. Pause, Adolf, Wotan, Thor and all the rest, before you sip! That fragile cup which passes among you was once a child. German, perhaps, or Polish, French or English. What does it matter now?

Drink deep if you will, and yet you cannot bring back the laughter which is gone. Even the shouted cadences of the Germanic gods cannot still the cries of terror and agony from those whose blithe spirits are such as the Kingdom of Heaven. When Herr Hitler put on the uniform he added accouterments not provided for in the regulations. He is weighted down by more than the Iron Cross. He has hung a millstone around his neck. "He had to save his face."

When Hitler became the first soldier of the Reich he commanded into conflict not only the youth of Germany but the young men of Poland, of England and France. And from play he called the children of a score of great thriving cities. They, too, are soldiers of the front line. Put down your toys, my baby, and put your gas mask on.

Adolf Hitler is first soldier only in the sense that he gave the marching orders. Beside him stand the generations of the past, today and of the years to come. Some little girl in Warsaw who is two or three years old runs the same risk as the gallant Fuehrer who is prepared to win or die. For this plunger who spreads his chips upon the table as the wheel spins does not move colored counters from one space to another but scatters about, upon the red and black, the hopes and ideals and aspirations of mankind. Indeed, like one of Pilate's Roman soldiers, he gambles for the sundered garments of Jesus Christ.

"He had to save his face." There is no seed which flowers as fast as sin. Dragon's teeth never fall on stony ground. Out of the blinding hatred of one man will rise the brutal, unreasoning anger of millions. In the beginning it will be said, "We have no quarrel with the German people." But soon inoffensive individuals will be harried in many lands.

Let us pray for deliverance. Let us war against unreason. And let us not forget in the dark hours that there will be again a resurrection. Even for Hitler there should be pity. "He had to save his face." Perhaps he will, but at a price which should stagger him in his secret heart. He is gambling for stakes far greater than those which he has mentioned. To save his face he has risked his immortal soul.

175. THE MASTER WORKMAN

"Could I have a mousetrap, please?" I asked. The old gentleman who was fussing around with a couple of wires and a hammer did not put his tools down upon the instant. This gave me a chance to wipe the blood off my face, which had been rather badly cut by the thorns and brambles of the wilderness.

The master workman adjusted his specs and said, "I guess you found it rather heavy going getting here to my little place."

"Yes," I answered, "I must have lost the path. There wasn't any sign of a road at all. I just had to hack my way through."

"Path," chuckled the skilled artist mirthlessly; "there isn't even a cow track."

Naturally I was surprised, and instinctively I quoted from Emerson, or whoever said it, "If a man can make a better mousetrap the world will beat a pathway to his door, even though it lie in the trackless forest"—or words to that effect.

My friend was not amused. "It's stuff and nonsense," he told me. "You're the first customer who's been here in ten years. In fact, I don't want 'em any more. They interfere with my work."

"But," I objected, "that is a mousetrap that you're making, isn't it?"

He fondled the model lovingly and answered, "It is, indeed. That's the finest mousetrap in the world. It's the best one I ever made. When I was a young man I couldn't do half so good. They keep getting better. I change the specifications every day.

That's what keeps me young. In the beginning I made only a pretty good mousetrap. This one is sheer genius."

"Maybe," I suggested, "it was your lesser mousetraps that the public wanted. Perhaps fifty years ago they beat a pathway to your door."

This time he fairly snorted with petulance. "I told you once already, stranger, that the pathway thing is just a lie. I've been a hermit all my life. Mousetraps don't sell on merit. If you want to sell mousetraps you've got to buy machines to make 'em. You can't pay any attention to the product yourself. To be a tycoon in the mousetrap field you've got to sit outside the tent and beat a drum and think up advertising slogans such as 'The Pied Piper was a sucker; he didn't have a Malcolm. It satisfies everybody but the mouse.' And then you've got to take newspaper advertising and go on the air with a jazz band, a blues singer and two comics. I hate radio and jazz and comics. I like mousetraps. That's why I never sell any."

He took the model on which he was working and placed it on the floor near the window. For the first time I noticed that every strand of wire was of a different color.

"Look," said the old man. "See how the sun plays on it. That might be a rainbow. It's better than a rainbow, because I know more about mixing colors. And look at the shape of it—round as a hill and just as much alive as any river."

"But in a cellar," I protested, "there isn't much sunlight. And maybe the mice don't care about the architectural perfection. It's the cheese they're after."

"Sure," he said, "it's just the same with mice and men. They want the golden stuff which satisfies the belly. My traps are made for the satisfaction of my soul."

This time I proffered money. After such an arduous trip I didn't want to go home empty-handed. But he shook his head.

"My traps are not for sale," he explained. "I make them for posterity. If a man makes a better mousetrap the world will stay away from his door in droves, but they will beat a pathway to his grave. After I'm gone these traps of mine will stand as ornaments on every mantel. I don't want to hurry you, young fellow, but the generations yet unborn become impatient. I must get on with my work. Tomorrow I may make an even better mousetrap."

When I picked up my hat I found that the felt was full of minute punctures. The brim was riddled.

"Really," I exclaimed, "I had no idea the thorns and brambles were quite as thick as all that in the forest."

This time he laughed in high good humor. "Not brambles or thorns," he said. "Them's mice, stranger. The house is full of 'em. They're my audience. They're the ones that have beat the pathway to my door through the trackless forest. They take things on faith without listening to the radio, and that's why I sit all day and build 'em little palaces."

176. NO ERSATZ FOR DEMOCRACY

During one of the blackest weeks in the last war, which was once called the great war, a bunch of American newspapermen were sitting in the parlor of the Hotel Providence in Neufchâteau. At the moment the Germans were sweeping everything before them. The submarine campaign threatened to starve out Great Britain. Success was with the arms of the Reich on every front. And, more than that, Allied morale was beginning to crack. Poilus in Paris sat in cafés and said in loud voices that further slaughter was useless and that they would not return when leave was up. American newspapers were snarling at the administration, and English journals were in full-throated revolt against the current leadership.

In Germany everything seemed serene. No dissenting voices were raised. And one of the men from a New York paper spoke up between drinks and said, "Now, fellows, get me right. You know I'm as much against this regimented stuff as anybody here. But let's be sensible. Our side is licked. Maybe the top men beat 'em over the head to get it, but there's no point in denying that the Germans have achieved complete unity. We haven't. A lot of us have been down to the British front and watched the way the Australians first-name their generals and refuse to salute their colonels. And can you imagine the Germans having a paper run by enlisted men like the *Stars and Stripes*, which even dares to kid Pershing? I'm all for that, but it just doesn't work. Every time you shut the Germans off from something they find an ersatz which is just as good. I like democracy. That's the way I was brought up, but I'm afraid the Germans have found an ersatz for that, too. Much as I hate to say it, I'm afraid that destiny is in their favor. I won't like it, but right now it seems to me that it's in the cards that Germany is going to rule the world."

A small man in the corner from an obscure paper in the Middle West said, "Let's wait a little while. I think there's something wrong in the German system. I don't think there is any ersatz for democracy."

And within the month it happened. I don't think anybody has ever put sufficient stress upon the miracle which occurred. The tide wasn't really swung wholly by the marines at Château-Thierry or by the entire impulse of American participation, important as that factor undoubtedly was. To some extent the American army came through in full strength about the time that Russia withdrew from Allied participation. In a measure, at least, these two factors counteracted each other.

The German divisions from the east came roaring back to the western front full of pep and power. And in their last swirling, clashing drive they almost broke through to the Channel. But overnight something smashed. It was not so much on the front as back home. It wasn't starvation, and I don't think it was the result of outside propaganda. But within twenty-four hours the German people sickened of having their thinking done for them. Men and women who had long been forbidden to say certain things or even think certain thoughts became articulate as if the gift of tongues had been conferred upon them. It can and will happen again. Suppression carried on too long breeds a counter-movement.

And so it will be again in the case of the Siegfried line. My belief is that France and Great Britain will be foolish to fling their young men against the concrete. Let them remember that when Siegfried was bathed in the magic stream of invulnerability he was not totally immersed. A spot remained between his shoulder blades untouched by the magic stream. It was the back door to his heart. And, sooner or later, those who bow down to Hitler not only as leader but as veritable god of the Reich will awake to a new concept and cry out, "Whatever are we fighting for?"

German men and women are really just like other human beings. They will shake themselves and fly out, far out, of the axis of regimentation. And no barrier or bomb or gun can stand against the nascent cry of "Before all else I am a human being."

177. NOT ALL THE LEOPARDS

Many things undoubtedly have been changed by the pact between Russia and the Reich. The whole course of world history may be affected. Hitler and Stalin may fight over the remains of Europe or divide it up in friendly fashion. There could be a common ideology between the dictators, although it is an exaggeration to say that already the difference exists in catchwords alone.

The chances of change both in physical fact and in world philosophy as well are profound. But I think it is unwise to be too cocksure about the result of Stalin's strategy, or lack of it, until there has been time for digestion. And though the current of history seems to have shifted for the worse, in my estimation, there remain in America some not very good eddies which retain their original character.

I am a little startled to find that Westbrook Pegler is under the impression that he had some sort of beat upon the matter. From his present chortling, one might think that he was the one to deliver Lepke to the G-men. I think it will be premature if the public follows his coy suggestion and immediately awards a halo to him. There are still some marked differences between the author of Fair Enough and the Little Flower.

Nor do I understand at all by what process Stalin's diplomacy has suddenly justified the assertion of Ben Stolberg that he, Benjamin, is a friend of labor. To my mind Fish remains Ham and John Nance Garner is still an old man with one foot in Uvalde.

Most curious of all is the drive of the celebrants who insist that now is the time to smash labor unions in America. There are those who set up finks and strikebreakers as brave men whose whole motivation was to thwart the move for appeasement between Berlin and Moscow.

I see things from precisely the opposite angle. Those who feel that fascism has been strengthened by Soviet action should fight all the harder for the maintenance and extension of democracy in America. Surely no logical answer will be made to the Russian action by those who insist that there should now be a non-aggression pact, if not a military alliance, between liberals and Herbert Hoover. Nothing has happened that in any way touches the gospel of trade unionism and the case for the New Deal is strengthened rather than weakened because it will be even sillier now than it was before to shout that Roosevelt is the conscious or unconscious agent of Communism.

Leaders of the left wing have laid themselves open to criticism because of the futility of the explanatory matter which they have put forth in regard to the pact. It is possible that a case can be made for Russia's choice of partners, but surely no coherent one is being set forth.

For all that, American Communists should not be denied the credit which is due to them for the effective work which they did in the case of Mooney, the Scottsboro defendants and in many other instances of legal injustice. And again I think that even the sharpest critic in the liberal and progressive ranks ought to admit that American Communists have done much to wake the public conscience to the facts of unemployment, the plight of sharecroppers and other defects in the functioning of our democracy.

No one need blush or apologize if he has willingly and eagerly been on the same side as radicals in causes which were just. Some absurd formulas might be drawn if the rule were to prevail that a liberal must choose his side in every public question by merely saying that he is against anything the Communists favor regardless of the merits of the controversy. Such a procedure would reduce the progressive to the estate of the fanatic who insisted that he wished to contract a venereal disease because he understood it was being fought editorially by the Chicago *Tribune*.

And it is well to remember that radical thought neither began nor ends with Josef Stalin. There is nothing novel in suggesting that now is an excellent time for us to look into the progressive and radical roots which are part of our own heritage. The weakness of Communism has always been in its basic dependence upon leadship which was far away and unfamiliar with American conditions.

The tie between left-wingers here and the authorities in Russia was probably pretty thin as far as detail went. Much was done here without any consultation whatsoever. But a tether rope remained and the sudden shift in the line as reflected in the pact must have come with an unexpected jerk to native party leaders. Their very floundering seems to show that they were neither tipped off in advance nor consulted as to what effect the move would have upon progressive and radical opinion here.

Earl Browder has testified that party members are subject to expulsion if they criticize this diplomatic coup of the Soviet Republic. Apparently American Communists are doing their gulping, if any, behind closed doors and officially putting as good a face as possible upon the matter. Defections, however, are rampant among so-called sympathizers. But the net result of this split may be very disappointing to the chortlers. For three or four years anybody, of a conservative trend, whose play or book or poem was criticized attributed the bad notices to "the malice of the fellow travelers."

There were some who held that Stalin received a clip sheet of the newspapers and magazines of the United States at least once a week and maybe every morning. And, according to the legend, he would look these over and call up party headquarters in New York with specific instructions as to which books and comedies and musicals were to be praised and which condemned by his agents in Manhattan.

For instance, Mr. Stalin might say, "Morrie Ryskind had a piece in the *Nation* last week which I found most objectionable. Please see that he gets a smearing at the hands of all the fellow-traveling critics."

I am of the opinion that the legend may now evaporate. George Kaufman once told the story of a man who was socially unpopular and very unhappy about it. When his best friends told him he had dandruff he was delighted. He felt that this fact explained everything. Purchasing the proper remedy he soon cured the dandruff, but to his horror he was just as unpopular as ever.

And it is my notion that even though Stalin has signed a pact with Hitler, many of the Red-baiters have the same spiritual dandruff as afflicted them before. Not all the leopards have changed their spots.

178. THE CHAMPION

Joe Louis, it seems to me, excels all other fighters in something which is only incidentally connected with his pugilistic practice. He makes the best after-the-battle remarks into the microphone.

Some have insisted that the champion is not quick-witted. He certainly belies this charge when hauled up suddenly after a grueling fight and asked to say a few words to the invisible audience.

Such things cannot be rehearsed unless the boxer chooses to use some stencil such as, "Hello, Mom; put on the pork chops." But I have never heard Joe pull a phony.

I am among the many who find it desperate work to speak over the air even at such times as I hold a script studded with brilliant remarks of my own culled out of old columns. The idea of first absorbing a few punches and then taking on a national hookup seems to me one of the most exacting ordeals which could be placed on any man. But the co-ordination of the Brown Bomber extends to casual conversation as well as right-hand hooks.

The announcer at the mike never is able to throw him off balance. And I must say that often the queries almost seem like traps for the unwary. The victor in a prize fight is tempted to exult and chortle over his rival's discomfiture.

Not so Joe Louis. He keeps his guard up while talking and invariably reports that his opponent, who at the moment is being carried out of the ring, gave him a desperate battle. Generally the next jab of the announcer is to ask, "Did he hurt you at any time during the fight, Joe?"

Now, there are plenty of pugilists who will fall for that one and make some ungracious answer, such as, "That bum! Why, he couldn't even rumple my hair."

Louis handles it with the keen force of implication and understatement. After the Pastor fight his answer ran, "Well, I knew he'd been hitting me."

Detroit, to my mind, marked an actual triumph for the champion, because I think it was the first occasion on which he ever coined an epigram. During the bout we had heard, as usual, a great deal about the dead pan of the champion. During a flurry of blows the radio audience was informed, "Out of all the 45,000 people here Joe Louis seemed the calmest of the lot."

So when it was all over and the fighter had come over right after the knockout to be interviewed the inevitable question was proffered, "Joe, were you worried at all at any time during the fight?"

Louis didn't have to think long on that one. He said, "It's nice to be champion, and so you're always worried."

That, I submit, is authentically an epigram. "Uneasy lies the head which wears the crown" is much less colorful. In fact, I think the remark was self-revelatory. I imagine that a tolerably erroneous picture of this particular fighting man has been built up by the sports commentators. Too much has been made of the dead pan. The fact that it is merely a ring accessory has been ignored. Joe wears it as he would a rubber mouthpiece.

A lack of expression can be a kind of camouflage. The so-called dead pan may conceal the fact that the last body punch the other fellow landed was really agonizing.

Most fighters play it in reverse. Thus when anybody all but swept the block off Maxie Baer he would break into a wide grin in an effort to convey the impression that he was not hurt at all.

Joe Louis plays it more mysteriously by neither glaring nor grinning while the fight is on. There is no facial indication as to his feelings or his intentions. Baer often telegraphed his right-hand punch by feinting with his eyebrows. But nobody can tell by looking into the eyes of Louis whether he is about to give ground, jab or lash out with full power.

And yet I'm sure he spoke accurately. The fires go on under the crater crust. A man incapable of worry would be incapable of ever becoming a champion. The prince in the fairy tale found that out. In order to amount to anything a man must learn how to shiver and shake and still keep coming in.

179. THERE IS NO HIDING PLACE

"Senator Borah," says an editorial in the Hearst papers, "reveals his own strict neutrality, both as an eminent member of the Senate and as the ranking member of the Senate Foreign Relations Committee, by not mentioning by name the combatants in the European war."

This, I agree, is the ultimate in isolation. Indeed, it goes all the way back to an ancient tribal taboo under which even the names of individuals were secret lest they fall into the clutches of evil spirits. But no harm could come to Tom or Dick or Harry if the demons had no identifying tag around which they might weave a spell. If there were safety in such a retreat from reality, it would, without question, constitute a magnificent way of life. Death itself could not prevail if its existence might be obliterated by never mentioning it even in whispers. And here would be the sure way to abolish poverty, disease, fear and every other misery known to man. In passing a graveyard the practitioner of this magic would either refer to the place as a conservatory or keep silent. And possibly even the pauper would feel no belly pains if he could only stuff his ears against the sound of words such as "breakfast," "dinner" or "a crust of bread."

We might even pretend that Hitler and the guns and bombers over Europe are all part of some nightmare not worth discussion among the wakeful. Keep a stiff upper lip and pinch yourself and Fascism will fly out the window.

To be sure, this theory was given quite a workout for a number of years in the matter of venereal disease. Nice people never mentioned the maladies. Newspapers co-operated in cutting out all shocking words and gave no space to any stories of the situation in hospitals and homes. Unfortunately, syphilis and gonorrhea did not disappear when sent to Coventry.

And I very much fear that the canker of conflict cannot be cured by the device of pretending that here in America its echoes are quite inaudible.

Only the other day I was rereading *Lost Horizon*, and one episode in Mr. Hilton's book had a prophetic quality. I can't remember whether it was included in the motion picture version. You may remember that the head of the monastery was an ancient who had managed to add centuries to his life by an ability to withdraw not only from the world but actually from consciousness during trancelike periods in which there came to his muted senses not even so much as the ticking of a clock. And he urged the hero to follow in his steps. His argument was based upon the fact that the world outside was about to destroy itself and that there should be a small corner of the earth where civilization might be preserved as if in a vacuum. Ideals might be kept alive within that small valley protected by its giant mountains and in a kingdom whose existence was unknown.

It was a romantic conceit. It is a story; there really is no such land and no such valley. The author quite frankly put his tale forward as a fantasy. It would be nice, and all of us, I imagine, might like it very well to dwell with Senator Borah in a big apartment at No. 277 Linden Avenue, Shangri-la, somewhere in Tibet. But there is a man called Hitler. There is a Nazi nation. There is a Russian bear that has stepped beyond his borders—for what purpose time will tell.

It is not a dream that bombs fall from the sky and kill and blister. Buildings burn. Women mourn. It is expedient that we pray and work for peace here at home. It will be well, if it lies within our power, to call the nations out of conflict.

But we will be useless even to our own interests if we close our eyes and pretend our world ends at the misty line where some wooded American hill keeps its rendezvous with the sky. That is not the end of the world or the end of the road. There are sounds louder than the ticking of the clock. Time and space cannot be discarded, nor can we throw off the circumstances that we are citizens of the world. The blood of one is the blood of all. Our Lord dies once again.

180. SIGMUND FREUD

Sigmund Freud, the disturber of dreams, died in a nightmare world and has been gathered back to the father image. He has gone, I believe, to the heart of a dark continent whose fringes he explored. And yet if he never traveled more than half a day's journey across the divide which separates sleep from waking he remains a pioneer. Not since Orpheus has any mortal come closer to the secret springs.

And I imagine it will be as artist and philosopher rather than as physician that the little Viennese will be remembered. He suffered too much from a sort of Sherlock Holmes complex to be numbered among the scientists. Like the fictional detective, he would take a less than conclusive clew and say dogmatically to some convenient Watson, "That man was running for his life." He could take the fragment of a dream and build it into a case history as readily as Holmes might solve a murder mystery by looking at a cigar ash through a lens.

And yet, though psychiatry may reject Freud in whole or

part, the medicine men first must knock him down. Ironically enough, his name and fame will be best preserved by a motley crew, most of whom never read a line of his writing and got his teaching in distorted form at fourth or twentieth hand.

At the very moment Freud's ashes are being laid to rest somewhere an American prize-fight manager, sixth grade class of '98, will be saying: "The trouble with my heavyweight is the kid's inhibited. He don't know his own strength." And base-ball managers have begun to ask their southpaws with more than academic interest, "Tell me, Lefty, what's your sex life?"

Quite obviously, the philosophy inherent in the teaching of Sigmund Freud is insufficient for the salvation of human personality. It could not bring peace of mind to Freud himself when the dark days came, although it must be admitted that fate turned the iron in the soul of the proud old man. In some respects the lessons which he gave were harsh. He developed a point of view which shocked many religious people. And still it seems to me that in many respects he restated spiritual truths.

The discipline of analysis and rationalization might go far to nourish a more kindly civilization than exists today. Certainly Freud was a scourge to the Pharisees of the earth. He crusaded against cant; the method he espoused served to strip the mask from men who clothed mean motives under phrases of high pretensions. He did suggest that health and integration lay in the individual's ability to keep open covenants with himself, and it is my notion that he forged a wedge with which to split the hypocrisy of race and religious prejudice.

In going to the sources he is able to furnish much evidence that a publicly proclaimed principle may be no more than a shield behind which lurk spites and jealousies of the most base and bitter kind. And some day the world will learn to differentiate between what the leader says and the actual motivation which animates his conduct.

The Freudian approach is competent to bring Hitler down from the mountain to his own little dunghill. The tragedy of

Freud lay in the fact that, although his philosophy may endure to save others, he could not save himself, one of the indubitably great men of our age. He was persecuted, scored and exiled in his old age.

The Communists quarreled with his theories because they warred against the notion that every man is conditioned solely by his economic background and interest. The Fascists would have no part of him, since he saw the totalitarian state as a kind of national adolescence in which the Duce or the Fuehrer set himself up in the father role as a herdsman demanding sheep-like and childlike obedience. Since the researches of Freud dealt with the problem of the maladjusted individual, he was a force for social good. He was the champion of the weak and the oppressed. Indeed, I think it is not too much to say that here was a man who in his own way fought through a long life for the dignity and survival of the human soul. He dealt with dreams, for he himself was a dreamer.

181. TO OUR SUBSCRIBERS

Nutmeg nods. And that is putting it mildly. The little publication is reeling around the ring and occasionally sinking to the canvas. It seems to think that it is home in bed. Kindhearted people all over the Garden are shouting, "Stop it! Stop it!"

But they don't know what *Nutmeg* is made of. Neither does the editor until just before press time.

We have only just begun to fight. We'll hold her nozzle against the bank until the last galoot's ashore. ETC.

Besides, didn't the printer say, "Never mind about the bills for the present"? Just funning, Gillespie Brothers. We will pay on the barrel head as soon as a barrel can be obtained.

In the last issue you may have read a notice that certain

things were left out on account of "reorganization." That was just eyewash and might better have been expressed by the phrase "after looking at our bank account."

That long serial of Peter Neale's called *The Sun Field* although far from being ended was tossed out of the sleigh to the wolves. So far nobody has complained except the wolves.

Several friends and a number of utter strangers have called to tell us what is wrong with *Nutmeg*. The sum total which I gather is that there ought to be a punch in every line. A few compromise by saying that we might get by with a punch in every paragraph. We ought to be fearless and should invariably begin, "That is a lie," or "This is an outrage."

Next there should be more bulk, more subscribers and more advertisers. But you can't get more bulk unless you get more advertisers and you can't get more advertisers unless you get more subscribers. This is known in the trade as a vicious circle.

Among all our advisers there is general agreement that what *Nutmeg* needs is more working capital. Or at any rate more capital. But upon close question it turns out that not a single one of the suggesters is himself a capitalist. Indeed I have yet to find that any one of them has got a friend.

However, I urge our subscribers to be calm. Don't crowd or stone the stockholders. Sicker enterprises than *Nutmeg* have eventually recovered and lived to blossom and burgeon. Several such cases can be found in the *Lives of the Saints*.

This is not farewell or even adieu. Some sort of *Nutmeg* will be out again next week. It may be just as voluminous as the present issue or we may go into leaflet form in order to give you a more handy size to stick away in your pocket. Eventually the subscriber may be receiving a calendar each week with no more text than the dates and the motto "Love and Kisses."

Under such circumstances would it be fair or wise to urge anyone to subscribe here and now to *Nutmeg* even at the one dollar rate for twelve numbers if, when and as if issued? It would not be fair or just in a strict business sense. *Nutmeg* has ceased to be an investment and now moves into the field of speculation. Just think of the fun you could have in waiting each week and saying to yourself, "Do I get the blamed thing or don't I?"

And let me point out to advertisers what an amazing medium *Nutmeg* might be if, in spite of its rather limited clientele, every single subscriber were a confirmed gambler who had indicated his willingness to take a chance. Indeed I have recommended to all our advertising solicitors a new sales talk which runs, "Listen, Mr. Merchant, a person who purchases the *Nutmeg* will buy anything."

After listening to the excellent and kindly advice of many I have decided on a constructive plan of action in regard to *Nutmeg's* future. My first idea was to try and raise a little extra dough from my wife Connie who has had me on an allowance lo these many years. So far all advances have been thrown back. That way madness lies.

So be it. My left is shattered. My right is crumpled. My center is disorganized. I shall attack at two-thirty this afternoon at the Aqueduct race track.

By getting to the mail first I have managed to hold out a stray check for a hundred dollars which I received from a literary magazine in return for an article entitled Some Modern Reverberations of William Congreve in the Comedies of Samuel Behrman.

I shall take the check to the West Fifty-seventh Street branch of the Chase National Bank, which handles all my funds. The paying teller is a friend of mine and we will play volleyball with the check from the literary magazine, which isn't so very much better off than *Nutmeg*. If we can manage to get the token payment to lie flat I will leave the bank with one hundred dollars in small bills.

Chartering a fast automobile, I will hiss through my teeth, "The clubhouse at Aqueduct." I have a pass for the clubhouse.

And I will add in a stern voice, "There's a dollar in it for you if we make the first race."

I purpose to risk every cent of my mess of pottage for dear old *Nutmeg*. I'll die for dear old *Nutmeg*. I purpose to come back with my shield, or on it, or without it.

No official announcement will be necessary. Just go to your neighborhood newsdealer next week. If you see a sixteen-page issue it will mean that once again righteousness has triumphed. Four pages will mean "Yes" and "No."

But if when you say *"Nutmeg"* the man replies, *"Nutmeg"* doesn't live here any more," you will know that the worst has happened and that the leaflets have begun to fall.

"Come on, Remorse."

182. A MATTER OF TASTE

Izvestia, which speaks officially for Russia, has placed a benediction on the head of Hitler, and the compliment is all the more surprising since it is given with the left hand. "One may respect or hate Hitlerism, just as any other system of political views," says the Soviet journal smugly. "This is a matter of taste."

Choose the red caviar, if you like, or the black. What's the difference? This is a matter of taste.

There was a day when Russian revolutionists insisted that Fascism was their foe. There was a time when Communist leaders expressed horror at the treatment of the Jews in Germany. And men and women were killed or went to concentration camps under the delusion that the way of life they espoused was one which clashed utterly with the Nazi philosophy. And many a Marxist was tortured and beaten by the Storm Troopers.

Hitler said before he came to power that when control was

his the heads would roll in the streets and the blood would run. This was a pledge he did not break. And the tongues of the flogged and tortured were caked and black.

And it is ironic as well as tragic, since it now seems that the whole vast battle between the official left and right has been a misunderstanding. It has been no more than a spat over a matter of taste. And concerning tastes there can be no dispute.

The Romans had a phrase for it. Hitler may not know much about freedom, but he knows what he likes. The partition of Poland is less a political issue than a problem in applied design. Didn't Hitler say before he poured the troops across the border and loosed the slaughter that his real ambition was to retire from the ardors of leadership and become one of the world's greatest artists?

Perhaps he put too much magenta on his palette, but if it is the whim of the artist to paint the moon blood red who can quarrel with his taste? This which was once a village has now become the canvas for the brush of Der Fuehrer. And out of the bodies of workers and peasants he has fashioned pigments. You like it or you don't like it, simply in accord with your own preference for houses with thatched roofs or blasted ruins.

Look again and observe the pattern of those shattered trees against the sky. All right, never mind. It is the way that Adolf paints. Take it or leave it. Perhaps he has made mistakes at times, but it is said that even the hand of the potter has been known to slip.

Who would be so graceless as to deny to the lord of German kultur the right to take a rag heavy with turpentine and rub out the existing map of the world? Let there be no weeping by the women and children should they be told they must not cry. Hitler will paint a new map and make the world all bright and Reich and Aryan. He has found a new way to abolish slums. He simply shells them.

What will this world be like when Adolf Hitler has added the last brush strokes and signed his masterpiece in the lower right-hand corner with a swastika? Who can tell? The artist toils furiously at his easel. We must wait. But here are one or two already who feel sure they do not like it. For them it is too tight a scheme. They would prefer more liberty and light.

These are men and women who have felt that freedom of worship and freedom of speech were the very things by which mankind lived. They feel that without them humanity will perish. Fellowship among all creeds and races was to them vital in any design for living. It cannot be found anywhere in the picture Hitler paints. Things which were the essence of existence are not, so Moscow says, worth arguing about.

It is a matter of taste. And a man in armor thrusts a sponge of vinegar to the crucified and says, "This shall ye drink."

183. MY UNIFORM

A short dispatch in the newspapers the other day said the American correspondents were going up to the British front along the West Wall. The story said that under army regulations the reporters would wear uniforms like those of officers, but that they would have the distinguishing identification of a green brassard with a red C on the left arm.

This had a nostalgic note for me. My first trip up to the line last time was with the British. This was early in the summer of 1917. My credentials came only a day or so before the newspaper party was supposed to start, and the job of making myself look like an officer on short notice was difficult. In fact, only charity permitted me a passing grade.

There wasn't time to have anything run up on the machine, so I went to a French store, called Galeries Lafayette, and explained to a young lady that I wanted to look like an officer— in a hurry. Although her English was flawless, she still seemed puzzled. Finally, with the help of everybody in the store, a burnt sienna tunic not unlike a smock was dragged out from the back of a shelf. The girl said it would look better under a Sam Browne belt. Finding a 48 measure was tough, but again something turned up among the remnants.

Next they brought out riding pants and puttees made of some composition approximately leather. They failed to sell me spurs. With those pants I could hardly sit in a chair, much less on top of a horse, even if an amiable one could have been discovered. Still, if I had asked the Galeries Lafayette for a horse I feel sure they would have reached under a counter and produced one.

Having managed to work my way into the garments of a warrior, I kept them on and put my good clothes in a paper bag. Flushed with success, I spoke to the saleslady in French, "Connaissez-vous le magicien Houdini?" She answered, "Oui." "Pas moi," I explained, "and so, I think, I'll keep this uniform on until the war has ended." Hitler not having been heard of at the time, we both laughed heartily.

Unfortunately, I forgot a hat to top the combination, and I wandered out into the streets of Paris wearing a rakish gray felt called the Sophomore, which was a big seller along Broadway at the time I quit the States. On account of the hat, I guess, no fewer than five military policemen challenged me and asked for my credentials before I reached the hotel. One of them confessed that he thought I was a fugitive from a labor battalion.

But my moment of triumph was to come. The headquarters where I was instructed to report was in Amiens. There was only one other newspaperman present, and the English officers were cordial, and nobody passed any cracks about my uniform. However, my fellow correspondent seemed ill at ease, although he himself was all done up regardless in handmade whipcord. I found after dinner that he was blushing on my account. He was more hurt than angry. In fact, he called me "Oofs," which was a nickname conferred on me by Floyd Gibbons under the assertion that this was a phonetic reproduction of my pronunciation of "des oeufs avec jambon."

"Try and look like an officer," he implored. "You don't want to make America seem foolish. Your puttees are on the wrong side, too." But early next morning when I wandered out alone I ran smack into a sentry who gave me the awe-inspiring salute of the British Army, which seems to be made up of three nip-ups and a swan dive. He stood rigidly at attention waiting to see what I would do. We both were petrified.

In addition to neglecting to get a proper hat I had also failed to equip myself with any sort of salute in the Galeries Lafayette. And so I smiled broadly and said, "Nice morning, sir," and went upon my way. It semed to me that it would be wrong to deceive him. I wasn't really an officer.

184. THE FAIREST DAYS

Among the ironic tragedies of modern warfare is the fact that the fairest days are the foulest along the front. The full moon is not a lure for lovers but a lamp to light the way of bombers. And a high sun in the skies means greater mobility for mechanized units. When nature does her best the worst of man is put on show. Bleak days and winter nights seem more appropriate for slaughter, but these are the very conditions under which a great offensive may break down. Up rises a red and giddy sun at dawn and troops go over the top behind the barrage of the big guns. Man thrusts aside all the brightest gifts of existence in order to kill and be killed.

To be sure, after fields have been fiercely contested the landscape itself takes on the look of nightmares. And when the earth and all the groves are shattered it may seem a little easier to leave the world behind in a last attack.

Trees are piteous as victims of shellfire. Their very tenacity makes them targets for a torture which leaves them skeletonized against the sky. After days and even weeks of pounding some part of the stump will still remain or the bony finger of a single branch continue to beckon as in the days when it offered shade and shelter. The scarred earth becomes a dirty chalk-white along the western front, and when the wind blows or high explosives fall a greasy geyser, like water from a ditch, splashes high in the air. But man has yet no weapon which can deface the sky for more than fleeting minutes.

They have bright stars in France, and at this time of year the bowl above the fighting men is far more blue than the uniforms of the poilus. I first saw planes in action on the British front, and the afternoon was one to fill anyone from the city with the excitement which comes when the ceiling is high and sunlit.

And suddenly I saw the white buds burst many thousands of feet above our heads. First these blossoms were single, and then they were grouped close to form a huge flower like a chrysanthemum. The anti-aircraft guns were pinning a machine within their far-flung petals. Perhaps the plane drew clear or was lost in the middle of the deadly bouquet. Beyond the garden of the guns two other machines were in combat, and it was not possible for artillery of either side to participate, since they dived and rolled too rapidly for any marksman to wing a foeman without endangering a friend.

All I could see was the quick spark of machine-gun fire, and this was no more than a lightning flash, hardly as big as your thumbnail. The sound of it remained inaudible. These men had sailed up and up into an element once reserved for the figures of mythology. But now the genius of mortals had made it possible for human beings to climb up to the clouds and through them. They soared like birds and angels, and each tried to go higher than his competitor, so that he might dive down suddenly and demolish him.

So much has man improved his lot on earth that now he may almost literally paint the face of the moon with blood. The sun goes down. Stars dance in their course. Up rides the moon —that silver galleon known to the poets, a thing of joy and delight. It is the same moon which is used in every popular song as the symbol of romance.

Shine on, shine on, harvest moon! Not any longer does it shine "for me and my gal." In the cities and along the battle line men become moles and go underground. These are the nights on which the sirens sound as the planes prowl. The very gifts of nature are turned into a curse. The war is on—

185. A ROVING O. HENRY

There is nothing in the popular delusion that a war in Europe is a boom to newspapers in America. Circulation may go up, but not as rapidly as costs, and the whole tendency of a period of conflict is a lowering of journalistic standards. It becomes even more difficult than usual to pin down the truth. Censorship caps a long list of hurdles which lie between the action and the printed story. War alternates between seeming to offer too little news and too much for digestion. The present contest, in particular, has had such a slight amount of action that all the decks and all the front lines are cleared for rumor and for rival propaganda.

But I have no desire to chime in with those who seem impatient at the fact that this has been to such a large extent a "phony" war. I have encountered people who act almost as if they were ringside ticket holders at a heavyweight bout in which both fighters were stalling.

Surely from every humane point of view the stalemate which goes on along the Western Front, at the time this is written, is preferable to the bloody sacrifices of 1917, when hundreds of thousands were sacrificed for salients which were of little moment. Moloch has known in all history no altar such as that of Verdun, where the youth of two nations spent itself fruitlessly. Out of stalemate peace can come.

Huge casualty lists may leave both sides standing precisely where they are at present. And I am not at all sure that a more inspired sort of journalism could not find a greater opportunity for expression than it has yet manifested in the very fact of inaction.

With all deference to tradition, I do not think that news, either in peace or war, is limited to the recital of overt acts. True reporting should be a great deal more than a recital of oddities. It should go deeper into the commonplace and ordinary.

Journalism at its best is current history, and in the long run history is compounded out of things which may seem trivial at the moment. There ought to be an eye for acorns as well as oaks. All too frequently a daily paper takes on the form of cataloguing the folk in a sideshow. The silliest sort of playboy can earn himself headlines by semi-insane antics. Lunatic acts and kindred deeds are overplayed, in my opinion.

There is no poorer rule for the approximation of news than the familiar adage about dogs and men. Unless there is some special setting for the event, I deny the existence of news in the fact that a man bites a dog. An editor's reaction to such an event should be to spike the story, saying, "It's just another nut or one of those press agents."

It is my notion that papers, on the whole, are too indifferent to things which are a matter of mass experience. Hurricanes, blizzards and electrical storms are quite justifiably written up in full, but I would like to see more front-page stories based upon the fact that some certain morning of June or November was a little gayer and more glorious than usual.

I remember that a certain Easter made the front page because of a ghastly triple murder by an insane man. I think that the coming of another Easter was in reality a more important story than the crime which marred it.

It would be snobbish to pretend no interest whatsoever in those departments devoted to the doings of people in night clubs and all along the amusement fringe. But I would like to see some columnists do the side streets and the suburbs and chronicle the joys and tragedies of the ordinary run of people. There could be a beat for a roving O. Henry. Indeed, I'd like to see some young man follow in the steps of St. Francis or of Thoreau.

I would like to know much more about the pigeons of Manhattan and of all small creatures in the streams and ponds which lie within the greater city. A newspaper at its best chronicles life, and life is deeper and more varied than murder, mass attack or any sort of death in the afternoon.

186. THE HAND OF HEROD

A news dispatch from Paris says that the authorities have decided that midnight Masses may not be celebrated in any of the churches of the city during the Christmas season. It is explained that it would be impossible to keep the light from filtering out through the great stained glass windows of a cathedral. A candle by a shrine sheds a beam which is too broad for the warring world in which we live. If the figure of the Christ child were illuminated it might serve as a beacon for the way of wise flying men from out of the East. And their gifts would not be gold and frankincense and myrrh.

Once again the hand of Herod is raised for the slaughter of the innocents. But those things which were are with us now. I have seen men and women moved by devotion into such a mood that they felt themselves not only followers but contemporaries in the life of Jesus. To them His death was a present tragedy and Easter morning marked a literal triumph. And to those who are like-minded there lies reassurance in the revelation of the past. Herod was a ruler who for a little time had might and power vested in himself. His word was absolute and his will was cruel. As captain over thousands he commanded his messengers to find and kill the newborn king. An army was set in motion against an infant in a manger.

But though the hand of Herod fell heavily upon Bethlehem and all the coasts thereof, Joseph, the young child and his mother escaped into Egypt. "In Rama was there a voice heard, lamentation and weeping and great mourning, Rachel weeping for her children, and would not be consoled, because they are not." The blood of the young was spilled upon the ground even as it is being shed today. And it may well have seemed, some two thousand years ago, that there was no force which could stay the ravages of the monarch and his minions.

Around the child there stood on guard only Joseph and Mary, three wise men and shepherds from the field who had followed the course set for them by a bright star. Death came to Herod, and the bright star was a portent of the perfect light which was to save the world from darkness. The light of the world was not extinguished then, and it lives today and will again transfix the eyes of men with its brilliance.

In the dark streets of Paris on Christmas Eve, even as in the little town of Bethlehem, a star will animate the gloom. The call comes once more to kings and shepherds to journey to the manger and worship at the shrine of the Prince of Peace. Quite truly the civil authorities of Paris have said that it is impossible to blackout the light which shines from the altar.

And if I were in France I would go at midnight to the little island on the Seine and stand before Notre Dame de Paris. At first the towers of that great Gothic structure might seem to be lost in the blackness of the night. And it has been ruled that no congregation shall raise its voice to welcome the tidings of great joy. But then I think all the windows will take on magnificence, and that the air will resound with the message which has been given to the sons of men and will be offered again to the fellowship of all mankind. "Glory to God in the highest and on earth peace, good will toward men." And that choral cry will rise above the hum of Herod's grim messengers. It will be much louder than the crash of guns and the roar of cannon. No hymn of hate can prevail if we will only heed the eternal cadence of the Christmas carol.

187. THIRD FIRING

I've been fired in the Spring, the Summer and the early Winter. I like it best in the Summer. Three times in thirty-one years isn't so much to be fired. The first firing is often worse than the last. It's very discouraging to get canned when you're young. That's the way it was with me. I was twenty-one and working on the *Morning Telegraph*. My stall in the old Eighth Avenue car barn was right next to Bide Dudley. He was getting thirty-five dollars a week and my salary was twenty-eight. I wanted thirty but when I asked for it they fired me.

The next job was a long time coming. Fortunately I was a man of character and living home and so I didn't go into insurance or business but just borrowed money from my father and sat around for six months doing nothing. Eventually Burdick gave me a job on the *Tribune*.

He was a shy city editor and when he mentioned the salary he didn't want to pronounce the fatal words. He gazed away off at a distant window and wrote on a piece of scratch paper $25. Newspaper work is like that. You can go perfectly straight down once you are over the top of the mountain but detours are necessary as you come up from the valley.

As a matter of fact it was a mountain which made me. Burdick gave me the *Tribune* job on the strength of a recommendation from Fred Pitney, his star reporter. Pitney remembered that when I covered the E. H. Harriman deathwatch for the *Evening Sun*, I had crawled up through the woods at Arden and come right to the door of the big house. Getting there didn't get me anything but a boot from the butler. Still after a year and a half Pitney remembered me as an energetic young man. I've seen that hill since and now I couldn't walk it, let alone make the grade on my belly.

Pretty nearly ten years went by before I got fired again. The *World* did it. I had gone to that paper on my own volition and through the seductive influence of Mr. Swope. The Sacco-Vanzetti case had something to do with it but only indirectly. First of all I went on a one-man strike because they said I wasn't to write about the case any more. They didn't disagree with my opinions but they objected to violence of language. "Is Harvard to be known hereafter as Hangman's House?" was the sentence which made the trouble.

At the end of six or seven months the good shoemaker and the poor fish peddler were dead and things were patched up for me to go back to the paper. Getting fired was something of a surprise. Being bereft of topics I had dashed off a little masterpiece for the *Nation* saying that I thought the editorial policy of the *Morning World* was a shade on the timid side.

Naturally I didn't expect the editors to like it, but after all the *Nation* isn't so big and umbrage wasn't in the scope of my vision. Blithely on the way home I bought a morning paper but I only looked at the sport page. Arriving home I was asked as I came in the door whether or not I had read the *World*. "Sure," I replied, "Yankees win, Giants win, Dodgers lose." Those were the old, old Giants.

"But have you seen your own page?" my wife persisted.

"I'm saving that up for later," I told her.

"You needn't," she said, "you're fired."

And so I was. There in my old spot was a box explaining that Mr. Broun had been dropped on account of "disloyalty." I did object to the word a little because the casual reader would hardly know whether I had robbed the till or sat on the editor's hat.

Still it was Summer and I was full of energy and I went around opening my shirt to show my scars and having a fine time in general. And presently I got a job with Scripps-Howard which lasted eleven years. This ran out in the Winter.

Since *Nutmeg* is a publication which belongs to what the Parisians wittily call "Le Presse Confidentiale," or French to that effect, I think I may reveal that the farewell conference with Roy W. Howard passed off in entire peace and amity.

He said, "I've talked it over with my associates and we've decided not to make you an offer. It would be just too much grief. The price of newsprint is going up and we think that the place to cut expenses is among the high-priced specialists in order to protect the run-of-the-mine reporter."

"Roy," I said (all Scripps-Howard executives are known by the first name even to the humblest employee), "I can't possibly make any squawk about that because I've made that same speech myself at dozens of Guild meetings."

And so we shook hands and had a drink and everything was very pleasant. But I still think it is better to be fired in the Summer.

188. THE FIFTY-FIRST BIRTHDAY

When I woke up the morning of December ninth at seven minutes past nine I found I was fifty-one years old. It would be pleasant but untrue to say that I could detect no change in myself. Calling for a mirror, a dish of ham and eggs and a sloe gin rickey I crawled out of bed more gingerly than usual.

I took the mirror first and was pleased to observe that when held close to my lips a slight mist could be detected upon its bright surface. But upon surveying my entire countenance the glass grew tarnished. I looked like hell and accordingly I quickly changed the order and substituted a second rickey for the slice of ham. At fifty-one it is well to keep a weather eye upon the diet.

Canceling all business appointments, I decided to go back to bed and check up on my spiritual accounts. This, I fear, is a symptom of being past fifty. The tendency to self-examination begins to gnaw in and express itself in the question so long and happily unheeded, "Did I do right or wrong?" But this self-criticism is sedative rather than tonic because all too often the half-centenarian under cross-examination tends to answer, "Well, what else would you expect me to do under the circum-stances?"

Perhaps this is one of the greatest weaknesses of the aged. We wander about with arched back hoping for a friendly pat from someone who will say, "Don't let them kid you. I've known worse jerks than you are."

I've only tried it one way but in my opinion it is better to have your fifty-first birthday drop on your head like a ton of bricks than to have senescence do a sneak-up on you. That, I am told, is the trouble with clean living. Persons afflicted with this complaint enter the icy water a toe at a time. Surely there is less shock in plunging in head first with a high nonny and a hoopla.

Still, if I were a go-getting evangelist I would keep a little list of men who had just passed fifty. They are suckers for any Billy Sunday. When a man is halfway home he begins to fret and ask himself, "Whatever did I do with my religion?" And often you will find him searching through the clothes closet and

turning the pockets of his last year's winter overcoat inside out.
But at fifty-one I have more faith than I ever had before.
People are better than I thought they were going to be—myself
included. In mere physical exertion there may be some let-up.
Instead of the daily constitutional of a hundred yards it will be
twenty-five from now on. But at fifty-one I'm a better fighter
than at twenty-one. Things which once were just a sort of senti-
mental solace are now realities. Brotherhood is not just a Bible
word. Out of comradeship can come and will come the happy
life for all. The underdog can and will lick his weight in the
wildcats of the world.

189. THE LAST COLUMN

The horsemen and the footmen are gathering at the capital
from many quarters of the country to see the major political
event of 1940. I think that they have the correct candidate in
mind and the likely party, but why pick on the city of Wash-
ington?

The more we announce our repugnance to dictatorial proc-
esses, eagerness to avoid these governmental devices may lead
us into the very blasphemies which we purport to shun. For
instance, it is held that the decision as to whether Mr. Roose-
velt shall run for a third term can only come after a very definite
word from him. I do not agree, although I grant that to a mild
extent it is up his alley. The public seemingly was dissuaded
from following after the feet of Calvin Coolidge. It was said
that Mr. Coolidge did not choose to run. You couldn't tell it
by his feet. I'm not sure he actually meant it. I think that a
small determined band of one man or less might have sneaked
up to Calvin's room the night before he refused the nomination
and by threatening him that refusal would have meant being

ridden into the White House on rails, the young man might have given way to the cowboys. But there were no cowboys.

Now, of course, we know Franklin D. Roosevelt a good deal better than Calvin Coolidge. Indeed, his newspaper mind is singularly open to the convenience of correspondents. Some of them don't think he is going to run, because they don't think he wants to run. A few believe it is more or less a matter of social hygiene. Naturally, anybody who knows anything about it thinks that if he is nominated he will be re-elected, and that's the way to bet.

We do Mr. Roosevelt a great disservice by constantly speaking as if the decision to run or not to run were his to make. If you please, that simply isn't in his province. He is a great man, but he is the servant of the people and they will have to tell him what he should do.

Franklin Delano Roosevelt moves about the world as a man with great charm because he has the gift of being able to listen to someone as if he were really paying attention. This piece of good manners is occasionally unfortunate. It flatters men into speeches which are far too long and often convinces a Washington visitor that he has scored a signal point, although in all truth his message was not much appreciated.

But if public men in Washington got together to wager on the basis of their international acumen, I have no doubt that Cordell Hull would play, that Borah could be nagged into it, that Johnson would not abstain, and that Roosevelt would be willing.

Now, if you think of yourself as among the group best situated to lead your country in a particular crisis, it is decidedly an unpatriotic duty to throw that leadership away until you know in which direction it is going.

There seem to be very many evidences now that Roosevelt is less keen for a third term than he was previously. If the chance to act as an international mediator does not come before the conventions of 1940 are held, it is not likely to come at all.

And the third term of any American President may be a constant grim-lipped enterprise of keeping our own barbed wire up when it is smashed by passing shell raids. Who wants such a third term in his right senses? Nobody. But to hold the office marks the man in history. Your son, and your son's son can look it up in the almanac, and there it will read, under some farmer's joke, "I told you," the boy said, "that my great-grandfather Fred used to be President of the United States. That's how he got his start. Now he is working in the shops in Wichita."

Depend upon it, there won't be very much of a show when Roosevelt makes up his mind yes or no on the third term issue. He'll go into a room and there will be three persons there: the President, his better nature, and his devotion to his country. That should be a committee quite satisfactory to anyone.

SOURCES

1. *The Nation*, September 5, 1936.
2. *Harvard Advocate*, March 5, 1909.
3. *The A. E. F.: With General Pershing and the American Forces*, 1918. Chapter IV.
4. *Our Army at the Front*, 1919. Part of Chapter XXV.
5. *Brown's Nutmeg*, August 19, 1939.
6 to 15. From *Seeing Things at Night*, 1921.
16 to 27. From *Pieces of Hate, And Other Enthusiasms*, 1922.
28, 29. *The Boy Grew Older*, 1922. Book 1, Chapters 1 and 10.
30 to 41. From *Sitting on the World*, 1924.
42. New York *World*, June 25, 1925.
43. *World*, October 24, 1925.
44. *World*, October 23, 1926.
45. *World*, November 29, 1926.
46. From *Gandle Follows His Nose*, 1926. Chapter II.
47. *World*, January 25, 1927.
48. *World*, February 8, 1927.
49. *World*, August 5, 1927.
50. *World*, August 6, 1927.
50a. *World*, August 12, 1927.
50b, 51, 51a. *World*, August 17, 1927.
52. *The New Yorker*, October 1, 1927.
53. *World*, February 6, 1928.
54. *Nation*, May 4, 1928.
55. New York *Telegram*, February 19, 1929.
56. *Telegram*, May 8, 1929.
57. *Telegram*, December 23, 1929.
58. *Telegram*, January 27, 1930.
59. *Telegram*, March 2, 1930.
60. *Telegram*, June 5, 1930.
61. *Telegram*, August 19, 1930.
62. *Telegram*, August 30, 1930.
63. *Telegram*, December 12, 1930.
64. New York *World-Telegram*, February 28, 1931.
65. *World-Telegram*, March 6, 1931.

66. *World-Telegram*, May 5, 1931.
67. *World-Telegram*, December 9, 1931.
68. *World-Telegram*, December 29, 1931.
69. *World-Telegram*, January 23, 1932.
70. *World-Telegram*, April 23, 1932.
71. *World-Telegram*, July 1, 1932.
72. *World-Telegram*, September 1, 1932.
73. *World-Telegram*, November 22, 1932.
74. *World-Telegram*, January 19, 1933.
75. *World-Telegram*, January 27, 1933.
76. *World-Telegram*, February 27, 1933.
77. *World-Telegram*, April 10, 1933.
78. *World-Telegram*, May 12, 1933.
79. *World-Telegram*, June 20, 1933.
80. *World-Telegram*, July 19, 1933.
81. *World-Telegram*, August 7, 1933.
82. *World-Telegram*, November 27, 1933.
83. *World-Telegram*, November 28, 1933.
84. *World-Telegram*, January 10, 1934.
85. *World-Telegram*, January 15, 1934.
86. *World-Telegram*, February 13, 1934.
87. *World-Telegram*, March 23, 1934.
88. *World-Telegram*, April 28, 1934.
89. *World-Telegram*, July 9, 1934.
90. *World-Telegram*, August 11, 1934.
91. *World-Telegram*, September 15, 1934.
92. *World-Telegram*, September 19, 1934.
93. *World-Telegram*, February 12, 1935.
94. *World-Telegram*, March 7, 1935.
95. *World-Telegram*, March 20, 1935.
96. *World-Telegram*, April 15, 1935.
97. *Nation*, July 17, 1935.
98. *World-Telegram*, November 22, 1935.
99. *World-Telegram*, January 6, 1936.
100. *World-Telegram*, January 10, 1936.
101. *World-Telegram*, January 20, 1936.
102. *World-Telegram*, January 27, 1936.
103. *World-Telegram*, February 22, 1936.
104. *World-Telegram*, March 10, 1936.
105. *World-Telegram*, April 10, 1936.
106. *World-Telegram*, April 30, 1936.

107. *World-Telegram*, May 5, 1936.
108. *World-Telegram*, June 11, 1936.
109. *World-Telegram*, June 12, 1936.
110. *World-Telegram*, June 16, 1936.
111. *World-Telegram*, June 29, 1936.
112. *Nation*, August 1, 1936.
113. *World-Telegram*, October 28, 1936.
114. *World-Telegram*, December 15, 1936.
115. *World-Telegram*, December 24, 1936.
116. *World-Telegram*, March 11, 1937.
117. *World-Telegram*, March 18, 1937.
118. *World-Telegram*, April 30, 1937.
119. *World-Telegram*, May 19, 1936.
120. *World-Telegram*, June 17, 1937.
121. *World-Telegram*, June 26, 1937.
122. *World-Telegram*, July 7, 1937.
123. *World-Telegram*, November 12, 1937.
124. *The New Republic*, November 17, 1937.
125. *World-Telegram*, November 20, 1937.
126. *World-Telegram*, December 6, 1937.
127. *World-Telegram*, December 11, 1937.
128. *New Republic*, December 15, 1937.
129. *New Republic*, February 16, 1938.
130. *New Republic*, February 23, 1938.
131. *World-Telegram*, February 25, 1938.
132. *World-Telegram*, March 1, 1938.
133. *World-Telegram*, March 21, 1938.
134. *World-Telegram*, March 26, 1938.
135. *World-Telegram*, April 5, 1938.
136. *New Republic*, April 6, 1938.
137. *World-Telegram*, April 18, 1938.
138. *World-Telegram*, April 23, 1938.
139. *World-Telegram*, April 27, 1938.
140. *New Republic*, May 4, 1938.
141. *World-Telegram*, May 10, 1938.
142. *World-Telegram*, June 6, 1938.
143. *New Republic*, June 15, 1938.
144. *World-Telegram*, June 28, 1938.
145. *The Connecticut Nutmeg*, July 14, 1938.
146. *World-Telegram*, August 24, 1938.
147. *World-Telegram*, September 16, 1938.

148, 149. *Connecticut Nutmeg*, November 10, 1938.
150. *World-Telegram*, November 16, 1938.
151. *Connecticut Nutmeg*, December 1, 1938.
152. *World-Telegram*, December 7, 1938.
153. *World-Telegram*, December 21, 1938.
154. *Connecticut Nutmeg*, December 22, 1938.
155. *World-Telegram*, December 24, 1938.
156. *World-Telegram*, February 6, 1939.
157. *Connecticut Nutmeg*, March 30, 1939.
158. *World-Telegram*, April 4, 1939.
159. *World-Telegram*, April 11, 1939.
160. *Broun's Nutmeg*, April 15, 1939.
161. *Broun's Nutmeg*, May 6, 1939.
162. *Broun's Nutmeg*, May 20, 1939.
163. *World-Telegram*, May 22, 1939.
164. *World-Telegram*, June 9, 1939.
165, 166. *Broun's Nutmeg*, June 10, 1939.
167. *World-Telegram*, June 14, 1939.
168. *World-Telegram*, July 6, 1939.
169. *World-Telegram*, July 13, 1939.
170. *New Republic*, July 26, 1939.
171. *World-Telegram*, August 9, 1939.
172. *World-Telegram*, August 17, 1939.
173. *World-Telegram*, August 19, 1939.
174. *World-Telegram*, September 2, 1939.
175. *World-Telegram*, September 14, 1939.
176. *World-Telegram*, September 15, 1939.
177. *New Republic*, September 20, 1939.
178. *World-Telegram*, September 22, 1939.
179. *World-Telegram*, September 23, 1939.
180. *World-Telegram*, September 26, 1939.
181. *Broun's Nutmeg*, September 30, 1939.
182. *World-Telegram*, October 11, 1939.
183. *World-Telegram*, October 13, 1939.
184. *World-Telegram*, October 18, 1939.
185. *World-Telegram*, November 8, 1939.
186. *World-Telegram*, November 27, 1939.
187, 188. *Broun's Nutmeg*, December 9, 1939.
189. The New York *Post*, December 15, 1939.

CHRONOLOGY

1888: Born in Brooklyn, December 7, son of Henrietta Brosé and Heywood Cox Broun. Named Heywood Campbell Broun.

1894-1906: Attended Horace Mann School, New York City.

1906: Entered Harvard.

1908: Got summer job on staff of *Morning Telegraph.*

1909: Contributed story to the *Harvard Advocate*, March 9.

1910: Left Harvard, joined *Telegraph* permanent staff. Fired the following spring, did free-lance work on the *Sun.*

1911: Joined staff of the New York *Tribune.*

1917: Married Ruth Hale.

1918: War correspondent for *Tribune.* Heywood Hale Broun, only son, born March 10.

1921: Joined staff of the New York *World.*

1927: Controversy with *World*, August, about Sacco and Vanzetti columns.

1928: Wrote *Nation* column, May 8, which led to his dismissal from the *World.* Joined staff of the New York *Telegram.*

1930: Ran for Congressman from the 17th District of New York City. Defeated by Mrs. Ruth Pratt, Republican candidate.

1931: Produced and played in *Shoot the Works*, a musical. Conducted the Give a Job Till June Campaign, free employment agency.

1933: Wrote A Union of Reporters (see page 295), which led to the founding of the Newspaper Guild. President, 1933 to 1937.

1935: Married Connie Madison, Jan. 5.

1938: First issue of the *Connecticut Nutmeg*, May 26. Changed to *Broun's Nutmeg*, April 15, 1939.

1939: Conversion to Catholic faith announced; received into Church, May 23; *World-Telegram* contract ended in December; last, and only, column appeared in *Post*, Dec. 14; died of pneumonia, Dec. 18.

BIBLIOGRAPHY

BOOKS

The A.E.F.: With General Pershing and the American Forces, D. Appleton and Company, 1918.

Our Army at the Front, Volume V of a series on "America in the War," Charles Scribner's Sons, 1918. Illustrated.

Seeing Things at Night, Harcourt, Brace and Company, 1921.

Pieces of Hate: And Other Enthusiasms, George H. Doran Company, 1922.

The Boy Grew Older, G. P. Putnam's Sons, 1922.

The Sun Field, G. P. Putnam's Sons, 1923.

Sitting on the World, G. P. Putnam's Sons, 1924.

Gandle Follows His Nose, Boni and Liveright, 1926.

It Seems to Me: 1925-1935, Harcourt, Brace and Company, 1935.

COLLABORATIONS

Anthony Comstock: Roundsman of the Lord, by Heywood Broun and Margaret Leech, Albert and Charles Boni, 1927.

Christians Only: A Study in Prejudice, by Heywood Broun and George Britt, Vanguard Press, 1931.

MISCELLANY

Nonsenseorship: Sundry Observations Concerning Prohibitions, Inhibitions and Illegalities, by Heywood Broun, Ben Hecht, Alexander Woollcott and twelve others, G. P. Putnam's Sons, 1922.

The Cream of the Jesters, by Heywood Broun, Robert Benchley, Ring Lardner, Dorothy Parker and twenty-one others, Albert and Charles Boni, 1931.

PAMPHLETS

If New York Were Socialist, by Heywood Broun, Morris Hillquit, Norman Thomas and four others, 1931.

What Is Freedom of the Press? by Heywood Broun, Will Irwin and Julian S. Mason, a Town Hall of the Air broadcast by NBC, edited by Lyman Bryson, 1936.

SPECIAL EDITION

A Shepherd, privately printed by William E. Rudge's Sons, 1924. 18 pages.

BOOKS ABOUT BROUN

Heywood Broun: As He Seemed to Us, by Franklin P. Adams, Kenneth G. Crawford, Father Edward Dowling, S.J.; Morris Ernst, Edna Ferber, Lewis Gannett, Charles Horowitz, A. J. Isserman, Gardner Jackson, Theodore S. Kenyon, Rollin Kirby, John Kieran, Fiorello H. La Guardia, John L. Lewis, Edward McNamara, Ernest L. Meyer, Carl Randau, Quentin Reynolds, Edward G. Robinson, Frank Sullivan, Herbert Bayard Swope, Karl Virag and Morris Watson, a stenographic record of the Heywood Broun Memorial meeting on February 12, 1940, published for the Newspaper Guild of New York, Random House, 1940.

The Conversion of Heywood Broun, by the Right Rev. Msgr. Fulton J. Sheen, a pamphlet published by The Saint Paul Guild, 117 East 57th Street, New York, 1940.

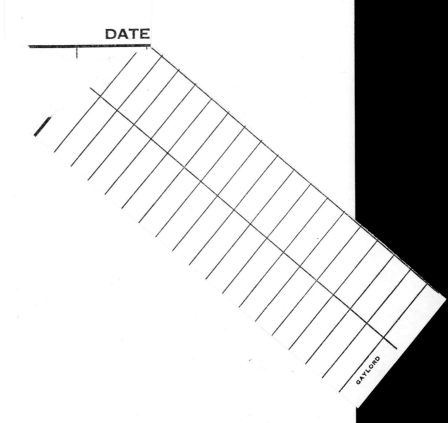

DATE